The Anointed Church

Toward a Third Article Ecclesiology

Gregory J. Liston

Fortress Press
Minneapolis

THE ANOINTED CHURCH

Toward a Third Article Ecclesiology

Cover design: Joe Reinke

Cover image: Rublev's famous icon showing the three Angels being hosted by Abraham at Mamre / Wikimedia Commons

Library of Congress Cataloging-in-Publication Data is available

Paperback ISBN: 978-1-4514-9706-9

eBook ISBN: 978-1-5064-0042-6

The paper used in this publication meets the minimum requirements of American National Standard for Information Sciences — Permanence of Paper for Printed Library Materials, ANSI Z329.48-1984.

Manufactured in the U.S.A.

This book was produced using PressBooks.com, and PDF rendering was done by PrinceXML.

The Anointed Church

Contents

Acknowledgements

The first vote of thanks goes to Myk Habets, who combines intelligence and wit with a generous spirit. His regular encouragement and detailed advice were both valuable and valued. The title of this work is a not-so-subtle allusion to the fact that I see it as a natural extension of Myk's research in *The Anointed Son.*

Other colleagues have been equally valuable. Thanks to Martin Sutherland (for an insightful, overarching perspective), Andrew Picard (for many Gunton-esque conversations), Brian Harris (for a last-minute overview), and Sarah Snell (for timely proofreading). I am grateful for all the honest and helpful feedback given by each of these excellent people, over many more years than this project encompassed. In addition, my discussions with many of the lecturers and students at Carey Baptist College and Laidlaw College, both past and present, have been stimulating and fruitful.

Much appreciation to AUT University, Pacific Park Christian Holiday Camp, and the Lam Family, who provided financial support for this research.

Spending more time with my wonderful family—Diane, Emily, and James—has been the greatest sideline blessing that has arisen from pursuing this project. All three are incredibly supportive and exceptionally loving. My parents have also been unswervingly encouraging and supportive of my research and ministry, and their interest and involvement in this project is no exception.

I have tried to live out the maxim that it is better to fail at something that matters than succeed at something that doesn't. The Father's love poured out in our Spirit-enabled union with Christ matters. And succeed or fail, writing of it is much more than just "something."

This research is dedicated to the memory of my sister, Helen Frances Abraham.

Soli Deo Gloria.

PART I

Toward a Third Article Ecclesiology

At the root of Christian ecclesiology lies a confidence that the church "can never fail, for it is based upon a rock."[1] It is "spread out through all time and space, rooted in eternity, terrible as an army with banners."[2] Furthermore, "the church is the hope of the world."[3] These affirmations are sourced not merely from reasoned thinkers throughout history, but from the Christian Scriptures themselves. The gates of hell will not prevail against the church (Matt. 16:18). It is being built into a dwelling place for God by the Spirit (Eph. 2:22). Through it the manifold wisdom of God is made known (Eph. 3:10). The ecclesiology revealed is one of impregnability, inspiration, and immeasurable importance.

Our experience, however, is vastly different. From a contemporary western vantage point, the church is crumbling. This diminution in size, status, and significance is often characterized through the phrase "*the collapse of Christendom*." Many responses simply urge the

1. T. S. Eliot, *The Complete Poems and Plays: 1909–1950* (Orlando: Harcourt, Brace, 1971), 30.
2. C. S. Lewis, *The Screwtape Letters: Letters from a Senior to a Junior Devil* (Glasgow: Collins, 1989), 15.
3. Charles H. Spurgeon, *The Treasury of David*, 6 vols. (London: Passmore & Alabaster, 1888), 4:169.

western church to rebuild. They argue that by being more organized and pragmatic—by simply *doing better* in some way—the western church can recover its numbers, regain its respect, and reexert its influence. But such effort, although well intentioned, simply repeats past mistakes.

There is an alternative response. Colin Gunton argues for a "greater emphasis on [the church's] constitution by the Spirit."[4] This enables us to "reappropriate an ecclesiology of the humanity of Christ."[5] He sees this as "the first and crying need if responses to the collapse of Christendom are not to take the form of new authoritarianisms, as they are indeed doing."[6]

From such a perspective, the collapse of Christendom is not a tragedy, but an opportunity. Through this loss of size, status, and significance—through our weakness—the western church can rediscover that it is a profoundly and irreducibly Spiritual entity. The church can learn again to walk by faith and not by sight, to understand itself not primarily as a player in society but as fundamentally constituted by God's Spirit.

This research finds its motivation in such a conviction. It examines ecclesiology through the methodology of Third Article Theology, in which all reality is viewed *through the lens of the Spirit*. Just as Spirit Christology has gained new insight by examining Christ's person and life through a pneumatological lens, this research suggests that the approach of Third Article Theology provides similar benefits to the study of ecclesiology.

The work broadly divides into three parts. Part one articulates the prolegomena to the development of a Third Article Ecclesiology. It outlines a dialogical framework in which the Spirit's identity and

4. Colin Gunton, "The Church on Earth: The Roots of Community," in *On Being the Church*, ed. C. Gunton and D. Hardy (Edinburgh: T. & T. Clark, 1989), 62.
5. Ibid., 65.
6. Ibid.

actions repeatedly inform the analogical link between other theological doctrines and ecclesiology. These doctrines become the theological vantage points from which ecclesiology is observed through the lens of the Spirit. The next two parts work out this methodological framework from the perspectives of Christology and the Trinity. Part two examines ecclesiology from the vantage point of Christology, utilizing the insight that the Spirit forms the church as Christ's body. Paralleling the Spirit's involvement in Christ and the church enables the constituent features of a *Christological* Third Article Ecclesiology to be determined. Part three employs the vantage point of the Trinity, examining ecclesiology through the recognition that by the Spirit believers participate in Jesus' communion with the Father. Identifying how the Spirit's immanent identity is reprised in the church enables the constituent features of a *Trinitarian* Third Article Ecclesiology to emerge. Of course, Christology and the Trinity are not the only doctrines that can be used as theological vantage points. While the advanced state of Spirit Christology and its well-developed implications for the Trinity make these two doctrines logical initial choices, others could certainly be considered. The research concludes with a brief discussion of how two other doctrines—eschatology and the world—could be used similarly as vantage points, with the ultimate aim of all four perspectives being integrated to provide a comprehensive Third Article Ecclesiology.

Given that the objective of this research is to demonstrate the viability of a Third Article Theology approach in examining ecclesiology, it is not intended to be exhaustive. Each part of the research interacts with those theologians, and distinguishes those ecclesial features that enable the validity of the approach to be established, and does not delve widely beyond them. In terms of dialogue partners, while virtually all those theologians who explicitly attempt to extend Third Article Theology beyond Spirit Christology are interacted with, beyond this core group dialogue partners are (predominantly) chosen as exemplars that enable the constituent features of a Third Article Ecclesiology to be contrastingly illustrated. So part two, for example, engages Zizioulas as a dialogue partner mainly to contrast how a Third Article Ecclesiology that logically distinguishes between the ecclesial roles of the Son and the Spirit without existentially separating them avoids collapsing ecclesiology into Christology.[7] Similarly, the ecclesial features that are determined and examined are those aspects most clearly illuminated from the vantage points of Christology and the Trinity. So, for example, while the ecclesial marks of oneness and catholicity are considered in detail, the mark of apostolicity is not considered as rigorously in this research, as these two vantage points do not illuminate it as clearly as would the vantage point of the world.[8] In short, the theologians interacted with and the ecclesial features discussed are those that demonstrate the value of applying a Third Article Theology to ecclesiology, and most clearly illuminate how a Third Article Ecclesiology is distinguished from ecclesiologies derived through other methodological approaches.

The close relationship between the Spirit and the church is not a new recognition. The Apostles' Creed places them side by side: "I believe in the Holy Spirit, the holy catholic church, the communion of saints."[9] But as is often noted, "the pervasive association between 'Spirit' and 'church' notwithstanding, theologians have reflected relatively little on precisely *how* the two are related."[10] While certainly not without historical forerunners and precedents, advocates of the

7. See section 4.2 and chapter 6.
8. See section 11.2 for a brief discussion of apostolicity and the vantage point of the world.
9. Jaroslav Pelikan and Valerie Hotchkiss, eds., *Creeds and Confessions of Faith in the Christian Tradition: Early, Eastern and Medieval* (New Haven: Yale University Press, 2003), 669.
10. Miroslav Volf and Maurice Lee, "The Spirit and the Church," in *Advents of the Spirit: An Introduction to the Current Study of Pneumatology*, ed. Bradford E. Hinze and D. Lyle Dabney (Milwaukee: Marquette University Press, 2005), 382. See also William R. Barr and Rena M.

newly emerging Third Article Theology acknowledge that it is still very much in its formative stages.[11] Consequently, this research begins by describing and justifying it as a methodology, with a particular focus on its extension beyond Christology to ecclesiology. Such a methodological development is logically necessary before the structural framework of the research can be explained in any more detail than the cursory outline given above. So the prolegomena in part one first describes the background from, motivation for, and methodology by which a Third Article Theology is undertaken (chapter 1). The focus then turns from a general discussion of Third Article Theology to its Christological implications (chapter 2). Examining this core doctrine where the most effort has been directed and the most progress made concretely demonstrates Third Article Theology's distinctive characteristics. Based on this preparatory material, chapter 3 explicitly examines how the approach of Third Article Theology can and will be applied and extended to ecclesiology, concluding with the outworking of this methodological framework in the detailed structure of the research.

Yocum, "Introduction," in *The Church in the Movement of the Spirit*, ed. William R. Barr and Rena M. Yocum (Grand Rapids: Eerdmans, 1994), 1–2.

11. Amos Yong, "Introduction: Pentecostalism and a Theology of the Third Article," in *Toward a Pneumatological Theology: Pentecostal and Ecumenical Perspectives on Ecclesiology, Soteriology, and Theology of Mission*, ed. Amos Yong (Lanham, MD: University Press of America, 2002), xvii.

1

Third Article Theology

Nearing his death in 1968, Karl Barth commented that his theological work could be replicated and complemented by a Third Article Theology: a theology that interprets reality through the lens of the Spirit. He wrote:

> What I have already intimated here and there to good friends, would be the possibility of a theology of the third article, in other words, a theology predominantly and decisively of the Holy Spirit. Everything which needs to be said, considered and believed about God the Father and God the Son in an understanding of the first and second articles might be shown and illuminated in its foundations through God the Holy Spirit.[1]

Interestingly, Barth did not think the time for pursuing such a Third Article Theology was ripe, arguing that it was "still too difficult to distinguish between God's Spirit and man's spirit." He suggested that after the turn of the century a genuine Third Article Theology

1. Karl Barth, "Concluding Unscientific Postscript on Schleiermacher," in *The Theology of Schleiermacher*, ed. D. Ritschl (Grand Rapids: Eerdmans, 1982), 278.

could begin to emerge.[2] This "prediction" has proved remarkably astute, as for the last several years theologians from many different traditions—Roman Catholic (Ralph Del Colle, David Coffey), Protestant (Lyle Dabney, Gary Badcock, Clark Pinnock, Myk Habets), and ecumenical (Veli-Matti Kärkkäinen, Amos Yong, Steven Studebaker)—have begun to move in this direction. While differences of approach exist,[3] the common conviction underlying this research stream is that pneumatology comes first. Third Article theologians specifically and intentionally examine theology through the lens of the Spirit.

1.1 What Is Third Article Theology?

What does it mean to start with the Spirit? Proponents of Third Article Theology most often describe this theological method by contrasting it with other approaches. While such contrasting descriptions are illustrative, Third Article Theology should primarily be understood as an important and necessary subset of the Trinitarian renaissance that has fueled much of twentieth-century theology.

First, Second, and Third Article Theologies

The United Methodist theologian D. Lyle Dabney characterizes Third Article Theology by contrasting it with two alternative theological strategies that have dominated western Christian thought, namely First and Second Article theologies.[4] His comparisons are

2. Karl Barth, *Karl Barth's Table Talk* (Edinburgh: Oliver & Boyd, 1963), 28.

3. Differences include whether the specific terminology of a "theology of the third article" or a "Third Article Theology" is adopted or not. Note also that many authors, including Barth, use the two phrases interchangeably. This research will make a distinction between them, as described in section 1.3 below.

4. The following subsection is based on D. Lyle Dabney, "Why Should the First Be Last? The Priority of Pneumatology in Recent Theological Discussion," in *Advents of the Spirit: An Introduction to the Current Study of Pneumatology*, ed. Bradford E. Hinze and D. Lyle Dabney (Milwaukee: Marquette University Press, 2005), 240–61. See also D. Lyle Dabney, "Starting

helpful if seen as broad generalizations rather than detailed historical critiques.

The first article of the Apostles' Creed states "I believe in God the Father, Almighty, Creator of heaven and earth."[5] So, First Article theologies start with the Father. Using this lens, the focus is initially on God's creation—our innate God-given abilities and capabilities—and traces a continuous path from nature through to grace. First Article theologies understand that there is a universal, inbuilt, human capacity for and tendency toward God. So grace fills out and purifies what is already in us and in all of creation—that which has been tarnished and diminished by sin—and brings it to perfection and completion. All of our reality—our humanity, our salvation, our relationships, our future—is interpreted and understood through this continuity. First Article theologies are most clearly evidenced in medieval scholasticism. Exemplars include Thomas Aquinas ("Grace does not destroy nature, but perfects it")[6] and perhaps even Augustine ("You made us for yourself, and our heart is restless until it finds rest in you").[7]

The second article of the Apostles' Creed states "And in Jesus Christ, his only Son, our Lord."[8] Second Article theologies thus start with the Son, and view reality through the lens of Christ and his redemptive work. In contrast to First Article theologies, which operate from the initial orientation of Patrology, Second Article theologies have a Christological orientation. So rather than starting

with the Spirit: Why the Last Should Now Be First," in *Starting with the Spirit*, ed. Stephen Pickard and Gordon Preece (Hindmarsh: Australian Theological Forum, 2001), 3–27; and D. Lyle Dabney, "Saul's Armour: The Problem and Promise of Pentecostal Theology," *Pneuma* 23, no. 1 (2001): 126–31.

5. Jaroslav Pelikan and Valerie Hotchkiss, eds., *Creeds and Confessions of Faith in the Christian Tradition: Early, Eastern and Medieval* (New Haven: Yale University Press, 2003), 669.
6. Thomas Aquinas, *Summa Theologica*, trans. Fathers of the English Dominican Province (London: Burns Oates & Washbourne, 1920), 13.
7. Augustine, *Confessions*, trans. E. M. Blaicklock (London: Hodder & Stoughton, 1983), 15.
8. Pelikan and Hotchkiss, eds., *Creeds and Confessions: Early, Eastern and Medieval*, 669.

with our openness to God as his creation, they focus on our universal rejection of God as sinners. Rather than tracing a continuous route from nature through to grace, they focus on the darkly impenetrable divide between humanity and God. Rather than concentrating on created humanity gradually making its way up to God, they center on a God who miraculously makes his way down to fallen humanity. For Second Article theologies, all of our reality is interpreted not through continuity but through discontinuity—through contrast and contradiction. God is completely pure; humanity completely depraved. God is totally powerful; humanity totally impotent. Second Article theologies are most clearly evident in the work of the Protestant Reformation. Exemplars include Luther ("on the part of man however nothing precedes grace except ill will and even rebellion against grace")[9] and perhaps even Barth himself, who clearly considers each theological doctrine from a Christological perspective. ("We see [Christ], and in this mirror we see ourselves, ourselves as those who commit sin and are sinners. We are here inescapably accused and irrevocably condemned.")[10]

The third article of the Apostles' Creed states "Who was conceived by the Holy Ghost, born of the Virgin Mary."[11] Third Article Theology operates from the initial orientation of pneumatology, and thus views reality through the lens of the Spirit and his transformative work. First and Second Article theologies focus respectively on our *universal* tendency toward or *universal* rejection of God. Third Article theologies focus on the *particular*—the specific reality of the Spirit in communities and relationships. And even more particularly they focus on one relationship—the Spirit's presence in Jesus Christ. Third

9. Martin Luther, *Luther's Works*, trans. H. J. Grimm, vol. 31 of 55 vols. (Philadelphia: Fortress Press, 1957), 11.
10. Karl Barth, *Church Dogmatics*, trans. G. W. Bromiley (Peabody, MA: Hendrickson, 2010), IV/1, 390.
11. Pelikan and Hotchkiss, eds., *Creeds and Confessions: Early, Eastern and Medieval*, 669.

Article theologies do not start from the continuity or discontinuity between humanity and divinity, but rather with the reality of *transformation.* Hence they balance and affirm both the continuity and discontinuity of nature with grace, of time with eternity, and ultimately of humanity with divinity. And arising from this basis of *particularity* and *transformation*, Third Article theologies search for an "emergent common," a *relational* reality as we are drawn together to God. For First Article theologies the key concept is *the beatific vision*—the perfection and completion of humanity. For Second Article theologies the key concept is *justification*—the restoring of a right standing. But for Third Article theologies, the key concept is *participation*—the drawing of individuals and communities into the life of God.

There is no claim that a Third Article Theology and its associated methodological commitment are entirely novel or unique. Irenaeus in the patristic period,[12] John Owen[13] or Jonathan Edwards[14] after the Reformation, or Edward Irving in the Enlightenment[15] are just a small sample of those who developed components of a Third Article Theology. Moreover, theologians who focus primarily on other approaches certainly do not neglect pneumatology, often using the

12. See for example Anthony Briggman, *Irenaeus of Lyons and the Theology of the Holy Spirit* (Oxford: Oxford University Press, 2012).
13. See for example K. M. Kapic, "The Spirit as Gift: Explorations in John Owen's Pneumatology," in *The Ashgate Research Companion to John Owen's Theology*, ed. K. M. Kapic and M. Jones (Farnham, UK: Ashgate, 2012), 113–40; Alan Spence, "The Significance of John Owen for Modern Christology," in *The Ashgate Research Companion to John Owen's Theology*, ed. K. M. Kapic and M. Jones (Farnham, UK: Ashgate, 2012); and Colin Gunton, "John Owen and John Zizioulas on the Church," in *Theology through the Theologians: Selected Essays (1972-1995)* (London: T. & T. Clark, 1996), 187–205.
14. See for example Myk Habets, "The Surprising Third Article Theology of Jonathan Edwards," in *The Ecumenical Edwards: Jonathan Edwards and the Theologians*, ed. Kyle Strobel (Farnham, UK: Ashgate, forthcoming), n.p.
15. See for example Colin Gunton, "Two Dogma's Revisited: Edward Irving's Christology," in *Theology through the Theologians: Selected Essays (1972-1995)* (London: T. & T. Clark, 1996), 151–68.

lens of the Spirit to complement and balance the views they gain in developing First or Second Article theologies.[16] Medieval scholarship is not entirely based on the first article, nor is Reformation theology entirely based on the second. Further, there is no implication that Third Article theologies should *replace* First and Second Article theologies. The methodological portraits above should be seen as stylized caricatures, not detailed, historically accurate photographs.[17] Nevertheless the claim of those promoting Third Article theologies is that the lens of the Spirit as a theological starting point provides a profound perspective that has not been comprehensively pursued with depth and rigor. "Such a theology of the third article is still truly in its infancy," writes Amos Yong, one prominent advocate of this perspective.[18] Although it has been hinted at, the development of a thorough, complete, and systematic Third Article Theology still lies in front of Christian endeavor. It promises a significant and valuable complement to the already well-developed First and Second Article theologies.

Theologies from Above and Below

A second contrast distinguishing Third Article Theology from other approaches is that it is a theology "from below" and not "from above." Unlike many other methodologies, Third Article Theology makes Spirit-enabled functionality its starting point rather than Trinitarian ontology. It focuses first on the Spirit-empowered works of God

16. So, both Augustine and Barth for example (used above as exemplars of First and Second Article theologies) certainly had robust pneumatologies.
17. Regarding the challenges of applying a "Kuhnian" paradigmatic approach in a complex theological and cultural landscape, see Martin Sutherland, "Pine Trees and Paradigms: Rethinking Mission in the West," in *Mission Without Christendom: Exploring the Site*, ed. Martin Sutherland (Auckland: Carey Baptist College, 2000), 132–36. Sutherland's work applies particularly to missiological categories, but has broader relevance.
18. Amos Yong, "Introduction: Pentecostalism and a Theology of the Third Article," in *Toward a Pneumatological Theology: Pentecostal and Ecumenical Perspectives on Ecclesiology, Soteriology, and Theology of Mission*, ed. Amos Yong (Lanham, MD: University Press of America, 2002), xvii.

rather than the internal makeup of his being. It starts from below and works upwards, rather than starting from above and working downwards. Although Barth's work exemplified a top-down approach, he recognized and endorsed this alternative method of doing theology:

> There is certainly a place for legitimate Christian thinking starting from below and moving up, from man who is taken hold of by God to God who takes hold of man . . . one might well understand it as a theology of the third article. . . . Starting from below, as it were, with Christian man, it could and should have struggled its way upward to an authentic explication of the Christian faith.[19]

In this movement from below to above, our theological reflection matches our discipleship. As we are drawn by the Spirit from our current fallen state into participation in the Godhead, so our theological reflections start from our current experience and knowledge (limited and tainted by creaturely mortality and sinfulness) and move upwards toward reflections on the nature and existence of God. So for example, in developing a Third Article Christology (or Spirit Christology), theologians start from Jesus' Spirit-empowered actions and move upwards from there to consider his divine status.

Two important clarifications are required. First, a key feature of Third Article theologies is the assumption of movement. Although the starting point for Third Article theologies is from *below*, this is merely a starting point *from* which movement occurs. The intent is to move upwards. As Gunton has written specifically of a Christology from below, "[T]here is every intention and indeed expectation to leave the ground, to speak theologically as well as anthropologically, and not to remain stranded on the earth."[20] Second, Third Article

19. Karl Barth, *The Humanity of God* (Richmond, VA: John Knox, 1972), 24–25.

theologies, as theologies from below, are intended to complement and not replace theological methods that start from above. While some argue for such replacement,[21] and others contend that theologies from below are preferable or prior to top-down alternatives,[22] this research argues that the two approaches are complementary. Third Article Theology fills out and corrects some of the over- or underemphases, the intractabilities, and particularly the dichotomies of other theological methodologies. As Dabney writes, a Third Article Theology may "bring together what we have so often let slip apart: worship and theology, service to God and service to God's world, the honouring of God's creation and the proclamation of God's redemption."[23] With its triple emphases of particularity, transformation, and relationship, starting with the Spirit holds great promise for theological insight.

Trinitarian Theology

More than the perceived inadequacies of other theological approaches, though, Third Article Theology finds its positive justification and impetus as a subset of the twentieth century's Trinitarian renaissance. Stanley Grenz, writing in 2004, comments that "whenever the story of the last hundred years is told, the rediscovery of the Trinity that sprouted and then came to full bloom during the eight decades following the First World War must be given center stage, and the rebirth of Trinitarian theology must be presented as one of the most far-reaching theological developments of the century."[24] This renewed interest has extended well beyond

20. Colin Gunton, *Yesterday and Today: A Study of Continuities in Christology* (London: Dartman, Longman & Todd, 1983), 11.
21. For example those Spirit Christologies that attempt to replace Logos Christology. See section 2.1 for further discussion of such proposals.
22. See for example Myk Habets, *The Anointed Son: A Trinitarian Spirit Christology* (Eugene, OR: Pickwick, 2010), 50–51. This aspect of priority is commented on further in section 1.3 below.
23. Dabney, "Starting with the Spirit," 27.

an investigation of the Trinity as a lone subject, to the impact that these newly derived or rediscovered Trinitarian understandings have on other theological doctrines. As Gunton famously remarked, "In the light of the theology of the Trinity, everything looks different."[25] Significant numbers of theologians are following the Trinitarian renaissance by reexamining soteriology, ecclesiology, Christology, and other theological aspects through interpretational grids developed from a Trinitarian starting point.

One pertinent insight that has emerged from this explosion of interest in the Trinity is the relative underemphasis historically on pneumatology—an oversight that is rapidly being redressed. McGrath's often-quoted witticism is that "the Holy Spirit has long been the Cinderella of the Trinity. The other two sisters may have gone to the theological ball; the Holy Spirit got left behind every time. But not now."[26] Yong comments similarly that "the resurgence of thinking about the Holy Spirit, long recognized as the shy, silent, or even forgotten member of the Trinity—has been underway at least since the middle of the twentieth century."[27] But just as a renewed interest in the doctrine of the Trinity led to a viewing of other theological loci through a Trinitarian lens, a renewed interest in pneumatology has led to the similar desire to view other theological loci through the lens of the Spirit. While such an approach fits within the subset of broader Trinitarian approaches to theology, it has shown

24. Stanley J. Grenz, *Rediscovering the Triune God: The Trinity in Contemporary Theology* (Minneapolis: Fortress Press, 2004), 1. Not all see the direction this Trinitarian renaissance has taken as positive, however. See for example Stephen R. Holmes, *The Quest for the Trinity: The Doctrine of God in Scripture, History and Modernity* (Downers Grove, IL: IVP Academic, 2012), 1–32, 198–200.

25. Colin Gunton, *The Promise of Trinitarian Theology* (Edinburgh: T. & T. Clark, 1997), 7.

26. Alister E. McGrath, *Christian Theology* (Malden, MA: Blackwell, 1994), 279. The nomenclature of the Spirit as a Trinitarian Cinderella can be traced back to (at least) G. J. Sirks, "The Cinderella of Theology: The Doctrine of the Holy Spirit," *Harvard Theological Review* 50, no. 2 (1957): 77–89.

27. Yong, "Introduction," xvi.

great potential for theological insight. As Dabney argues, "Christian theology has never come to grips with the fact that relationship to God through Jesus Christ starts with the Spirit. There may have been good reasons for that in the past. But now, a host of voices suggest, there are good reasons for beginning our theologizing where we begin our discipleship."[28] The discussion turns now to a brief explication of these reasons.

1.2 Why Should We Pursue a Third Article Theology?

What is to be gained by starting from the Spirit? What imperatives imply that starting with the Spirit will complement other more established theological approaches and yield valuable theological insight? The following discussion briefly considers five overlapping imperatives that point to Third Article Theology as an appropriate and timely theological method.

The Biblical Imperative

The first imperative is biblical. God's word reveals the Spirit as God's transcendent immanence. God is present to us by his Spirit in an immediate and not mediated sense.[29] This recognition allows us, and even encourages us to view God's other activity in the world as an aspect of the Spirit's mission, rather than the Spirit as an aspect of God's other activity. So, for example, the fact that the Bible speaks of the incarnation being facilitated through the Spirit (Matt. 1:18, 20) leads naturally to seeing the Son's mission as an aspect of the Spirit's, rather than the reverse.[30] The realization that God regularly initiates

28. Dabney, "Starting with the Spirit," 27.
29. See for example Steven M. Studebaker, *The Trinitarian Vision of Jonathan Edwards and David Coffey* (New York: Cambria, 2011), 164–65.
30. See particularly Clark H. Pinnock, *Flame of Love: A Theology of the Holy Spirit* (Downers Grove, IL: IVP Academic, 1996), 80.

his action in the world through the Spirit suggests a theological approach that views God's work in the world through a pneumatological lens.

There are multiple biblical examples of God initiating his action through the Spirit. In creation, even before the word of God was spoken, the Spirit hovered over the waters (Gen. 1:2). The Spirit or breath of God is viewed as both life's animator (Gen. 2:7; Job 27:3) and its *re*-animator (Ezek. 37:1-14). The nation of Israel was established through the Spirit (Exod. 15:8, 10; Isa. 63:11-14), and her prophets, priests, and kings were chosen and empowered through the Spirit (Zech. 7:11-12; 2 Chron. 24:20; 1 Sam. 16:13-14). Turning to the New Testament, Jesus' birth was facilitated by the Holy Spirit (Luke 1:35), his ministry was initiated by the Spirit (Mark 1:9-12), he was led to the cross by the Spirit (Heb. 9:14), and he was resurrected by the power of the Spirit (Rom. 1:4). The church similarly was born of the Spirit (Acts 2:1-41). Indeed, all of our Christian life is enabled by the Spirit: our conversion (John 3:5-8), our prayers (Jude 21), and our final resurrection (Rom. 8:11). The Spirit is the firstfruits of God's life in us and our life in him (2 Cor. 1:22). Even the very Bible that conveys these truths was inspired by the Spirit (2 Pet. 1:20-21).

Given that God, according to the clear biblical witness, so often initiates his work through the Spirit, there is motivation for adopting a theological approach that reflects this revealed reality—an approach that intentionally views God's activity through the lens of the Spirit. There is, of course, no definitive, logical link from "God works this way" to "We should learn of God this way." But it is nevertheless suggestive. At the very least it implies that a theological methodology that starts with the Spirit is congruent with Scripture and is well worth pursuing.

The Theological Imperative

A second imperative is theological. It is through the Spirit that we are united to Christ and increasingly conform to his image. By starting with the Spirit, then, our theological method matches our discipleship.

Analyzing the Spirit is difficult. "Understanding is often more incomplete and confused here than with most of the other doctrines."[31] There is less explicit revelation in the Bible concerning the Spirit than the other two persons of the Godhead.[32] While the Father and the Son have images enabling us to conceptualize them (however inaccurately), the Spirit is intangible and difficult to apprehend. When we turn from looking *at* the Spirit to looking *through* the Spirit, however, the picture quality changes dramatically.[33] It is only *through the Spirit* that we are convicted of our sinfulness (John 16:8-11), recognize Jesus as the Son of God (John 15:26), or approach the Father (Rom. 8:14-17; Eph. 2:18). It is *through the Spirit*, however implicitly, that we know about God and approach him in relationship. The suggestion of Third Article Theology, then, is that we make explicit what is implicit; that we intentionally begin our theological examinations by looking *through the Spirit*. In this way our theological method matches our reality, our experience, and our discipleship.

The image of the Spirit as a lens is helpful here. When we look *at* a lens—particularly a high-quality lens—it is transparent and difficult to focus on. When we look *through* a lens, the object in view comes

31. Millard Erickson, *Christian Theology* (Grand Rapids: Baker, 1983), 846–47.

32. Ibid., 847. See also Killian McDonnell, "The Determinative Doctrine of the Holy Spirit," *Theology Today* 39, no. 2 (1982): 142–45.

33. This echoes a distinction made by C. S. Lewis of looking *along* something rather than merely looking *at* it. See C. S. Lewis, "Meditation in a Toolshed," in *Compelling Reason: Essays on Ethics and Theology*, ed. W. Hooper (London: Fount, 1998), 52–55.

into perspective. Third Article theologies aim to use the Spirit as a God-given lens through which we can conduct theological inquiry. As Bobrinskoy writes, "Pneumatology is not so much one specific chapter of Christian theology as an essential dimension of every theological view of the church and of its spirituality and liturgical and sacramental life."[34] Third Article theologies thus explicitly aim to allow the Spirit to guide us into all truth (John 16:13).

The Philosophical Imperative

A third imperative is philosophical. The nature of created reality is irreducibly plural, and hence our theological examinations will benefit from starting with the relational category of Spirit.[35]

According to Steven Smith, twentieth-century philosophy has moved past classical ontology (which starts with the abstract concept of existence) and postfoundationalism (which starts with the limits of human capacity) and now begins its examination of reality through the medium of language and speech.[36] But language and speech are essentially interpersonal. Relationship undergirds and intrinsically indwells language. So before anything else, claims Smith, relationship must be the starting point of any examination of reality. But, as theologian Michael Welker notes, accepting this starting point of relationship and the irreducible plurality of our reality inevitably brings pneumatology to theology's forefront[37] because it is through the Spirit that we relate to God and others. Pneumatology thus becomes the primary lens through which we examine reality. As

34. Boris Bobrinskoy, "Holy Spirit," in *Dictionary of the Ecumenical Movement*, ed. Nicholas Lossky et al. (Grand Rapids: Eerdmans, 1991), 470.

35. See Dabney, "Starting with the Spirit," 5–11.

36. See Steven G. Smith, *The Concept of the Spiritual: An Essay in First Philosophy* (Philadelphia: Temple University Press, 1988), particularly pp. 3–5.

37. See Michael Welker, *God the Spirit*, trans. J. F. Hoffmeyer (Minneapolis: Fortress Press, 1994), particularly pp. ix–xiii. Note that it is the Holy Spirit and not a generalized notion of human spirit that is being referred to here. These two concepts need to be carefully distinguished.

Killian McDonnell writes, "Pneumatology is to theology what epistemology is to philosophy. Pneumatology determines the 'rules' for speaking about God."[38]

The Cultural Imperative

A fourth imperative is cultural. Third Article Theology, with its emphases on particularity and relationality, has significant potential to speak with relevance to contemporary western society in a way that can be heard.

Although the claims of cataclysmic shifts in cultural perception are exaggerated, there is nevertheless genuine validity in the notion of postmodernism. The way people view and understand the world around them has altered. Historical "givens" such as human rationality and the inevitability of progress are increasingly questioned. But if there is scant acknowledgment of human rationality or any Godward tendency in today's world, the potential for a First Article Theology to be heard is significantly diminished. Similarly, the claims of Second Article Theology can sound negative, and appear, at least initially, to offer little hope in a world that is already broadly acknowledged as chaotic and disintegrating. These theological approaches, quite appropriate to their time, have decreasing connection with a postmodern mindset.

In contrast, the themes of Third Article Theology—particularity, relationality, transformation—closely align with the leitmotifs of postmodernism. Good theology will always teach the church how to proclaim and live the truths we believe in a manner that is appropriate and understandable to our age. In a world that has rejected the

38. Killian McDonnell, "A Response to D. Lyle Dabney," in *Advents of the Spirit: An Introduction to the Current Study of Pneumatology*, ed. Bradford E. Hinze and D. Lyle Dabney (Milwaukee: Marquette University Press, 2005), 264. See also Killian McDonnell, "A Trinitarian Theology of the Holy Spirit," *Theological Studies* 46, no. 2 (1985): 214–18.

universal for the particular, Third Article Theology begins with the localized claim that in *this* people, at *this* time, the Spirit is present and drawing us as a community toward redemption with God. In a world that values community,[39] a Third Article Theology begins with the Spirit that draws us *together* to God. In a world where good and evil dwell side by side, a Third Article Theology that focuses on neither universal continuity nor discontinuity can "enable the Christian community both to socially and intellectually affirm some and yet contradict other aspects of the age we live."[40] Through its theme of transformation it can speak hope to a world whose fundamental fabric is threatening to unravel.

The Ecumenical Imperative

A fifth imperative is ecumenical. A Third Article Theology has the potential to speak with relevance not just to contemporary society but also to the current church. Naturally, no single methodology will result in practical catholicity, but if hopes are realized, starting with the Spirit will provide an approach that begins to cross theological spectra and draws diverging groups together.[41]

If the world is changing, the church is changing too. First, Christianity's influence is rapidly declining as Christendom "collapses." Religion is increasingly privatized and Christianity is just one choice among many. Second, the sociological and historical barriers that separate us from our Christian brothers and sisters are diminishing. In many cases, the major remaining causes of division between distinctive Christian groupings are theological dichotomies

39. Even if that community is a pale imitation of true Christian communion.

40. Dabney, "Starting with the Spirit," 25–26.

41. See Veli-Matti Kärkkäinen, *Toward a Pneumatological Theology: Pentecostal and Ecumenical Perspectives on Ecclesiology, Soteriology, and Theology of Mission* (Lanham, MD: University Press of America, 2002), 65–79. This article outlines ways the ecumenical imperative is being fulfilled through Third Article Theology.

that the vast majority even within those groups neither recognize nor understand. Third, and most significantly, Christianity has spread globally. The western missionary endeavor, for all its failings, has been immensely successful. Christianity exists and thrives in an increasingly vast variety of contexts. Furthermore, not just the sociological and historical barriers, but the practical barriers of distance and communication with other believers are diminishing.

In this changing context, what is needed is an ecumenical way of doing theology—a methodology that stretches wide to embrace different aspects of Christian diversity, drawing them into an emerging and common doctrinal unity.[42] Third Article Theologians claim there are several reasons to be hopeful that starting with the Spirit has ecumenical potential. First, pneumatology as a relatively unexamined theological subject allows Christian groups a new meeting place for dialogue, which can be approached without too many preconceived opinions and agendas.[43] Second, the starting point of particularity as opposed to universality enables the contextual distinctiveness of each position and community to be acknowledged up front, while also affirming the common reality of the Spirit in each particular expression. Third, there is hope that the both/and approach of Third Article Theology (rather than Second Article Theology's emphasis on discontinuities) will enable new ways to resolve or minimize longstanding internal disputes and dichotomies. Fourth, a Third Article Theology may be able to redefine what ecumenism means altogether, enabling a meaningful "unity within diversity" framework applied not just to individuals within local churches but to groups and traditions within the global Christian community.

42. For a lucid summary of the aims and limitations of an ecumenical theology see George Hunsinger, *The Eucharist and Ecumenism* (Cambridge: Cambridge University Press, 2008), 1–18. Particularly insightful is the list of seven guidelines, pp. 9–10.
43. See for example Philip J. Rosato, "Called by God, in the Holy Spirit: Pneumatological Insights into Ecumenism," *Ecumenical Review* 30, no. 2 (1978): 110–26, particularly pp. 110–11.

Fifth, Third Article Theology as a method invites, and in many ways requires, a strong integration of spirituality and intellectualism.[44] Given that the Spirit has always been understood as the binding factor, not just within the Trinity but historically within the church, it does not seem a vain hope that by starting with the Spirit we may find means to develop an emerging commonality not just in our thinking, but in our practice.

1.3 How Do We Do Third Article Theology?

How does starting with the Spirit actually work? Third Article Theology as a phrase is used in two senses: first as a specific theological *method* that starts with the Spirit, and second as the theological *understanding* that emerges when this method is adopted. Focusing particularly on the former sense, Third Article Theology locates itself within the broader stream of Trinitarian methodologies. But how does one go about following such a methodology? In particular, how is Third Article Theology distinguished from other approaches? Extending the work of Dabney, Habets has developed a set of ten methodological criteria that characterize Third Article Theology. What follows is my own theological articulation of these ten points.[45]

1. It starts with the Holy Spirit. Pneumatological considerations are not left to a postscript or conclusion but are, rather, incorporated into theological discourse right from the beginning.

44. See for example Kärkkäinen, *Toward a Pneumatological Theology*, 78–79.

45. These were listed most comprehensively in Habets, "The Surprising Third Article Theology of Jonathan Edwards," n.p. (Note that Habets's article lists the criteria without further explanation, although [as noted in the detailed explanations below] he has more detail in other published work.) Criteria 1, 6, 7, and 10 are sourced from Dabney, "Starting with the Spirit," 24–27. Criteria 3 and 8 have been independently suggested by Andrew Grosso, "Spirit Christology and the Shape of the Theological Enterprise," in *A Man of the Church: Honoring the Theology, Life, and Witness of Ralph Del Colle*, ed. Michel René Barnes (Eugene, OR: Pickwick, 2012), 206–22.

In contrast to First Article Theology which (in Dabney's characterization) starts with human capacity, or Second Article Theology which starts with human incapacity, Third Article Theology begins not with universals but with a particular claim, that through the ages a particular community has been and is being moved toward a redemptive relationship with God *by his Spirit*. From this theological baseline, a Third Article Theology views every aspect of God's action in the world intentionally through the lens of his Spirit, from creation to incarnation to eschatology. So, for example, employing a Third Article Theology approach, Clark Pinnock suggests exploring Christology as follows: "Let us see what results from viewing Christ as an aspect of the Spirit's mission, instead of (as is more usual) viewing Spirit as a function of Christ's."[46] The underlying assumption is that the Word of God is not the most basic reality, but exists only in and through an equally fundamental reality: the Spirit of God. As Pinnock writes, "Far from being an incidental or isolated topic in theology, Spirit is a major theme, supplying a standpoint, in fact, for surveying the whole vista of Christian truth."[47]

2. It looks *through* the Spirit rather than looking *at* the Spirit, thus it is a "Third Article Theology" and not a theology of the third article (which would simply be pneumatology).

Although closely related to it, Third Article Theology is not pneumatology. The doctrine of the Holy Spirit (characterized in this criterion as "a theology of the third article") is sometimes divided into a study of the person and the work of the Spirit, and while connected, is often examined separately from other theological loci. Third Article Theology, in contrast, examines the full range of

46. Pinnock, *Flame of Love*, 80.
47. Ibid., 10.

theological loci, but for each uses the Spirit as a lens. The Spirit thus becomes a means rather than an end to the theological task; it is looked *through* rather than merely being looked *at*. Pertinent here is the Spirit's role in connecting theological doctrines. Examined through the lens of the Spirit, it is virtually impossible to treat theological topics in isolation. So, for example, it is the Spirit that forms the members of the church into the body of Christ (1 Cor. 12:13), connecting ecclesiology and Christology. Third Article Theology thus focuses on the connection between and not just the content of specific theological subjects.

3. It should precede First and Second Article theology, as the most consistent way of coordinating the *ordo salutis*, from which we derive the *ordo cognoscendi*, and come to know the *ordo essendi*—from the Father, through the Son, to the Holy Spirit, and back by the Holy Spirit, through the Son, to the Father.

There are two reasons why Habets claims that Third Article Theology should precede First or Second Article Theology. The first is temporal and argues that this methodology should have priority at this moment in history. Reasons for this include historical context (in which both First and Second Article theologies have been rigorously mined as methodologies, leaving Third Article Theology as the methodology with the greatest untapped potential), theological context (in which the influence of Schleiermacher is increasingly distant, allowing for a distinguishing between the human spirit and God's Spirit),[48] and cultural context (in which the themes of particularity and relationality overlap with postmodern emphases and hence have potential to be more easily heard).[49] But Habets goes

48. As noted by Barth and discussed in section 1.1 above.
49. See section 1.2 above.

further and argues that Third Article Theology should be prior in an atemporal sense as well. The logic he uses relates ontology with epistemology. It is the Spirit who is our immediate (as opposed to our mediated) point of connection with God. We know of God and we know God first through the Spirit. Consequently, according to this criterion, our scholarly understanding of God should also always start with an examination through the Spirit.

At this point, my own understanding diverges from that of Habets. While I acknowledge the contextual imperatives for the priority of Third Article Theology, I would argue (atemporally) for First, Second, and Third Article Theology (and other methodological approaches) to be given equal priority, or better, for none to be given priority. Although an imperfect illustration, the situation can be compared to an understanding of scientific method. A theory can be sourced from anywhere, and in many ways the source is secondary and unimportant. All that matters is the extent to which the predictions of the theory match experimental evidence, something that is decided *after* the theory has been tested and not before. In a similar way all methodologies of determining knowledge about God and the world are permissible, and in many ways the methodology chosen is secondary and unimportant. What matters is the extent to which the outcomes of that methodology match God's revelation.[50] It may be argued (as I believe Habets would, and with some justification) that because Third Article Theology aligns our epistemological approach with our existential reality, it will be more likely to result in an understanding closely aligned with God's revelation. This may be the case, but it ought to be evaluated *after* the methodology has been worked out, and not before. Just as it is unwise to have an *a priori* prejudice toward one scientific theory over

50. See for example John Polkinghorne, *The Faith of a Physicist* (Minneapolis: Fortress Press, 1996), 5–7.

another, it is unwise to advance one theological method as being prior to others.[51]

4. It complements and thus does not compete with First and Second Article theologies. It is thus a contribution toward a fully Trinitarian theology.

As a theology that self-consciously starts with the Spirit, Third Article Theology is not a methodological replacement for First and Second Article Theology, but is intended to complement them and in some cases correct their extremes. The most developed outworking of this is again in Christology, where Spirit Christology is seen as a complement and not a replacement for Logos Christology. If Third Article Theology intentionally "competed" with Second Article Theology, then it would argue that Jesus' divinity could be entirely explained through the Spirit, in contrast to the more common but equally flawed argument that Jesus' divinity is entirely explained through the Logos. Certainly there are some theologians who argue for such a replacement,[52] but a more nuanced understanding sees both as complementary, by arguing that Jesus is *fully and uniquely the person of the Son and fully and uniquely anointed by the Spirit.*[53] The Third Article Theology developed in this research argues that if either of these aspects is neglected or downplayed, then neither Jesus' divinity nor his humanity can be adequately understood or explained.

5. It recognizes that the Spirit continues to speak today to the church in a retroactive movement of triune discourse. This retroactive hermeneutic is first applied to Scripture and then to

51. The question of priority in theological method will be addressed further in section 3.2, which discusses a "Wolterstorffian" methodological approach.

52. See Roger Haight, "The Case for Spirit Christology," *Theological Studies* 53 (1992): 257.

53. This Christological proposition, and the post-Chalcedonian Spirit Christology it explicitly rejects, is discussed further in section 2.1.

> the communicative acts of the church empowered and inspired by the Spirit of the resurrected Christ.

Despite human limitations, a Third Article Theology maintains that the Spirit is at work in the observer as well as in the revelation being observed. Habets terms this a "retroactive hermeneutic."[54] "Retro" refers to the role of the Spirit in the lives of biblical authors, enabling them to accurately recall and record Jesus' words and works (John 16:12). "Active" refers to the role of the Spirit in guiding the interpreters to the true message of the text and its correct application to the new situations the community finds itself in (John 14:26). Habets writes, "It is the Spirit of Light who illuminates the significance of the Christ event (*retro*); it is the presence of the Spirit of Life that moves the church on (*active*); and it is the Spirit of Truth who brings the word of God into new situations (*retroactive*)."[55] Two further features of a retroactive hermeneutic are noted. First, following Vanhoozer, it is intrinsically communal. Recognizing the problems of individual subjectivity, the church community has a Spirit-derived "charismatic authority,"[56] evidenced for example in the Jerusalem council: "for it seemed good to the Holy Spirit and to us" (Acts 15:28). Second, following Gunton, a retroactive hermeneutic leads to an understanding of doctrinal development as enrichment. Habets writes, "Enrichment . . . is a Spirit inspired reading of the past from the vantage point of the future."[57] This is contrasted with

54. For more detail see Habets, *The Anointed Son*, 103–17. Also, Myk Habets, "Developing a Retroactive Hermeneutic: Johannine Theology and Doctrinal Development," *American Theological Inquiry* 1 (2008): 77–89. For a similar discussion see Dabney, "Saul's Armour," 134–36.

55. Habets, *The Anointed Son*, 105–6. This terminology is also used by Philip J. Rosato, "Spirit Christology: Ambiguity and Promise," *Theological Studies* 38 (1977): 444.

56. As opposed to a canonical authority, to which it is subject. See for example Kevin J. Vanhoozer, *Is There a Meaning in This Text?* (Leicester: Apollos, 1998), 411.

57. Habets, *The Anointed Son*, 114.

an *evolutionary* development, where new understandings are loosely (or simply not) related to those of the past, and could be contrasted with a *static* resistance, where no development beyond the canon is permitted. A retroactive reading of the gospels thus opens us to an encounter with Jesus the Messiah—he who was uniquely and completely anointed by the Spirit of God.[58]

6. It unfolds the story of the Trinitarian mission of God in the world.

Because of its "particular" starting point of a community being moved toward redemptive relationship with God by the Spirit, Third Article Theology is intrinsically dynamic and narrative-based, and therefore missional. Looking through the lens of the Spirit, the story we are drawn into is one where all things are being brought together to the Father in Christ by the Spirit. The key term is "transformation," as Dabney explains: "[A] theology of the third article is a theology of God's mission of a transforming re-creation of creation, a theology of continuity in God's presence and purpose in creation and re-creation through the discontinuity of human sin and death. It is thus a theology of neither continuum nor of contradiction, but rather of transformation."[59] Moreover, Third Article Theology is not merely an examination of God's mission but intends, through understanding, to further it. As a Spirit-driven theology, it is intentionally an active player and not merely an observer of the Trinity's mission in the world.

7. It finds its focus in the center of that story—in the life, death, and resurrection of Jesus Christ.

58. This research uses but does not exegete the significant and complex interrelationship between the Spirit, the Scriptures, and the church. A detailed examination and development of a Third Article Hermeneutics is a valuable task that still lies ahead for Third Article Theology.
59. Dabney, "Starting with the Spirit," 25.

While a Third Article Theology maintains that the Spirit is at work through the ages, it also recognizes that our view of the Spirit's work is often marred and muddied through human failings. There is one episode in the story, however, where the Spirit's work is seen with particular clarity, namely the incarnation: the life, death, and resurrection of Jesus Christ. Here, the manner in which the Spirit interacts with and indwells humanity in order to draw us toward God can be most easily examined and understood. Third Article Theology has for this reason focused primarily to this point on Spirit Christology: understanding the identity and mission of Jesus through the lens of the Spirit. Various authors have given attention to this subject matter and produced useful and new understandings of both the hypostatic union and Christ's activity.[60] Spirit Christology is thus central to Third Article Theology, just as Christ is central to Christianity. We may be looking *through* the lens of the Spirit in Third Article Theology, but the center of our view is Christ. Consequently Third Article theological examinations of other theological doctrines often go through Spirit Christology as a first point of access. Of particular note here is the way that Spirit Christology informs our understanding of the immanent Trinity. There are significant risks inherent in starting with God's unity and "solving" his diversity, or starting with his diversity and "solving" his unity.[61] In contrast, a Third Article Theology focuses on that aspect of the revelation where the unity and diversity of the Godhead are most clearly and simultaneously evident—Spirit Christology—and from there draws implications about the immanent Trinity. For this reason, it is often claimed that Spirit Christology provides a more

60. For a useful overview see Habets, *The Anointed Son*, 188–227.

61. Karl Rahner, *The Trinity*, trans. Joseph Donceel (Tunbridge Wells, UK: Burns & Oates, 1997), particularly pp. 15–20.

secure route to understanding the immanent Trinity than other economic launching points.[62]

8. It highlights the eschatological nature of God's Trinitarian mission and proleptically incorporates such eschatology throughout its pneumatological dogmatics, whereby the mission of God in Christ remains the center of the divine drama.

Third Article Theology is not static. Being based on the transforming work of the Spirit in the community, it recognizes and requires constant movement. But the motion inherent in this understanding is neither purposeless nor endless. It has an endpoint and a goal. And that endpoint is the eschatological reality where our union with Christ and full human participation in his life in God are finally consummated. The Bride of Christ is not being endlessly purified; she is being prepared for a wedding. So Third Article Theology is constantly mindful of the realization that the Spirit's work in the world has as its goal the presentation of the church fully and finally to Christ. It is in this *telos* that the present transformation of the community finds its context and character.

9. It emphasizes the sanctifying work of the Spirit to move believers into further holiness or christification—thus it is existentially viable and apologetically effective in today's postmodern milieu.

With this point, the methodological criteria move beyond epistemology to existential reality, and beyond knowledge to transformation, and indeed beyond transformation to participation

62. For a more detailed discussion of the route from Spirit Christology to the Trinity, see chapter 7, or the collection of essays in Bradford E. Hinze and D. Lyle Dabney, eds., *Advents of the Spirit: An Introduction to the Current Study of Pneumatology* (Milwaukee: Marquette University Press, 2001), 302–46.

(as evidenced in the deliberate choice of the Eastern Orthodox–inspired term: *christification*). There is no sense in which the Third Article Theologian is a distant observer, observing God and humanity from afar through the lens of the Spirit with detached objectivity. Just as the Spirit is the means of union or the bond of love in the Trinity, so the Spirit forms the relational bond drawing humanity into union with Christ and in him into the life of the Trinity. Third Article Theology does not merely acknowledge this but takes it as a starting reference point. We are a community being redemptively drawn into the life of God by the Spirit. The intent is to deliberately and consciously align our scholarship with the Spirit's work so that in this area, as in other areas of our lives, we may be drawn together by the Spirit into the life of God. As Kärkkäinen writes: "Hardly any other theological topic has such a potential for integrating spirituality and discursive theologizing. . . . The hegemony of one-sided Western theologizing, notwithstanding its massive accomplishments, must give way to a more comprehensive, intercultural theologizing where the whole life, not just intellectualism, comes to bear on our living and thinking."[63]

10. It is a thoroughly ecumenical theology. Ecumenical is used here in two senses; first it indicates a commitment to the ecumenical creeds and confessions of Christendom, and second; it indicates the potential for doctrinal unity among the currently divided traditions of Christianity.

The point that Third Article Theology has ecumenical potential was made in the previous section. In listing it as a methodological criterion Habets (and Dabney) are making a bolder claim. Not only does Third Article Theology have ecumenical potential, it *must* be

63. Kärkkäinen, *Toward a Pneumatological Theology*, 78.

developed in a way that draws believers together as God's community rather than driving us apart. A Third Article Theology that does not intentionally point in this direction is not a Third Article Theology at all. Of course, our understanding of what it means to be united as God's people will be impacted and changed through our analysis, but at its core Third Article Theology is based on our journeying together into God's life by the Spirit. As Dabney writes:

> A theology of the third article, a theology of the Holy Spirit, could very well be a way we could begin to do that together now. Ecumenical theology, in this sense, would thus be best understood not simply as the task of resolving our "internal" disputes concerning faith and practice, but rather as the common task of living and thinking as disciples of Christ in the new "external" situation in which we now find ourselves, of participating in God's ongoing mission of reconciliation.[64]

Having discussed its distinctive features, motivational imperatives, and methodological criteria, the discussion turns now from Third Article Theology in general to its particular Christological outworking. Exploring Spirit Christology at this point has several advantages. First, it is difficult to speak of a theological method in abstract terms. Examining the theological doctrine where most effort has been directed and most progress made enables these features, imperatives, and criteria to be concretely demonstrated. Spirit Christology illustrates what a Third Article Theology looks like (in terms of content), not merely how it works (in terms of method). Second, Spirit Christology forms the natural focal point for a Third Article Theology. The Spirit Christological insights developed in the next chapter, together with the ten methodological criteria outlined in this chapter will be used extensively later in the research to apply a Third Article Theology approach to ecclesiology.

64. Dabney, "Starting with the Spirit," 26.

2

A "Chalcedonian" Spirit Christology

The last few decades have seen a significant rise in attention paid to Spirit Christology: theologies that interpret Christ's identity (at least partly) through the category of the Spirit, and not solely through the category of the Son. Spirit Christology's foundational claim is that we cannot understand the identity and mission of Jesus Christ without introducing the category of the Spirit at the most fundamental level. Andrew Grosso comments on this research stream that "the direction of theological studies in the late modern period bears more than a passing resemblance to the development of the tradition in the fourth and fifth centuries."[1] He adds: "Whether or not it will be possible (or desirable) to achieve relative to pneumatology anything like the same degree of specificity that was achieved at Chalcedon relative to Christology remains to be seen."[2]

1. Andrew Grosso, "The Anointed Son (Review)," *International Journal of Systematic Theology* 14, no. 3 (2012): 368.
2. Ibid.

The Spirit Christological propositions outlined in this chapter are "Chalcedonian" in two respects. First, they are intentionally compatible with Chalcedon. Perhaps the key Chalcedonian insight is that in Christ God's Son—the second Trinitarian person—became human. This chapter does not just affirm this insight, but more deeply engages with it through a fuller analysis of the Spirit's Christological mission. So the propositions below are intended to complement and not replace the Chalcedonian Creed or the Logos Christology it underpins. Positively, they provide a succinct and concise summary of some key Christological insights gained through applying the approach of Third Article Theology to Christology. Negatively, they explicitly recognize that theological proposals that inadequately deal with the category of the Spirit do not produce a Christology compatible with Chalcedon.

Second, the propositions are Chalcedonian in attempting to be similarly rigorous and unambiguous. In a series of carefully crafted phrases, the Chalcedonian Creed clearly describes how the human and divine natures operate within the incarnate Son. In a similar manner, this chapter takes steps toward clarity in the study of Spirit Christology, outlining and defending two carefully crafted propositions regarding how the Son and Spirit operate within Christ. There is no claim that these propositions either are or should be considered equal in status to the Chalcedonian propositions. Indeed, particularly toward the latter part of the chapter, they reflect my own understanding and not even a broad consensus of those exploring Spirit Christology. These caveats aside, the propositions are being proposed as constitutive of Spirit Christology, and will be used as foundational building blocks for constructing a Third Article Ecclesiology in the remainder of this research.

2.1 Neither the Son nor the Spirit Can Be Neglected

Proposition 1: Our Lord Jesus Christ is fully and uniquely the person of the Son and fully and uniquely anointed by the Spirit.

The Chalcedonian Creed affirms that

> our Lord Jesus Christ, the same perfect in Godhead and also perfect in manhood; truly God and truly man, . . . consubstantial with the Father according to the Godhead, and consubstantial with us according to the Manhood; . . . one and the same Christ, Son, Lord, only begotten, to be acknowledged in two natures . . . one and the same Son, and only begotten God, the Word, the Lord Jesus Christ.[3]

The pivotal point established in these creedal clauses is that Jesus Christ is one person, the Son, the second person of the Trinity, but having two natures, identified as a divine nature ("according to the Godhead") and a human nature ("according to the Manhood"). The first Spirit Christological proposition divides into two clauses, the first of which simply restates this "one person" point of the Chalcedonian Creed. The second clause, which parallels the first, emphasizes the complementary recognition that the Spirit dwells within Christ, and that the Son's incarnation cannot be understood or explained without acknowledging his anointing by the Spirit at a basic and foundational level. As Del Colle writes: "who Jesus Christ is and the salvation that he brings proceeds from a basic and foundational pneumatological orientation."[4]

On what basis do Del Colle and other advocates of Spirit Christology make such a claim? Consider the challenges that arise

3. Jaroslav Pelikan and Valerie Hotchkiss, eds., *Creeds and Confessions of Faith in the Christian Tradition: Early, Eastern and Medieval* (New Haven: Yale University Press, 2003), 181.
4. Ralph Del Colle, "Spirit-Christology: Dogmatic Foundations for Pentecostal-Charismatic Spirituality," *Journal of Pentecostal Theology* 3 (1993): 95–96.

when the Son's incarnation is understood without any reference to the Spirit—an *exclusive* Logos Christology. Such an understanding has Jesus revealing God to humanity substantially; he is God in the flesh. And because of this substantial, hypostatic union our salvation can and should be understood as genuinely ontological. The challenge comes when such an *exclusive* Logos Christology (which defines Jesus' divinity solely through the Son without any reference to the Spirit) tries to reconcile its ontological understanding with the biblical accounts of Jesus' activity. Consider some of Jesus' more obvious supernatural actions. How on earth did Jesus do miracles, control nature, and resist temptation? If he utilized the resources of his divine nature directly, then he has not experienced our condition—he is not *fully* human. But according to an *exclusive* Logos Christology, Jesus has (by definition) no other divine resources to draw on.

An *exclusive* Logos Christology is thus not capable of providing a comprehensive explanation for how divinity and humanity function within Jesus. Being exclusively a theology "from above," it understands the God-man in purely ontological terms, but neglects his activity. The core problem is that Jesus' divinity is fully contained and explained in the hypostatic union between his human and divine nature, with the latter defined only as the Son's divine nature. But this single divine reality within Jesus proves inadequate to explain how such a hypostatic union is feasible.[5] If Jesus' actions were achieved even partly by directly employing the divine resources of his Sonship, then precisely to that degree his humanity is denied. In any simplistically bipolar interaction, Jesus' divinity overwhelms his humanity with an unavoidably Docetic result. Given this,

5. See for example Ivor Davidson, "Theologizing the Human Jesus: An Ancient (and Modern) Approach to Christology Reassessed," *International Journal of Systematic Theology* 3, no. 2 (2001): 129–53.

Christologies that deny or neglect the genuineness of the Spirit within the person of Jesus can be grouped under a category labeled as Spirit-Docetism. Their error is to deny or neglect the Spirit, but their inevitable result is to minimize Christ's humanity.[6]

Many theologians argue that following Chalcedon, the accepted Christological position swung too far toward what I am terming a Spirit-Docetism. As Rosato asserts, "Had Spirit Christology's weaknesses not been so exaggerated, its strength would have remained a permanent legacy to the later Christological treatises of classical Scholastic and Protestant theology."[7] Some, for example, see evidence of this tendency in the writings of Athanasius. Given his historical context, this eminent theologian's significant emphasis on the Son was entirely justified as a necessary defense of orthodoxy. But viewed ahistorically, and particularly from the basis of our current "postmodern" context, some question whether this emphasis on the Son leads to an underemphasis on the Spirit and a consequent diminution of Christ's humanity.[8] Athanasius certainly affirmed the genuine humanity of Jesus,[9] but it is argued by some that he does not give an adequate account of it. For example, Athanasius does not consider the implications of Christ having a human soul, and consequently "appears incapable of accounting for the ignorance,

6. While Docetism was originally a historical appellation, it is used (and extended) here in an ahistorical manner. Such ahistorical usage is neither uncommon nor unjustified. For example, many ecclesiologists extend the category of Docetism beyond Christology and apply it to an inadequate understanding of the church's nature. The concept of Spirit-Docetism will be extended to ecclesiology in a similar manner. See particularly chapters 4 and 6.

7. Philip J. Rosato, "Spirit Christology: Ambiguity and Promise," *Theological Studies* 38 (1977): 435.

8. Note that as described in section 1.3 above, Third Article Theology embraces an "enrichment" understanding of theological development, a "Spirit-inspired reading of the past from the vantage point of the future." As such it is entirely appropriate to both recognize the relevance of Athanasius' work for its context, and to critique it from the basis of our contemporary and (hopefully) enriched perspective.

9. Thomas F. Torrance, *Theology in Reconciliation: Essays Towards Evangelical and Catholic Unity in East and West* (London: Geoffrey Chapman, 1975), 151–56.

emotions, agony, and suffering of Jesus."[10] Gunton argues similarly: "While it is unfair, for example, to charge Athanasius with anticipations of Apollinaris, his language is undoubtedly unguarded at times, as when, for example, he speaks of the Word as wielding his body like an implement . . . the humanity of Jesus lacks historical particularity in Athanasius."[11]

While these critiques of Athanasius have some merit, his emphasis on the Logos was at least partly a justified response to early Spirit Christologies, which tended toward the opposite error of denying the person of the Son in the incarnation. From early adoptionist proposals (for example, Theodotus the elder, who characterized Christ as merely an inspired man)[12] through to the much more nuanced Christologies of the Antiochene school (for example, Theodore of Mopsuestia, who qualitatively distinguished between God's indwelling in Christ and humans),[13] the key feature of early Spirit Christologies was that Jesus' divinity was interpreted *solely* through the category of the indwelling Spirit of God. These early theologians claimed that Jesus "was 'the man' in whom God dwelt, and accordingly that he was 'the man' who uniquely among other humans turned himself fully to God's indwelling presence."[14] If understandings that define Jesus' divinity solely through the Son are described as *exclusive* Logos Christologies, then these early understandings may be described as *exclusive* Spirit Christologies, as they define Jesus' divinity solely through the Spirit, and thus deny (or neglect) the place of the Son in the incarnation. Certainly, such

10. Myk Habets, *The Anointed Son: A Trinitarian Spirit Christology* (Eugene, OR: Pickwick, 2010), 73.
11. Colin Gunton, *Theology through the Theologians* (London: T. & T. Clark, 1996), 151.
12. See Robert M. Grant, *Jesus After the Gospels: The Christ of the Second Century* (London: SCM, 1990), 68–82.
13. See Gary D. Badcock, *The House Where God Lives: Renewing the Doctrine of the Church for Today* (Grand Rapids: Eerdmans, 2009), 136–37.
14. Ibid., 137.

an understanding has some positive features. It matches the scriptural description of Jesus being prompted and enabled by the Spirit,[15] and so provides a natural explanation for Jesus' spiritual development, together with an exemplary path to follow in imitating Jesus' submission to God's presence.

But an *exclusive* Spirit Christology has two significant and essentially irresolvable challenges. The first is that it requires Jesus the man to exist first, with God indwelling him either chronologically or logically after. This implies the existence of two distinct persons within Jesus, effectively two "sons" of God—traditional Nestorianism. The second challenge is revealed in the question: "Why Jesus?"[16] What is it that makes Jesus "the man" in whom God specially dwells? Why is this specific human open and obedient to God's presence, in contrast to the rest of us? The only way these questions can be answered is by endowing "the man" Jesus with some unique and intrinsic God-like characteristics—precisely that which an *exclusive* Spirit Christology denies by definition.

The core problem with an *exclusive* Spirit Christology is that it understands and explains the God-man Jesus based entirely on his activity. It is a theology developed purely "from below." While this approach is necessary and important, it is as inadequate on its own as a theology purely "from above." To fully understand Jesus we have to explain not just what he did, but who he was. Jesus must be ontologically God for salvation to be understood ontologically, as the biblical witness indicates it should.[17] Many proponents of an *exclusive* Spirit Christology explicitly (and all implicitly) start from an *a priori* assumption that Jesus' ontological humanity precludes his

15. Gerald F. Hawthorne, *The Presence and the Power: The Significance of the Holy Spirit in the Life and Ministry of Jesus* (Dallas: Word, 1991), chs. 2–6.
16. This parallels the previous "How Jesus?" question that illuminated the challenges of an exclusive Logos Christology.
17. See for example Gal. 6:15; 2 Cor. 5:17; John 1:13; 3:1.

ontological divinity.[18] Consequently, Jesus' divinity is understood as an inspirational presence rather than an intrinsic, ontological nature. God's Spirit indwells a preexisting man, rather than God's Son being hypostatically united to a human nature—a nature that anhypostatically had no existence before the union. As Moltmann compellingly expresses: "*Incarnation* has no presuppositions. *Inhabitation* presupposes human existence. If incarnation is identified with inhabitation, Christology is dissolved in anthropology."[19] An *exclusive* Spirit Christology thus leads directly and inevitably to traditional Ebionism, in that it fails to adequately account for Jesus' full ontological divinity. Given this, Christologies that deny (or neglect) the genuineness of the Son within the person of Jesus can be grouped into a category labeled Spirit-Ebionism.[20] Their fundamental error is to deny or neglect the reality of the Son in Christ, but the inevitable result is to minimize Christ's divinity.

Interestingly, the last few decades have seen a renaissance not just in Spirit-Christological proposals that embrace Chalcedon and Trinitarian theology, but also several that go much further by arguing that Spirit Christology should not complement but replace Logos Christology.[21] Their motivation arises from thinking that postmodernity finds an indwelling Spirit more accessible and palatable than an incarnate Son. Roger Haight, for example, writes "by a Spirit Christology I mean one that 'explains' how God is present

18. Newman states this explicitly: "If Jesus was human he could not at the same time be deity. His relationship with God had to be adoptive." Paul W. Newman, *A Spirit Christology: Recovering the Biblical Paradigm of Christian Faith* (Lanham, MD: University Press of America, 1987), 217.

19. Jürgen Moltmann, *The Way of Jesus Christ: Christology in Messianic Dimensions* (San Francisco: HarperCollins, 1990), 84.

20. Similarly to the use of Docetism earlier, Ebionism (and other Christological categories) should be understood ahistorically here. Each of these Christological categories will be analogously applied to ecclesiology at a later point in the research.

21. Theologians whose proposals openly embrace such a formulation include Roger Haight, Norman Hook, Geoffrey Lampe, Paul Newman, Hendrikus Berkhof, Piet Shoonenberg, and James Dunn. For further details see Habets, *The Anointed Son*, 194–200.

and active in Jesus, and thus Jesus' divinity, by using the Biblical symbol of God as Spirit, and not the symbol of Logos."[22] The parallels between early Spirit Christologies and this latter renaissance run very deep, and as such these modern proposals can also be grouped under the heading of Spirit-Ebionism. In attempting to replace the category of Logos with the category of Spirit in the person of Jesus, this stream of researchers essentially replicates the errors of the early church in its initial Spirit Christological explorations. Openly rejecting the Chalcedonian and Nicene formulations, they invite the same critique and suffer from the same flaws as their early-church counterparts. To fully understand Jesus' identity, neither the Spirit *nor the Son* can be denied or neglected.

The first Spirit Christological proposition thus argues that Jesus' identity cannot be understood simply by examining the relationship between his divine and human natures. These two categories, when viewed exclusively, are neither adequate nor complete. A third category is needed. More specifically, the divine category needs to be divided into two separate realities: the Son and the Spirit, and Christ's ontology needs to be expressed not only in how each of these relates to Jesus' human nature, but also in how they relate to each other. Taking the insights of Spirit Christology seriously means Trinitarian theology needs to be thoroughly integrated into Christology, so that the doctrine of the immanent Trinity accurately informs our apprehension of the incarnate Son. As the first proposition affirms:

22. Roger Haight, "The Case for Spirit Christology," *Theological Studies* 53 (1992): 257. There is a second Spirit Christological research stream (with which I align myself) that aims to complement rather than replace traditional Logos Christology. Contrast Haight's understanding with a definition from this second stream: "By Spirit Christology, I mean . . . reference to Jesus Christ is true to the gospel only when the Christological event is understood to be a thoroughly Trinitarian event, an event in which God effects salvation through the Son and the Spirit." Del Colle, "Spirit-Christology: Dogmatic Foundations," 93. For a detailed comparison of these two streams, see Ralph Del-Colle, "Spirit Christology: Dogmatic Issues," in *A Man of the Church: Honoring the Theology, Life, and Witness of Ralph Del Colle*, ed. Michel René Barnes (Eugene, OR: Pickwick, 2013), 3–19.

Our Lord Jesus Christ is fully and uniquely the person of the Son and fully and uniquely anointed by the Spirit.

2.2 Without Priority, without Confusion, without Separation

Proposition 2: Within the incarnation the identity and missions of the Son and the Spirit are logically and chronologically synchronous (without priority), distinct (without confusion), and interdependent (without separation).

Once the relatively simplistic errors that deny the reality of the Spirit or the Son within the incarnation are rejected, the question turns to how the identities and missions of the Spirit and the Son interact within the incarnation. If an exclusive Logos Christology has an adequate ontology but an inadequate understanding of Christ's activity, and an exclusive Spirit Christology has precisely the reverse, then the obvious theological move is to combine the two—to develop a theology that integrates and combines the missions of the Son and the Spirit in the Incarnation. Spirit and Logos Christology are not mutually exclusive, as Badcock explains: "Spirit Christology and Logos Christology are surely no more incompatible than Spirit and Logos themselves. According to strict Trinitarian orthodoxy, after all, the two are one as much as they are distinct."[23] Very broadly, such a proposal would have Jesus being ontologically the Logos, substantially the Son of God, and yet the Son's divine nature does not act directly on Christ's humanity. Rather, the incarnate Son voluntarily submitted his actions (not subordinated his person) to the Spirit, who guided and empowered him. Smail expresses this combined proposal succinctly: "This new man, Jesus Christ, is the

23. Gary D. Badcock, *Light of Truth and Fire of Love: A Theology of the Holy Spirit* (Grand Rapids: Eerdmans, 1997), 161.

work of the Son of God operating in his own human nature in the power and energy of the Holy Spirit."[24] But where does one start in constructing such a proposal? The second Spirit Christological proposition proposes some guidelines on how the Spirit and the Son can be understood to operate within the incarnation.

Perhaps the most famous and pivotal collection of phrases in the Chalcedonian Creed are the four "withouts": "*to be acknowledged in two natures, inconfusedly, unchangeably, indivisibly, inseparably.*"[25] George Hunsinger explains that these four exclusionary phrases within the Creed do not "isolate a point on a line that one either occupies or not. It demarcates a region in which there is more than one place to take up residence."[26] The second proposition of a Spirit Christology adopts a similar approach, in that it demarcates a "region" through a series of "without" clauses, rather than specifying the incarnate relationship between Son and Spirit in rigid and unyielding detail.

Without Priority

The first affirmation is that the identity and missions of the Spirit and the Son in the incarnation are synchronous; that is, the Father sent both the Son and the Spirit into the world so that the Son could become incarnate, and in the manner of their sending, both during the period of Jesus' earthly incarnation and now in glory, neither has logical or chronological priority over the other.[27] The following discussion first examines Christological proposals that prioritize the

24. Thomas Smail, *Reflected Glory: The Spirit in Christ and Christians* (Grand Rapids: Eerdmans, 1975), 64.
25. Pelikan and Hotchkiss, eds., *Creeds and Confessions: Early, Eastern and Medieval*, 181.
26. George Hunsinger, *Disruptive Grace: Studies in the Theology of Karl Barth* (Grand Rapids: Eerdmans, 2000), 132.
27. It will be argued (see chapters 7 and 9) that the fundamental reason for this is that in the immanent Trinity the Spirit and Son proceed and are begotten from the Father in a single action: the Father breathes the Spirit in speaking the Word. The Son and Spirit's incarnational features of interdependence and distinctness are thus ultimately sourced to their immanent Trinitarian identities.

Son over the Spirit, followed by the reverse, and argues that neither option is satisfactory.

Christological proposals that prioritize the Son over the Spirit (often abbreviated below as "Son-priority" proposals) do so either chronologically or logically. Chronological priority has the hypostatic union occurring first and then at some later point (often identified as Jesus' baptism) the Holy Spirit empowers Jesus for ministry.[28] This divides Jesus' life into two sections—a period where he had the Spirit's empowering and another where he did not. For those periods where he was not empowered, chronological Son-priority proposals strike the same problems as the Spirit-Docetic approaches. Before the indwelling, how did Jesus remain sinless; how did he grow and develop spiritually? The only possible answer is through the power of the divine Logos, which means Jesus has not truly experienced our humanity.

A more nuanced understanding avoids this challenge by giving the hypostatic union logical, but not chronological, priority. Jesus is first understood ontologically as the God-man according to an exclusive Logos Christology, and then the indwelling Spirit is layered on as an energizing, empowering influence. The scholastic doctrine of "habitual" sanctification provides an illustrative example.[29] This doctrine distinguishes between Christ's "essential" sanctification: Jesus' intrinsic anointing by virtue of his ontological union, and his "habitual" sanctification: his specific functional anointing by the Spirit in order to live a life of godliness. The "habitual" sanctifications are logically distinct from the "essential" grace of union, and

28. See for example Roger Helland, "The Hypostatic Union: How Did Jesus Function?" *Evangelical Quarterly* 65, no. 4 (1993): 325.

29. See Badcock, *Light of Truth and Fire of Love*, 146–53. Also, Declan O'Byrne, *Spirit Christology and Trinity in the Theology of David Coffey* (Oxford: Peter Lang, 2010), 59–62.

"derivative in the sense that they flowed from it."[30] Badcock critically assesses this approach as follows:

> The intention . . . was . . . to provide a distinctive role in Christology for the Holy Spirit in its relation to that humanity. However, the concept of human nature it involved was defective. It allowed no growth or movement in Jesus' human relation to God, whereas development is essential to human existence; without it, one cannot be a human being in a physical, psychological, social, or, we might add, spiritual sense. . . . The problem was that, in the end, the doctrine of the hypostatic union was interpreted in a timeless and static rather than a dynamic and temporal way. It was a conception that did not permit the humanity of Christ to be considered apart from its once-for-all assumption by the Logos.[31]

The twentieth-century Roman Catholic scholar Heribert Mühlen insightfully developed this scholastic doctrine by positing that the Spirit gradually "sanctified" the human nature of Jesus so that it could be increasingly united with the divine Logos. The Son, however, remains logically prior to the Spirit in the incarnation, because (according to Mühlen's presuppositional acceptance of the *filioque*) the Spirit proceeds from the Son in eternity.[32] Consequently, the sanctification of Christ's human nature comes *directly* from the indwelling Spirit, but *ultimately* is derived from the hypostatic union with the Son, which enables the Spirit's presence. However, intractable problems remain. First, the biblical witness contrastingly suggests the hypostatic union was *originally* facilitated by the Spirit (e.g., Matt. 1:18, 20). Second, it leaves unanswered the question of how the divine and human natures were originally united. If the

30. Badcock, *Light of Truth and Fire of Love*, 146.
31. Ibid., 149.
32. O'Byrne perceptively notes that "the idea of deducing conclusions for Christology from premises in Trinitarian theology will today strike many as untenable from the point of view of theological method." O'Byrne, *Spirit Christology and Trinity in the Theology of David Coffey*, 62. Note that Mühlen's work, and particularly its ecclesial application, is analyzed in greater detail in section 8.3.

Holy Spirit is required for *increasing* connection of the divine and human natures, how can it be absent in their *initial* union?[33] Son-priority proposals assert *that* the Word was made flesh; but on *how* the Word was made flesh they remain silent.[34] The only way this question can be answered is by positing a role for the Holy Spirit in the incarnation *from the very beginning*, precisely that which Son-priority proposals—with their *a priori* assumption that the hypostatic union is logically prior to the Spirit's indwelling—deny by definition.

If proposals that prioritize the Son over the Spirit lead to inconsistency, what about prioritizing the Spirit over the Son (abbreviated below as "Spirit-priority" proposals)? In a similar way, these can be categorized respectively into proposals that prioritize the Spirit chronologically and logically. An example of the former are *plerosis* Christologies (e.g., Dorner),[35] which posit that the union of the Logos with a human nature was a gradual process facilitated by the Spirit, resulting in a completely unified God-man only and finally at the resurrection. But just as the chronological Son-priority proposals led directly to the Spirit-Docetic challenges, so the chronological Spirit-priority proposals lead directly to the challenges of Spirit-Ebionism. In particular, *plerosis* Christologies require Jesus the man to exist first, and consequently two clear and distinct persons within Jesus: traditional Nestorianism.

33. It is at precisely this point that Studebaker finds Pinnock's Spirit Christology deficient. Steven M. Studebaker, "Integrating Pneumatology and Christology: A Trinitarian Modification of Clark H. Pinnock's Spirit Christology," *Pneuma* 28, no. 1 (2006): 18–19. See also Clark H. Pinnock, *Flame of Love: A Theology of the Holy Spirit* (Downers Grove, IL: IVP Academic, 1996), 79–112.
34. Kasper calls this Christology's central problem. See Walter Kasper, *Jesus the Christ*, trans. V. Green (London: Burns & Oates, 1977), 230–74. See also Badcock, *Light of Truth and Fire of Love*, 153–55.
35. See the description in Louis Berkhof, *Systematic Theology* (Edinburgh: Banner of Truth, 1939), 329–30.

More nuanced Christological proposals that give the Spirit logical priority strike related problems.[36] The thinking behind such proposals is that the Spirit "enhances" or "enables" human nature so that the divine Son, kenotically limited in some substantial way, can be incarnated as a human person. But the being concocted is neither truly God nor truly human. Jesus' human consciousness is simply a divine will "stripped down" to fit into the constraints of a mortal body. He is a *tertium quid*, occupying a space between divinity and humanity but containing the core essence of neither.[37]

The issue here is conceptual. Spirit-priority proposals view the incarnation as compositional—the "substantial compositional union of two natures forming a new being."[38] But in any such union, the divine being will overwhelm the human unless it is substantially limited. Consequently Spirit-priority proposals are forced into limiting the divine being.[39] The genius of the early church fathers, however, was that they did not view the hypostatic union as compositional, enabling them to make a logical (but not existential) distinction between person and nature.[40] For these early crafters of orthodox theology, the Son of God becoming human *did not mean*

36. David Coffey's work (examined in chapter 7 of this research) presents a contemporary example of a Spirit-priority Christological proposal.

37. There are clear parallels here with traditional Arianism. Where traditional Arianism creates a third category between God and humanity *in eternity*, Spirit-priority Christological proposals create a third category between God and humanity *in time*. For this reason one might be tempted to term the Spirit-priority proposals in this grouping Spirit-Arianism (paralleling the previous two categories that were termed Spirit-Docetism and Spirit-Ebionism). Son-priority proposals could then be labeled Spirit-Apollinarianism, and so on. The problem that is encountered in using this nomenclature is that (unlike the previous two proposal groupings) Spirit-Arianism (Spirit-Apollinarianism) does not lead directly to traditional Arianism (Apollinarianism), even when these terms are used ahistorically. Most people hearing these terms simply assume (incorrectly) that such a connection is being proposed given the commonality of the name. As such, it is prudent to choose clarity over rhetorical parallelism.

38. See Thomas Weinandy, *Does God Change?* (Still River, MA: St. Bede's, 1985), 119.

39. The discussion in Weinandy's book on kenotic theologies is relevant here. See ibid., 114–23.

40. If the Spirit-indwelled human nature (even logically) has an independent existence, as Spirit-priority proposals assert, then we cannot (even logically) distinguish between a person and a nature.

that the divine nature must *become* human (or vice versa). As the Chalcedonian Creed states: "The difference in natures being by no means removed because of the union."[41] Kenosis thus occurs through the Logos "taking on" a human nature rather than "giving up" some portion of the Son's inherent divinity. As such, "compositional" problems can only be avoided if the human nature of Christ is viewed as anhypostatic and enhypostatic, that is, if its existence depends on the hypostatic union, which Spirit-priority proposals *deny* by definition.

Summarizing, the first clause in this second Spirit-Christological proposition affirms that the identity and missions of the Spirit and the Son in the incarnation are logically and chronologically synchronous (without priority). But as is regularly noted, Christological conclusions have Trinitarian implications.[42] For example, T. F. Torrance writes, "We have to remember the inseparable relation in the Bible of . . . pneuma and logos, where the basic conception is of the living Breath of God uttering his Word, so that the reception of the Spirit is through the Word. The Spirit thus comes from the Father in the name of the Son, uttering the Word made flesh."[43] Protestant theologian Myk Habets has recently drawn a direct link between this synchronous Spirit Christological insight and an immanent Trinitarian understanding where the Father begets the Son in or by the Spirit in a single unified action.[44] Such exploration, however, need not only happen in the direction *from* the economy *to* the immanent Trinity. Not only should the insights of Spirit Christology be read into our understanding of who God is in himself, but the (perhaps altered) doctrines of the immanent Trinity should be read

41. Pelikan and Hotchkiss, eds., *Creeds and Confessions: Early, Eastern and Medieval*, 181.
42. Chapter 7 addresses this economic/immanent connection in detail.
43. Thomas F. Torrance, *Royal Priesthood: A Theology of Ordained Ministry* (Edinburgh: T. & T. Clark, 1993), 24.
44. Habets, *The Anointed Son*, 188–227. Also see section 7.3.

back into the economy to accurately inform our apprehension of the incarnate Son and so too the nature of our own existence. Accurate and rich understandings of the immanent Trinity will lead to accurate and rich understandings of Christology, together with other theological loci.

But equally, inadequate conceptions of the immanent Trinity will lead directly to inadequate Christologies. And it is here that the two final clauses of the second proposition are encountered. An overemphasis on God's numerical unity leads directly to Christological proposals that insufficiently distinguish between the Son and the Spirit within the incarnation. And an overemphasis on God's personal plurality leads directly to Christological proposals where the identity and missions of the Spirit and Son in the incarnation are insufficiently interdependent. Spirit Christology thus affirms the need for the identity and missions of the Son and the Spirit to be not just without priority, but also without confusion and without separation.

Without Confusion

Chalcedon's "inconfusedly" affirmation is a clear rebuttal of Eutychianism. While Eutyches maintained separate divine and human natures before the hypostatic union, he argued for a co-mingling after it, with the human nature being subordinate to the divine. A similar and closely related error is to *confuse* the Spirit and the Son within the incarnation (abbreviated here as Spirit-Son-confusion proposals). Such Christological misunderstandings too greatly meld or co-mingle the persons of the Son and the Spirit within the incarnate Jesus. They are ultimately derived from a misunderstanding of unity within the Godhead.

Similarly to traditional Eutychianism, the lens of time is significant for Spirit-Son-confusion proposals. While both Son and Spirit are often acknowledged, it is in the movement toward or from the reality of these two persons that confusion arises. While there are many variants, typically a monotheistic God in eternity—a single entity—is passed through the lens of time to end with a Trinitarian framework. This results in three often-repeated features: the denial of any real pre- (or eternal) existence of the "person" of the Son; the ontological equivalence of the Spirit with the risen Jesus; and consequently, a rejection of Trinitarian orthodoxy—particularly the denial of an eternal Trinity with three persons and one substance. These features are illustrated through the work of two theologians separated by 1600 years: Marcellus of Ancyra in the fourth century,[45] and Hendrikus Berkhof in the twentieth.

Regarding the Son's preexistence, Berkhof argues that Sonship has its origin in eternity, but realizes itself in a historical struggle for obedience. In his understanding, at a particular stage in covenantal history, the monotheistic God performs a new act in the creation of "the perfect covenanted man, the new man, the eschatological man."[46] This happens through God's Spirit, who is not (at this point) a separate person within the Godhead, but simply "the name for God in action toward the world."[47] But this newly created Jesus is part of history, and out of free will allows his "I" to be "fully and permanently permeated by the 'I' of God; and in virtue of this permeation becomes the perfect instrument of the father,"[48] as validated in the resurrection. While similar, Marcellus' understanding centers on the Logos rather than the Spirit. For Marcellus, the Father,

45. Having been tainted as a heretic, little remains of Marcellus' work. Mostly it is cobbled together from others' refutations of his work. Young comments: "These texts are not set in Marcellus' own context or connecting narratives or arguments: it is notoriously difficult to make sense of so much silence." Frances M. Young and Andrew Teal, *From Nicea to Chalcedon: A Guide to the Literature and Its Background* (Grand Rapids: Baker Academic, 2010), 57.

46. Hendrikus Berkhof, *Christian Faith: An Introduction to the Study of the Faith* (Grand Rapids: Eerdmans, 1979), 287.

47. Ibid., 331.

48. Ibid., 287.

Son, and Spirit emerge from God's activity, but are not eternally distinguished even as *hypostases*. The Logos is thus immanent but inactive before creation, "just as our speech is inactive when we are silent, but active when we speak."[49] Regarding the incarnation, only the Logos *together with the human body* is considered as the "Son." At the end of Christ's reign, the flesh is abandoned, the Son ceases to exist, and the Logos (necessarily) returns to God who again becomes a single unity or *hypostasis*.[50] Such denial of the Son's preexistence as made by Berkhof and Marcellus clearly runs counter to the Scriptures, which make such a claim explicitly (John 1:2; Phil. 2:6; Heb. 1:2f.) and implicitly (Rom. 8:3).

The second common feature of such proposals is the ontological equivalence of the Spirit with the risen Jesus.[51] For Berkhof, after the resurrection, Jesus is (humanly) taken into the realm of God, and his "I" (now molded into God's shape) becomes the "I" which controls God's Spirit. Before the resurrection the Spirit was the action of God in the world; now the Spirit is the action of Jesus. Berkhof summarizes: "[T]he Spirit is always and everywhere the Spirit of Jesus Christ."[52] Marcellus' approach is similar. For Marcellus, the coming of the Spirit is simply an "extension of an extension."[53] "The Spirit remains inevitably in God, but goes forth as activity . . . from the Father and the Logos."[54] So the Spirit is not just

49. Eusebius, "Contra Marcellum," I.i.4. As quoted in R. P. C. Hanson, *The Search for the Christian Doctrine of God: The Arian Controversy 318–381 AD* (Edinburgh: T. & T. Clark, 1988), 224.

50. Marcellus may have retreated from some of these understandings. See Hanson, *The Search for the Christian Doctrine of God*, 231–34. For an interesting discussion of Marcellus' assertion that the incarnation would end, see also Sophie Cartwright, "The Image of God in Irenaeus, Marcellus, and Eustathius," in *Irenaeus: Life, Scripture, Legacy*, ed. Paul Foster and Sara Parvis (Fortress Press: Minneapolis, 2012), 177–78.

51. Or even more clearly between *Father*, Son, and Spirit in Marcellus' work.

52. Hendrikus Berkhof, *The Doctrine of the Holy Spirit: The Annie Kinkead Warfield Lectures* (Richmond, VA: John Knox, 1964), 24.

53. As quoted in Hanson, *The Search for the Christian Doctrine of God*, 229.

54. W. G. Gericke, *Marcell von Ancyra* (1940), 128. Quoted by Hanson, *The Search for the Christian Doctrine of God*, 229.

consubstantial, but "of identical being" with the Father, just as the Logos is similarly "of identical being." He writes: "If anyone divides the . . . *Logos* from almighty God, he must either think that there are two gods . . . , or confess that the Logos is not God. I have learnt strictly that the Father's power (*dynamis*), the Son, is undivided and unseparated."[55] Regarding this ontological identification, Fee's weighty biblical counterargument notes pertinently that in only three of 140 pneumatic references does Paul refer to the Spirit as the "Spirit of Christ." He argues that ontologically identifying the risen Christ with the Spirit begins with and focuses on a small number of obscure texts that are superficially ambiguous, while ignoring many other texts that clearly distinguish between the two persons.[56] Numerous theological challenges can be added to Fee's exegetical arguments. As one example, an ontological identity of Spirit and Son precludes worship. For us to participate in Christ's relationship with his Father, someone must stand on humanity's side to enable believers to hear the words *from* Christ as they are spoken, and to intercede for believers *to* Christ. If the person relating believers *to* Christ is ontologically identified *with* Christ, then there is no genuine relationship.[57]

Both Berkhof's and Marcellus' proposals do not fall neatly into any standard theological categorization. They can both be misunderstood as modalistic,[58] and Berkhof's theology may be misunderstood as

55. As quoted in Hanson, *The Search for the Christian Doctrine of God*, 231. This is a quote from Marcellus' Letter to Julius, written at a later point when he is more willing to call the Logos the Son. The key point is his refusal to see distinctions within the Godhead, beyond mere action.

56. See Gordon Fee, *God's Empowering Presence: The Holy Spirit in the Letters of Paul* (Peabody, MA: Hendrickson, 1994), 834–40.

57. These themes are worked out further in chapter 9 of this research.

58. For Marcellus, this comes from the strong emphasis on a single *hypostasis*, while for Berkhof, the human person of Jesus is totally subordinated to the personality of God, so there is (likewise, but only eventually) one subject. See for example, N. A. Nissiotis, "Theological Rapprochement: The Doctrine of the Holy Spirit (Review)," *Ecumenical Review* 17, no. 3 (1965): 274–76. Nissiotis only claims that Berkhof "leaves the reader with the impression that he hides a kind of

binitarian.[59] The point that separates both understandings from each misinformed critique is their dynamism. This is a point that Berkhof himself makes emphatically.[60] The relationship between God as Father, Son, and Spirit changes over time as God works out his salvation plan in the world. The Trinity is a genuine temporal aberration of a single eternal unity. God remains in eternity a single subject, but in time is enriched permanently (Berkhof) or altered temporarily (Marcellus) through his double movement toward humankind and drawing them back into himself. The consequence is a denial of Trinitarian orthodoxy. So, Hanson writes of Marcellus: "There was for him in God only one 'Person' in the later Trinitarian sense of that word."[61] In Berkhof's case, the denial is explicit: "We must ask the question whether a radical return to a pneumatic Christology would not do more justice to the biblical message, and be more relevant to the modern mind, than our traditional categories. It is clear that such a rethinking would not leave the Trinitarian dogma unaffected."[62]

The analysis above suggests that, contra Berkhof's claim, approaches that meld the Son and the Spirit within the incarnation do not do "more justice to the biblical message," so what motivates Berkhof, Marcellus, and others in this direction? In part, they are reacting to an ever-present tendency to overemphasize the distinction between Christ and the Spirit, an approach they

Modalism" (ibid., 275). Note that both Eusebius and the Catholic Encyclopedia label Marcellus' work as Sabellianism. See Hanson, *The Search for the Christian Doctrine of God*, 224; and John Arendzen, "Marcellus of Ancyra," in *The Catholic Encyclopedia*, ed. William J. McDonald (Palatine, IL: Jack Heraty & Associates, 1967), 9:191.

59. So Jesus is not merely another form of God, but a separate subject, with a separate consciousness. This is why he struggles to subordinate himself to the Spirit. See for example, Donald Bloesch, *The Holy Spirit: Works and Gifts* (Downers Grove, IL: IVP, 2000), 256–57.
60. Berkhof, *Christian Faith*, 312. Marcellus' understanding can be similarly defended against Sabellianism (although less forcefully).
61. Hanson, *The Search for the Christian Doctrine of God*, 230.
62. Berkhof, *The Doctrine of the Holy Spirit*, 21.

(correctly) claim leads to tritheism and an unbelievable Christian gospel.[63] And in their defense, a strong unity between the Spirit and the risen Christ must be affirmed. Even Barth uses language that, when viewed in isolation, appears to confuse the Son and the Spirit: "[The Spirit] is no other than the presence and action of Jesus Christ himself: his stretched out arm; he himself in the power of his resurrection."[64] But where Barth and others shrink back from ontological identity, what pushes Berkhof, Marcellus, and others in this direction? The core problem is that they lack a nuanced understanding of the meaning of person. Embracing an overly individualized understanding that has insufficient regard for indwelling or *perichoresis*, these theologians are forced into the dichotomous alternatives of either tritheism or complete identification of the Spirit and the Son.[65] A more considered analysis opens a middle road, which recognizes that Paul's fluid language about Christ and the Spirit is primarily soteriological and experiential, and from that basis derives ontological implications.

One key consequence of Son-Spirit-confusion proposals is their tendency toward monophysitism. When the Spirit and Son are melded, the union of the divine and human is reduced to a bipolar interaction, with the divine inevitably overwhelming the human. This is seen in the work of both Berkhof (for whom the divine nature gradually overwhelms the human) and Marcellus (for whom the divine nature is always predominant and the flesh lacks a human *psyche*). Such a tendency toward monophysitism justifies using the label Spirit-Eutychian for Spirit-Son-confusion proposals. The

63. This understanding is caricatured in the oft-repeated comment from Pentecostals to Evangelicals: "You know the risen Christ, but you do not know the Spirit." See N. M. Watson, "Risen Christ and Spirit/Paraclete in the Fourth Gospel," *Australian Biblical Review* 31 (1983): 81.

64. Karl Barth, *Church Dogmatics*, trans. G. W. Bromiley (Peabody, MA: Hendrickson, 2010), IV.2, 322–23.

65. See for example Nissiotis, "Theological Rapprochement," 275–76.

confusion of Son and Spirit leads to the confusion of the divine and human, with the divine overwhelming the human.

Occam's razor states that "entities should not be multiplied unnecessarily," or as Einstein (reputedly) put it: "Everything should be made as simple as possible, but not simpler." Spirit-Eutychians develop a doctrine of Christ and the Holy Spirit that bypasses and rejects the complicated and mysterious orthodox Trinitarian understanding. The direction of their movement is from one to three. The immanent and monotheistic God seen through the lens of time leads to an economic, triadic theology. But their wielding of Occam's razor cuts into orthodox Trinitarian theology too deeply. It is necessary to ontologically distinguish between the Son and the Spirit within the incarnation if Christology is to match the biblical revelation, and enable authentic worship.

Without Separation

If Spirit-Eutychianism confuses the persons of the Son and the Spirit in the incarnation, there is an opposite error that excessively separates them (abbreviated here as Spirit-Son-separation proposals). Rather than working from one to three, these proposals often have an initially triadic God interact with time to obtain an eventual unity. Such proposals can be divided into those where God's immanent self genuinely changes through interaction with the world, reaching eventual unity only eschatologically, and those where God's worldly interaction has a proleptic effect on his being, so that he always was and is who he is becoming. God is thus open to the world but not changed by it. From the above descriptions, it is evident that proposals that excessively separate the Son and the Spirit often reject either or both traditional notions of God's immutability and impassibility. This, together with the strongly monotheistic starting point of the early church fathers, means Spirit-Son-separation proposals were uncommon in Christianity's early centuries. They have become prevalent in recent years, though, as God's openness to the world and his ontological suffering is increasingly considered.[66]

Dealing with the broad variety of proposals that excessively separate the Son and the Spirit within the incarnation is unfeasible, but the prominent Christological proposals of Jürgen Moltmann illustrate well the key challenges involved. While there is great strength and incredible creativity in Moltmann's work, it has core challenges directly related to its inclusion in this category.[67] Moltmann's theology has three presuppositional starting points. First, it is intrinsically eschatological. "God is a reality ahead of us, coming to us out of a future that breaks into the present bringing what is genuinely new."[68] Second, Moltmann intentionally starts from the threeness of God as described in the biblical narrative. He writes, "It seems to make more sense theologically to start from the biblical history, and therefore to make the unity of the three divine Persons the problem, rather than to take the reverse method—to start from the philosophical postulate of absolute unity, in order then to find the

66. Sarot's claim that "almost all theologians agree that God does suffer" hints at the tendency toward such proposals in contemporary theology. See Marcel Sarot, "A Critical Discussion of Thomas G. Weinandy's *Does God Suffer?*" *Ars Disputandi* 1 (2001). Retrieved September 18, 2013 from Utrecht Publishing and Archiving Services: http://www.arsdisputandi.org/.

67. Choosing Moltmann as an example raises a question about which of the two categories mentioned above he fits into. This is a surprisingly difficult question to answer, and commentators on Moltmann's work differ. Thompson, for example, places Moltmann in the first category. God is "an evolving event between three divine subjects and the world . . . wherein the triune God is not complete until the end." John Thompson, *Modern Trinitarian Perspectives* (New York: Oxford University Press, 1994), 51. Otto, in contrast, places Moltmann in the second category. "God is instead a 'possible God' (Gott-möglich), coming from the future, from the non-Being of potentiality, which for Moltmann, 'must be higher ontologically than reality.'" Randalf Otto, "The Use and Abuse of Perichoresis," *Scottish Journal of Theology* 54, no. 3 (2001): 375. The fact that both these positions can justifiably argue to be valid interpretations suggests Moltmann evidences theological imprecision on this point.

68. David J. Bryant, "God's Body or Beloved Other? Sallie McFague and Jürgen Moltmann on God and Creation," in *Theology as Conversation: The Significance of Dialogue in Historical and Contemporary Theology: A Festschrift for Daniel L. Migliore*, ed. Bruce L. McCormack and Kimlyn J. Bender (Grand Rapids: Eerdmans, 2009), 179.

problem in the biblical testimony."[69] Third, at an ontological level God is open to the world and affected by his interactions with it. So, to choose a trenchant example, for Moltmann it is important, necessary, and accurate to say that God in his inmost being suffers and dies. "The pain of the cross determines the inner life of the triune God from eternity to eternity."[70] Two implications Moltmann derives from these presuppositions illustrate particularly common features of Spirit-Son-separation proposals—panentheism and defining unity perichoretically. But both of these implications have significant biblical and logical challenges.

Panentheism—the belief that the world is an intrinsic and essential part of God—is the first key implication of Moltmann's theological presuppositions, and exists (to some extent) in most Spirit-Son-separation proposals, although it is not always referred to explicitly. The traditional problem plaguing panentheistic theologies is that they limit God's freedom. God becomes dependent on the world. Moltmann responds to this challenge by tying necessity and freedom together. "In God necessity and freedom coincide; they are what is for him axiomatic, self-evident. For God it is axiomatic to love, for he cannot deny himself. . . . This does not make him 'his own prisoner.' It means that he remains true to himself."[71]

Despite such dogged attempts at finding solutions, Moltmann's panentheistic Trinitarian theology retains significant issues. First, there is no biblical support for panentheism. "No Biblical text suggests or implies that the world is a part of God, either of his eternal nature or his actual existence."[72] Even in those few texts that can

69. Jürgen Moltmann, *The Trinity and the Kingdom: The Doctrine of God* (Minneapolis: Fortress Press, 1981), 149.
70. Ibid., 161.
71. Ibid., 107–8.
72. John W. Cooper, *Panentheism: The Other God of the Philosophers* (Grand Rapids: Baker, 2006), 323.

potentially be interpreted as panentheistic[73] a close reading clearly reveals significant distinction between Creator and creatures, and not an ontologically necessary indwelling.[74] Second, there are deep logical problems. In making creation a necessity for God, Moltmann removes a significant distinction between the eternal begetting of the Son and the creation of the world. God's creation of the world is a contingent necessity in the same way as is his begetting of the Son. But this immediately raises questions of how we distinguish sufficiently between the Son and creation. So for example, why does creation fall/endure suffering/need saving, when the Son does not? Molnar critically notes that Moltmann cannot simultaneously and consistently hold that God is free and that he needs the world.[75] At its core, Moltmann's panentheistic theology can provide a compelling description of God suffering as he absorbs evil and iniquity into himself, but it cannot provide a convincing explanation of why there should or could be sin and suffering in the first place.

Defining unity perichoretically—where *perichoresis* logically precedes and causes the Godhead's unity rather than following it—is the second key implication. By starting theologically with three separate persons of the Godhead, the obvious question is how the three are also one. Moltmann rejects the idea of God's unity as essence, being, or subject, and in contrast defines it as both eschatological ("The unity of the Father, Son and Spirit is then the eschatological question about the consummation of the Trinitarian history of God")[76] and perichoretic ("The concept of God's unity … must be conceived in the *perichoresis* of the divine Persons").[77]

73. For example, birth metaphors for creation (Deut. 32:18), the church as Christ's body (1 Corinthians 12).

74. Cooper, *Panentheism*, 322–24.

75. See Paul D. Molnar, *Divine Freedom and the Doctrine of the Immanent Trinity* (London: T. & T. Clark, 2002), 226–27.

76. Moltmann, *The Trinity and the Kingdom*, 149.

77. Ibid., 150.

By *perichoresis*, Moltmann means that the three constitute a unity in their mutual relations together as a single community. "The persons themselves constitute both their differences and their unity. If the divine life is understood perichoretically, then it . . . is bound to consist of the living fellowship of the three Persons who are related to one another and exist in one another. Their unity does not lie in the one lordship of God; it is found in the unity of their tri-unity."[78]

But defining unity perichoretically is deeply problematic, evidencing biblical selectivity, historical inaccuracies, and logical inconsistencies. First, despite Moltmann's claims otherwise,[79] the epistemological methodology of starting with the three and "solving" the problem of unity does not match the biblical record, which makes God's monotheism in the Old Testament at least chronologically prior to the "three" Gods of the New. It is thus more justifiable (although it eventually becomes just as problematic) to argue that the biblical record makes God's threeness the "problem" to be solved. Better than both approaches, however, is a simultaneous recognition of the Godhead's threeness and oneness, which a growing number of scholars recognize as both orthodox and coherent.[80] Second, *perichoresis* is not traditionally understood as the grounds of God's unity, but rather as its consequence. There appears to be little recognition in Moltmann's theological proposals that he is using the concept of *perichoresis* to mean something quite different from the traditional understanding.[81] Third and most significantly, there are logical inconsistencies. First, how can a God who takes suffering into his ontological being from eternity to eternity conceivably *overcome*

78. Ibid., 175.

79. See for example ibid., 149–50.

80. See for example Molnar, *Divine Freedom*, 232. Or more generally see the brief discussion at the beginning of chapter 7.

81. See for example Veli-Matti Kärkkäinen, *The Trinity: Global Perspectives* (Louisville: Westminster John Knox, 2007), 116–17.

suffering? Rahner makes this point forcefully, "In Moltmann and others I sense a theology of absolute paradox. . . . It does not help me escape from my mess and mix-up and despair if God is in the same predicament. . . . From the beginning I am locked into [the world's] horribleness while God—if this word continues to have any meaning at all—is in a true and authentic, consoling sense the God who does not suffer, the immutable God."[82] A second logical problem is how the Father or the Spirit, who are determined by their relationship with the Son,[83] can have that relationship with that Son completely severed and yet still remain the Father or the Spirit? Why did the ontological death of God the Son not immediately lead to the termination of God the Father and God the Spirit? Kärkkäinen's conclusion here is telling: "The most that can be said about the unity of the triune God in Moltmann's theology is that he has not successfully satisfied even the most moderate critics."[84]

Moltmann's work, together with many other Spirit-Son-separation proposals, pushes beyond the traditional position of having God the Son suffering and dying *according to his human nature*, and proposes God taking suffering and death into his ontological, eternal being. In order for this position to not end in immediate theological absurdity with the cessation of God's existence, it must significantly distinguish between the Trinitarian persons, leading to an excessive separation between the Son and the Spirit in both the Trinity and the life of Christ. But, as has been shown above, the consequences of adopting such a position—panentheism and defining unity perichoretically—neither match the biblical witness, nor stand up to theological scrutiny. Spirit-Son-separation proposals distinguish between the persons of the Trinity in order to allow God to

82. Karl Rahner, *Karl Rahner in Dialogue: Conversations and Interviews 1965-1982*, ed. Paul Imhof and Hubert Biallowons, trans. Harvey D. Egan (New York: Crossroad, 1986), 126–27.

83. Moltmann, *The Trinity and the Kingdom*, 172.

84. Kärkkäinen, *The Trinity*, 117.

ontologically suffer. But placing suffering within God's very nature neither explains its existence nor rescues us from its presence.[85]

Historically the study of Christology has been focused on the relationship between Christ's divine and human natures. Erickson wittily portrays this by commenting:

> Someone has said that there are only seven basic jokes, and every joke is merely a variation on one of them. A similar statement can be made about heresies regarding the person of Christ. There are basically six, and all of them appeared within the first four Christian centuries. They either deny the genuineness (Ebionism) or the completeness (Arianism) of Jesus' deity, deny the genuineness (Docetism) or the completeness (Apollinarianism) of his humanity, divide his person (Nestorianism) or confuse his natures (Eutychianism). All departures from the orthodox doctrine of the person of Christ are simply variations of one of these heresies.[86]

Applying a Third Article Theology approach to Christology suggests that this dualistic distinction of natures is no longer adequate, and that not only should the relationship between the Son's divine nature and human nature be examined, but also the way the Son and Spirit relate to each other within the incarnation.

From a negative standpoint, this analysis has enabled six complementary Spirit-Christological errors to be identified: those that deny within the incarnation the genuineness of the Spirit's anointing (an exclusive Logos Christology or Spirit-Docetism) or the genuineness of the Son's personhood (an exclusive Spirit Christology or Spirit-Ebionism); those that deny the full anointing of the Spirit (Son-priority proposals) or the full personhood of the Son (Spirit-priority proposals); those that excessively meld or confuse the Son

85. A point granted by even sympathetic commentators: "In Moltmann's understanding, the cross does not solve the problem of suffering, but meets it with the voluntary fellow-suffering of love." Richard Bauckham, *The Theology of Jürgen Moltmann* (Edinburgh: T. & T. Clark, 1995), 12.

86. Millard Erickson, *Christian Theology* (Grand Rapids: Baker, 1983), 738.

and the Spirit during the incarnation (Spirit-Son-confusion proposals or Spirit-Eutychianism) or excessively distinguish between them (Spirit-Son-separation proposals). From a positive standpoint, applying a Third Article Theological method to Christology has enabled two "Chalcedonian" propositions to be affirmed. First, that Jesus Christ our Lord is fully and uniquely the person of the Son and fully and uniquely anointed by the Spirit. Second, that within the incarnation the identity and missions of the Son and the Spirit are logically and chronologically synchronous (without priority), distinct (without confusion), and interdependent (without separation). While these propositions in no way encapsulate the full breadth of Christological insight enabled through a Third Article Theology approach, they do provide a succinct summary of some key Spirit Christological insights. In the next chapter, the discussion turns from an examination of Christology, to exploring how a Third Article Theology methodology can yield insight into the theological doctrine of ecclesiology.

3

Constructing a Third Article Ecclesiology

Recent investigations of Third Article Theology have concentrated on Christology, examining how Christ's divine and human natures are hypostatically united *through the Spirit*, and the implications this pneumatological perspective has for Christ's activity and mission. Myk Habets maintains that (broadly conceived) there are at least fifty theologians currently pursuing Spirit Christological research.[1] There are significantly fewer explicitly extending Third Article Theology beyond Christology. In 1996 Clark Pinnock published a monograph that examines the main theological loci through a pneumatological lens.[2] Being the first (and so far, the only) complete Third Article Theology, the volume adopts a bird's-eye view, but nevertheless indicates some profitable directions for the subject. Three years later,

1. Myk Habets, *The Anointed Son: A Trinitarian Spirit Christology* (Eugene, OR: Pickwick, 2010), 200.
2. Clark H. Pinnock, *Flame of Love: A Theology of the Holy Spirit* (Downers Grove, IL: IVP Academic, 1996). Similarly to Pinnock's examination through a pneumatological lens, Yong has examined a number of theological doctrines through the related and overlapping lens of Pentecostalism. See Amos Yong, *The Spirit Poured Out on All Flesh: Pentecostalism and the Possibility of Global Theology* (Grand Rapids: Baker Academic, 2005).

Lyle Dabney called for the development of a detailed systematic theology that intentionally starts with the Spirit.[3] He is rumored to be working toward such an accomplishment individually,[4] although his published work to date only contains pointers.[5]

Various other authors also prioritize the Spirit, but without developing a complete and systematic Third Article Theology. The work of Wolfhart Pannenberg,[6] Jürgen Moltmann,[7] the late Stanley Grenz,[8] and Gary Badcock[9] are indicative. Pannenberg and Grenz are truly systematic, and both give the Spirit more priority than other contemporary theologians. While there is quite some overlap between their work and Third Article Theology, their starting point is the Trinity and not the Spirit specifically. In contrast, Moltmann and Badcock more explicitly start with the Spirit, but their research is better categorized as exploratory rather than comprehensive. Also

3. See particularly D. Lyle Dabney, "Starting with the Spirit: Why the Last Should Now Be First," in *Starting with the Spirit*, ed. Stephen Pickard and Gordon Preece (Hindmarsh: Australian Theological Forum, 2001), 26–27.
4. See Amos Yong, "Introduction: Pentecostalism and a Theology of the Third Article," in *Toward a Pneumatological Theology: Pentecostal and Ecumenical Perspectives on Ecclesiology, Soteriology, and Theology of Mission*, ed. Amos Yong (Lanham, MD: University Press of America, 2002), xvii.
5. Dabney's significant publications to date on Third Article Theology include the following: a series of four chapters given as presentations in 1999 (see Pickard and Preece, eds., *Starting with the Spirit*, 3–110); D. Lyle Dabney, "Otherwise Engaged in the Spirit: A First Theology for a Twenty-First Century," in *The Future of Theology: Essays in Honor of Jürgen Moltmann*, ed. Miroslav Volf et al. (Grand Rapids: Eerdmans, 1996), 154–63; and a similar article in an introductory collection focused on pneumatology: D. Lyle Dabney, "Why Should the First Be Last? The Priority of Pneumatology in Recent Theological Discussion," in *Advents of the Spirit: An Introduction to the Current Study of Pneumatology*, ed. Bradford E. Hinze and D. Lyle Dabney (Milwaukee: Marquette University Press, 2005), 240–61.
6. Wolfhart Pannenberg, *Systematic Theology*, trans. G. W. Bromiley, 3 vols. (Grand Rapids: Eerdmans, 1991, 1997).
7. Relevant works include Jürgen Moltmann, *The Church in the Power of the Spirit: A Contribution to Messianic Ecclesiology* (New York: Harper & Row, 1977); and Jürgen Moltmann, *The Trinity and the Kingdom: The Doctrine of God* (Minneapolis: Fortress Press, 1981).
8. Relevant works include Stanley J. Grenz, *The Social God and the Relational Self: A Trinitarian Theology of the Imago Dei* (Louisville: John Knox, 2001); and Stanley J. Grenz, *Theology for the Community of God* (Grand Rapids: Eerdmans, 1994).
9. Relevant works include Gary D. Badcock, *Light of Truth and Fire of Love: A Theology of the Holy Spirit* (Grand Rapids: Eerdmans, 1997); and Gary D. Badcock, *The House Where God Lives: Renewing the Doctrine of the Church for Today* (Grand Rapids: Eerdmans, 2009).

of note are Pentecostal theologians Amos Yong, Steven Studebaker, and Veli-Matti Kärkkäinen. Yong's theology of religions begins with (common) pneumatological concerns while "temporarily bracketing" the (divisive) Christological concerns as much as possible.[10] Putting aside questions regarding the validity of this approach, Yong's work overlaps significantly with Third Article Theology. Studebaker has focused primarily on Spirit Christology, but his most recent work extends into a Third Article soteriology, Trinity, and a theology of religions.[11] Kärkkäinen's research similarly explores the development of a Third Article Theology, particularly summarizing and categorizing others' work while adding his own contributions.[12] Finally in this brief summary is Habets's echoing of Dabney's call for a complete and systematic Third Article Theology. He outlines the beginnings of such an enterprise, focusing primarily on the constituent features of a Third Article prolegomenon, anthropology, and soteriology.[13]

The only sustained work to date on what is termed here a Third Article Ecclesiology comes from one of Dabney's students, Cheryl Peterson, who has published a fascinating investigation exploring one way in which an ecclesiology that starts with the Spirit can

10. See for example Amos Yong, *Beyond the Impasse: Toward a Pneumatological Theology of Religions* (Grand Rapids: Baker, 2003), particularly p. 22.

11. For an example of his Spirit Christology, see Steven M. Studebaker, "Integrating Pneumatology and Christology: A Trinitarian Modification of Clark H. Pinnock's Spirit Christology," *Pneuma* 28, no. 1 (2006): 5–20. For an extension into other areas, particularly Trinitarian theology, see Steven M. Studebaker, *The Trinitarian Vision of Jonathan Edwards and David Coffey* (New York: Cambria, 2011). Also Steven M. Studebaker, *From Pentecost to the Triune God: A Pentecostal Trinitarian Theology* (Grand Rapids: Eerdmans, 2012).

12. Relevant works include the collection of articles in Veli-Matti Kärkkäinen, *Toward a Pneumatological Theology: Pentecostal and Ecumenical Perspectives on Ecclesiology, Soteriology, and Theology of Mission* (Lanham, MD: University Press of America, 2002); and the first volume of a comprehensive systematic theology: Veli-Matti Kärkkäinen, *Christ and Reconciliation*, vol. 1 of *A Constructive Christian Theology for the Pluralistic World* (Grand Rapids: Eerdmans, 2013).

13. Habets, *The Anointed Son*, 228–57. Note that Habets's work on *theosis* could also be seen as a natural extension of his interest in Third Article Theology in a soteriological frame. See Myk Habets, *Theosis in the Theology of Thomas Torrance* (Farnham, UK: Ashgate, 2009).

be developed. After discussing the ecclesiological context in North America, she explores three alternative theological conceptions: the church as word-event, communion, and missional; respectively using Barth, Jenson, and Guder as exemplars (among others). Favoring the missional conception, she goes on to develop a narrative method for ecclesiology that intentionally starts with the Spirit in exploring "the 'story of the church' in the Holy Scriptures and . . . in answering the question of the church's identity."[14] While there are significant differences between Peterson's narrative approach and the more intentionally systematic framework developed in this research, there is nevertheless also substantial convergence between the themes and outcomes of both studies. These points of overlap will be noted in the following chapters.

This research aligns itself with efforts to extend Third Article Theology beyond Spirit Christology. Its intent is to move toward a systematic Third Article Ecclesiology, by first developing a methodological framework through which key ecclesiological features can be observed, and then by beginning to clad that framework with ecclesial features leading toward the development of a comprehensive Third Article Ecclesiology. This chapter examines the framework design.

3.1 Framework Design

The first two methodological criteria mentioned in chapter 1 were that a Third Article Theology starts with pneumatology, and that it looks through, rather than at the Spirit. Looking through the Spirit at the subject of ecclesiology, however, it is clear that this doctrine cannot be viewed in isolation. For it is primarily through the Spirit that ecclesiology is connected with other theological doctrines.

14. Cheryl M. Peterson, *Who Is the Church? An Ecclesiology for the Twenty-First Century* (Minneapolis: Fortress Press, 2013), 99.

A comprehensive framework and methodology for a Third Article Ecclesiology emerges directly from this recognition. Rather than looking directly at ecclesiology through the Spirit, the constituent features of a Third Article Ecclesiology are illuminated by looking *through* the lens of the Spirit *from the vantage point* of other theological loci.

To illustrate, consider the view of ecclesiology seen from the vantage point of Christology. First, the link between the two subjects is primarily pneumatological. The church is connected historically, metaphorically, and organically with Christ, and each of these connections is pneumatologically enabled.[15] For example, just as the Spirit birthed and empowered Jesus during the incarnation, so the Spirit births and empowers the church. Second, the link between the two loci is analogical. The church's identity is related to but not identical with Jesus' identity. The continuities are real, but not exact, and determining the limits to which the analogy can be taken and how the analogy can best be used is pivotal in obtaining an accurate ecclesiological understanding. Third, the particular vantage point employed illuminates some but not all ecclesiological features. So the link from Christology to ecclesiology illuminates the ontology of the church, but (because of Jesus' individuality) sheds little light on ecclesial relationships. Another vantage point needs to be taken in order to clearly view this aspect of ecclesiology.

Recognizing these features of the Spirit-enabled connection between theological doctrines, how is a comprehensive and systematic ecclesiology to be developed? Working backwards, the third insight above (that each vantage point only sheds light on particular features of ecclesiology) means that a variety of vantage points will be needed to move toward a truly comprehensive

15. The church was founded by Christ (historical); the church is like Christ (metaphorical); and the church is in Christ (organic). See chapter 5 of this research for further discussion.

understanding of ecclesiology. It is not sufficient to view ecclesiology only from the vantage point of Christology. The pneumatological perspectives from other theological loci—the Trinity, eschatology, and others—also need to be included. Section 3.2 outlines this multiple vantage point approach using some seminal concepts from Nicholas Wolterstorff's work *Reason within the Bounds of Religion.*[16] Wolterstorff outlines a rigorous, postcritical, and dialogical epistemological approach that is particularly suited to the integrated nature of Third Article Theology.

The second insight regarding the analogical link between theological doctrines is initially problematic. By what criteria can we determine whether a Christological or Trinitarian "truth" can be applied to ecclesiology? It is wise to be extremely cautious in too closely identifying the two. Indeed it could justifiably be questioned whether anything concrete can be determined by regarding humanity as analogous to deity. Thankfully, this "analogous" pathway has been traveled by former theological giants, on whose shoulders we stand. For example, Barth's examination of reconciliation in *Church Dogmatics* IV extensively uses the notion of analogy, or as Barth often terms it, correspondence.[17] For Barth, the relation between Christ's divine and human natures provides a viable means to consider the corresponding relationship between Christ and the church. Section 3.3 will examine how these correspondences can be deployed and extended within a Third Article Theology. The final section, 3.4, outlines the structure of the remainder of the research.

16. See Nicholas Wolterstorff, *Reason Within the Bounds of Religion* (Grand Rapids: Eerdmans, 1976).

17. See for example Karl Barth, *Church Dogmatics*, trans. G. W. Bromiley (Peabody, MA: Hendrickson, 2010), IV/3.2, 532–33. Also see Kimlyn J. Bender, *Karl Barth's Christological Ecclesiology* (Aldershot, UK: Ashgate, 2005), 5–7.

3.2 Multiple Vantage Points

This research will adopt a postcritical,[18] realist,[19] and dialogical epistemology. The dialogical approach adopted follows that outlined by Nicholas Wolterstorff,[20] who rejects the enlightenment ideal of foundationalism, claiming that there is no indubitable knowledge. Yet he also asserts that scholars can approach a true understanding of reality through the analysis and interchange of background beliefs, data beliefs, and control beliefs.

To take an illustrative example, consider the way an astronomer measures a star's position. Put simply, the optical features of a telescope are used to determine the star's coordinates. Indeed, astronomers usually integrate several measurements to obtain the most accurate results possible. Applying Wolterstorff's framework to this example, the star's position is the data belief—the reality the astronomer is determining. The telescope's optical features are the control beliefs—the basis on which the astronomer determines the star's position. Everything else, such as Newton's laws of motion, are simply assumed. These are background beliefs.

18. Michael Polanyi, *Personal Knowledge: Towards a Post-Critical Philosophy* (London: Routledge & Kegan Paul, 1969).
19. Recognizing the caveats of postfoundationalism, this research presupposes that it is a "real reality" being examined. For a brief discussion of presuppositions of reality within a (post-) critical epistemology, see Egon G. Guba and Yvonna S. Lincoln, "Competing Paradigms in Qualitative Research: Theories and Issues," in *Approaches to Qualitative Research: A Reader*, ed. S. N. Hessie-Biber and P. Leavy (New York: Oxford University Press, 1976), 36. A general introduction to postcritical realism can be found in José López and Garry Potter, eds., *After Postmodernism: An Introduction to Critical Realism* (London: Continuum, 2001). The more detailed species of critical realism adopted in this work may be found in Roy Bhaskar, *A Realist Theory of Science* (Brighton, UK: Harvester, 1978). See also, Roy Bhaskar, *Dialectic: The Pulse of Freedom* (London: Verso, 1993). Theological adoptions of this methodology are most evident in Thomas F. Torrance, *Theological Science* (Oxford: Oxford University Press, 1969); Thomas F. Torrance, *Reality and Evangelical Theology* (Downers Grove, IL: IVP, 1992); and Alister E. McGrath, *A Scientific Theology*, 3 vols. (Grand Rapids: Eerdmans, 2001–2003).
20. See Wolterstorff, *Reason Within the Bounds of Religion*. Wolterstorff does not use the word "dialogical" but the idea is implied.

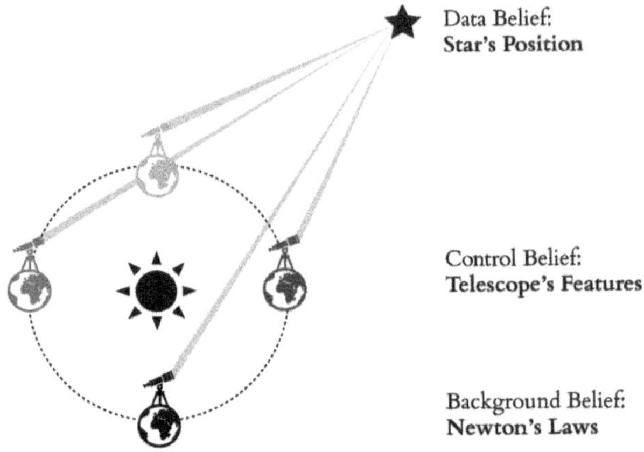

Wolterstorffian Framework — Initial Setup

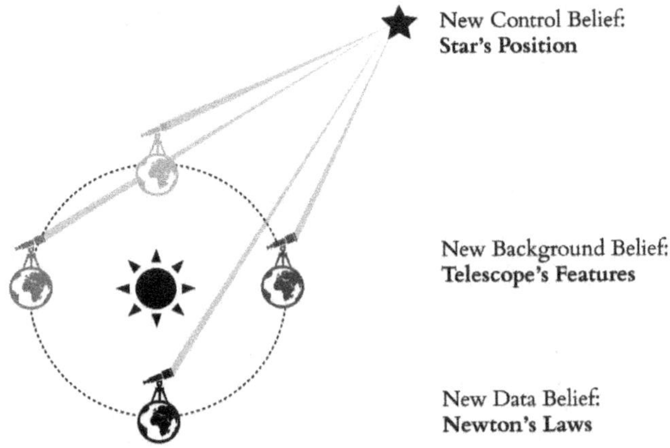

Wolterstorffian Framework — Subsequent Setup

Wolterstorff claims that scientists regularly swap the positions of the data beliefs, control beliefs, and background beliefs. So, for another experiment, the astronomer will simply assume how the telescope works (background belief) and measure a star's position (control belief) in order to test Newton's laws of motion.[21] The star's position in the sky, which was originally a data belief, becomes a new control belief.

In order to illustrate a Wolterstorffian epistemological approach's applicability to contemporary theology, consider the prominent contemporary issue of the relationship between the economic and the immanent Trinity.[22] A simple and direct application of Rahner's *grundaxiom*[23] implies an approach where we examine God's biblical revelation of himself and deduce from this the nature of God's immanent being. The direction of consideration is thus always vertically upwards, from the economy to God's immanent reality. Using Wolterstorff's terminology, in this approach the biblical, economic Trinitarian accounts are the control belief, the immanent Trinity is the data belief, and everything else is in the background. With Rahner's approach, each of these beliefs permanently stays in its initially assigned position. The biblical Trinitarian accounts are always the control; the immanent Trinity is always the data.

Coffey suggests an extension of this approach, where initially the biblical accounts are used to gain an understanding of the Trinity, from which the immanent reality of the Godhead is deduced. Then,

21. Interestingly, this is exactly what happened when Eddington observed the relative shift of a star's position during a solar eclipse in 1919. His new control belief disproved the data belief of Newton's laws of motion, and was a confirmation of the new data belief of Einstein's General Theory of Relativity. Apparently, when Einstein was asked what his reaction would have been if his new data belief of General Relativity had not have been confirmed by the experiment, he replied, "Then I would feel sorry for the dear Lord. The theory is correct anyway."

22. This topic will be considered in significant detail in chapter 7.

23. "The economic Trinity is the immanent Trinity and the immanent Trinity is the economic Trinity." Karl Rahner, *The Trinity*, trans. Joseph Donceel (Tunbridge Wells, UK: Burns & Oates, 1997), 22.

as a second step, this understanding of the Trinity is applied to other doctrines such as soteriology and ecclesiology.[24] Describing this approach in Wolterstorff's terminology, the first stage matches the simple and direct application of Rahner's *grundaxiom* above. But in Coffey's second stage, the immanent Trinity becomes the control belief, other theological loci such as soteriology and ecclesiology become the data belief, and the biblical Trinitarian data becomes the background belief.

While this is a positive step forward, a Wolterstorffian approach would go further. It would apply the *new* control belief of the immanent Trinity not just to other loci, but also to the *original* control belief of the biblical accounts of the Trinity. In other words, a Wolterstorffian approach would say that our newly derived immanent Trinitarian understanding should inform even our reading of the text—what is currently termed a theological interpretation of Scripture.[25] Further, it would also use the revised understandings of soteriology and ecclesiology as control beliefs. Indeed, every area of knowledge is used as a vantage point to examine every other area, and the revised understanding gained from this examination immediately becomes a new vantage point from which to observe all others. This is the crux of the Wolterstorffian approach to theology. All aspects of our understanding—our biblical interpretation, our

24. Coffey outlines this approach in several of his theological papers. Most clearly in David Coffey, *Deus Trinitas: The Doctrine of the Triune God* (New York: Oxford University Press, 1999), 9–32. For a comparison of the methodological approach of Rahner and Coffey see Declan O'Byrne, *Spirit Christology and Trinity in the Theology of David Coffey* (Oxford: Peter Lang, 2010), 155–84.

25. See for example Daniel J. Treier, *Introducing Theological Interpretation of Scripture: Recovering a Christian Practice* (Grand Rapids: Baker Academic, 2008). It has been demonstrated that T. F. Torrance, among others, adopts this method. See Myk Habets, "Theological Interpretation of Scripture in Sermonic Mode: The Case of T. F. Torrance," in *Ears That Hear: Explorations in Theological Interpretation of the Bible*, ed. Joel Green and Tim Meadowcroft (Sheffield: Sheffield Phoenix Press, 2013), 44–71. For one example using the Third Article of the Apostles' Creed, see Richard Hays, "Spirit, Church, Resurrection: The Third Article of the Creed as Hermeneutical Lens for Reading Romans," *Journal of Theological Interpretation* 5, no. 1 (2011): 35–48.

apprehension of the immanent Trinity, our understanding of the Trinity's actions in the church, all other theological loci and even beyond this to other areas of human knowledge—each of these are to be used as both control and data beliefs, so that our entire system of knowledge is consistent, coherent, and always developing.

So the application of Wolterstorff's epistemological approach to theological methodology does not ascribe a definitive theological starting point—a single indubitable foundation from which all other understandings are derived. Theologies from below are not preferenced over theologies from above. Third Article theologies are not preferenced over First or Second Article theologies. Indeed, even revelatory or experientially based starting points are not preferenced over philosophical starting points. The *subjective source* of an understanding is of secondary importance in Wolterstorff's framework; of primary importance is the consistency and coherence of the understanding developed—the extent to which it matches the breadth of experimental evidence (from a scientific perspective), or the breadth of revelation (from a theological perspective).[26] Having said that, a Third Article Theology fits very naturally with a Wolterstorffian approach, as looking through the lens of the Spirit emphasizes the links between theological loci. Perhaps in this sense, Catholic theologian Heribert Mühlen is correct in asserting that "[t]he doctrine and person of the Holy Spirit is not one doctrine among others, but a fundamental doctrine and reality in the church."[27]

Wolterstorff's framework describes the overall methodology adopted in this research for moving toward a complete and coherent

26. See John Polkinghorne, *The Faith of a Physicist* (Minneapolis: Fortress Press, 1996), 5–7.

27. Heribert Mühlen, *Una Mystica Persona. Die Kirche als das Mysterium der heilsgeschichtlichen Identität des Heiligen Geistes in Christus und den Christen: Eine Person in vielen Personen* (Paderborn: Ferdinand Schöningh, 1967), 5. As quoted in and translated by Wolfgang Vondey, *Heribert Mühlen: His Theology and Praxis* (Dallas: University Press of America, 2004), xv.

Third Article Ecclesiology. There are background beliefs—Holy Scripture and the Creeds—which are crucial reference points, but not the focus area of this particular research project. There are several control beliefs—Third Article doctrines such as Spirit Christology—which form the basis or vantage points from which the examination occurs. And finally there is the data belief—ecclesiology—which is the specific area being examined. Each of the ecclesiological views gained from the different perspectives is integrated to determine as complete and coherent a view of a Third Article Ecclesiology as possible. While such a combined ecclesiological understanding represents the ultimate goal of a Third Article Ecclesiology, it does not form the end of the theological program. This understanding should then be used as a control belief—a vantage point from which other Third Article Theological loci can be examined.[28] One of these next steps includes an examination of Scripture through the lens of the ecclesiological insights gained.

The intent of this research is to take some initial steps along this path that lead to a robust, coherent, and comprehensive Third Article Theology. Particularly it examines ecclesiology from the perspectives of Christology and the Trinity, through the lens of the Spirit. There are, of course, other perspectives from which ecclesiology can be examined. Christology and the Trinity have been chosen not just because to date they are the furthest-developed Third Article Theological doctrines and consequently provide readily available vantage points, but also because the relationship between each doctrine and ecclesiology is clearly pneumatologically derived.

28. Grosso develops a similar understanding of how a comprehensive Third Article Theology could be developed but uses the epistemological framework of Polanyi rather than Wolterstorff. See Andrew Grosso, "Spirit Christology and the Shape of the Theological Enterprise," in *A Man of the Church: Honoring the Theology, Life, and Witness of Ralph Del Colle*, ed. Michel René Barnes (Eugene, OR: Pickwick, 2012), 215–22.

Regarding Christology, it is the Spirit that forms the church as the body of Christ (1 Cor. 12:13). For the Trinity, it is by the Spirit that the church joins in the life of the Trinity. As James Torrance writes, we participate "by the Spirit in the Son's communion with the Father."[29] The final chapter discusses how this research may be extended so that other vantage points such as eschatology and the world can be utilized and the views they give of ecclesiology incorporated to construct a coherent and comprehensive Third Article Ecclesiology.

3.3 Analogical Connections

In Wolterstorff's terminology, then, this research uses two doctrines as control beliefs—Christology and the Trinity—and looks from these vantage points through the lens of the Spirit at the data belief of ecclesiology. The immediate question arising from this Wolterstorffian design is how an analogical connection can be made between each doctrine and ecclesiology. How is it determined if a truth about Christology or the Trinity can be analogously applied to ecclesiology?

Focusing first on the Christological vantage point, Barth extensively employs the notion of analogy (or correspondence) in *Church Dogmatics* IV. He writes that Christ is

> . . . that which men become as they are called to be Christians. That is to say, He is originally the Son of God. And in analogy and correspondence, which means with real similarity for all the dissimilarity, they may become sons of God. Their new and distinctive being as Christians is their being in this real similarity, for all the dissimilarity, to His being as the Son of God. They may become and thus be what He is originally and does not have to become.[30]

29. James B. Torrance, *Worship, Community and the Triune God of Grace* (Downers Grove, IL: IVP Academic, 1996), 31.
30. Barth, *Church Dogmatics*, IV/3.2, 533.

Barth argues that the correspondence between ecclesiology and Christology, and indeed the relationship between all human and divine interactions parallels the correspondence between the human and divine natures of Christ.

Following Kimlyn Bender's analysis, we note three repeated elements within this parallel.[31] The first element is the "Chalcedonian pattern."[32] Between the divine and human nature of Christ—and consequently, according to Barth, between all divine and human relationships—there is unity, differentiation, and asymmetry: unity in that the two need to be considered together—"without division or separation"; differentiation in that they cannot be so mingled that either loses its own integrity—"without confusion or change"; and asymmetry in that the relationship is ordered so the first is independent and superior, the second dependent and subordinate. According to Hunsinger: "There is virtually no discussion of divine and human agency in the *Church Dogmatics* which does not conform to this scheme."[33] The second element expands on the asymmetry of the Chalcedonian pattern. Within Christology it is expressed as the *anhypostasia/enhypostasia* formula, which establishes (negatively) that the human nature of Jesus has no existence without the Word (*anhypostasia*), and (positively) that the human nature has a true, genuine existence in the Word (*enhypostasia*). Barth analogically affirms similar truths about all divine/human relations, noting that

31. For a more detailed discussion see Bender, *Karl Barth's Christological Ecclesiology*, 3–8. In developing these three elements, Bender is building upon the work of Hunsinger, Holloway, Torrance, and Gollwitzer, among others. See George Hunsinger, *How to Read Karl Barth: The Shape of His Theology* (New York/Oxford: Oxford University Press, 1991); James Y. Holloway, ed., *Barth, Barmen and the Confessing Church Today* (Lewiston, NY: Edwin Mellen, 1992/1995); Thomas F. Torrance, *Karl Barth, Biblical and Evangelical Theologian* (Edinburgh: T. & T. Clark, 1990); and Helmut Gollwitzer, "Kingdom of God and Socialism in the Theology of Karl Barth," in *Karl Barth and Radical Politics*, ed. George Hunsinger (Philadelphia: Westminster, 1976), 97–99.

32. Hunsinger, *How to Read Karl Barth*, 185.

33. Ibid., 187.

the human side depends on the divine in a manner akin to the *anhypostasia/enhypostasia* formula. The third and final element expands on the *enhypostasia* and its analogical extension into all divine/human relationships. This element is termed "correspondence," and refers to human actions reflecting the divine in a manner appropriate to the creature. Focusing on ecclesiology, Bender explains:

> Barth's notion of correspondence describes the character of human life and activity that exists enhypostatically in the divine Word in the incarnation, and by analogy the character of the life of the Church and the Christian established by God within the covenant of grace. . . . The action of the human partner does not replace nor supplement the divine activity, but does have a real, true and important place that reflects and bears witness to God's salvific work.[34]

In this work, these three elements together—the Chalcedonian pattern, the anhypostasia/enhypostasia formula, and the notion of correspondence—are termed Barth's Chalcedonian logic.

Applying this logic to the relationship between Christ and the church, it can be asserted that as Christ's divine and human natures are one, so Christ and his church are one. In the same way that Christ's divine and human natures must be differentiated and not confused, so Christ and the church must be differentiated and not confused. In the same way that there is an asymmetry between Christ's divine and human natures so there is an asymmetry between Christ and the church, with Christ always the source and life of the church.[35] Such a straightforward examination of the correspondence between a traditional Logos Christological understanding and ecclesiology simply revisits Barth's work, but a Third Article

34. Bender, *Karl Barth's Christological Ecclesiology*, 6–7.

35. For a discussion of how Barth viewed the relationship between Christ and the church, see Bender, *Karl Barth's Christological Ecclesiology*—in particular the discussion of the *totus Christus* on pp. 202–5.

Theology approach enables a valuable extension. Spirit Christology not only gives a new vantage point from which to examine ecclesiology (i.e., from a Spirit Christology and not just a Logos Christology) but also a new way of forming the analogy (as Spirit Christology has enabled a more nuanced view of the hypostatic union). Just as Spirit Christology has provided new insights into not just what the hypostatic union is but how it functions, a Third Article Ecclesiology provides insights into what the entire church—the *totus Christus*—is and how it functions. Such an examination is undertaken in part two of this work.

The correspondence of the church with the Trinity is more complicated than the Christological connection, as in the latter both entities "contain" divinity and humanity, while in comparing the Trinity and the church this similarity no longer holds. While a number of theologians have characterized the church as an image or reflection of the Trinity and developed an ecclesial understanding from that basis,[36] others directly refute their work, arguing that such a direct correlation excessively minimizes the distinction between Creator and creature.[37] Expanding on the work of such theologians as J. B. Torrance,[38] Heribert Mühlen,[39] and Kathryn Tanner,[40] this research takes a different approach by arguing that the link between the Trinity and ecclesiology is not primarily to be understood as an image or reflection but rather a pneumatological participation. The church participates "by the Spirit in Jesus's communion with

36. Most notable in this group is Miroslav Volf, *After Our Likeness: The Church as the Image of the Trinity* (Grand Rapids: Eerdmans, 1998), although others such as Moltmann, Boff, and LaCugna could also be included.

37. See particularly Kathryn Tanner, *Christ the Key* (Cambridge: Cambridge University Press, 2010), 207–46.

38. Torrance, *Worship, Community and the Triune God of Grace.*

39. Mühlen, *Una Mystica Persona.* For a recent analysis of Mühlen's work in English, see Vondey, *Heribert Mühlen.*

40. Tanner, *Christ the Key*, 140–206.

the Father."[41] It is by examining the Trinitarian acts in terms of both their immanent grounding and their creaturely fruits that the two sides of the analogy can be effectively compared and contrasted. This understanding enables the development of a pneumatologically enabled but Christologically conditioned approach to illuminate the continuities between the Trinity and the church. Such a pneumatological approach begins by noting that there are significant continuities between the Spirit's ecclesial role and his immanent identity. These continuities are not derived from any intrinsic similarity between God and humanity, but rather from the reality that the same Spirit indwelling the Trinity (by nature) also indwells the church (by grace). Further, the Spirit's presence in the church unites us with Christ, and this union illuminates significant continuities between Christ the Son's immanent Trinitarian identity, and the church's identity and participation in the Trinity. By the Spirit, the church is united with Christ and participates in both the status and experience of his Spirit-enabled Sonship. An examination of these analogical connections is undertaken in part three of this work.

3.4 Research Structure

Following a Wolterstorffian approach, then, the first step is to determine the Spirit-enabled parallels between each theological vantage point and ecclesiology. From these, points of continuity, of discontinuity, and asymmetry emerge. The second step is to draw out implications for the particular aspects of ecclesiology that are seen most clearly from this vantage point. This overall approach is worked out in the structure of the research as follows.

In working "*Toward a Third Article Ecclesiology,*" part one has summarized the subject's background and the methodological

41. Torrance, *Worship, Community and the Triune God of Grace*, 31.

approach. Chapter 1 introduced Third Article Theology, together with its motivation and methodological distinctives. Chapter 2 illustrated the methodology of Third Article Theology through an examination of Spirit Christology. Chapter 3 has described the framework through which a Third Article Ecclesiology will be developed. This "Wolterstorffian" framework uses two different theological doctrines as control beliefs—Christology and the Trinity—each providing a vantage point from which the data belief of ecclesiology can be viewed through the lens of the Spirit.

Part two examines ecclesiology from the vantage point of Christology through the lens of the Spirit, characterizing "*The Church as Sequel to the Incarnation*," an image that incorporates the continuity, discontinuity, and asymmetry that exists between the two doctrines. The argument centers on two key premises. First, that insight into the ontology of the church can be gained through comparison with the ontology of Christ. Second, that examining this correspondence requires giving prominence to the Spirit. In discussing the first premise (chapter 4), the work of Barth and Zizioulas is considered. While both their developed ecclesiologies have significant strengths, it is argued that Barth overemphasizes (slightly) the "without confusion" aspect of the relationship between Christ and the church, while Zizioulas overemphasizes (significantly) the "without separation" aspect. The discussion of the second premise (chapter 5) explores five pneumatologically inspired parallels between Christ and the church to determine points of continuity, discontinuity, and asymmetry, enabling detailed insights regarding the church's ontology to be developed. Chapter 6 gathers these insights together and compares the resulting Christological Third Article Ecclesiology with alternative ecclesial ontologies that over- or underemphasize the Son or the Spirit.

As has already been noted, using the vantage point of the Trinity to view ecclesiology through the lens of the Spirit is a great deal more complicated than using that of Christology. Following a Wolterstorffian approach requires a rather circuitous route to be traversed. First, the question of which understanding of the Trinity to use as a vantage point needs to be answered. Chapter 7 argues that Spirit Christology is that aspect of the biblical revelation where God's unity and diversity are most clearly and simultaneously evident, and so provides the optimal vantage point from which to view the immanent Trinity. The recent attempts of Coffey, Moltmann, and Habets to trace this path are considered, and it is argued that a "reconceived" understanding of the Trinity similar to that outlined by Thomas Weinandy where the Father begets the Son in or by the Spirit most clearly matches the economic revelation. The question of how to apply this immanent Trinitarian understanding to ecclesiology is addressed in chapter 8. A "reflective" or "direct" correlation between the Trinity and the church is rejected in favor of a more nuanced approach that understands "*The Church as Participant in the Life of the Trinity*," and consequently determines an analogical linking mechanism between the church and the Trinity that is pneumatologically enabled but Christologically conditioned.

Based on this preparatory work, chapter 9 argues that the identities of the Son and the Spirit in a "reconceived" immanent Trinitarian understanding are reprised (with inevitable continuities and discontinuities) on a series of expanding stages: Christologically in the hypostatic union, soteriologically in the mystical union, and most pertinently, ecclesiologically in relationships between individual church members. This examination of Trinitarian identity and action reveals a vantage point from which to view inter-ecclesial relationships (as we analogously compare our relationship with the Father to that of Christ, given that by grace we share Christ's

Trinitarian Sonship) and intra-ecclesial relationships (for the Spirit relates us to other ecclesial persons in an analogous way to how we are related to the person of Christ). Chapter 10 examines the understanding that emerges of a church that exists in any and all relationships where, by the Spirit, the love of Christ is offered and returned. The ecclesial characteristics of this Trinitarian Third Article Ecclesiology are described and contrasted with others that emerge through viewing the church from alternative Trinitarian starting points.

The final chapter summarizes the Third Article Theology approach used and the ecclesial insights gained from the vantage points of Christology and the Trinity, before outlining how this research could be extended to view ecclesiology from other perspectives such as eschatology or the world, and how the different ecclesial viewpoints gained can be integrated into a complete and coherent Third Article Ecclesiology.

PART II

The Church as Sequel to the Incarnation

In Christ, the Son of God exists bodily; in the church, Christ indwells his ecclesial body. The first major premise of part two of this work is that significant insight into the ontology of the church can be gained through comparison with the ontology of Christ. The parallels between the two are not identical, but examining the continuities, discontinuities, and asymmetry between them provides significant insight into our understanding of the church—what it is, who is in it, how it is recognized, and what it does.

Such a comparison is hardly novel, however.[1] Karl Barth, for example, points to the correspondence between a traditional Logos (or Chalcedonian) Christology and ecclesiology. The aim here is to expand on such ecclesiological understanding through the

1. See for example Vladimir Lossky, *The Mystical Theology of the Eastern Church* (London: James Clarke, 1957), 186. Also, *Lumen Gentium*, ch. 1, part 8. Retrieved September 26, 2013 from http://www.vatican.va/archive/hist_councils/ii_vatican_council/documents/vat-ii_const_19641121_lumen-gentium_en.html.

methodology of Third Article Theology. Consequently, the second major premise is that the correspondence between Christ and the church cannot be adequately examined without giving the Spirit prominence. Two key reasons justify this premise. First (as argued in chapter 2), Christ's ontology cannot be understood without introducing the category of the Spirit at a fundamental level. Second (as argued in chapter 3), Spirit Christology not only gives a new vantage point from which to examine ecclesiology (i.e., from a Spirit Christology and not just a Logos Christology) but also a new way of forming the correspondence. Pneumatological insights into how the eternal Son became human inform our understanding of how the perfect Christ indwells an imperfect church. Spirit Christology has enhanced comprehension of the hypostatic union, and the approach of Third Article Theology similarly enhances comprehension of the church's ontology. Kärkkäinen asserts that "the only way to construe a viable pneumato-ecclesiology is to reflect very carefully on the relationship between Christ and the Spirit on the one hand, and on the relation of the Spirit to the church on the other hand, and then try and see these three as mutual entities that inform each other."[2] In Wolterstorff's terms, Spirit Christology is the *control belief*, ecclesiology is the *data belief*, and Scripture and the creeds form the *background beliefs* for this examination.[3]

The discussion proceeds as follows. Chapter 4 examines the premise that the ontology of Jesus Christ provides insight into the ontology of the church. Two contrasting formulations connecting Christology and ecclesiology are reviewed: Barth's Chalcedonian logic and Zizioulas's notion of Eucharistic communion. While

2. Veli-Matti Kärkkäinen, *Toward a Pneumatological Theology: Pentecostal and Ecumenical Perspectives on Ecclesiology, Soteriology, and Theology of Mission* (Lanham, MD: University Press of America, 2002), 93.
3. See section 3.2.

acknowledging the significant strengths of both proposals, it is argued that Barth overemphasizes the "without confusion" aspects of the divine/human ecclesiological relationships and underemphasizes the "without separation" aspects, while Zizioulas does the reverse. Applying the terminology of Spirit Christology developed in chapter 2 to ecclesiology, the root cause of both imbalances is argued to be an ecclesial Spirit-Eutychianism: both theologians too greatly merge and confuse the Son and the Spirit's involvement in the church's life. For Barth, the Spirit's ecclesial involvement is partly subsumed into that of the Son, while for Zizioulas the reverse occurs, with the Son's ecclesial involvement almost completely subsumed into the Spirit. In many ways this ecclesial logic parallels the Christological logic of chapter 2 where the identities and missions of *both* the Son and the Spirit within the incarnation needed to be recognized and distinguished for a satisfactory Christology to emerge. Formulating a pneumato-ecclesiology that balances the "without confusion" and "without separation" aspects of divine and human engagement within the church similarly requires both the Son and the Spirit's ecclesial involvement to be logically distinguished without being existentially separated.

Chapter 5 corrects the perceived imbalances of Barth and Zizioulas and extends on their ecclesial insights. Five pneumatologically inspired parallels are observed: (1) The Spirit conceives (Christ and the church); (2) The Spirit sustains the communion (of Christ and the church); (3) The Spirit conforms (Christ and the church); (4) The Spirit directs and empowers (Christ and the church); (5) The Spirit is displayed and mediated (by Christ and the church). Examining these points of continuity together with their complementary discontinuities and asymmetries enables several pneumato-ecclesial insights to be gathered. The church is recognized as tripartite in nature, relational in identity, unique in context, Christ-centered in orientation, Christotelic in momentum, indivisible in constitution, cruciform in shape, missional in purpose, and narrative in character.

Chapter 6 arranges these insights into a Christological Third Article Ecclesiology that coherently addresses the following pivotal questions: (1) What is the church? (2) Who is in the church (with a focus on baptism)? (3) How do we recognize the church? And (4) What does the church do? For each characteristic, a contrast is outlined between a balanced ecclesiology and those errors that arise from overemphasizing either the Son or the Spirit's ecclesial involvement.

The logic of part two confirms Clark Pinnock's insight that the church can be viewed as "a continuation of the Spirit-anointed event that was Jesus Christ."[4] There is one significant modification, however. Pinnock's key descriptor—*continuation*—suggests too strong a continuity between Christ and the church. Recognizing a more nuanced relation, the title of part two refers to the church as the incarnation's "sequel."[5] The term was originally literary, but now is commonly associated with filmography. In this context, Jess-Cooke defines a *sequel* as a "framework within which formulations of repetition, difference, history, nostalgia, memory and audience interactivity produce a series of dialogues and relationships between a textual predecessor and its continuation, between audience and text, and between history and remembrance."[6] Three of these features are of particular significance in this discussion. First, a sequel has a

4. Clark H. Pinnock, *Flame of Love: A Theology of the Holy Spirit* (Downers Grove, IL: IVP Academic, 1996), 113.

5. The only other references I have encountered to the church (or an ecclesial aspect) as *sequel* refer specifically to Pentecost. Cook writes: "Pentecost is not the continuation of the incarnation but its sequel or result, the final goal of the divine economy." Michael L. Cook, *Trinitarian Christology: The Power That Sets Us Free* (New York: Paulist, 2010), 28. Similarly, "The work of the Spirit is not subordinate to the work of the Son, nor is Pentecost a 'continuation' of the Incarnation, but rather its sequel, its result." Kärkkäinen, *Toward a Pneumatological Theology*, 85.

6. Carolyn Jess-Cooke, *Film Sequels: Theory and Practice from Hollywood to Bollywood* (Edinburgh: Edinburgh University Press, 2009), vi.

necessary unity with the original (a clear continuity). Many of the same characters emerge and similar themes are explored. Second, for all the similarities, a sequel is evidently and purposefully differentiated from the original (a recognizable discontinuity). Disaster awaits attempts to too closely imitate the original. Third, it has an asymmetric relation. There is no sequel without an original. It is completely dependent, connected not just sequentially but often intertwining and reinterpreting the original storyline. These three features correlate closely with the relationship existing between Christ and the church illuminated in Barth's Chalcedonian logic. The church can be viewed as continuous with the incarnation, being Christ's body, his physical presence on earth at the present time. There is, however, also a necessary discontinuity. The church is not Christ. It can and should not attempt to replicate or add to Christ's already completed work. Disaster awaits attempts to identify the church too closely with Christ. And finally there is an asymmetrical relationship. Christ is the source and life of the church, but Christ is not similarly dependent on the church. The relationship is heavily one-sided. Jesus is the embodied Son independent of what the church is or does. In contrast, the church is Christ's or it is not the church at all. Labeling the church as the "sequel" to the incarnation metaphorically alludes to all three of these aspects,[7] and as such is an underlying image that accurately illustrates the analogical link between Christ and the church.[8]

7. These three features are not the only points of similarity. For example, Jess-Cooke comments that the "reason why a sequel disappoints—and why the very concept of sequelisation is often met with a collective groan—seems to do with how the sequel re-imagines and extends its source in ways that impose upon our memories and interpretation of the previous film" (ibid., vii). There are resonances here between how the church's activity can (re)interpret people's understanding of Jesus, for both good and ill. While detailed exploration of other parallels such as this may be profitable, they are not pursued further in this work. The "sequel" terminology is used merely as an evocative, high-level illustration.

8. Indeed, it captures the notion of correspondence better than even Barth originally did in terming the church a "repetition" of the incarnation, admittedly with significant qualifications.

Karl Barth, *Church Dogmatics*, trans. G. W. Bromiley (Peabody, MA: Hendrickson, 2010), I/2, 215. Interestingly, in later volumes Barth moves away from the terminology of "repetition," choosing a more careful use of "reflection" and "analogy." See for example ibid., IV/1, 767–70; III/2, 511–15. See also Thomas F. Torrance, *Royal Priesthood: A Theology of Ordained Ministry* (Edinburgh: T. & T. Clark, 1993), 25.

4

Two Contrasting Christological Ecclesiologies

In the incarnation, the eternal Son united himself to a human nature; in the church, Christ unites himself with humanity. The importance of a nuanced theological understanding of the continuities and discontinuities between Christ and the church can thus scarcely be overstated. At stake is an understanding of what the church is, how we recognize it, who is in it, and how they enter it. But it also can scarcely be overstated just how difficult such questions are. An adequate ecclesial ontology encapsulates two things that are extraordinarily different. In the church, we claim that something immortal, invincible, infallible, and altogether divine is present and real in something mortal, weak, flawed, and all too human.

This chapter examines the first major premise of part two—that significant insight into the ontology of the church can be gained through comparison with the ontology of Jesus Christ. This is done specifically by investigating the Christological ecclesiologies of Barth and Zizioulas. Particular attention is paid to the connection they develop between Christ and the church, the implications they derive for the ontology of the church, the characteristics and challenges of their theological positions, and how those challenges can be overcome.

Both Barth and Zizioulas note that the most important New Testament image connecting Christology and ecclesiology describes the church as Christ's body. There are four epistles that either allude or explicitly refer to the church this way. Particularly in the more extended outworkings (1 Cor. 12:12–27; Rom. 12:3–8), the primary point of these references is that unity and diversity can and should exist mutually in the church. Just as a body has many organs with many differing functions that act synergistically to form one united organism with a common purpose, so the church has many members with many functions that act synergistically to form one united community with a common purpose. The outworking of the metaphor is relatively obvious—don't undervalue or envy others' roles, but rather inhabit your role in such a way that the entire community will be purposeful and united.

This point about unity in diversity, were that to be the entirety of the author's intention, however, could be made equally powerfully by reference to a generic body. In each of these passages, however, the church is identified as not just any "body" but the body *of Christ*. As a metaphor, this correlation cannot be pushed excessively beyond its explicit intent.[1] Metaphorical language takes clearly evident truths in one particular sphere of life and applies them to another sphere. In this case evident truths in the field of biology are applied to the

1. For a detailed discussion on the use of metaphor within Scripture, focused particularly on the "body of Christ," see Andrew Perriman, "'His Body, Which Is the Church . . .' Coming to Terms with Metaphor," *Evangelical Quarterly* 62, no. 2 (1990): 123–42. Also, Barbara Field, "The Discourses behind the Metaphor 'the Church is the Body of Christ' as Used by St. Paul and the 'Post Paulines,'" *Asia Journal of Theology* 6, no. 1 (1992): 88–107.

spiritual reality of Christ and the church. But this naturally leads to the question of just how far into genuine ontology and activity this metaphor applies, and further, to what reality this analogical language is pointing. Theological judgements on this question are far from unified. Broadly, opinion can be divided into three categories on the metaphorical–literal continuum. First, there are those that claim the church is an extension of the incarnation. In this viewpoint (held by Roman Catholics and some high Lutherans), the church is literally the body of Christ, and Christ has no human body outside his ecclesial body. For example, Robert Jenson claims "Paul's teaching [about the church being the body of Christ] can be exploited for the similes it enables, and thus does Paul exploit it. But the teaching itself is a proposition and not a trope."[2] The viewpoint at the other end of the continuum (held by many evangelical or free churches) is that reference to the ecclesial body of Christ is entirely metaphorical, and Jesus' body literally resides *only* at the right hand of the Father.

Regarding these two extremes, there is certainly some biblical motivation for the assertion that the church is more than just *metaphorically* Christ's body, while strict and exclusive identification goes well beyond the biblical position. Briefly working through some key references makes this clear. The writer of Colossians refers to Christ as the "head" of the body (Col. 1:18). Then, only a few verses later, the author specifically refers to Christ's *physical* body to distinguish between the two, which is unusual and quite possibly unnecessary if the first connection is taken *either* literally or merely metaphorically. Even more clearly, in Ephesians Christ is again described as being the "head" of the church which is his body, but this reference is surrounded with ontological language: "his body, the fullness of him who fills everything in every way" (Eph. 1:22-23).

2. Robert Jenson, *Systematic Theology*, 2 vols. (Oxford: Oxford University Press, 1997, 1999), 1:204.

In 1 Corinthians 12 the words "Christ" and "the church" are used virtually interchangeably. Particularly the phrase "so it is with Christ" (12:12) in the introduction to the passage is surprising if the connection between Christ's body and the church is *merely* metaphorical. Similarly surprising is Jesus' questioning why Paul is persecuting *him* rather than his church (Acts 9:4). Even in the reference to the church as Christ's body in Romans (Rom. 12:5), which has primarily metaphorical application, Paul says that "*in Christ*, we though many form one body"—organic language referring to a genuine reality. None of the above examples is definitive. Each reference *can* be interpreted as metaphorical. But taken together, there is a strength of connection between Christ and his church that, while falling well short of strict identification, certainly seems to imply more than just a figurative link.

The biblical material thus points toward a third category, an intermediate position between these two extremes. The statement "The church is the body of Christ" is literally true in some ways and not in others, and a coherent understanding of the phrase requires theological nuance.[3] This chapter examines two such nuanced understandings that avoid the extremes of identifying the church as either always and completely Christ's literal body, or "merely" metaphorical and containing no literal truth. John Zizioulas (coming from an Eastern Orthodox perspective) suggests the church only becomes the body of Christ at particular times doing particular actions—particularly at or around the Eucharist. Karl Barth (coming from a Reformed perspective) claims that the church is only a part of Christ's body, so that the risen Christ (at the Father's right hand) and the ecclesial body of Christ together form the *totus Christus*, the entirety of Christ's body. Barth and Zizioulas's Christological

3. For a general discussion of metaphor within Christian theology, see J. A. N. Muis, "Can Christian Talk about God Be Literal?," *Modern Theology* 27, no. 4 (2011): 582–607.

ecclesiologies are examined here because they illustrate well how the pneumatological understanding adopted impacts the relationship between Christ and the church. What is being sought is an ecclesiology within which Christ and the church interact "*inconfusedly, unchangeably, indivisibly, inseparably.*"[4] In other words, the same Chalcedonian criteria that describe the relationship between the divine and human natures in Christ are used to evaluate the relationship between Christ and the church. The following discussion argues that despite their many strengths, the ecclesiological formulations of both Barth and Zizioulas do not meet these balanced criteria precisely because they too greatly confuse and merge the ecclesial involvement of the incarnate Son and the Spirit.

4.1 Barth's Chalcedonian Ecclesiology

Writing in an era that elevated the human spirit and sociological ecclesiologies, Karl Barth swung the theological pendulum back toward theological objectivity. While such a correction was timely and necessary, the question is whether Barth's pendulum swung too far. The following discussion argues that while Barth's Chalcedonian ecclesiology demonstrates the value of examining ecclesiology from a Christological vantage point, it lacks balance. In particular Barth's ecclesiology emphasizes the "without confusion" aspect of human and divine interaction to the detriment of the "without separation" aspect, and hence does not rigorously work out its Chalcedonian underpinning. Further, it is argued that this imbalance is rooted in Barth's insufficient distinguishing between the roles of the Son and the Spirit in the church's life, what could be labeled an ecclesial Spirit-Eutychianism, following the Spirit Christological terminology developed in chapter 2.

4. See Jaroslav Pelikan and Valerie Hotchkiss, eds., *Creeds and Confessions of Faith in the Christian Tradition: Early, Eastern and Medieval* (New Haven: Yale University Press, 2003), 181.

Barth's most detailed outworking of ecclesiology falls within his development of reconciliation in volume IV of *Church Dogmatics*. This volume explains salvation as a divine act (IV/1 Jesus Christ, The Lord as Servant; focused on Christ's priestly office), a human act (IV/2 Jesus Christ, The Servant as Lord; focused on Christ's kingly role) and a divine-human act (IV/3 Jesus Christ, The True Witness; focused on Christ's prophetic role). Barth's part-volume IV/1 explains how divine substitution is universal in bearing, and that in the cross God bears sin's consequences and reorients himself to humanity. In IV/2, Barth argues that the resurrection's related universal bearing is *eschatological*. Sanctification occurs only for those who have been awakened by faith. Moving to IV/3, Barth notes that Christ's mediation which awakens faith is revelatory. More than information, this involves *encountering* an "alien history" to which believers give themselves. Humans "respond" and "correspond" to the Christ-effected reconciliation. Believers follow Christ's pattern, living lives that are neither confused nor separated from his, but imitating his life in discipleship. And from this arises Barth's ecclesial context, as Bender comments:

> This task of response and correspondence bears directly upon the issue of ecclesiology, for it is the church, the Christian community, which is called to live and serve in response to this altered situation achieved in reconciliation. The church lives in correspondence to the reconciliation completed in Christ and serves the role of witness to this event. This is its primary purpose and task.[5]

For Barth, the church is not just metaphorically *like* but literally is Christ's body, just not its entirety.[6] Christ exists outside of his ecclesial

5. Kimlyn J. Bender, *Karl Barth's Christological Ecclesiology* (Aldershot, UK: Ashgate, 2005), 140.
6. The church is thus *totus Christi*, but not *totum Christi*. Essentially, the whole person of Christ dwells in the church, but the church is not the sum total or the entirety of Christ. See for example Karl Barth, *Church Dogmatics*, trans. G. W. Bromiley (Peabody, MA: Hendrickson, 2010), IV/3.1, 216. For definitions see R. A. Muller, *Dictionary of Latin and Greek Theological*

body, as a "kind of ecclesiological *extra Calvinisticum*, that protects the divine freedom of Christ."[7] He thus has two forms of existence: a "heavenly historical form," which is his incarnate body, and an "earthly historical form," which is the church. Barth understands both forms through his *Chalcedonian logic*: the Chalcedonian pattern, the *anhypostasia/enhypostasia* formula, and the notion of correspondence.[8] Just as there is a Chalcedonian correspondence between Jesus' divine and human natures, a similar correspondence exists within ecclesiology.[9] The invisible work of the Spirit (the event) forms the basis for the real society of persons in history (the institution), with the latter corresponding to the former. The visible institution is an embodiment of an invisible (and repeated) event whereby the Spirit (who ecclesiologically is closely identified with the risen Christ) brings Jesus' past work into the believer's present. *Constructively*, each of the three elements of the Chalcedonian logic can be applied to this intra-ecclesial relationship. First, the event cannot be separated from or confused with the institution. The Spirit is not captive or equivalent to the institutional church. Second, the institution has no genuine life without the event, but the event imbues it with genuine reality. Institution without event is no longer church, meaning the church cannot be analyzed *merely* sociologically any more than Jesus can be analyzed *merely* historically. Third, the institution reflects the event. Consequently, the church is an article of faith—a place where heaven and earth truly meet. *Critically*, Barth rejects erroneous ecclesiological tendencies that, like Christological heresies, emphasize

Terms (Grand Rapids: Baker, 1985). For historical usage see E. David Willis, *Calvin's Catholic Christology: The Function of the So-Called Extra Calvinisticum in Calvin's Theology* (Leiden: E. J. Brill, 1966), 31–33.

7. Bender, *Karl Barth's Christological Ecclesiology*, 200.
8. See section 3.3 for further details. This research uses the term "Chalcedonian logic" to refer to all three aspects. Bender, in contrast, uses the term "Christological logic." See particularly ibid., 3–7.
9. See for example Barth, *Church Dogmatics*, IV/1, 643–50.

one side of the tension too greatly. The Docetic tendency sees the church primarily as invisible event, while the Ebionite tendency does the reverse.[10] A third error, which could be labeled Eutychian, occurs when the event and the institution are confused and melded.[11]

Barth further employs this Chalcedonian logic not just *within* Christology and ecclesiology, but *between* them.[12] The church (including event and institution) corresponds to Christ (including divine and human natures). First, Christ and the church cannot be separated or confused, but together form the *totus Christus*, the total (physical and ecclesial) body of Christ. Second, the church has no independent existence outside of Christ. Third, the church's actions and deeds correspond to Christ's; the life of the church is modeled on the life of Christ. The church's *modus operandi*, then, is to *correspond* to Christ in obedience. And the limit of ecclesial activity is to bear witness to the divine event that reconciles us to Christ. When the church attempts to be more than a witness, it ironically becomes not more but less.[13] This point is pivotal. Barth rejects all forms of sacramental mediation because in the present historical period Christ is not absent.[14] Although Christ is obviously not *physically* present on earth since his ascension, Barth claims Christ is truly present through his Spirit. Christ *cannot* be absent; otherwise his presence would need to be mediated through the sacraments, and the ecclesial role would go beyond mere witness. Consequently, for Barth, the Spirit *must* be closely identified with Christ. Barth certainly makes a close connection between the two in his ecclesiological language—a

10. See for example ibid., IV/1, 653.

11. Although to my knowledge (and Bender's) Barth never explicitly uses the term this way. See Bender, *Karl Barth's Christological Ecclesiology*, 7.

12. See for example Barth, *Church Dogmatics*, IV/1, 650–62. Also, ibid., IV/2, 59–60.

13. See particularly ibid., IV/1, 657. Also Bender, *Karl Barth's Christological Ecclesiology*, 179.

14. See for example Barth, *Church Dogmatics*, IV/3.1, 46; IV/3.2, 514–16. Also the discussion in Douglas Farrow, *Ascension and Ecclesia: On the Significance of the Ascension for Ecclesiology and Christian Cosmology* (Edinburgh: T. & T. Clark, 1999), 250–54.

virtual identity.[15] For example, in IV/3.1 Barth directly identifies the Holy Spirit twice as "Jesus Christ Himself in the power of His resurrection."[16]

Given the theological climate Barth was responding to, with both the mysticism of Schleiermacher and the existentialism of Bultmann sacrificing the objectivity of the Christ event for a subjectively conceived reality that divorced Christ from the Spirit, it is not surprising that Barth swung significantly toward hard objectivity, and the Son and Spirit's close identification. But perhaps his pendulum swung too far. For, as argued below, Barth is at risk of an *ecclesial* Spirit-Eutychianism (confusing/melding the Son and the Spirit). Some even claim that Barth minimizes the Spirit to such a degree that his proposals are susceptible to an ecclesial Spirit-Docetism (where the Spirit's role is subsumed into Christ's in the church's being and life). While the former critique is probably more justified, some evidence points in the latter direction. Below are some of the more justified critiques of Barth's ecclesiology that arise from his ecclesial Spirit-Eutychianism, moving from the weakest and narrowest to the broadest and most significant.

First, Barth's close ecclesial identification of Christ and the Spirit implies a sharp distinction between the true and false church. Given that for Barth the institution of the church exists only through its embrace of the Spirit's event, the institutional church is divided into two parts—a true aspect and a false aspect. McFarland comments, "This dichotomization of Christ and community is problematic not because it posits an absolute distinction between divine and human action, but because it so identifies the former with the inner spiritual realm as to cut it off from the earthly-historical plane of human

15. His Trinitarian explanations, in contrast, always recognize the Son and the Holy Spirit as distinct "modes of being." See for example Barth, *Church Dogmatics*, I/1, 348–83.

16. Ibid., IV/3.1, 352–53.

exteriority."[17] This is illustrated in Barth's characterization of the church as the body of Christ, with minimal reference to other metaphors that enable greater distinction.[18] Christ does not sin, so it follows that when the church sins it is not Christ and therefore not the church.[19] The church ceases to exist, at least in that locality. Nicholas Healy argues that for Barth, "Sometimes, at least, the unfaithful Bride of Christ is a different entity than the true Body of Christ."[20] Such an understanding threatens the historical continuity of the church. It should be noted that both Bender[21] and Hunsinger[22] vigorously (and quite successfully) defend Barth against this particular critique by arguing that the relation between the true/sanctified and false/sinful church is in fact another of Barth's dialectic tensions. Even if their response is granted, Bender nevertheless notes that "while Barth is masterful at protecting and delineating the distinction and irreversibility between ecclesiological strands, he is often less adept at describing their unity and relation."[23] This is a common theme in the critiques below.

17. Ian A. McFarland, "The Body of Christ: Rethinking a Classic Ecclesiological Model," *International Journal of Systematic Theology* 7, no. 3 (2005): 230. See this reference and the following article from Healy for a more extended explanation of this critique. Nicholas M. Healy, "The Logic of Karl Barth's Ecclesiology: Analysis, Assessment and Proposed Modifications," *Modern Theology* 10, no. 3 (1994): 253–70.
18. Bender notes that Barth understands the church almost exclusively as the "body of Christ," and neglects other biblical images. Bender, *Karl Barth's Christological Ecclesiology*, 277–78. Healy similarly suggests that Barth's "systematic use of a single definition" is "methodologically misguided." Healy, "The Logic of Karl Barth's Ecclesiology," 226. For a general discussion of the problems of not using a broad range of biblical models and images, see Nicholas M. Healy, *Church, World and the Christian Life: Practical-Prophetic Ecclesiology* (Cambridge: Cambridge University Press, 2000), 25–51.
19. Note that the critique here isn't that the church isn't concrete (as some claim), but rather that the concrete church is sharply divided into two parts—a true and false aspect.
20. Healy, "The Logic of Karl Barth's Ecclesiology," 259.
21. Bender, *Karl Barth's Christological Ecclesiology*, 273–74.
22. George Hunsinger, "The Mediator of Communion: Karl Barth's Doctrine of the Holy Spirit," in *Disruptive Grace: Studies in the Theology of Karl Barth* (Grand Rapids: Eerdmans, 2000), 148–85.
23. Bender, *Karl Barth's Christological Ecclesiology*, 274.

Gunton, in a largely positive article focused on Barth's doctrine of salvation, notes the "relative underweighting of the pneumatological and ecclesial dimensions of Barth's way of speaking about the appropriation of salvation,"[24] and thus adds a second and third critique of Barth's ecclesiology.[25] Gunton notes that in Barth's account Jesus mediates knowledge of himself, while the biblical witness assigns this function to the *Paraclete* (cf. John 16:12-15). It could be added that such pneumatological minimization leads directly to the truly remarkable comment that "the world would not necessarily be lost if there were no Church."[26] In both cases then, historical objectivity trumps subjective personal appropriation, rather than working in concert with it. Rogers consequently (and perhaps exaggeratedly) suggests that "there is a developing consensus that [Barth's] doctrine of the Spirit subsides into Christology, as if there's nothing the Spirit can do that Christ can't do better."[27]

Another of Gunton's critiques is more telling. Recognizing Barth's "rather non-participatory conception of knowledge," Gunton would prefer that Barth spoke of *participation* in Christ's body rather than merely *encountering* another history. Gunton argues that Barth's focus is on Christ "bringing home to the believer his past work," and "the miraculous transfer of what happened then to ourselves now" rather than the Spirit's present transformative work and the current relationship to Christ so enabled.[28] The reason for Barth's imbalanced ecclesiology is precisely Barth's imbalanced Christology. This is very

24. Colin Gunton, "Salvation," in *The Cambridge Companion to Karl Barth*, ed. John Webster (Cambridge: Cambridge University Press, 2000), 152. Jenson makes a similar point about Barth's overall framework. See Robert Jenson, "You Wonder Where the Spirit Went," *Pro Ecclesia* 2 (1993): 302–4.

25. Both critiques focus particularly on volume IV/3 of *Church Dogmatics*.

26. Barth, *Church Dogmatics*, IV/3.2, 826.

27. Eugene F. Rogers, "The Mystery of the Spirit in Three Traditions: Calvin, Rahner, Florensky or, You *Keep* Wondering Where the Spirit Went," *Modern Theology* 19, no. 2 (2003): 243.

28. See Gunton, "Salvation," 152.

significant. Gunton maintains that Barth's excessive ecclesial separation of the human and the divine is derived directly from a tendency to diminish the Spirit's ecclesial role relative to the Son. He explains: "In dogmatics, a proper distribution of weight between the various topics is important, so that the underweighting of the place of the Spirit in relation to the humanity and ministry of Jesus in Barth's thought carries implications for pneumatology elsewhere."[29] Recognizing that Barth's Christ has a genuine humanity, Gunton argues that a lack of reference to the Spirit leads to Christ's humanity not being particular. Consequently Jesus' temptation, ascension, and his pneumatologically enabled filial relationship are scarcely mentioned. Gunton's argument, then, is that Barth's *Christological* tendency toward what I have termed a Spirit-Docetism leads directly to an ecclesial Spirit-Eutychianism, with its emphasis on encounter over participation.

Bender, after an exhaustive but largely affirming account of Barth's ecclesiology, draws a similar conclusion.[30] He notes the common accusation that Barth's work is underdetermined by pneumatology, and pertinently remarks that Barth was the first to acknowledge this tendency.[31] Bender also recognizes some validity in the charge that Barth considers redemptive history to be complete at the cross, leaving little for the Spirit or the church still to do. While he rightly rejects the mistaken conclusion that Barth leaves no place for human agency (referencing Barth's rich notion of correspondence), Bender notes that "Barth often speaks of a parallelism of action, rather than an embodied action. . . . The point might be illustrated by asking

29. Ibid.

30. This paragraph briefly summarizes the argument in Bender, *Karl Barth's Christological Ecclesiology*, 277–84.

31. For a considered statement of this position, see for example Gary D. Badcock, *The House Where God Lives: Renewing the Doctrine of the Church for Today* (Grand Rapids: Eerdmans, 2009), 88–96, particularly pp. 92–93.

whether Christ comes to us *through* the proclamation of the Church or *alongside* of it."[32] This parallels Gunton's concern above about participation being reduced to encounter. In Bender's analysis Barth's outworking emphasizes divine and human distinction and irreversibility, but is "less successful in describing their relation and inseparability."[33]

The final weakness in Barth's Christological ecclesiology regards his analysis of ecclesial mediation. Barth rightly rejects strong notions of ecclesial mediation (which suggest that human actions add to or complete Christ's work), but also, and particularly in his later work, he rejects even weak notions (that Christ comes through human words and actions). While Christ *can and does* present himself to us by his Spirit outside of the church, the question is whether Christ *also* acts through the church by the Spirit; indeed whether this latter mechanism is primary. Barth's response is strongly negative: "All real acquaintance with Him rests on the fact that He makes Himself known. All adequate conception rests on the fact that He introduces Himself. No other can do this for Him."[34] But such rejection of weak ecclesial mediation is problematic. For one thing, and perhaps a trifle simplistically, witness itself surely implies at least some form of creaturely mediation. As Yocum writes, "If the witness is a witness visible to other human beings, how can one eliminate the mediating role of the human actor, and preserve any content to the term 'witness'?"[35]

32. Bender, *Karl Barth's Christological Ecclesiology*, 282.
33. Ibid., 279.
34. Barth, *Church Dogmatics*, IV/3.1, 46.
35. John Yocum, *Ecclesial Mediation in Karl Barth* (Aldershot, UK: Ashgate, 2004), particularly pp. 65–67.

This line of critique of Barth has become quite common.[36] Even after recognizing that some supposed failings are overdrawn,[37] and that backtracking on previous criticisms of Barth's work is not uncommon,[38] concerns remain. Hauerwas expresses them pungently: "Barth, of course, does not deny that the church is constituted by the proclamation of the gospel. What he cannot acknowledge is that the community called the church is constitutive of gospel proclamation."[39] More precisely, Mangina notes a distinction between active and passive ecclesial mediation.[40] *Passive* ecclesial mediation is simply that the church "serves in God's hands as a sign or an instrument of grace."[41] But this sign is only constituted by the event of the Spirit who conveys the work of Christ to the church in the present moment. *Active* ecclesial mediation, in contrast, is the understanding that "the Church is *actively* involved in the

36. Healy, "The Logic of Karl Barth's Ecclesiology," 253–70. Also Nicholas M. Healy, "Karl Barth's Ecclesiology Reconsidered," *Scottish Journal of Theology* 57, no. 3 (2004): 287–99. In this latter article Healy steps back a little from some of his earlier (and potentially overdrawn) criticisms. See also: Joseph L. Mangina, "The Stranger as Sacrament: Karl Barth and the Ethics of Ecclesial Practice," *International Journal of Systematic Theology* 1, no. 3 (1999): 322–39; Joseph L. Mangina, "Bearing the Marks of Jesus: The Church in the Economy of Salvation in Barth and Hauerwas," *Scottish Journal of Theology* 52 (1999): 269–305; Reinhard Hütter, "Karl Barth's 'dialectical catholicity': Sic et Non," *Modern Theology* 16, no. 2 (2000): 137–57; Reinhard Hütter, *Suffering Divine Things: Theology as Church Practice*, trans. Doug Scott (Grand Rapids: Eerdmans, 2000); Eugene F. Rogers, *After the Spirit: A Constructive Pneumatology from Resources outside the Modern West* (Grand Rapids: Eerdmans, 2005), 19–22; and McFarland, "The Body of Christ," 226–32.
37. An example of this is the suggestion that Barth forces an implicit choice between the invisible and visible church, or sets them up in opposition to one another. See for example Yocum, *Ecclesial Mediation in Karl Barth*, 121. Also Hütter, "Karl Barth's 'dialectical catholicity': Sic et Non," 149–52. Hütter critiques Barth for lacking ecclesial concreteness while surprisingly not mentioning Barth's description of twelve specific practices (see Barth, *Church Dogmatics*, IV/3.2, 864–901).
38. See Healy, "Karl Barth's Ecclesiology Reconsidered," 287–99. Also, Badcock, *The House Where God Lives*, 93.
39. Stanley Hauerwas, *With the Grain of the Universe* (London: SCM, 2002), 145.
40. Specifically Mangina labels these as strong and weak forms of ecclesial mediation, but as these labels differ from those we used in the previous paragraph, we have chosen different descriptive words to unpack Mangina's point.
41. Mangina, "Bearing the Marks of Jesus," 293.

communication of saving grace."[42] This position holds that the church cooperates with God, rather than just pointing to him and his work. "The medium is, if not the message, the binding medium in which faith takes shape."[43] For Barth, passive ecclesial mediation is acceptable, but active ecclesial mediation is forbidden. The church stands alongside the story it bears witness to.

Barth often illustrated this distinction by referencing the medieval artist Grünewald's depiction of the crucifixion and John the Baptist pointing with a crooked finger to Christ.[44] A similar but less common image is that of Joseph, who Barth sees as a model of the quiet witness the church should imitate.[45] Joseph is contrasted with Mary, an active participant in the gospel narrative. But "could there not be a place for *both* Joseph and Mary?"[46] Bender's insight here is profound:

> This divine visitation, this perfect and complete work of singular and uncompromised grace, is an act that God chooses to bring about through a human partner. And this suggests a real, though radically chastened, form of mediation. In the end, it is questionable whether a choice can be made between such witness and mediation. Are not both needed to qualify each other and together point to a deeper and inexpressible reality, the one protecting against a synergistic understanding of grace, as the other protects against a monistic one? Both Joseph and Mary were present at the manger, and both testify to the mystery and miracle of Christmas.[47]

42. Ibid., 294.
43. Ibid., 295.
44. For example, "In this connexion one might recall John the Baptist in Grünewald's Crucifixion, especially his prodigious index finger. Could anyone point away from himself more impressively and completely . . . ? And could anyone point more impressively and realistically than here to what is indicated?" Barth, *Church Dogmatics*, I/1, 112. See also ibid., I/1, 262; I/2, 125; III/3, 492.
45. See for example Karl Barth, *Letters: 1961-1968*, trans. Geoffrey W. Bromiley (Edinburgh: T. & T. Clark, 1981), 75, 84, 94, 245.
46. Bender, *Karl Barth's Christological Ecclesiology*, 282.
47. Ibid., 283.

The distinction is between whether Christ merely *comes* to the church by the Spirit, or whether Christ *works* through the church by the Spirit. Barth affirms only the former, whereas the latter seems equally biblical. Questions thus arise again about whether Barth's emphasis on the distinction and asymmetry between divinity and humanity has led him to undervalue the Chalcedonian truth that their actions are also without separation.

Barth's ecclesiology contains a wealth of theological insight. Most crucially, it argues that the church (*enhypostatically*) exists only because of Christ, and (*anhypostatically*) cannot exist apart from him. Within the climate Barth was writing, this emphasis on revelation's objective reality and the church's theological basis was timely. Barth's development of a Chalcedonian logic and the consequent relationship between Christ and the church is rigorous and valuable. From Barth's outworking alone the first premise, that significant insight into the ontology of the church can be gained through comparison with the ontology of Jesus Christ, can certainly be affirmed.

The critique above argues that Barth's explication of this Chalcedonian logic is nevertheless imbalanced. His overemphasis on the "without confusion" aspect of the divine/human interaction leads to its "without separation" aspect being relatively underemphasized. The root cause of this imbalance is Barth's leaning toward ecclesial Spirit-Eutychianism: the ecclesial roles of the Son and Spirit are insufficiently distinguished. At times, Barth even slips toward an ecclesial Spirit-Docetism, where the Spirit's work is subsumed into the Son's. An understanding of the Holy Spirit's ecclesial involvement as logically distinct from and yet eternally intertwined with the Son could enable an ecclesiology that extends and balances Barth's developments, yet retains all its majesty and mastery. The aim in moving forward then is "not to go around, but to go through Barth's doctrine of the Church."[48] Mangina insightfully (and perhaps exaggeratedly) writes, "The way beyond Barth at this point, it seems to me, lies in the direction of a 'concrete' pneumatology that is able to recognise the Spirit as a salvific economy in its own right—a demand that Eastern theologians have consistently made of their Western counterparts."[49] A pneumatological lens provides insight into how divine and human actions correspond in the church without being confused or merged, but also without being excessively separated. As such, our investigation turns to the contemporary Eastern Orthodox theologian John Zizioulas, and his pneumatological approach to connecting ecclesiology with Christology.

4.2 Zizioulas's Eucharistic Ecclesiology

Zizioulas's ecclesiology may be summarized as follows: Christ institutes the church while the Spirit constitutes the church.[50] In contrast to an understanding that sees the church existing first as Christ's body *and only then* being empowered through the Spirit, Zizioulas argues that the Spirit has an ontological and constitutive ecclesial role. In his opinion, this brings a much-needed ecclesial corrective to a traditional western overemphasis on Christology.[51] The following discussion argues that while Zizioulas's ideas are profound, in direct contrast to Barth he overemphasizes the "without separation" and minimizes the "without confusion" aspect of divine/

48. Ibid., 284.
49. Mangina, "Bearing the Marks of Jesus," 301. Note that the words Mangina uses here, giving the Spirit "salvific economy in its own right," are probably unnecessarily exaggerated. There is no suggestion that the Spirit saves apart from Christ. Rather, the course of salvation history is not accomplished exclusively by Christ. It is best to see the Spirit and Christ as having logically distinct roles within existentially united actions.
50. See John Zizioulas, *Being as Communion: Studies in Personhood and the Church* (Crestwood, NY: St. Vladimir's Seminary Press, 1985), 140. Also John Zizioulas, "The Doctrine of God the Trinity Today: Suggestions for an Ecumenical Study," in *The Forgotten Trinity*, ed. Alasdair I. C. Heron (London: BCC / CCBI, 1991), 28.
51. Zizioulas, *Being as Communion*, 126.

human relations in ecclesiology. This leads to an overrealized eschatology and an overemphasis on sacramentalism and ecclesial mediation. Further, the root cause for this imbalance is the same as Barth's—insufficiently distinguishing between the Son and Spirit's involvement in the church's life: the now-familiar category of ecclesial Spirit-Eutychianism. But while Barth's ecclesial Spirit-Eutychianism tended *slightly* toward ecclesial Spirit-Docetism, Zizioulas's ecclesial Spirit-Eutychianism leans *strongly* in the opposite direction toward ecclesial Spirit-Ebionism, with the Son virtually subsumed into the all-pervading role of the Spirit.

The major outworking of Zizioulas's ecclesiology occurs in his two acclaimed collections of essays: *Being as Communion*[52] and *Communion and Otherness*.[53] In the first volume Zizioulas unpacks his primary theological theme: that ontology is relational, or *being is communion*: "It is communion that makes beings 'be': nothing exists without it, not even God."[54] Zizioulas bases this understanding on God's existence. In his reading, the Greek Fathers located the "ground" of God's existence not in his substance (as became common in the west) but in the Father's *hypostasis*. ". . . God, as Father, and not as substance, perpetually confirms through 'being' His *free* will to exist."[55] He does this by freely begetting the Son and spirating the Spirit—by existing in communion. Love, then, is not a secondary

52. Ibid.

53. John Zizioulas, *Communion and Otherness: Further Studies in Personhood and the Church* (London: T. & T. Clark, 2006).

54. Zizioulas, *Being as Communion*, 17.

55. Ibid., 41. Many theologians question Zizioulas's characterization of Athanasius and early fathers on this point. They note particularly that for these patriarchs, the monarchy resides in the entire Godhead and not with the Father alone. Moreover, they claim that this latter understanding has more theological justification. See for example Alan J. Torrance, *Persons in Communion: An Essay on Trinitarian Description and Human Participation* (Edinburgh: T. & T. Clark, 1996), 288–95. Also, Gunton, *The Promise of Trinitarian Theology*, 196–97. For the purposes of this argument, it is not significant whether Zizioulas is accurately interpreting the work of the early fathers, merely that Zizioulas believes them to be making these claims and owns them himself.

feature of God added once he exists, but constitutes his existence. God exists in, by, and through love. "Love . . . 'hypostasizes' God."[56] Zizioulas identifies God's *ousia* precisely with his triune communion, arguing that this is Athanasius' primary contribution to Christian theology. "Substance, in as much as it signifies the ultimate character of being, can be conceived only as communion."[57]

Zizioulas then transposes divine ontology onto human ontology, consistently elaborating a distinction between individuals ("substantial" entities) and persons (who are defined by their relationships). To expand, an individual is constituted by their *own* substance (e.g., physical body or existential consciousness) rather than *another's* substance. This understanding naturally flows from humanity's biological existence as separate beings. Zizioulas views sin as the realization of this inherent weakness of our biological, creaturely existence.[58] The fall is precisely the refusal to make our being entirely dependent on communion[59] and consequently leads to death.[60] Persons, in contrast to individuals, are constituted not by substance but by communion. While persons *have* bodies and consciousness, they are not *equated* with these things. They transcend their natural boundaries (ecstatic), and bear within themselves the reflection of all others (catholic).[61] As such, humans cannot become persons through their own choice. While humans are individuals biologically, they do not become persons simply by opening up

56. Zizioulas, *Being as Communion*, 46. See here also Stanley J. Grenz, *Rediscovering the Triune God: The Trinity in Contemporary Theology* (Minneapolis: Fortress Press, 2004), 141.
57. Zizioulas, *Being as Communion*, 84.
58. Ibid., 52.
59. Ibid., 102.
60. Ibid., 51, 105. Volf analyzes Zizioulas's understanding here as follows: "Creation and Fall coalesce into a single entity in Zizioulas's thinking. The Fall consists merely in the revelation and actualization of the limitations and potential dangers inherent in creaturely existence." Miroslav Volf, *After Our Likeness: The Church as the Image of the Trinity* (Grand Rapids: Eerdmans, 1998), 82–83.
61. See Zizioulas, *Communion and Otherness*, 206–49.

relationally. Rather, an ontological change is required, in which they become constituted by their relationships.[62]

The triune God as unoriginated true person[63] enables humanity to enter into *ecclesial* personhood rather than endure *biological* individuality, which inevitably leads to death. How is this realized? First, the hypostatic union demonstrates the possibility of human personhood, as Christ is *constituted* by his relationship of Sonship with the Father. Second, Christ instituted the church, through which humans enter into the personal existence Jesus demonstrated—a communal and not merely biological existence. The ecclesial existence entered is not just the same *kind* as Christ's, but actually Christ's existence. For Zizioulas, Christ is a corporate personality who incorporates the many into the one—his incarnate *and* ecclesial body—by the Spirit. "The Holy Spirit, in making real the Christ-event in history, makes real at the same time Christ's personal existence as a body or community. Christ does not exist first as truth and then as communion; He is both at once. All separation between Christology and ecclesiology vanishes in the Spirit."[64] As ecclesial persons united to Christ, by the Spirit, we transcend our natural boundaries (ecstatic), and bear within ourselves all others in Christ (catholic)—thus experiencing a genuinely new personal-relational ontology.

62. See John Zizioulas, "Human Capacity and Incapacity: A Theological Exploration of Personhood," *Scottish Journal of Theology* 28 (1972): 401–47. Or Volf, *After Our Likeness*, 82–83.

63. See Zizioulas, *Being as Communion*, 42–49. For Zizioulas, God the Father as a "person" chooses to be in relation by begetting the Son, and thus his personhood, freedom, and irreducibly communal existence coincide. In contrast, "man cannot exercise his ontological freedom completely, because he is tied by his createdness, by the 'necessity' of his existence, whereas God as 'uncreated' does not experience this limitation" (ibid., 44). Also, "This communion is a product of freedom as a result not of the substance of God but of a person, the Father . . . who is Trinity not because the divine *nature* is ecstatic but because the Father as a *person* freely wills this communion" (ibid.).

64. Ibid., 111.

Personhood, then, only occurs in the church.[65] Indeed, the church is not primarily an institution, but a way of being.[66] "Christ's existence is applied to our existence not *in abstracto* or individualistically, but in and through a community."[67] This existence is entered through baptism,[68] where we die as individuals, but are resurrected as ecclesial persons, a new birth "in the Spirit" just as Christ was born "in the Spirit." Through this ecclesial existence, humans experience the truth, by which Zizioulas refers to the way it is for God and will be for us. Our ecclesial existence is thus eschatological in character, in that the future of humanity is brought into present-day reality. This eschatological nature of our ecclesial existence is only truly and completely experienced in the Eucharist. Here our body and blood are transformed by and united with Jesus' body and blood. We receive Christ and become part of him, not just reflecting but actually participating in the eschatological event where the two become one: "[T]here is no room for the slightest distinction between the worshipping Eucharistic community on earth and the actual worship in front of God's throne."[69] In summary then, the local church community, as it celebrates the Eucharist through the Spirit, becomes the true and complete body of Christ, a genuine eschatological reality. Originally through baptism and repeatedly through the Eucharist, individuals become persons as together they exist as part of Christ's communion with the Father.

65. Interestingly, the ecclesiological outworking of Zizioulas's understanding receives much less attention than his Trinitarian communion ontology, while Zizioulas clearly sees the two as intimately connected. See for example Stephen R. Holmes, *The Quest for the Trinity: The Doctrine of God in Scripture, History and Modernity* (Downers Grove, IL: IVP Academic, 2012), 12. And as an example, Grenz, *Rediscovering the Triune God*, 140.
66. Zizioulas, *Being as Communion*, 15. See also Zizioulas, "The Doctrine of God the Trinity Today," 27–28.
67. Zizioulas, *Being as Communion*, 113.
68. As an Eastern Orthodox, Zizioulas is referring to infant baptism. In the detailed examination of baptism in chapter 6, the meaning is intentionally broader.
69. Zizioulas, *Being as Communion*, 233.

For Zizioulas, it is axiomatic that the Son became incarnate only through the Spirit, and consequently only through the Spirit that the church becomes Christ's ecclesial body. So there is no distinction between Son and Spirit in the church:

> . . . the Holy Spirit is not one who *aids* us in bridging the distance between Christ and ourselves, but he is the person of the Trinity who actually realizes in history that which we call Christ, this absolutely relational entity, our Saviour. In this case, our Christology is *essentially* conditioned by Pneumatology . . . in fact it is *constituted* pneumatologically. Between the Christ–truth and ourselves there is *no gap to fill* by grace.[70]

Christ's involvement in and relation to the church is thus "melded" with the Spirit (ecclesial Spirit-Eutychianism) and even subsumed into it (ecclesial Spirit-Ebionism). This leads directly to Zizioulas collapsing Christology into ecclesiology, existence into communion, and eschatology into sacramentology, three instances of overemphasizing the "without separation" aspect of divine/human relations at the expense of them being "without confusion."

First, subsuming the Son's ecclesial role into the Spirit results in the "one" Christ collapsing into the "many" of the church. Zizioulas adopts an almost complete identification not just between Christ's physical and ecclesial body, but Christ's Eucharistic body as well.[71] The three are virtually interchangeable terms and thus indistinguishable entities—three ways of talking about the same thing.[72] Volf explains: "The Eucharist is the place where church and Christ become one body, the body of *Christ*, and thus 'completely' identical."[73] In critiquing this understanding, Volf argues that the

70. Ibid., 110–11.
71. See for example Paul McPartlan, "Who Is the Church? Zizioulas and von Balthasar on the Church's Identity," *Ecclesiology* 4, no. 3 (2008): 271–88.
72. Zizioulas, *Communion and Otherness*, 289–91.
73. Volf, *After Our Likeness*, 99.

reason Zizioulas neglects other biblical images for the church is because they emphasize the distinction between Christ and the church.[74] Further, he (perhaps exaggeratedly) argues that such strong identification means the church participates not just in God's inner life, but also in his actions toward humanity.[75] This circular argument has significant soteriological consequences: we are virtually saving ourselves.[76] Gunton raises other concerns, writing of "a tendency to identify the Church with Christ. However, such an identification comes at a price, and it is that of marginalizing the continuing humanity of Christ."[77] Put simply, the problem is that Zizioulas's theological proposals are perilously close to binitarianism. Christologically, his focus is on the Spirit and the humanity of Christ, with the divine Logos playing no substantive role except to be incarnate. Ecclesiologically, the Spirit makes the church Christ's body, with the human Christ retaining little further importance. Zizioulas's Christological Spirit-Ebionism translates directly into ecclesial Spirit-Ebionism.

A related problem is that the unity only becomes total at the Eucharist and so (like the Eucharist itself) the church becomes a repeated event in history. For Zizioulas, the church is the entire body of Christ, but it is not always the body of Christ. An individual's personhood and the church's existence as Christ's body is "received again in the present from the future"[78] and not carried into the future from the past. The implication is that between Eucharists the church is not the body of Christ, but exists only "rhythmically."[79] McPartlan explains: "The identity experienced in the Eucharist is immediately

74. Ibid., 100. See also McPartlan, "Who Is the Church?" 278.
75. Volf, *After Our Likeness*, 100.
76. Ibid., 91.
77. Colin Gunton, "Persons and Particularity," in *The Theology of John Zizioulas*, ed. Douglas H. Knight (Aldershot, UK: Ashgate, 2007), 105.
78. Paul McPartlan, *The Eucharist Makes the Church: Henri de Lubac and John Zizioulas in Dialogue* (Edinburgh: T. & T. Clark, 1993), 192.

lost again, to be abidingly acquired only on the last day."[80] Zizioulas attempts to resolve this odd conclusion by arguing that time between Eucharists is bridged by the Spirit's transtemporality, through which "time is redeemed from fragmentation and history acquires a different sense."[81] It is not at all clear, though, why time acquiring a "different sense" makes the church any more the body of Christ between Eucharistic gatherings.[82]

A second challenge with Zizioulas's ecclesiology is that human existence collapses almost completely into communion. For Zizioulas, communion constitutes not just being or essence but existence, for both God and humanity. Consequently nothing can precede communion either causally or chronologically, as it is only in communion that there is a "person" who is truly free to choose. Zizioulas is forced in this direction (again) because of his close identification of the Spirit (through whom humans enjoy personal communion) and the Son (through whom humans enjoy personal existence).[83] But such close identification causes significant problems. From the divine perspective, the Father's choice to *exist* through begetting the Son contains within it the priority of existence over communion.[84] Consequently, many suggest that God's monarchy and his decision to exist should be viewed as belonging to the entire

79. For a detailed discussion see Volf, *After Our Likeness*, 101–2. Also see McPartlan, *The Eucharist Makes the Church*, 287–88.
80. McPartlan, *The Eucharist Makes the Church*, 287.
81. Zizioulas, *Being as Communion*, 183.
82. It may be that Zizioulas considers that the church's continuity depends on the Spirit *sustaining* true personhood by virtue of his repeated self-giving. Such an interpretation certainly makes more sense theologically, and removes from Zizioulas's work any of the "rhythmic" implications suggested by McPartlan above. To my knowledge, though, this "sustaining" interpretation is not explicitly stated in *Being as Communion*, and even if granted in its entirety, does not disqualify the overarching point that for Zizioulas Christology collapses into ecclesiology.
83. Whether or not it is the close identification of the Spirit and the Son that causes the close identification of being and communion, or vice versa, is a question I will not be addressing here. Suffice it to say that the two are very closely connected.
84. Volf, *After Our Likeness*, 79.

triune Godhead and not the Father alone.[85] From the human perspective, if the freedom to make cognitive decisions—a crucial yet incomplete part of the conversion process—precedes communion, then it implies that there is a *person* existing prior to the ecclesial communion and as a logical cause of it.

There are many other issues. Volf, for example, claims Zizioulas's understanding cannot particularize either the laity or the bishops. Ecclesial persons can't be differentiated in their biological existence (which individualizes by definition) or by their participation in God (as all ecclesial persons enjoy the same relationship of the Son with the Father).[86] How then are different members of the laity distinguished? Similarly, because each Eucharistic gathering is precisely identified with eschatological worship, the actions of different bishops must be a single action, so the particularity of the bishops also vanishes.[87] While pointing toward a valid critique, Volf is overreaching here. These particularity-based problems assume that no remnant of biological existence can impact ecclesial existence. But reading Zizioulas's hospitably,[88] it is probably more justified to claim that the latter encompasses and dwarfs the former, rather than overwhelming it completely. Characterizing Zizioulas's ecclesial personhood as "anhypostatic"[89] or claiming that cognitive choice is the *exclusive* prerogative of such ecclesial persons is overexaggerating. Zizioulas does not diminish the role of our biological existence to the point

85. See Gunton, *The Promise of Trinitarian Theology*, 196–98. And Torrance, *Persons in Communion*, 292–95. Also, Thomas Weinandy, "Zizioulas: The Trinity and Ecumenism," *New Blackfriars* 83, no. 979 (2002): 409–11.

86. Volf, *After Our Likeness*, 87.

87. Ibid., 111. From Volf's perspective, the particularity of the bishops cannot be found in their biological hypostasis, as that individualizes by definition.

88. For an example of the "hermeneutics of hospitality," see Thomas R. Thompson, "*Interpretatio in bonem partem*: Jürgen Moltmann on the Immanent Trinity," in *Theology as Conversation: The Significance of Dialogue in Historical and Contemporary Theology: A Festschrift for Daniel L. Migliore*, ed. Bruce L. McCormack and Kimlyn J. Bender (Grand Rapids: Eerdmans, 2009), 159.

89. Volf, *After Our Likeness*, 100.

of complete absence.[90] For example, he writes, "[T]ruth is not *just* something 'expressed' or 'heard,' a propositional or logical truth; but something which *is*, i.e. an ontological truth: the community itself becoming truth."[91] The word *just* here implies that Zizioulas doesn't completely remove the biological individual's cognitive rationality, but rather it is engulfed and transformed by something more fundamental and significant.[92]

Volf's critique, although exaggerated, certainly points in the right direction.[93] The divine in Zizioulas's framework so overwhelms the human that little of our biological existence remains. Zizioulas's error here is to equate human existence with being. For the triune God, communion, being, essence, and existence *are* identical.[94] For humanity, the situation is more complex. Communion cannot be identified with existence as we do exist outside of communion, if only temporarily. So biological existence is not *merely* individual and has traces of the personal within it. Gunton's comments here are pertinent:

> If Christ is the mediator of creation as well as being mediator of salvation and the head of the Church, his body, does it not follow that even our biological selves are already personal, as created? Zizioulas is right, surely, in his assertion that person is an eschatological concept; but is not the person's eschatological realisation anticipated already in creation,

90. As Volf claims. See ibid., 96.
91. Zizioulas, *Being as Communion*, 115 (italics mine).
92. Volf recognizes the quote and its implications, but suggests that given Zizioulas's conviction that rationality always individualizes this cannot be what he really means. Volf, *After Our Likeness*, 96. However, the references that Volf points to in order to justify this reversal are not emphatic enough to be convincing, e.g., Zizioulas, *Being as Communion*, 121n26.
93. Gunton also recognizes that Volf exaggerates this critique. He writes: "Miroslav Volf may exaggerate, but he exaggerates something that is there when he asserts Zizioulas' 'conviction that human personhood is not of this world, but rather is divine.'" Gunton, "Persons and Particularity," 104n35.
94. Although such an understanding (contra Zizioulas) does require that the decision to exist resides in the Godhead entire, and not in the Father alone.

> albeit less truly under the conditions of sin and death than in the community of salvation?[95]

A third challenge for Zizioulas is that his theological proposals collapse eschatology into sacramentology. The Eucharist "is not to be understood as a reality *parallel* with that of heaven, but rather as *identical* with it."[96] Once again this collapse derives directly from his overemphasis on the Spirit. The Spirit "bring[s] into history the last days, the eschaton,"[97] and with no compensating present historical role of the Son, Zizioulas has no theological means to distinguish between present reality and the coming Kingdom. On this point, Volf correctly argues that such identity removes any sense of ecclesial progression, as the future is completely identified with the already-experienced Eucharist.[98] To this can be added that not only progression but transformation and even worship itself have no theological justification in his framework. By collapsing the involvement of the Son and the Spirit in the church, the Spirit cannot be identified as a distinct person within us leading us into the (logically distinguishable) life of the Son. The risen Christ is simply the Spirit drawing us into himself. Another equally troubling consequence of collapsing eschatology into sacramentology is that elevating present activity (specifically Orthodox structures and practice) does not protect sufficiently against the remnants of the biological and sinful individual existence. Human actions simply do not justify such confidence.[99] Perhaps Gunton's insight is more

95. Gunton, "Persons and Particularity," 105.

96. John Zizioulas, "L'eucharistie: quelques aspects bibliques," in *L'eucharistie*, ed. J. Zizioulas et al. (Paris: Mame, 1970), 40. As quoted in Volf, *After Our Likeness*, 101.

97. Zizioulas, *Being as Communion*, 100.

98. Volf, *After Our Likeness*, 101.

99. See the helpful discussion in ibid., 109–16. Mawson's critique that Jenson and Hütter confuse the Holy Spirit and the objective spirit of the church could also be applied to Zizioulas here. See Michael Mawson, "The Spirit and the Community: Pneumatology and Ecclesiology in Jenson, Hütter and Bonhoeffer," *International Journal of Systematic Theology* 15, no. 4 (2013): 453–68.

ironically accurate than he intends, when he writes that Zizioulas "allows the weakness of the [Orthodox] tradition to come into view while operating in faithfulness to it."[100]

In the context of this discussion, the greatest critique and compliment that can be made regarding Zizioulas's Eucharistic ecclesiology are the same—the positives (and excesses) of his formulations directly counter the negatives (and excesses) in Barth's ecclesiology. Barth problematically rejects all notions of ecclesial mediation; Zizioulas in contrast makes baptism and the Eucharist a central part of ecclesiology; indeed he goes too far in collapsing eschatology into sacramentology. Barth problematically overemphasizes knowledge so that Christ merely encounters the church, rather than it participating in his life; Zizioulas in contrast makes communion the very basis of ecclesial personhood—indeed he goes too far in collapsing human existence into communion and thus minimizing the personhood of created but sinful humanity. Alan Torrance makes an interesting comparison here between the two theologians:

> Bonhoeffer accused Barth of revelational foundationalism—a "positivism of revelation"—and it has been suggested that this can lead to a form of isolationism. What we are required to ask of Zizioulas here is whether his account is not open to a parallel charge of operating an ontological "positivism of communion" or "personalist foundationalism" which fails to take seriously human continuity with society at large and the ontological implications of this.[101]

Continuing, Barth problematically tends to neglect the "without separation" aspect of the divine and human roles in ecclesiology, and consequently overemphasizes the "without confusion" aspect and

Specific church structures and their theological underpinnings are addressed in section 9.1 of this research.

100. Gunton, "Persons and Particularity," 107.

101. Torrance, *Persons in Communion*, 300.

asymmetry between them. For Zizioulas, in contrast, the "without separation" aspect is adequately recognized and in fact overemphasized with Christology collapsing into ecclesiology, particularly in its repeated performance of the Eucharist.

The argument above is that the imbalances of both Barth and Zizioulas derive from an ecclesial Spirit-Eutychianism that too greatly melds the ecclesial roles of the Son and the Spirit. For Barth, this ecclesial Spirit-Eutychianism tips *slightly* in the direction of ecclesial Spirit-Docetism, with the role of the Spirit relatively underemphasized. For Zizioulas, precisely the reverse occurs, with his ecclesial Spirit-Eutychianism tipping *significantly* toward ecclesial Spirit-Ebionism, as the Son's ecclesial involvement is subsumed into the Spirit's. It follows that formulating an ecclesial ontology that does not "fall over" into either of these excesses and suitably balances the "without confusion" and "without separation" aspects of divine and human engagement requires developing a Christological ecclesiology that logically distinguishes between the involvement of the Son and the Spirit in the church without existentially separating them. In many ways this ecclesiological development parallels the Spirit Christological analysis in chapter 2, where the understanding derived from Christ having merely divine and human natures was not sufficient, and there arose a need to clearly distinguish within the divine category two realities—Son and Spirit—and examine how *both* relate to Christ's human nature and each other. Establishing a similar distinction between the persons and roles of Son and Spirit in the life of the church is required. The development of such a viable and balanced Christological ecclesiology is the subject of the next chapter.

5

The Pneumatological Union between Christ and the Church

Part two is based on two premises: first, that significant insight into the ontology of the church can be gained through comparison with the ontology of Christ; second, that examining this correspondence requires giving prominence to the Spirit. The first premise was explored in the previous chapter through the Christological ecclesiologies of Barth and Zizioulas. While this chapter builds on these previous insights, it primarily uses the second premise to determine analogical insights about ecclesiology from the vantage point of Christology. In so doing, constituent features of a pneumato-ecclesiology begin to emerge, as viewed from a Spirit-Christological foundation. As Kärkkäinen asserts, "[T]he only way to construe a viable pneumato-ecclesiology is to reflect very carefully on the relationship between Christ and the Spirit on the one hand, and on the relation of the Spirit to the church on the other hand, and then try and see these three as mutual entities that inform each other."[1]

Two recognitions underlie the importance of viewing the connection between Christ and the church through a pneumatological perspective. First, Christ's identity cannot be understood apart from the Spirit.[2] Second, pneumatology *enables* the relationship between Christ and the church. It is *by the Spirit* that the church forms Christ's body. The most extended biblical outworking of the image asserts precisely this reality: "For we were all baptised by one Spirit so as to form one body—whether Jews or Gentiles, slave or free—and we were all given one Spirit to drink" (1 Cor. 12:13). This key verse is not merely saying that the Spirit enables believers to embrace unity in diversity as a functional community. More profoundly, it is claiming that the Spirit makes the church *Christ's* body. Badcock comments, "The church as the body of Christ cannot be considered apart from [the Spirit's presence], for the ecclesiastical 'body' of Christ is something that is mediated by the work of the Spirit, and cannot exist without the Spirit."[3]

Such an insight is restricted neither to the *image* of the church as the body of Christ, nor to merely *metaphorical* connections between Christology and ecclesiology. The biblical text connects these two doctrines in three significant ways: historically (the church was

1. Veli-Matti Kärkkäinen, *Toward a Pneumatological Theology: Pentecostal and Ecumenical Perspectives on Ecclesiology, Soteriology, and Theology of Mission* (Lanham, MD: University Press of America, 2002), 93. This pivotal quotation was also noted in the introduction to part two. Volf and Lee comment similarly that "we have before us a *triplicity* of relations that is of fundamental significance for ecclesiology: the relation between the Spirit and the church, the relation between Christ and the church, and a complex relation between the Spirit and Christ in which Christ appears as both bearer and giver of the Spirit. No ecclesiology which fails to take into account the particularities of all these relations can be adequate to the biblical testimonies, to the tradition, or, for that matter, to experiences of the divine presence in the church." Miroslav Volf and Maurice Lee, "The Spirit and the Church," in *Advents of the Spirit: An Introduction to the Current Study of Pneumatology*, ed. Bradford E. Hinze and D. Lyle Dabney (Milwaukee: Marquette University Press, 2005), 384.
2. See chapter 2.
3. Gary D. Badcock, *The House Where God Lives: Renewing the Doctrine of the Church for Today* (Grand Rapids: Eerdmans, 2009), 85.

founded by Christ), metaphorically (the church is *like* Christ), and organically (the church is *in* Christ), and for each of these the connection is pneumatologically facilitated.[4] This point is significant. If the Bible so strongly emphasizes the pneumatological nature of this connection, then a coherent theological understanding of the union and correspondence between Christ and the church simply cannot be formed without reference to the Spirit.

Adopting the approach of Third Article Theology, one that views reality through a pneumatological lens, parallels between a Spirit Christology and a pneumato-ecclesiology immediately become clear: (1) The Spirit conceives (Christ and the church); (2) The Spirit sustains the communion (of Christ and the church); (3) The Spirit conforms (Christ and the church); (4) The Spirit directs and empowers (Christ and the church); (5) The Spirit is displayed and mediated (by Christ and the church). This chapter applies these pneumatological parallels to analogically view ecclesiology from the perspective of Christology. Using Wolterstorff's terminology, Spirit Christology is the *control belief*, ecclesiology is the *data belief*, and Scripture and the creeds form the *background beliefs*. As noted in the titular labeling of the church as the incarnation's *sequel*, each parallel above has points of continuity (because the church is united with Christ) and discontinuity (because the church is not merely a continuation or repetition of the incarnation). Moreover, as with all divine/human correspondences each parallel also has a clear asymmetry, for the existence and function of the church depends completely on the existence and function of Christ.[5] By examining these points of continuity, discontinuity, and asymmetry in detail, the constituent features of a Christological Third Article Ecclesiology come into clear focus. In particular, the church is revealed as being

4. This chapter gives a detailed justification of this claim.
5. See section 3.3.

tripartite in nature (the pneumatological union between Christ and the church), relational in identity, unique in context, Christ-centered in orientation with a Christotelic momentum, indivisible in constitution, cruciform in shape, missional in purpose, and narrative in character.

5.1 The Spirit Conceives (Christ and the Church)

The *continuity* in this parallel is simple and clear. Just as Jesus' conception and birth was "by the Spirit" (Luke 1:35), so the conception and birth of the church itself was "by the Spirit" (Acts 2). It is by the Spirit that the eternal Son became hypostatically united with a human nature, and it is similarly by the Spirit that Christ was (and is) mystically united with his church. The consequence is that the church is not just irreducibly human (as is clearly evident) but also irreducibly divine (as is sometimes omitted). The church is not solely (or even primarily) a human institution, but exists substantially because of its pneumatological communion with Christ. The church cannot be understood merely sociologically any more than Christ can be examined merely historically. In contrast, the church has a *tripartite nature*—it is the pneumatological union between Christ and the church's human community.[6] Talking or thinking of the church's human community independently of its connection with Christ through the Spirit is as nonsensical as talking or thinking of the human nature of Christ independently of its hypostatic union with the eternal Son by the Spirit.[7]

6. This phrase—the church's human community—refers to the entity to which Christ unites himself to form the church. By definition, such an entity cannot include Christ within it, because it needs to be united with him in order to form the church. The sole purpose in categorizing such an entity is to recognize that talking or thinking in such a way is nonsensical, for the church cannot and does not exist apart from Christ.
7. In other words, enhypostatic and anhypostatic are descriptors not just of the relationship between the divine and human nature of Christ, but also of the relationship between Christ and the church.

The discontinuity associated with this parallel regards the sending and receiving of the Spirit. In terms of the incarnation, Christ "receives" the Spirit who is sent from the *Father*. In contrast, the church "receives" the Spirit who is "sent" to us by *Christ*.[8] Christ is thus both the receiver and giver of the Spirit, a discontinuity that requires explanation.[9] God normally acts in the world by the *Father* speaking the Word *through the Spirit*. In this case, though, the Spirit appears to come *through the Word*. How can this be?

Catholic theologian David Coffey provides a positive pointer toward the explanation by employing the "mutual love" model of the Trinity.[10] He maintains that within the Trinity, the focus of the Father's love is on the Son, but when in the divine plan that love is directed beyond the Godhead, it is creative (creating Christ's humanity) and unitive (in "that the result is not a mere union of persons but *unity of person* within the Son").[11] The Spirit hypostatically unites the humanity of Christ with the person of the Son. As Coffey explains: "In the *one act of nature and grace* the humanity of Christ was created by the triune God *and* so radically sanctified by the Holy Spirit, sent thereto by the Father, *that it*

8. The word "receives" is in quotes here, as it is used purely in a directional, and not in a temporal sense. Explicitly rejected is any implication that Christ or the church existed before the "receiving" of the Spirit. The conceiving (by the Spirit) and the receiving (of the Spirit) should be considered as chronologically and logically synchronous. The word "sent" is in quotes because, as will be discussed further in chapter 7, the action of the Son and the Spirit in the world are also best viewed as synchronous, so that Christ's "sending" is best interpreted as a sending *through* Christ and not a sending *from* him.
9. See for example Thaddeus D. Horgan, "Biblical Basis and Guidelines," in *The Church in the Movement of the Spirit*, ed. William R. Barr and Rena M. Yocum (Grand Rapids: Eerdmans, 1994), 15.
10. Coffey's work is used here because of its suggestive nature. As noted at several points (and detailed further in chapter 7), it certainly has challenges. But nevertheless it points in a direction that is suggestive and worthy of reflection. The intention here is to use the "positive suggestions" in Coffey's work without accepting the problematic associations.
11. David Coffey, "The 'Incarnation' of the Holy Spirit in Christ," *Theological Studies* 45 (1984): 472. It could appear here that the Spirit creates the human first and then the Son is hypostatically united with that human, but such a chronological sequence is clearly not Coffey's intention.

became one in person with the eternal Son, and so Son of God in humanity."[12] Moreover, Coffey identifies not just the love of the Father for the incarnate Christ as the Holy Spirit, but also (and pivotally) the love of the human Jesus for the Father. So as the Son is incarnated in creation as the human Jesus, in an analogous way, the Holy Spirit is "incarnated" in creation as the love of the human Jesus for the Father.

During his life and ministry, the love that Jesus has for the Father as the Son (identified as the Holy Spirit)[13] is progressively realized in Jesus' humanity. According to Coffey, this stamps Jesus' imprint on the so-called "incarnate" Spirit, so that when Jesus dies, is resurrected, and gains the beatific vision *in his humanity*, not only has the incarnate person of Jesus fully realized his divine Sonship (to the full measure that humanity can accommodate it), but the "incarnate" love of Jesus has fully realized his divine "Spiritship." Finally, Coffey notes Rahner's proposition that human love for God is indistinguishable from and inextricably bound to human love for our neighbors,[14] and concludes that the sending of the Holy Spirit on the church by the human Jesus is simply the intrinsic and necessary counterpart of Jesus' human but fully realized love for the Father.

Without owning all of Coffey's theological positions above,[15] or his nomenclature (particularly his unusual application of the term

12. Ibid., 469 (italics mine). By using the words "radically sanctified" Coffey may be implying that as an infant (or embryo even) the human Christ had attained the beatific vision, with a full human knowledge of the Father. Further, Coffey appears to be suggesting that Jesus "becomes the Son" rather than being identically the Logos by virtue of the hypostatic union. Whether or not either of these implications accurately reflects Coffey's position is beyond the scope of this chapter, but neither is required or adopted for the following argument.
13. Coffey's identification of the Holy Spirit as the mutual love of the Father and the Son calls into question the full personhood of the Holy Spirit. For further discussion see chapter 7.
14. Karl Rahner, *Theological Investigations*, trans. Karl-H. Kruger and Boniface Kruger, 23 vols. (London: Darton, Longman & Todd, 1974), 6:231–49.
15. Several theologians strongly critique Coffey's position. The two most comprehensive critiques are from Paul Molnar (from a Barthian perspective) and Neil Ormerod (from a classical western perspective). These are discussed in chapter 7.

"incarnate" for the Holy Spirit), the direction in which his explanation heads is nevertheless suggestive.[16] The fact that in the moving Paraclete passages of John 14–16 the Spirit comes to believers through Christ and not directly from the Father, and the close connection made between Christ physically leaving and the Holy Spirit coming (e.g., John 16:7) suggest that through Jesus' life and culminating in his death, resurrection, and ascension there is growth and development not just in the incarnate Son's human nature, but also in his relationship with the Spirit. Indeed, if one thinks in terms of a relational ontology[17] then the two are interdependent by definition. Further, if the Spirit is sent fully, permanently, and completely onto the church only *after* Christ has departed, then one can reasonably conclude that it is Christ (as opposed to the eternal Son *simpliciter*) through whom the Spirit is sent, and further that the Spirit's sending is specifically and uniquely determined by Christ's humanity and its relation to the human nature of the church. In other words, the Spirit is sent through the incarnate Christ specifically to unite the church with Christ's humanity. Our humanity is joined with Christ's humanity by the Spirit.

16. Also, see Steven M. Studebaker, "Integrating Pneumatology and Christology: A Trinitarian Modification of Clark H. Pinnock's Spirit Christology," *Pneuma* 28, no. 1 (2006): 5–20. In this article Studebaker effectively applies Coffey's ideas to Clark Pinnock's Spirit Christology.

17. A relational ontology is adopted in Third Article Theology to more clearly identify and critique a substance ontology. The terms "relational" and "substance ontology" are used in broad terms, with the former referring to the commonly noted "turn to relationality" in theological understanding of the last few decades, and particularly in Spirit Christology. So rather than a person being an individual substance with a rational nature, as tradition (Boethius) would have it, the ontology of a person is understood as intrinsically and irreducibly relational. See for example Stanley J. Grenz, *Rediscovering the Triune God: The Trinity in Contemporary Theology* (Minneapolis: Fortress Press, 2004), 117–62, for a discussion of the relational ontology of the Godhead. See also Thomas Smail, *Like Father, Like Son: The Trinity Imaged in our Humanity* (Grand Rapids: Eerdmans, 2006), for a corresponding discussion on the relational ontology of humanity. See also Myk Habets, "Getting Beyond the *Filioque* with Third Article Theology," in *Ecumenical Perspectives on the Filioque for the 21st Century*, ed. Myk Habets (London: Bloomsbury / T. & T. Clark, 2014), 211–30. The phrase "relational ontology" will be further discussed in chapter 7.

Just as the Godhead experienced what it was like to create by creating, and the eternal Son experienced what it was like to become human in the incarnation, so the Holy Spirit in his (initial and continuing) anointing and his (final and eternal) resurrection of the incarnate Son experienced or "learned" through his actions what it meant to transform and redeem humanity. In particular, the Spirit experienced or "learned" what it meant/cost for humanity and divinity to be permanently and unalterably united together in the person of the Son. It is this experienced Spirit, the Spirit of Jesus the incarnate Son, who is sent to the church, drawing and wooing us, uniting our humanity to that of the incarnate Son. And as he makes us one with Christ we share in the incarnate Son's permanent and unique relationship with his Father, a relationship that is itself Spirit-enabled. The church then, should be understood precisely as the pneumatologically enabled relational union between believers' humanity and that of the incarnate Son.

The continuity of this parallel, then, is that just as the Spirit conceived and sustained Christ during the incarnation, so he conceived and sustains the church. The discontinuity is that while the Spirit is sent *to* Christ during the incarnation, the Spirit who has experienced uniting humanity and divinity is sent *through* Christ *to* the church to unite our humanity with his. And this leads directly to the asymmetry. The church exists only because the Spirit of God is fully sent to indwell humanity *through the incarnate Son.* A common biblical image profoundly illustrates this point. The epistles often describe Christ as the church's foundation (1 Cor. 3:11) or cornerstone (Eph. 2:20), or in the most detailed outworking its living capstone (1 Pet. 2:4, 6–8). But in each case, the metaphor is Christological *and* pneumatological. The church's foundation, cornerstone, or living cornerstone (which is Christ) is for the building of a human temple where God's Spirit dwells (1 Cor. 3:16; Eph. 2:22; 1 Pet. 2:5).[18]

The conclusions of John and Luke's Gospels both emphasize the church's pneumatological conception through the incarnate Son.[19] In John's Gospel, Jesus' final commissioning words to the community of his followers are about being sent into the world filled with the Holy Spirit that *he* gives to them (John 20:21-23). Luke similarly concludes with Jesus' assurance that *he* will send the promised Holy Spirit (Luke 24:45-49).[20] In fact, viewed together, Luke-Acts provides a compelling description of this "historical" link between Christ and the church. New Testament scholar Graham Twelftree notes clear and significant parallels between the life of Jesus and the early church, in preaching (both proclaim the good news of the kingdom of God), healing and exorcising (both perform extraordinary signs and wonders), prayer (a priority for both) and in character qualities (both are described as full of power, grace, and joy), and both elicit responses of fear through their ministry.[21] But primarily, Twelftree notes the parallels between the Spirit's involvement in Jesus' conception and the inauguration of his ministry, and the similar involvement of the Spirit in the church's early life and ministry. "Just as Jesus' ministry was inaugurated and empowered by the Spirit so the followers of Jesus were and, by implication, should continue to be empowered by the same Spirit."[22]

18. See for example Gordon Fee, *God's Empowering Presence: The Holy Spirit in the Letters of Paul* (Peabody, MA: Hendrickson, 1994), 873–74.
19. The Gospel of Matthew finishes with a similar promise to that in Luke and John, but in this gospel Jesus claims that he himself will be with his disciples (Matt. 28:19-20). Reading the text theologically, we would interpret this as a reference to the Spirit, but it is not explicit in the text. Mark, in contrast to the other three gospels, finishes quite rapidly without any parting words to the community (excluding the additional section not contained in the earliest manuscripts).
20. The parallel passage in Acts specifically identifies this gift from Jesus as the Holy Spirit.
21. For more information see Graham H. Twelftree, *People of the Spirit: Exploring Luke's View of the Church* (Grand Rapids: Baker Academic, 2009), 32–34. See also K. N. Giles, "The Church in the Gospel of Luke," *Scottish Journal of Theology* 34 (1981): 121–46.
22. See Twelftree, *People of the Spirit*, 31–32.

The Spirit, however, should not be seen as simply the *primary* parallel between the early life of Jesus and the early life of the church. The Spirit is the source and root cause of them all. Texts beyond Luke-Acts significantly strengthen these parallels, portraying the Spirit as their root cause. For just as the Spirit anointed Jesus to preach (Luke 4:18), so he anoints the early church to do so (Acts 2:14). As the Spirit empowered Jesus to heal (Luke 4:18), so he empowers the early church (1 Cor. 12:9). As the Spirit enabled Jesus' prayers to connect him with the Father (Luke 10:21-22), so the Spirit connects our prayers with the Father—even those we cannot express (Rom. 8:26-27). As the Spirit reveals Jesus' character and nature (John 16:32-35), so the Spirit enables the fruit of Jesus' character to be seen in the church (Gal. 5:22-25). The Spirit is consequently not just one parallel among many, or one characteristic connecting the church historically with the incarnation, but in connecting the church with Christ he is the one who enables the church to be the church.[23] As Twelftree rightly concludes, "Luke establishes the coming of the eschatological Spirit as the defining event and experience of the church. Christians are people of the Spirit. Thus, if Luke was asked what determined and characterized Christianity or the church, he would probably say that those who are part of it are people of the Spirit."[24] From a biblical perspective, the asymmetrical connection

23. Twelftree makes the argument in his analysis of Luke-Acts that the church is Christocentric and not pneumacentric. Ibid., 205–7. (All references in this footnote refer to Twelftree's book.) The primary basis for his claim is that Jesus instituted the church in the calling of the disciples *before* the coming of the Spirit. Such an understanding, however, unnecessarily diminishes the role of the Spirit in the life of Jesus, and assumes an unnecessary mutually exclusive distinction between characterizing Christ and the Spirit as the defining center of the church. Further, and ironically, making such a distinction runs directly against the gamut of evidence in Luke-Acts presented in the remainder of Twelftree's book. If, as Twelftree notes, this Jesus who was conceived by the Holy Spirit (p. 31), who had a ministry that was inaugurated and empowered by the Holy Spirit (p. 31), who founded a church that has the Spirit as its defining characteristic (p. 208), at a time that Luke looks back on and calls the church's beginning (p. 28), then surely it is safe to suggest that the church is centered on not just Christ but the Spirit as well.

24. Ibid., 208.

between Christ and the church is because the historical person Jesus Christ, fully and completely anointed with the Holy Spirit as a human, founded the church by breathing the Spirit onto it, thereby giving it life.

5.2 The Spirit Sustains the Communion (of Christ and the Church)

The Bible, however, doesn't focus merely on Christ's foundational role in the church. Christ is very much active in and connected to the church throughout its history. So a direct and significant corollary to the Spirit's conceiving Christ and the church is that it is not a once-off event but a continuous action. The Spirit sustained Christ in the hypostatic union through his communion with the Father, and the Spirit similarly sustains the church in its life-giving connection with Christ and his filial relationship with the Father.

Perhaps the most convincing evidence for the "organic" identity between Christ and the church is the repeated New Testament use of phrases referring to the church being "in Christ" or Christ being "in us." Although the phrases are used in different ways, most commonly they refer to the church's present status. For example, Paul's repeated description of his fellow believers in Romans 16 as "in Christ" suggests he uses the term not dissimilarly to contemporary use of the word "Christian." Being "in Christ" simply means that by grace, and in various particular senses depending on the context, what is true of Christ is true of us.[25] A primary implication is that just as Christ is the Son of God, we too are sons (and daughters) of God. But being *related* to the Father like Christ does not mean we are *relating* to the Father like Christ. Having the status of being sons and daughters does not mean that we are actually experiencing a filial relationship with our

25. See for example C. F. D. Moule, *The Origin of Christianity* (Cambridge: Cambridge University Press, 1977), 47–69.

heavenly Father. How does our "sonship" become more than a status, but a reality of fellowship—an active relationship? Paul explains by noting that "because we are sons [i.e., our status], God sends the Spirit of his Son into our hearts, the Spirit who calls out 'Abba Father' [i.e., our relationship]" (Gal. 4:6). So in grace, sonship is conferred on us as an active experience through the Spirit. We call the Father "Father" because the Spirit testifies to us that we are actually children of God (Rom. 8:16).

Again, there are clear continuities here, particularly when Jesus' life is viewed through the insights of a Spirit Christology. Just as the Spirit sustained Jesus' filial communion with the Father during the incarnation and now in glory, so he sustains the church's filial communion with the Father. Jesus in his incarnation always had the status of Sonship, but he chose not to act independently of his human nature, and as such did not use the "power" of his divinity to enable him to do more than a human being can intrinsically achieve. Rather, Jesus remained in active fellowship with the Father through the Spirit. Jesus' status was that of being God's Son, and during the incarnation this Sonship was appropriated in intimate fellowship with the Father through the Spirit. Similarly, we have the status of being sons and daughters, and we appropriate that status in the reality of intimate relationship with the Father through the Spirit in union with Christ.

The associated asymmetry is that the church's relationship with the Father is only "in Christ." It is only because the church is in Christ that we relate to the Father as his sons and daughters. Indeed it is precisely Christ's filial relationship with his Father in which the church participates. Thomas Torrance explains this pivotal asymmetry through a cautious analogy with the *anhypostasia/ enhypostasia* of Christ:

> *Anhypostasia* would then mean that the Church as Body of Christ has no *per se* existence, no independent *hypostasis*, apart from atonement and communion through the Holy Spirit. *Enhypostasia*, however, would mean that the Church is given in Christ real *hypostasis* through incorporation, and therefore concrete function in union with him. That is why to speak of the Church as the Body of Christ is no mere figure of speech but describes an ontological reality, enhypostatic in Christ and wholly dependent on Him.[26]

The implication is that the church's ontology is not just *intrinsically tripartite* but also *intrinsically relational*. The church is constituted by its participation in the Son's filial relationship with the Father. Just as the *ousia* of God is intrinsically relational, so the church's identity is constituted relationally. In Christ we experience the fatherhood of God through the mediation of the Spirit. Using the Christological vantage point leads to viewing the church as a single entity, which communes as this single identity—a single subject—with the Father. The Christological perspective enables us to view the church as a whole in its unity with God (i.e., the vertical relationship).[27] What is being emphasized from this perspective is the mark of the church as "one." The church is one primarily because there is one Christ (Eph. 4:4-6), and together by the one Spirit we as one church participate in Christ's one relationship of Sonship with his one Father.

The discontinuity regards our entry point. Christ's filial relationship with the Father is one of nature; the church's is one of grace. He is Son by virtue of being begotten. We are sons and daughters by virtue of being adopted. Christ began his human life

26. Thomas F. Torrance, "Atonement and the Oneness of the Church," *Scottish Journal of Theology* 7, no. 3 (1954): 254.

27. This is not to say that the horizontal perspective is absent or diminished in a comprehensive and coherent Third Article Ecclesiology, but simply that this particular aspect is not clearly visible from the present vantage point. The view through the lens of the Spirit from the starting point of Christology does not illuminate well the *horizontal relationships* that exist *between* church members. The Trinity provides a better vantage point, as discussed in part three of this research.

in relation with the Father, and we must undergo a qualitative transformation—a change not just of degree but of kind—in order to participate in his filial relationship. The church is thus formed or created through the transformation of individuals into the body of Christ, whereby we as many persons and yet one people are united with Christ by the Spirit, and thus participate in Christ's filial relationship with his Father. The transformational change that we undergo is thus "qualitative" and "individual."[28] In the ontologically defining new relationship through the Spirit that connects us with Christ and in him to the Father, we (unlike Christ) are fundamentally altered. In biblical language, we are born again (John 3:1-19); we become new creations (2 Cor. 5:17). The church is thus both *Christ-centered in orientation* and *unique in context*, for our ontological transformation is defined by a new relationship with Christ—becoming a member of his body—and cannot take place otherwise.

Perhaps the most balanced description of this transformation is in the work of Scottish theologian Thomas Torrance's notion of onto-relationships.[29] He maintains that human existence, even at the created, biological level is relational: "[I]t is apparent that man must be regarded as an essentially relational being, who is what he is as man through subsisting in the being-constituting relation of the Creator with him."[30] But people have "fallen" from this created, relational state so that "they are no longer the beings they ought to be either in relation to God or in relation to one another."[31] Nevertheless, a

28. This is in contrast to the "quantitative" and "communal" conformation to Christ's image that the church undergoes, as discussed in the next subsection.

29. In the explanation that follows we use Thomas F. Torrance, "The Goodness and Dignity of Man in the Christian Tradition," *Modern Theology* 4, no. 4 (1988): 309–22. There are, however, many sources where Torrance addresses these themes. For an overview, see Myk Habets, *Theosis in the Theology of Thomas Torrance* (Farnham, UK: Ashgate, 2009), 39–42.

30. Torrance, "The Goodness and Dignity of Man," 311.

31. Ibid., 312.

remnant of our original state remains, in that we are aware that we ought to be other than we are, even though we can do nothing to change our ontological, fallen state.[32] God's determination that people should be with him, however, triumphs over our fallen nature. Torrance points to Jesus as the true *imago Dei*, and thus identifies him as the only genuine human being. "Moreover, in . . . Jesus it became finally established that . . . for man to live in union with God is to become fully and perfectly human."[33] Further, because Jesus unites divine and human nature within his one person, "the humanity of every man . . . is ontologically bound up with the humanity of Jesus, and determined by it."[34] The consequence according to Torrance is that we "are but humanised men and women, for we are not human in virtue of some essence of humanity that we have in ourselves, but only in virtue of what we receive from his Humanity."[35] Strictly, God is the only true person, as an inherently relational being. We, in contrast, are "personed persons"; we are persons "only through what we receive from Jesus Christ and become in union with him and indeed in communion with the fullness of personal Being in the Holy Trinity. For us really to be personal, therefore, is to be in Christ."[36]

This new ontological relationship ("onto-relationship") of persons in communion with Christ occurs by the Spirit. Indeed it is not too exaggerated to say that for Torrance Jesus is the means, with the Holy Spirit as the end of our salvation.[37] What has happened through

32. Note the contrast here between Torrance's understanding and that of Zizioulas discussed in the previous chapter, who argues that there is no trace of intrinsic relationality in fallen humanity. For example, Gunton writes in a rebuttal of the latter position that "if Christ is the mediator of creation . . . is not the person's eschatological realisation anticipated already in creation, albeit less truly under the conditions of sin and death than in the community of salvation?" Colin Gunton, "Persons and Particularity," in *The Theology of John Zizioulas*, ed. Douglas H. Knight (Aldershot, UK: Ashgate, 2007), 105.
33. Torrance, "The Goodness and Dignity of Man," 315.
34. Ibid., 317.
35. Ibid., 318.
36. Ibid. See the further discussion of being personed persons and the role of the Spirit in chapter 9.

Christ's incarnation and atoning sacrifice is that "the profound ontological tension between our human being and the Holy Spirit has been healed so that the Holy Spirit is now freely given to us in all the fullness of his life-giving and sanctifying presence."[38] A person in Christ "is affirmed with a spiritual wholeness and a new ontological interrelation with others that transcends his original creation, for now he exists not just alongside of the Creator, but in such a way that his human being is anchored in the very Being of God."[39]

Summarizing, then, in terms of continuity, the parallel of communion reveals that the church is ontologically constituted in *relationship* with the Father through the Spirit. In terms of asymmetry, it illustrates that the church is ontologically constituted *in Christ* through the Spirit, and only by virtue of this position *in Christ* do we share his filial relationship. In terms of discontinuity, it points us to the ontological transformation undergone as biological individuals enter Christ's body the church. The church is thus *relational in identity, Christ-centered in orientation, and unique in context*: we are identified precisely as the one community of those who through the Spirit share in Christ's filial relationship with his Father.

5.3 The Spirit Conforms (Christ and the Church)

Humans are not static. Our minds develop; our wills sharpen; our emotions deepen. Development is of the very essence of humanity; it is our nature to change and grow. Jesus, as fully human, changed, developed, and grew throughout his life (Luke 2:52). And as this

37. On this point there are close parallels between Torrance's understanding and Eastern Orthodoxy. For example, Habets notes that "Torrance's pneumatology is in general agreement with this [i.e., an Eastern Orthodox understanding]." Habets, *Theosis in the Theology of Thomas Torrance*, 149. Habets then quotes Lossky, saying "For the true end of the Christian life is the acquiring of the Holy Spirit." Vladimir Lossky, *The Mystical Theology of the Eastern Church* (London: James Clarke, 1957), 186.
38. Torrance, "The Goodness and Dignity of Man," 321.
39. Ibid.

happened, Christ was increasingly conformed into the image of God by the Spirit. As such, the Spirit not only conceived the eternal Son as human in the hypostatic union, but enabled his human nature to develop in such a way that it increasingly revealed who he was. As Catholic scholar Heribert Mühlen correctly recognized, the Spirit "sanctified" or conformed the human nature of Jesus so that it could be more and more fully united with and revealing of the divine Logos.[40] The parallel here is that just as Christ was conformed into the image of God by the Spirit, so the church is conformed into the image of Christ by the Spirit. By the Holy Spirit the church is being "sanctified" so that it can be more fully united with Christ, and so more fully reveal and reflect him.

The implication is that the church's identity should be recognized as having an intrinsically dynamic disposition toward Christlikeness—a *Christotelic momentum*.[41] The church is not static, something that just "is." Rather, the church grows and develops, just as it is in the nature of humanity (and Jesus' humanity in particular) to grow and develop.[42] The analogy reveals a nuanced understanding of the church as Christ's body. In contrast to both Barth's understanding (where the church is fully and always the body of Christ, but only a part of it) and Zizioulas's understanding (where the church is "rhythmically" the body of Christ), Third Article Theology implies the biblical references to Christ's body can be interpreted not merely as a state of being but also of becoming. The church both "is" the body of Christ and is "becoming" the body of Christ. It is "becoming" the body of Christ in that as the church grows and develops through

40. See Gary D. Badcock, *Light of Truth and Fire of Love: A Theology of the Holy Spirit* (Grand Rapids: Eerdmans, 1997), 145–53.

41. Note that the Third Article Theology methodological criteria briefly discussed sanctification and Christification in section 1.3(ix).

42. This is not to imply that nature is independent of person, in some way. Rather, that as a nature (either human or ecclesial) matures, so the personal reality is increasingly clearly displayed.

time, it is increasingly transformed by the Spirit to achieve greater communion with Christ, fully realizing this potential for ontological union and identification at the eschaton. The church is "becoming" the body of Christ in the sense that it is being prepared for that day. And it already "is" the body of Christ in that Christ has already united himself to the church, with the promise of a fuller and greater communion to come. Just as the "not guilty" verdict of the final judgment is enacted "at the present time" (Rom. 3:26), the future union is (in a nuanced sense) enacted at this moment, through the *arrabōn* (deposit) of the Spirit.[43] Through the Spirit, the church both *is* the body of Christ, and *becoming* what she already is.

One clear benefit of the continuities arising from this parallel of communion, then, is that it paints a picture of ecclesial journey and development that naturally incorporates many similar biblical images, particularly the prominent image of the church as Christ's bride.[44] Although this metaphor is perhaps less commonly used in contemporary theology,[45] its biblical significance is in no way inferior. The body metaphor is predominantly Pauline, while the

43. See note 47 below.

44. There is some biblical motivation for interpreting this "bride of Christ" image as being more than merely a metaphor. Brewer, for example, notes the extreme lengths that Paul goes to in order to explain why the marriage covenant between Christ and the church applies not just to Gentiles but to Jews who had an existing marriage covenant (Rom. 7:1-4). He writes, "Paul must have been tempted to say that the analogy of a marriage covenant breaks down at this point. However, like the prophets, he regarded it as more than an analogy. This marriage of God to Israel was a solemn binding covenant which could not simply be disregarded." David Instone Brewer, "Three Weddings and a Divorce: God's Covenant with Israel, Judah and the Church," *Tyndale Bulletin* 47, no. 1 (1996): 22. Most commentators are content with acknowledging a literal covenant between God and Israel (or Jesus and the church), which parallels in very many respects an Ancient Near East marriage covenant, but is not to be literally identified as one.

45. Although it may be becoming less neglected. See for example, Hans Urs von Balthasar, *Explorations in Theology: Spouse of the Word*, trans. A. V. Littledale, vol. 2 (San Francisco: Ignatius, 1991). Migliore notes some of the challenges in Barth's ecclesiology arise from Christ's body being his controlling metaphor. See "Vinculum Pacis: Barth's Theology of the Holy Spirit," 20. Unpublished English Manuscript. Published in German as Daniel L. Migliore, "Vinculum Pacis—Karl Barth's Theologie des Heiligen Geistes," *Evangelische Theologie* 6 (2000): 131–52.

bridal metaphor is both contiguous with the Old Testament picture of Israel's betrothal (and unfaithfulness) to God,[46] and gets broadly repeated across the entirety of the New Testament, appearing in the Gospels (e.g., Matt. 9:14-17; 25:1-13; Mark 2:19; Luke 5:33-35), the epistles (e.g., Rom. 7:2-4; 2 Cor. 11:2; Eph. 5:25) and coming to fruition with the wedding supper of the lamb (Rev. 19:9-27). While the body image implies a unity of subject, metaphorically melding Christ and the church into a single organism, the bride image emphasizes the intimacy of relationship while the pair remain distinct identities. The metaphor's primary thrust is on the church's journey of preparation. Just as a future bride in the Ancient Near East was set apart for one husband, and prepared for her wedding by keeping pure and making herself ready, so the church is set apart for Christ, and prepares by keeping pure and making herself ready. The implication is clear: the church is Christ's and his alone; we must remain faithful, preparing ourselves for the day when he returns and unites us with him fully, completely, and forever.

But the Spirit is just as pivotal for the bridal image as for the body image. If the church is beholden to Christ, how has this "engagement" been confirmed? By the Spirit. "When you believed, you were marked in him with a seal, the promised Holy Spirit, who is a deposit guaranteeing our inheritance until the redemption of those who are God's possession—to the praise of his glory" (Eph. 1:14-15). (See also 2 Cor. 1:22; 5:5.)[47] And how does the church go about

46. For a description of the continuity between the OT and NT images, see Brewer, "Three Weddings and a Divorce," 1–25.

47. None of the three passages noted above are "bridal images," and it is difficult to make the case directly from the New Testament that the word translated "deposit" here (*arrabōn*) refers (even obliquely) to an engagement ring, although some commentators do use it this way. See for example Warren W. Wiersbe, *Be Rich: An Expository Study of the Epistle to the Ephesians* (Wheaton, IL: Victor, 1977), 24. Whatever the terminological usage of *arrabōn*, however, the truth being alluded to in such an identification (i.e., that the Holy Spirit is the present confirmation of the future promise of full union with Christ) is undoubtedly valid. See David J. Williams, *Paul's Metaphors: Their Context and Character* (Peabody, MA: Hendrickson, 1999), 53.

keeping pure and making herself ready? By the Spirit. It is the work of Christ that initially made the church pure and hence eligible for marriage. The old covenant united people to Yahweh by the law, but the church could not and Israel did not remain faithful to God through this means. But Jesus' death has released us from the law (Rom. 7:1-4), so that we are no longer prisoners of sin. But having thus been purified and hence become eligible for marriage, we are to remain pure and make ourselves ready. A bride prepares by putting on garments of fine linen; the church prepares by clothing herself with "righteous acts" (Rev. 19:8) or "by bearing fruit for God" (Rom. 7:4). To do this is to serve "in the new way of the Spirit and not in the old way of the written code" (Rom. 7:5), to demonstrate lives filled with the "fruit of the Spirit" (Gal. 5:25). It is by the work of Christ, then, that the church is eligible for marriage; but it is by the Spirit that we are marked as his future bride. Similarly, it is by the Spirit that believers remain pure and prepare ourselves for the coming wedding. Just as it is by the Spirit that the church becomes Christ's body, so it is by the Spirit that the church grows into being not just eligible but worthy to be Christ's bride.

The parallel between the Spirit's role in conforming Christ's humanity (to the Son) and conforming the church (to Christ) paints an illuminating picture of the church "growing up," becoming more aware over time of who she is, and through this increasing knowledge and obedience being molded into an increasingly perfect image of Christ. This coincides closely with the picture of the church as Christ's bride being prepared by his Spirit for the eschatological wedding day when union and communion are fully and finally realized. Both biblical images are often mentioned simultaneously (e.g., Eph. 5:25-33; 1 Cor. 6:12-17) and thus almost certainly refer (at least metaphorically) to a common truth. Whether the church is understood primarily as the body or the bride of Christ, it has a *Christotelic momentum*, becoming increasingly Christ-like in appearance.

There are two key discontinuities within this parallel, however. The first relates to our entry into the conformation process, and the second concerns the extent to which the church "lives up" to it. The former is simply a clearer statement of the discontinuity discussed in section 5.2. Christ in his humanity was increasingly *conformed* to who he already was; we in entering the church are first changed into something fundamentally new. We are *transformed* before being *conformed*. The change that occurred in Christ is "quantitative," in the sense that he started life in relationship with the Father. Christ was intimately connected by the Spirit from his conception, but was nevertheless limited by his inherent createdness and humanity. As his human characteristics grew and developed, and as the Spirit increasingly conformed his human will to the divine will, so he increasingly "became who he was." C. S. Lewis wrote of one of his fictional characters as having "at every age the beauty proper to that age."[48] We might similarly speak of Christ as "having at every age the perfection proper to that age." So Christ was perfect, and a perfect reflection of God was ever and always in Christ, but as a human this perfection included change, growth, and development, so that, in his humanity and within both its age-defined and creaturely limitations, Christ was increasingly *con-formed* into the image of the Son by the Spirit. The church, in contrast, is both *trans-formed* and *con-formed* into Christ's image. More accurately, the church is formed or created through the trans-formation of individuals into the body of Christ, whereby we as many persons and yet one people are united with

48. C. S. Lewis, "Till We Have Faces," in *Selected Readings* (London: HarperCollins, 2002), 462. The quote's extension is equally applicable and profound: "she was 'according to nature'; what every woman, or even every thing, ought to have been and meant to be, but had missed . . ." (ibid.).

Christ by the Spirit, and thus participate in Christ's filial relationship with his Father. The change that we undergo is thus "qualitative" and "individual" before it is "quantitative" and "communal."

But even following this transformation, the church's "quantitative" and "communal" conformation to the image of Christ must be distinguished from Christ's. For while Jesus' conformation is perfect within his creaturely and age-based limitations, the church's conformation is certainly not so. MacFarland calls this a "fundamental disanalogy between the incarnation and the life of the church," commenting that "while all the acts of the human being Jesus are *eo ipso* acts of God, there is no parallel relation between the acts of the church and the acts of Jesus."[49] The action of the church is (at times) sinful, because its being is (in part) sinful. It is precisely because of this second discontinuity that Barth made such a strong distinction between the true and false, or the sanctified and the sinful church. But adopting a "thick" pneumatological doctrine that recognizes the Spirit's unique "bridging" role in the redemption of humanity enables such sharp distinctions to be avoided.

Anglican theologian Gary Badcock, for example, examines the time when the Father turned his face away from Jesus on the cross—a point at which many scholars agree that Jesus was truly "full of sin"—and notes that even then Father and Son were united through the Spirit.[50] From this Spirit Christological basis, he comments, "It is not something foreign to God to be at one with himself in 'otherness.' The way of the triune God is not only such that God can be both 'here' and 'there' without contradiction, but that God can condescend to exist in the contradiction of sin and death, and yet remain one with

49. Ian A. McFarland, "The Body of Christ: Rethinking a Classic Ecclesiological Model," *International Journal of Systematic Theology* 7, no. 3 (2005): 245.

50. This paragraph summarizes one particular "exploration in theology" contained in Badcock, *The House Where God Lives*, 194–209.

himself."[51] Badcock then looks from this Spirit Christological vantage point at the church, noting that just as at the cross the Spirit united two things that were alien to each other (the Father in his holiness and the incarnate Son in our sinfulness), so he does in the community of the church. The Spirit "reaches beyond the small grasp of our own community and embraces not only those who seem alien to us, but supremely what seems strictly alien to God."[52] Badcock goes on to develop a theology of otherness, the way the church through the Spirit can and should embrace people who don't belong in a church. He concludes with these words, "The Spirit's 'passing over' into what seems incompatible with it is . . . a fundamental dimension of the Spirit's work, and a fundamental possibility with which the discipline of ecclesiology has scarcely begun to grapple."[53]

The consequence of a "thick" doctrine of the Spirit is that there can be no sharp distinctions made between the "holy" and "sinful" sections of the church. Indeed no sharp intra-ecclesial divisions—true/false, sanctified/sinful, visible/invisible—can be justified, meaning the church must be viewed as *indivisible in constitution*. For just as the Spirit maintained the union between Christ and the Father on the cross—a Christ who (at that point at least) was credited with our sinful nature and actions—so the Spirit unites both the sinful and the sanctified parts of the church with Christ, and consequently with each other. Moreover, just as by the power of the Spirit Jesus triumphed over the sin he bore for us, moving from death to life and glory, so by the power of the Spirit the church in its entirety will move from death to life and glory. For it is in the nature of the Spirit that where he exists he conforms, sanctifies, and perfects, so that just

51. Ibid., 203.
52. Ibid., 204.
53. Ibid., 208.

as he triumphed over the sin that caused Jesus' suffering and death, so he will conform and perfect the entirety of the church.

So the continuity inherent in such a parallel is that just as the Spirit conforms the humanity of Christ to the image of God, so the Spirit conforms the church to the image of Christ. The associated discontinuities are first, that individuals must be transformed before the church can be conformed, and second, that the church's conformation to the image of Christ is not gradual, steady, and perfect. The related asymmetry is that it is Christ to whom the church is being conformed. This is the repeated argument of Paul (Phil. 2:5; 2 Cor. 4; Ephesians 1–2; and Colossians 1) who urges that the life and death of Christ, his humiliation and exaltation, be increasingly translated into the life of the church. Perhaps even more explicitly, the Epistle to the Hebrews urges that the church look to "Jesus, the pioneer and perfecter of our faith. For the joy set before him he endured the cross, scorning its shame, and sat down at the right hand of the throne of God" (Heb. 12:2-3), and then goes on to urge that the church's life should analogically imitate his.

Thomas Torrance notes the twin poles of this asymmetry (Christ as goal) and the first asymmetry mentioned (Christ as founder).[54] He terms these the "eschatological" and the "ontological" views of the church. Insightfully, he recognizes that focusing on the latter leads to a view of the church as merely *enhypostatic*, and thus as an extension of the incarnation. Similarly focusing on the former leads to a view of the church as merely *anhypostatic*, with the result that the church has no present existence as the body of Christ but is rather defined solely by its eschatological future. But Torrance concludes that as both are centered on Christ, they

54. Torrance, "Atonement and the Oneness of the Church," 255–56.

> . . . belong together inseparably. . . . If we think of the Church consistently in terms of Christ who died and rose again and apply that analogically to the Church so that we understand it not only as constituted by the substitutionary work of Christ but as so incorporated into Him that it bears about in its body the dying and rising of the Lord Jesus, then we cannot have an "eschatological" view of the Church that is not also "ontological," nor an "ontological" view of the Church which is not also "eschatological."[55]

If we add to this the recognition that both the present existence of the church in Christ and the future attainment of the church being fully like Christ are pneumatologically enabled, then we end with a profound and balanced picture of the church in the Spirit as being and becoming Christ's body. In summary, the ecclesial parallel with the Spirit conforming Christ implies the church is not only *Christ-centered in orientation*, but also has a *Christotelic momentum.* Further, the "bridging" of the Spirit, and particularly a "thick" understanding, enables a characterization of the church as being continually transformed in its entirety, and hence *indivisible in constitution.*

5.4 The Spirit Directs and Empowers (Christ and the Church)

With the last two pneumatological parallels between Christ and the church, the focus moves from ontology to activity, from what the church is (and is becoming) to how it becomes so. Examining the church's functionality is a vast undertaking, even if viewed only from the single vantage point of Christology through the lens of the Spirit. Such a detailed examination goes well beyond the constraints of this chapter.[56] The intent of the following two sections is thus merely to recognize the overarching themes that arise in a pneumato-ecclesiology from these two parallels. In particular, the key question

55. Ibid., 256.
56. Section 11.2 discusses how the vantage points of eschatology and the world can be used to illuminate these issues more completely.

being addressed is *how* the church journeys toward its future and complete union and communion; how is the church conformed into the image of Christ? Insight into this question is gained by investigating the parallel question of *how* Christ grew and developed as a human.

The fourth parallel, then, is that just as the Spirit directed and empowered Christ, so the Spirit directs and empowers the church. The continuity here can be seen in the reality that the synoptic accounts of Christ being directed (and perhaps even compelled? e.g., Mark 1:12) by the Spirit are echoed in the accounts of the early Christians being similarly directed (and perhaps similarly compelled? e.g., Acts 8:39).[57] And not just directed, but empowered. After an exhaustive review of the gospel accounts, Hawthorne concludes that all the words and actions of Jesus, including his prayers and worship, were "spoke[n] and performed not by virtue of his own power, the power of his own divine personality, but by virtue of the power of the Holy Spirit at work within him and through him."[58] The church, similarly, acts only through the power of the Holy Spirit working within and through us (e.g., Rom. 8:5–17).

Perhaps the key recognition here is that the ontology and functionality of either Christ or the church simply cannot be distinguished to any great extent. Christ is what he does, and he does what he is. Viewed through the lens of the Spirit, it becomes clear that Christ's ontology, and particularly his human growth and development, is determined by his actions, and his actions are in turn determined by his ontology. So Christ's actions of obedience and suffering enable him to "become who he is." Christ learns obedience

57. Integrating this understanding with the Johannine statements about Christ doing and saying only what the Father does and says (John 5:19, 36, etc.) clearly imply that these Spirit-given directions are originally sourced from the Father.

58. Gerald F. Hawthorne, *The Presence and the Power: The Significance of the Holy Spirit in the Life and Ministry of Jesus* (Dallas: Word, 1991), 146.

in suffering, and he suffers in obedience. And as a human, his (ontologically defining) relationship with the Father is enabled through this growth and learning (see particularly Heb. 5:5–8). So too the church. The church's (ontologically defining) relationship through the Spirit with Christ and in him with the Father is determined by our obedience and suffering. It is as we keep Christ's commands that we remain in his love, just as Christ remained in the Father and the Father in him through his obedience (John 15:10). The Spirit conforms the church into the image of Christ, therefore, as she suffers and obeys, or better, as she suffers in obedience.[59]

The church is thus *cruciform in shape*, as Torrance explains:

> It is through baptismal incorporation, through self-denial and bearing the Cross, through Holy Communion that the Form of the Son of Man becomes the form of the Church His Body. . . . As the body of Christ, the Church is cruciform, but that has to be understood as active analogy, of daily crucifixion and resurrection. Wherever in obedience to the blood of Christ the Church is found engaged in the ministry of reconciliation, pouring out its life like the Son of Man that the Word of reconciliation might be delivered to all men for whom He died, wherever the Church shows forth His death until He comes and presents its body a living sacrifice, there the image of Christ is to be seen and His Body is to be discerned in the Church.[60]

Significantly, it could be added here that there the church is increasingly conformed to the image of Christ, as the Spirit increasingly unites the church to her founder and perfecter.

The discontinuity is that whereas Christ always obeyed the Spirit's direction, and submitted himself entirely to the Spirit's empowering, the church does not. Jesus could have sinned but didn't;[61] the church

59. See particularly John 15:1–25.

60. Torrance, "Atonement and the Oneness of the Church," 259.

61. Note that an exclusively *Logos* Christology, because of its inbuilt Docetic leaning, brings into question whether Jesus could actually have sinned. This chapter, however, is using a Spirit Christological perspective that fully acknowledges the reality of Christ's humanity.

can sin and does. The discontinuity discussed previously is applicable here. A "thick" understanding of the Spirit enables the church to still be the church even in those times when she is decidedly less than she should be. For not just when we are sinners, but even when we sin, even then the Spirit binds us to Christ. The asymmetry here is also most significant: the church is not a suffering servant in the way that Christ was. Christ's suffering obedience was uniquely effective in the ministry of reconciliation. The church does not repeat his ministry, nor does it contribute to it, but rather it *participates* in Christ's own ministry, and does so by serving *him* and suffering for *him*. Torrance again, "The Church's ministry as prophetic, priestly and kingly is correlative to Christ's whole ministry but entirely subordinate to it and fulfilled *alterius rationis*, in a way appropriate to the Church as the Body of which Christ is the Head, as the servant of which He is the Lord, as the Herald of which He is King."[62] The task of the church then is to be as transparent as possible, so that by looking at (or better, through) it people may see Christ, and so that by joining it people will be conjoined to Christ. It is precisely through the church being *cruciform in shape*, that she will increasingly fulfill her missional purpose.

5.5 The Spirit Is Displayed and Mediated (by Christ and the Church)

The continuity within the fifth and final parallel is that just as Christ displayed the existence of the kingdom of God as a present reality within the world, so too does the church. But this continuity is again Spirit-driven. In both cases, it is the presence of the Spirit that establishes the reality of the Kingdom. Jesus makes this explicitly clear

Consequently, there is both a recognition that Jesus could have sinned, and an affirmation that he did not.

62. Torrance, "Atonement and the Oneness of the Church," 258.

when he replies to the accusation of driving out demons through Beelzebub: "[I]f I drive out demons by the Spirit of God, then the Kingdom of God has come upon you" (Matt. 12:28).

The discontinuity is that whereas the Spirit is always displayed by Christ, it is not always displayed by the church. The Spirit is not captive to the church, nor restricted to it. But the existence of this discontinuity forces us to address the issue of whether the church has any mediatorial role at all. Two key questions arise. First, what role does the church play in the *transformation* of individuals, that is: What does the church do to embody, assist, or facilitate the Spirit in enabling individuals to make the "qualitative" passage from biological individuals to ecclesial persons in Christ? Second, what role does the church play in the *conforming* of itself (and as a corollary the persons that constitute it) to the image of Christ? In other words, what does the church do in order to aid its quantitative development epistemologically and practically?

There are two excesses to be avoided, both discussed in the previous chapter, and illustrated to some degree in the ecclesiologies of Barth and Zizioulas respectively. First, the rejection of all ecclesial mediation, where the church is restricted to mere witness and only encounters or "stands alongside" the work of the Spirit, but does not participate in it. Second, the overemphasis on ecclesial mediation, where the church is the unique context and means by which the transformation of the individual and the conformation of the church occurs, essentially making the church the sole and exclusive mediator of the Spirit. It was argued that both of these extremes are rooted in an ecclesial Spirit-Eutychianism, which too greatly melds the ecclesial roles of the Son and the Spirit. Logically distinguishing between the involvement of Christ and the Spirit within the church, however, enables both excesses to be avoided, and a real but limited role for ecclesial mediation to be affirmed. First, although the church witnesses to the world the reality of the Spirit and the kingdom of God, and although (as argued above) the church provides the *unique context* within which transformation occurs, it certainly does not accomplish that transformation. The grace by which we become part of the church is solely the work of the triune God. The Bible repeatedly and clearly maintains that we have no part in saving ourselves (e.g., Eph. 2:8).

Second, the church, which is a historical institution in which the Spirit abides even when we fall and fail, contributes to its own conformation into the image of Christ through suffering and obedience. This claim uses the parallel between the incarnate and ecclesial body of Christ. The Spirit enabled Christ to grow into who he was as his human nature developed. As he surrendered himself in obedient submission, the Spirit led him down the path of suffering and into glory. Similarly, the church as a whole, unified, historic institution grows into what it is over its history, and this growth happens through obedient submission to the Spirit that leads us along the same path of suffering and into glory. There is an extra dimension to our journey, in that the church is not merely growing into the fullness of its created potential, but is also conquering and overwhelming its fleshly or sinful nature.[63] But just as the Spirit has demonstrated mastery over this added impediment by raising Jesus from the dead, so he will triumph over our sinfulness as well; indeed we participate in Jesus' Spirit-enabled triumph. Further, as we submit to the Spirit in obedience, and walk the path of suffering into glory that he lays out for us, we increasingly provide a more complete

63. T. F. Torrance, for example, would not see this as an "extra" dimension but one that Christ also struggled with and overcame in the power of the Spirit. See for example Thomas F. Torrance, *The Trinitarian Faith: The Evangelical Theology of the Ancient Catholic Church* (Edinburgh: T. & T. Clark, 1988), 188–90. While I agree with Torrance, it is not necessary for the present argument, and consequently not included nor emphasized here.

picture of the kingdom of God on earth, and consequently, a more compelling witness.

The best descriptor for this ecclesial aspect is the church's *narrative character*, a common theme in the recent work of such theologians as Balthasar,[64] Vanhoozer,[65] Horton,[66] and Hauerwas.[67] As Vanhoozer comments: "If theology is about the speech and action of the triune God and the church's response in word and deed, then doctrine is best viewed as direction for the church's fitting participation in the drama of redemption."[68] Noted below are three clear points of intersection between the pneumato-ecclesiology being developed here and a narrative or "dramatic" understanding.

First, it recognizes that the church's primary role is simply to be. Or, to use Hauerwas's often-quoted dictum: "[T]he first social task of the Church . . . is to be the Church."[69] In this the church plays an important mediatory role as the context in which conformation occurs. A key feature of dramatic theology is that it recognizes that Scripture reveals who Jesus is only when it is employed as the script by which the Christian community lives. As Mangina explains, "The

64. Hans Urs von Balthasar, *Theo-Drama: Theological Dramatic Theory*, trans. G. Harrison, 5 vols. (San Francisco: Ignatius, 1988).
65. Kevin J. Vanhoozer, *The Drama of Doctrine: A Canonical-Linguistic Approach to Christian Theology* (Louisville: Westminster John Knox, 2005).
66. Michael S. Horton, *Covenant and Eschatology: The Divine Drama* (Louisville: Westminster John Knox, 2002). Also, Michael S. Horton, *People and Place: A Covenant Ecclesiology* (Louisville: Westminster John Knox, 2008).
67. Stanley Hauerwas, *The Peaceable Kingdom* (Notre Dame: Notre Dame University Press, 1983). Also, Stanley Hauerwas, *With the Grain of the Universe* (London: SCM, 2002), 145. For a brief summary of Hauerwas's dramatic outworking of ecclesiology in comparison with Karl Barth, see also Joseph L. Mangina, "Bearing the Marks of Jesus: The Church in the Economy of Salvation in Barth and Hauerwas," *Scottish Journal of Theology* 52 (1999): 269–305. Note that Hauerwas himself has endorsed Mangina's understanding of his theology on this point. See Hauerwas, *With the Grain of the Universe*, 144–45. The presentation here does not own all of the constituent features of these authors' (often contrasting) ecclesiologies, let alone their entire theologies. For a brief overview of dramatic theology see Myk Habets, "'The Dogma Is the Drama': Dramatic Developments in Biblical Theology," *Stimulus* 16, no. 4 (2008): 2–5.
68. Vanhoozer, *The Drama of Doctrine*, 31.
69. Hauerwas, *The Peaceable Kingdom*, 100.

otherness that brings me to myself, then, is not simply God as revealed in Scripture, but God as revealed in the lives of those persons who are my companions in the way of discipleship. A stronger statement of churchly mediation at this *local* level can scarcely be imagined."[70]

Second, it recognizes the essential narrative character of the church—the church is the living narrative of the Kingdom. In contrast to both Barth and Zizioulas, the church is not to be understood as merely a series of moments at which humanity encounters Christ through the Spirit. Nor is it a collection of many stories of various individuals who encounter Christ. It is rather the common, developing narrative of a community that lives in light of the death and resurrection of Jesus, is journeying inexorably toward a final and complete union and communion with him, and is even now in constant connection to the risen Jesus by the Spirit. This is why the church is often understood by these "dramatic theologians" as a journey, a procession, or an adventure.[71] Recognizing the dramatic nature of ecclesiology reinforces the terminology of the church as the incarnation's *sequel.*

Third, there is an emphasis on the everyday actions and life of the church—its obedience and suffering—as the means by which the journey is enacted and thus that God makes himself increasingly known to us. Hauerwas, for example, comments: "It is through gestures that we learn the nature of the story that is the very content and constitution of that kingdom."[72] By "gestures," Hauerwas is referring to the full breadth of Christian life: the day-to-day practices of community, the moral practices of ethical significance, and even the place of liturgy and sacraments. On the latter, Hauerwas notes

70. Mangina, "Bearing the Marks of Jesus," 297.

71. See for example, Hauerwas, *The Peaceable Kingdom*, 87. Horton, *People and Place*, 259–307.

72. Stanley Hauerwas, *Christian Existence Today: Essays on Church, World and Living in Between* (Durham, NC: Labyrinth, 1988), 289.

that "baptism and eucharist stand as crucial gestures which are meant to shape us rightly to hear as well as enact the story. . . . We cannot be the Church without them."[73]

There are clear points of convergence, then, between a narrative or "dramatic" ecclesiology, and the pneumato-ecclesiology being developed here. In particular, the church provides the context in which the transformation of individuals occurs, and further, in analogy with the humanity of Christ, it dynamically grows and develops through its actions of obedience and suffering. Indeed it could easily be argued that a "dramatic" ecclesiology fits best *within* the overall setting of a pneumato-ecclesiology, and as a subsection of it.[74] Mangina recognizes this as he wisely cautions against a potential tendency toward "impotent protest" in Hauerwas's ecclesiology:

> Without attention to the Spirit and to the specifically mandated ways by which we encounter the gospel, [Hauerwas's] political interpretation of the Church might easily slide into a Christian politics of identity, on the one hand, and as a corollary to this an impotent protest against liberal society. In other words, a developed pneumatology might offer resources for keeping the community of Jesus' followers focused on *his* story. An authentic theology of discipleship or imitation—"bearing the marks of Jesus," as I have put it—depends on situating the Church within the larger context of the Spirit's work.[75]

Such a "developed pneumatology," or (better) a pneumato-ecclesiology that looks through the lens of the Spirit at the ontology

73. Ibid., 107. While it is not outworked further here, placing church practices within an overarching Third Article Ecclesiological framework (and particularly using a "thick" understanding of the Spirit) may go some way to allaying Healy's concerns of "misplaced concreteness" that he perceives as occurring in recent ecclesiological studies. See Nicholas M. Healy, "Practices and the New Ecclesiology: Misplaced Concreteness?" *International Journal of Systematic Theology* 5, no. 3 (2003): 287–308.

74. See for example Cheryl M. Peterson, "Who Is the Church?," *Dialog* 51, no. 1 (2012): 24–30. Also Cheryl M. Peterson, *Who Is the Church? An Ecclesiology for the Twenty-First Century* (Minneapolis: Fortress Press, 2013), 99–120.

75. Mangina, "Bearing the Marks of Jesus," 292.

and functionality of the church is precisely the aim of this research in general, and the next chapter in particular.

Chapter 5 started from the vantage point of Christology and examined the theological loci of ecclesiology through the lens of the Spirit. By doing this, several ecclesial characteristics emerged: the church's tripartite nature, indivisible constitution, unique context, Christ-centered orientation, Christotelic momentum, cruciform shape, narrative character, missional purpose, and relational identity. The next chapter gathers and systematizes these ecclesiological insights in order to articulate the constituent features of a *Christological* Third Article Ecclesiology.

A slightly revised version of this chapter has been previously published. See Greg Liston, "Towards a Pneumato-Ecclesiology: Exploring the Pneumatological Union between Christ and the Church," *Colloquium* 44, no. 1 (2012): 31–58.

6

A Christological Third Article Ecclesiology

The final chapter in this second part of the research constructs a coherent pneumato-ecclesiology as viewed from the vantage point of Christology—a *Christological* Third Article Ecclesiology. In the earlier chapters, two major premises were engaged. The first premise was that insight into the church's ontology can be gained through comparison with Christ's ontology. Through examining the Christological ecclesiologies of Barth and Zizioulas, chapter 4 argued that the ecclesial roles of the Son and Spirit must be not only existentially inseparable but also logically distinguished for the coherent development of an ecclesiology that neither confuses nor separates its inherent divinity and humanity. The second premise was that the correspondence between Christ and the church cannot be adequately examined without giving prominence to the Spirit. Chapter 5 built upon this premise by viewing ecclesiology from the vantage point of Christology through the lens of the Spirit, enabling several broad characteristics of the church's ontology to be recognized. It characterized the church as tripartite in nature, relational in identity, unique in context, Christ-centered in orientation with Christotelic momentum, indivisible in constitution, cruciform in shape, missional in purpose, and narrative in character. This chapter systematically groups and examines these characteristics under the following pivotal questions: What is the church? Who is in it (with an emphasis on baptism)? How do we recognize it? And what does it do? As each characteristic of a Christological Third Article Ecclesiology is discussed, it is distinguished from alternative ecclesial formulations that underemphasize the roles of the Son or the Spirit.

6.1 What Is the Church?

The primary ecclesial feature illuminated from the Christological vantage point is that the church is *tripartite in nature*: the church is the pneumatologically enabled union that exists between the incarnate Christ and the human community of the church as Christ's body. This ecclesial understanding corresponds in some ways to the tripartite nature of Christ, who is the pneumatologically enabled hypostatic union between the Son and his enhypostatic humanity. The best way to unpack this tripartite understanding of the church is to outline the excesses it endeavors to avoid. The first two excesses are categorized using traditional Christological terminology. So ecclesial Ebionism overemphasizes the humanity of the church. The church is understood merely as a human community. Christ instituted the church but there is little active acknowledgment of Christ's current presence within the church's human community in terms of its structures and practices. Second, there is the directly opposite error of ecclesial Docetism that minimizes the place of human activity within the church. This error can be evidenced, for example, in a hyper-Calvinism (perhaps most typically evident in the English Baptists in the late eighteenth century) that so emphasizes God's sovereignty there is virtually no role left for the church, not even witness.

These are not the only pertinent ecclesial errors arising from the above understanding, however. A pneumato-ecclesiology recognizes the Spirit's role as the means of communion between the human church and Christ.[1] There are, consequently, a further pair of errors to consider. Ecclesial Spirit-Ebionism overemphasizes the role of the Spirit, requiring a communion between Christ and the human church that is so deep and profound and extensive that Christ and the human church are *confused* and essentially coalesce. At its extreme, Christ collapses into the human church, so that (particularly post-resurrection) there is no distinction between the two at all, and the incarnate Christ only exists in the church. The church is thus an essentially divine institution with a merely human exterior. Zizioulas's ecclesiology has Spirit-Ebionitic tendencies. Ecclesial Spirit-Docetism in contrast minimizes the Spirit's role, which minimizes the communion between humanity and Christ, and leads to an excessive *separation* in the resultant ecclesiology. Often the result is a church divided into two parts—a true and a false church. The *true* church corresponds to Christ and is in relationship with him. The *false* church doesn't and isn't, while remaining connected institutionally to the true church in some manner. Some accuse Barth's ecclesiology of trending in this direction.

Directly related to its tripartite nature is the church's *indivisible constitution*. In short, the church is one—the "mark" of the church most clearly visible when viewed from the vantage point of Christology through the lens of the Spirit. As a traditionally recognized ecclesial "mark," such an observation is far from novel, but it is vital nonetheless. Moreover, a pneumato-ecclesiology provides insight into this traditional mark in that it directly contradicts the often-used visible/invisible ecclesial division. Put at

1. The term "human church" is used to distinguish this particular entity from the true church, the *totus Christus*, the union of the incarnate Christ with his church.

its simplest, there is one church because there is one Christ, and one Spirit, by which we as one church participate in Christ's one relationship of Sonship with his one Father (Eph. 4:4-6). The immediate challenge with the theological observation that the church is *indivisible in constitution* is that it lacks phenomenological support. There are two issues. First, that the "one" church is divided into many local churches and (even more so) into localized individuals. This "geographical" and "biological" aspect of church unity will be discussed in part three. Second, and more pertinently here, there exist ideological distinctions and relational divisions within the church. The church may be one theologically, but sociological observation suggests it is far from united. Both Barth and Zizioulas recognize this and provide explanations.

Zizioulas claims that each local church, during the Eucharist, is not just a reflection of but actually participates in the eschatological fulfillment.[2] He explains this not just by claiming that the church institution between Eucharists is not a church,[3] but that a church that performs the Eucharist incorrectly (for example by discriminating between races, sexes, ages, professions, or by not being in communion with local churches in other localities) is also not a church. According to Zizioulas, such a Eucharist is not a bad Eucharist, but a non-Eucharist.[4] Gatherings of believers that make such errors are consequently not just bad churches, but non-churches.[5] Within this grouping Zizioulas includes (or hints at including) all confessional churches, which exclude those who don't agree with their particular confession. Zizioulas concludes, "[W]e

2. This confuses the necessary distinction between what the church is and what it will be, which is illuminated from an eschatological vantage point. See the discussion in section 11.2.
3. See the discussion on this feature of Zizioulas's work earlier in section 4.2.
4. John Zizioulas, *Being as Communion: Studies in Personhood and the Church* (Crestwood, NY: St. Vladimir's Seminary Press, 1985), 255n11.
5. Ibid., 255–56.

must be ready to admit that as long as confessionalism prevails no real progress towards ecclesial unity can be made."[6] For Zizioulas, then, the evidential disunity between churches results from many (if not most) of them being non-churches.

Barth's explanation is not quite so drastic.[7] He resolves the "evidential" lack of unity by distinguishing between the invisible and visible church,[8] noting that visible disunity is evidence of something wrong in the invisible church. The horizontal disconnection is evidence of a vertical disconnection. In particular, he outlines two opposite errors in relation to the church's oneness, corresponding directly to Christological errors. First, there is an ecclesial Docetism, which sees unity only in the invisible church and distances itself from the problems of the visible church. Second, there is ecclesial Ebionism, which attempts to establish the unity of the church within history. Looking through the lens of the Spirit, however, it becomes clear that the division of the church into invisible and visible sections is not only unnecessary but in fact unhelpful. These two errors that Barth has distinguished arise as subcategories of a deeper error that can be made—the error of ecclesial Spirit-Docetism, which minimizes the Spirit's ecclesial role and thus forces a logical division within the human church. The ecclesial error of Spirit-Docetism underemphasizes the Spirit's role in joining humanity to Christ within the church, and consequently overemphasizes the distinctions

6. Ibid., 260.

7. See Karl Barth, *Church Dogmatics*, trans. G. W. Bromiley (Peabody, MA: Hendrickson, 2010), IV/1, 668–85. For a briefer summary see Kimlyn J. Bender, *Karl Barth's Christological Ecclesiology* (Aldershot, UK: Ashgate, 2005), 184–85.

8. The terms "invisible" and "visible church" can be used in a variety of ways. Here the invisible church refers to that subsection of the church that is genuinely saved, while the visible church refers to the institution that evangelizes and performs the sacraments. The terms imply the existence of a subset of genuinely saved people—a true church—who exist within the overall framework of the institutional shell—the false church. See for example Louis Berkhof, *Systematic Theology* (Edinburgh: Banner of Truth, 1939), 565–67. Although their usage can be somewhat variable, for the most part Barth and Zizioulas offer these explanations.

between sections of the church that are seen as close or distant to Christ, such as visible/invisible, false/true, or even current/eschatological. This error excessively separates distinctions within the church, compromises ecclesial unity, and leads to a naïve and unwarranted ecclesial pessimism where a substantial section of the church is viewed as virtually hopeless. It is precisely this error that some claim Barth makes,[9] and that Gunton rightly rejects when he writes: "[T]here is no invisible Church—at least not in the sense in which it has usually been understood—not because the Church is perfect, but because to be in communion with those who are ordered to Jesus by the Spirit is to be the Church."[10] The Eastern Orthodox theologian Vladimir Lossky similarly denies the distinction, terming it "ecclesial nestorianism."[11]

The opposite ecclesial error of Spirit-Ebionism, in contrast, subsumes the role of the Son into that of the Spirit, collapsing the church into Christ with the result that the church is identified with its eschatological endpoint. Such an understanding lacks sufficient recognition that the present historical church is not all it should and will be. This error excessively confuses divinity and humanity within the church and consequently leads to a naïve and unwarranted ecclesial optimism. Moreover, and somewhat counterintuitively, it also compromises ecclesial unity by simply denying that any part of the church that doesn't correspond to the eschatological fulfillment can be accurately labeled as church. Zizioulas's ecclesiology fits in this

9. As mentioned previously. See Nicholas M. Healy, "The Logic of Karl Barth's Ecclesiology: Analysis, Assessment and Proposed Modifications," *Modern Theology* 10, no. 3 (1994): 259. As noted earlier, and in contrast to Healy's position in this paper, Barth's position is a little more complex than a simplistic ecclesial Spirit-Docetism due to the dialectical relation he develops between the sanctified and sinful church. Barth actually criticizes the visible/invisible distinction at times. See for example, Barth, *Church Dogmatics*, IV/3.2, 783–84.

10. Colin Gunton, "The Church on Earth: The Roots of Community," in *On Being the Church*, ed. C. Gunton and D. Hardy (Edinburgh: T. & T. Clark, 1989), 79–80.

11. Vladimir Lossky, *The Mystical Theology of the Eastern Church* (London: James Clarke, 1957), 186.

category. And one could justifiably ponder in response whether any community can rightly be labeled a church in this understanding. For what human community, even within its performance of the Eucharist, is without flaws of discrimination or broken relationship?

As described above, the excesses related to church unity correspond directly to Spirit Christological errors. Consequently, it is true but not sufficient to say that the historic church is one because there is one Christ. One Christ does not guarantee one church, because Christ without the communicative, crossing-over role of the Spirit into the present state of fallen and sinful humanity leads inexorably to a logically and practically divided church. Similarly, it is true but not sufficient to say that the historical church is one because there is one Spirit. One Spirit does not guarantee one church, because the present Spirit without the eschatological goal and distinct otherness of Christ means the church now is identified with its eschatological fulfillment, and such perfection simply doesn't presently exist. The historical church is one because there is one Christ *and* one Spirit, by which we as one church participate in Christ's one relationship of Sonship with his one Father.

The question remains: How can the earthly church's evidential disunity be resolved with the theological affirmation of its indivisible constitution? The contention here is that, viewed through a pneumatological lens, there is no discrepancy to resolve. After all, the church is on a journey. It should not be viewed simplistically as only the body of Christ (i.e., an already-perfect entity), but it also must be viewed as the bride of Christ being prepared for her wedding (i.e., a being-perfected entity). Such tensions and divisions within and between congregations are entirely to be expected. If the Spirit transforms, then it should thoroughly be expected that the church is something that needs to be transformed! Rather than being used as evidence against its unity, the church's continuing engagement with struggles and tensions should be seen as a sign of the Spirit's presence and action and consequently of the church's present union with Christ.

6.2 Who Is in the Church? (Spirit- and Water-Baptism)

The church is the Spirit-enabled union that exists between the incarnate Christ and the human community of the church (*tripartite in nature*). It is, moreover, a single entity (*indivisible in constitution*). These ecclesiological characteristics are immediate consequences of developing a Third Article Ecclesiology from the perspective of Christology. But they raise a number of questions, the first being: "Who is in the church?" A Christological Third Article Ecclesiology argues that the church is *unique in context*. In other words, having a relationship with Jesus and being part of the church cannot be separated or distinguished. If a person is united with Christ, they are part of his body (the church). If a person is not a part of Christ's body (the church), they do not have a relationship with him. To love Jesus is to love his ecclesial body. To separate yourself from Christ's ecclesial body is to separate yourself from Jesus. The church is thus the *unique context* in which the Spirit unites humanity to Christ. This is not to suggest that the Spirit is controlled by or limited to the church. Indeed, quite the reverse. It is the church that is controlled by and limited to the Spirit. But when a person is united to Christ by the Spirit, then that uniquely occurs through the *transformation* of that person into the church, the body and bride of Christ. To express the same thing differently: the church is precisely identifiable as the human community of the baptized.[12]

12. This would include those who (intentionally or unknowingly) are being prepared for baptism. See the discussion below.

A key argument for this understanding is exegetical. The biblical record portrays the Spirit as a gift to the church and only secondarily and consequently to individuals.[13] The church is the exclusive sphere within humanity of the Spirit's communing activity, and it is only as individual people are part of the church that they participate in the Spirit-enabled union of humanity with Christ. Goheen, for example, comments: "The temple of the Holy Spirit is first of all a corporate or communal image. Our regrettable tendency to limit this image to our physical bodies (another manifestation of our individualism) has the effect of diminishing the importance of Christian community. Only once does 'temple' refer to (the indwelling of) an individual person (1 Cor. 6:19)."[14] Interestingly, a persuasive grammatical argument can be made that even this exceptional reference is communal. The verse is most accurately translated, "Do you not know that the body (singular) of you (plural) is the temple of the Holy Spirit?" Consequently, Badcock argues that "the word 'body' is to be taken in the technical Pauline sense as 'body of Christ,' in which case, once again, the reference would be to the people joined with Christ rather than to the individual."[15] Given this, in every biblical reference the Spirit resides in the church, so that only by being part of the church is a believer relationally connected through the Spirit to Christ. Gunton claims similarly that "the Spirit works in the Church: his is a churchly rather than an individual sphere of activity."[16]

The argument here is not for precedence, however (as if a person is first a member of the church and only then united with Christ), but for equivalency. A person's relational connection to Christ by

13. The discussion below argues that separating the two is a false antithesis, however.
14. Michael Goheen, *A Light to the Nations: The Missional Church and the Biblical Story* (Grand Rapids: Baker Academic, 2011), 179.
15. Gary D. Badcock, *The House Where God Lives: Renewing the Doctrine of the Church for Today* (Grand Rapids: Eerdmans, 2009), 125n16.
16. Colin Gunton, "Baptism: Baptism and the Christian Community," in *Father, Son and Holy Spirit: Toward a Trinitarian Theology* (London: T. & T. Clark, 2003), 213.

the Spirit and their participation in the church are indistinguishable; the phrases are just two different ways of saying the same thing. Schleiermacher famously distinguished between the two major denominational streams by noting, "Protestantism makes the individual's relation to the church dependent on his relation to Christ" while Catholicism "makes the individual's relation to Christ dependent on his relation to the Church."[17] Whether this statement is theologically and historically accurate or not,[18] Third Article Theology goes to neither extreme, but logically identifies one's relationship to Christ with one's membership in the church.

Consider the implications of this understanding. What about those claims made by some to have a relationship with Jesus, but no involvement with the church? They are false. What of a person who claims no relationship with Jesus but increasingly commits themself to a Christ-centered church community? Their claim is also false. The line separating true and false, sanctified and sinner, does not run *between* individuals within a church, but *through* each individual. All those in the body of Christ are true and false; we are all sanctified and sinner, and we are so all the time. And all the time the Spirit is drawing us who together form the church into a closer relationship with Christ and with each other. Using Hiebert's helpful analogy of set theory,[19] this understanding characterizes a church as a centered set: it is relational (in that members are defined through relationship to Christ) and well formed (in that those with a relationship to Christ are clearly distinguished from those who do not).

So who is in this corporate body known as the church? The church consists of those individuals who are pneumatologically united with

17. Friedrich Schleiermacher, *The Christian Faith* (London: T. & T. Clark, 1999), 103.

18. See Veli-Matti Kärkkäinen, *An Introduction to Ecclesiology: Ecumenical, Historical and Global Perspectives* (Downers Grove, IL: IVP Academic, 2002), 11–12.

19. P. G. Hiebert, "The Category Christian in the Mission Task," in *Anthropological Reflections on Missiological Issues* (Grand Rapids: Baker, 1994), 107–36.

Christ. Or, to use more thoroughly biblical language, it consists in those who have been baptized into the body of Christ by the Spirit (Spirit-baptism). But this invisible relationship has clear and visible markers, of which water-baptism is primary.[20] Spirit-baptism and water-baptism thus have a complementary relationship, which can be understood according to Barth's Chalcedonian logic.[21] First (following the Chalcedonian pattern), Spirit-baptism cannot be separated from or confused with water-baptism. Second (following the anhypostasia/enhypostasia formula), water-baptism has no meaning beyond being a human rite without an accompanying Spirit-baptism, but the Spirit-baptism imbues the water-baptism with a genuine reality. Third, water-baptism corresponds to and reflects the genuine reality of Spirit-baptism. It thus can be said that through baptism a person genuinely becomes united to Christ in his body the church. Just as all who are in a marriage relationship have had a wedding, all who are in the church and participate in his body have been baptized. The church is precisely the community of the baptized: those who are a part of the body of Christ, which is relationally connected to him through the Spirit. This understanding, of course, requires some alteration to the "conventional" understanding of baptism. As Gunton notes, "It is not first of all the expression of the faith of an individual or some invisible inner

20. In using the term "water-baptism" the immediate question arising is whether it is infant baptism or believers baptism that is being referred to. As shall become clear in the following discussion, a pneumato-ecclesiology does not draw a sharp distinction between the two competing interpretations of water-baptism, and both can fit within this framework. The key recognition is the correspondence between Spirit- and water-baptism, as discussed below. Believers baptism fits perhaps more naturally with the pneumato-ecclesial perspective, as the rite of water-baptism chronologically follows the event of spirit-baptism that it corresponds to and from which its significance and meaning is drawn. But infant baptism, if considered as a proleptic anticipation of Spirit-baptism can also fit within the framework, through a pneumatologically enabled time reversal. See the brief introductory discussion of the relationship between the Spirit and time in section 11.2.

21. See for example George Hunsinger, "Baptism and the Soteriology of Forgiveness," *International Journal of Systematic Theology* 2, no. 3 (2000): 247–69.

cleansing, but it is public and communal: it is the means by which a person is brought into relation with Christ through the medium of his body, the Church."[22]

Perhaps more than any other Christian sacrament, the baptismal initiation symbolically incorporates both Christological and pneumatological components. From a Christological perspective, in baptism we are united with Christ's death and resurrection in a watery "burial" (e.g., Rom. 6:1-11). From a pneumatological perspective, the symbolism is that of a new birth, not just of water but of the Spirit in whose presence we are saturated and now live and breathe (e.g., John 3:1-8). Baptism must therefore be viewed not just Christologically, as merely a sacrament where the divine and the human meet, but pneumatologically, as it is in and through the Spirit that we are united with Christ.

Again, the clearest way of demonstrating this understanding of baptism is by recognizing the potential errors it seeks to avoid. The initial two errors correspond to the classical Christological heresies. An ecclesially Docetic understanding of baptism excessively focuses on Spirit-baptism at the expense of water-baptism, reducing water-baptism to merely a responsive gesture, a "public testimony to an inner spiritual transformation."[23] This is a common position espoused in certain Baptistic settings, and at the extreme can even treat baptism as a nonessential practice (e.g., the Quakers or the Salvation Army). The opposite error is ecclesial Ebionism, which completely neglects any mystical aspect of water-baptism, and views it merely as an initiatory rite into the human community of the church. Examples can be seen in some liberal mainline churches and nominal Roman Catholics.

22. Gunton, "Baptism," 208.
23. Millard Erickson, *Christian Theology* (Grand Rapids: Baker, 1983), 1096.

More prevalent, however, than these two are the pneumatological errors that excessively meld or disconnect the spiritual and human aspects of baptism. The ecclesial error of Spirit-Ebionism *confuses* water- and Spirit-baptism. Many theologians of the Middle Ages, for example, claimed that baptismal regeneration occurred *ex opere operato*.[24] But the act of baptism, in and of itself, is not regenerative. Union with Christ cannot be brought about through the performance of a physical act as if by magic. Further, as Grenz notes, "Baptismal regeneration survives in some form in the contemporary expressions of the more sacramental traditions, including the Roman Catholic and Eastern Orthodox churches and also among certain Lutherans."[25] Zizioulas's overemphasis on the Spirit at the expense of Christ in the life of the church, for example, leads directly to his holding such a position.[26] His Spirit-Ebionitic understanding of baptism comes as a direct consequence of lacking an understanding of Christ's person external to his corporate personality in the church. Because an individual's connection to Christ and to Christ's church is literally and not just logically identified, Spirit- and water-baptism also must be literally identical and not just logically complementary.

The opposite error of ecclesial Spirit-Docetism, in contrast, excessively distinguishes between water- and Spirit-baptism. This view doesn't neglect the importance of either form of baptism, but it views them as separate and (more importantly) separable. For example, toward the end of *Church Dogmatics*, on the basis that Jesus Christ is the one and only sacrament of God, Barth maintains the nonsacramental nature of water-baptism,[27] a claim that perplexes

24. Stanley J. Grenz, *Theology for the Community of God* (Grand Rapids: Eerdmans, 1994), 526.
25. Ibid.
26. See John Zizioulas, *Communion and Otherness: Further Studies in Personhood and the Church* (London: T. & T. Clark, 2006), 80. Also, Jonathan Martin Ciraulo, "Sacraments and Personhood: John Zizioulas' Impasse and a Way Forward," *The Heythrop Journal* 53, no. 6 (2012): 995–97.

even his most ardent supporters. Hunsinger writes that Barth's "argument is peculiar. Although, for Barth, Jesus Christ is the Word of God in the strict and proper sense, that did not prevent God's Word from having a threefold form. . . . A similar logic immediately suggests itself for thinking about baptism and the Lord's supper as sacraments."[28] As has already been noted, Barth's tendency is to overemphasize the human and the divine being without confusion, resulting from his ecclesial Spirit-Eutychian tendency to meld the role of the Spirit and the Son in ecclesial life. It is perhaps in his understanding and characterization of the sacraments that the problematic implications of this tendency are seen at their clearest.

Gunton, in contrast to both of these tendencies, intentionally walks the fine line between excessively confusing and distinguishing between Spirit- and water-baptism. In a fascinating discussion of infant baptism, he notes two particular errors he wishes to avoid.[29] First, the view that *anyone* may be brought into the church by baptism (equivalent to ecclesial Spirit-Ebionism), a view he regards as dangerously magical and that essentially puts the church in control of the Spirit by virtue of its physical actions. Second, the view that baptism must *follow* a particular experience (equivalent to Spirit-Docetism), a view he regards as ignoring the presence of the Spirit within children who have not yet made an adult profession of faith. In this latter point, Gunton (presumably) maintains the intimate connection between water- and Spirit-baptism, but understands it (as Hunsinger notes explicitly) as a "proleptic form of adult baptism."[30]

27. See Barth, *Church Dogmatics*, IV/4, 100–109. While it is true that Christ is the ultimate sacrament, this truth does not necessarily reduce baptism to a mere ordinance. See for example W. Travis McMaken, *The Sign of the Gospel: Toward an Evangelical Doctrine of Infant Baptism After Karl Barth* (Minneapolis: Fortress Press, 2013).
28. Hunsinger, "Baptism and the Soteriology of Forgiveness," 254.
29. Gunton, "Baptism," 212.
30. Hunsinger, "Baptism and the Soteriology of Forgiveness," 262 (slightly altered).

Putting aside the question of infant versus believers baptism, which is well beyond the scope of this research, Gunton's efforts reveal the gain obtained from viewing the church, and this sacrament in particular, through the lens of the Spirit. Moreover, it affirms the pneumato-ecclesial understanding of the church as the *unique context* in which a person's relationship with Christ is worked out and enabled. As Gunton rightly asserts, "[T]he Holy Spirit is the agent of our incorporation into Christ through the medium of the community of faith."[31] It is also worth noting that this pneumato-ecclesial understanding has significant ecumenical potential,[32] in that it doesn't merely draw a middle line between some traditional understandings of Protestantism and Catholicism, but provides potential resolutions in areas of long-held practical difference, notably here the area of infant baptism. Hunsinger recognizes this position's ecumenical potential, where believers baptism can be seen as the norm, but infant baptism—by virtue of its proleptic nature—is considered as "not impermissible."[33]

6.3 How Is the Church Recognized?

The Christological Third Article ecclesiology being developed here has so far examined two questions: "What is the church?" and "Who is in the church?" The first question was answered through the affirmations that the church is *tripartite in nature* (being the pneumatologically enabled union between Christ and the church's human community) and *indivisible in constitution* (with no invisible/visible or true/false distinctions). The second question was answered through the affirmations that the church is *unique in context* (in that

31. Gunton, "Baptism," 212–13.
32. See the original discussion of the ecumenical potential and imperative of Third Article Theology in sections 1.2 and 1.3.
33. See for example Hunsinger, "Baptism and the Soteriology of Forgiveness," 263.

membership in the church and a relationship with Jesus are logically equivalent) so that the church exists precisely as the community of the baptized (referring here to the correspondence of water- and Spirit-baptism). These questions lead naturally to another: "How is the church recognized?"

The question has an ironic undertone. C. S. Lewis, for example, reflects on the query "What are we to make of Jesus Christ?" by writing "the real question is not what are we going to make of Christ, but what is He going to make of us?"[34] Similarly, the real question here is not how *we* are going to recognize a genuine church, but how does *God* recognize it? For the church simply is, and it is because of Christ and the Spirit. It exists from him and in him and for him, whether humans recognize it or not. But given that in a pneumato-ecclesiology church, membership and having a relationship with Christ are so closely identified, and moreover that there is no true inner-core within an existing church, the question of which institutional communities are churches and which are not becomes pivotal.[35]

History reveals many varying ways of recognizing a community's ecclesial validity. The church fathers Irenaeus and Ignatius offer two contrastingly broad perspectives, focused on pneumatology ("where the Spirit of God is, there is the church and every kind of grace")[36] and Christology ("wheresoever Christ Jesus is, there is the Catholic Church")[37] respectively. The former viewpoint tends toward a more experientially based recognition, with the latter favoring a more

34. C. S. Lewis, *God in the Dock* (Glasgow: Fount, 1979), 79.

35. Or, similarly, which local communities are part of the global universal church and hence can be identified correctly as churches?

36. Irenaeus, "Against Heresies," in *The Ante-Nicene Fathers: Translations of the Fathers down to A.D. 325*, ed. Alexander Roberts and James Donaldson (Peabody, MA: Hendrickson, 1996), 3.24.1, 1:458.

37. Ignatius, *The Epistles of St. Ignatius: Bishop of Antioch*, trans. J. H. Strawley (London: Society for Promoting Christian Knowledge, 1900), 96–97.

structural understanding.[38] In the Protestant Reformation, Luther's criteria included functionality: "The church is the assembly of the saints in which the Gospel is taught purely and the sacraments are administered rightly."[39] Calvin's similar understanding also emphasized "correct faith and an upright Christian life" along with associated disciplines and a particular ministerial order.[40] The radical left wing of the Reformation (i.e., Anabaptists) and their "Free Church" descendants (e.g., Quakers, Baptists, etc.) claim the church is recognized not through functional sacraments but the voluntary gathering of true believers who each individually have direct, unmediated access to God. Volf, in arguing for this tradition, extends the formulation of Irenaeus by describing the church as an "intimate communion of independent persons,"[41] which exists wherever the Spirit "is present in its ecclesially constitutive activity."[42]

The pneumato-ecclesial perspective being developed here adopts a broad understanding of which communities are churches, and a broad range of evidences by which they can be determined as a genuine church. Such breadth is required because the church is Christ's bride and still journeying toward its intended goal. Given that the church both globally and locally is in the process of being

38. Note that this tendency is apparent even in Ignatius himself, as evidenced in the context surrounding this famous quote: "Wheresoever the bishop appears, there let the people be, even as wheresoever Christ Jesus is, there is the Catholic Church. It is not lawful apart from the bishop either to baptize or to hold a love-feast. But whatsoever he approves, that also is well-pleasing to God, that everything which you do may be secure and valid" (ibid., 96–98).

39. From the Augsburg Confession. See Jaroslav Pelikan and Valerie Hotchkiss, eds., *Creeds and Confessions of Faith in the Christian Tradition: Reformation Era* (New Haven: Yale University Press, 2003), 62. See also Veli-Matti Kärkkäinen, *An Introduction to Ecclesiology: Ecumenical, Historical and Global Perspectives* (Downers Grove, IL: IVP Academic, 2002), 40.

40. Kärkkäinen, *An Introduction to Ecclesiology*, 50. See also John Calvin, *Institutes of the Christian Religion*, trans. Henry Beveridge (Peabody, MA: Hendrickson, 2008), 4.1.8, 677–78; 4.12, 811–26; and John Calvin, *Calvin's Commentaries*, trans. John Pringle, 23 vols. (Grand Rapids: Baker, 2009), 20:349–51.

41. Miroslav Volf, *After Our Likeness: The Church as the Image of the Trinity* (Grand Rapids: Eerdmans, 1998), 213.

42. Ibid., 129.

transformed by the Spirit, it is unwise to make definitive proclamations regarding how a church must presently behave. A church cannot be recognized through such an approach. Looking from a Christological vantage point through a pneumatological lens reveals only two features that distinguish a true church. First, a church is recognized by being *Christ-centered in orientation.* In other words the origin, present existence, and future purpose of the community are centered on Christ. In biblical terms, it is a community that by intention (if not always in practice) lives out the reality that "Jesus is Lord." Second, a church is recognized by having a *Christotelic momentum.* Over time, genuine movement is seen toward increasing union with Christ. In other words, there is clear evidence of the Spirit working in the life of the church to draw it closer toward its ultimate goal. The key features by which a church is recognized thus correspond closely to its primary ontological constitution. Given that the church is the pneumatologically enabled union between Christ and humanity, it is recognized as such by its focus on Christ (*Christ-centered in orientation*) and its pneumatologically enabled movement deeper into that union (*Christotelic momentum*). In essence, a church is recognized through its existing and growing connection with Christ.

Again, this understanding is explained best through observing the excesses from which it needs to be distinguished. The first two correspond with classic Christological errors. The ecclesial error of Ebionism recognizes a church primarily from the practical human actions it performs. It focuses on having *Christotelic momentum*, particularly having a Christ-like appearance, and neglects being *Christ-centered in orientation.* Examples include churches that focus on good works and serving the community, but minimize true worship, a prevalent error in the contemporary west. Also common is the opposite excess—ecclesial Docetism—where human activity is discounted, and the church's actions are deemed largely irrelevant. In this understanding, the church's status as a church is (correctly) derived from its relationship to Christ, but (incorrectly) there is no consequent expectation on or realization of this relationship to impact a community's behavior. An overexaggerated example of this error is seen in early Gnosticism. Based on a strong dualism that regarded the material world as evil, gnostics responded either by being deliberately licentious or rigidly ascetic. Nevertheless their common core was that little value was to be attached to human activity. The focus was on the secret *gnosis* of their (supposed) *Christ-centered orientation*, and the impact of that on the community's behavior in terms of *Christotelic momentum* was negligible. Yamauchi notes, interestingly, that "most Gnostics were Docetics."[43]

Clearly the correct path forward in terms of recognizing a church is to again see a Barthian-type correspondence between divine and human activity. Churches ought to be recognized not merely from human attitudes or activity, nor merely from divine orientation, but the former should reflect and correspond to the latter. Badcock articulates this approach, commenting, "One might even suggest that just as classical Christology sought to hold together the two sides of the Christological definition, 'without confusion' and 'without separation,' so ecclesiology, following the Christological analogy, needs to hold together its two moments of divine outreach and human response."[44] This leads the argument logically toward a second set of excesses, based on the Spirit-Christological errors, for it is by the Spirit that these two characteristics are held together.

43. E. M. Yamauchi, "Gnosis, Gnosticism," in *Dictionary of Paul and His Letters*, ed. Ralph P. Martin Gerald F. Hawthorne, and Daniel G. Reid (Downers Grove, IL: InterVarsity, 1993), 352.

44. Gary D. Badcock, *Light of Truth and Fire of Love: A Theology of the Holy Spirit* (Grand Rapids: Eerdmans, 1997), 168.

If the communing role of the Spirit is overemphasized (Spirit-Ebionism) the divine union and the human action are confused, so that a church being *Christ-centered in orientation* and having *Christotelic momentum* are virtually equivalent. In this category, Barth notes the contrasting errors of both sacramentalism (where a church is defined as those who have participated in particular human rites or ceremonies) and moralism (where a church is defined by the attitudes and actions that the community holds in distinction from the world).[45] Of the former he writes, "What kind of conception of the Holy Spirit is it, of His presence and operation, of the awakening to faith, and of membership of the body of Christ, when all this can be imparted to a man simply by the correct fulfilment of an action initiated by men?"[46] Of the latter, he writes, "But where is the law that can serve as a measure to distinguish who has or has not the Holy Spirit, who believes or does not believe, who belongs to the community of the saints or does not belong? What decides and distinguishes in this case is not a sacramental *opus operatum* but a religious and moral *opus operantis*—as though the Lord, the Holy Spirit and His gift could be enclosed in the sphere of certain human works thought out by men."[47] Barth notes that even though moralism and sacramentalism are reactions against each other, they both make the same mistake. Further, no middle approach exists: "If we try to combine the two, will not the combination simply aggravate the evil which attaches to both?"[48] This "evil," which has been here labeled as the error of ecclesial Spirit-Ebionism, is to excessively confuse

45. See Barth, *Church Dogmatics*, IV/1, 695–96. Barth does not use the term "ecclesial Spirit-Ebionism" to describe these excesses. See also Kärkkäinen, *An Introduction to Ecclesiology*, 56–58; and Craig A. Carter, "Karl Barth's Revision of Protestant Ecclesiology," *Perspectives in Religious Studies* 22, no. 1 (1995): 35–44.
46. Barth, *Church Dogmatics*, IV/1, 696.
47. Ibid.
48. Ibid.

the human activities of the church and its divine orientation, as if divine activity is identified with and therefore constrained by human activity. It recognizes a true church by being both *Christ-centered in orientation* and having a *Christotelic momentum*, but it excessively *confuses* the two, and in extreme cases tends toward viewing them as synonymous.

Zizioulas's claim that the Eucharist makes the church clearly tends in this direction. In asserting this equivalence, Zizioulas diminishes neither the need for the church to act like Christ (recognizing their need to be a nonexclusive Eucharistic community), nor diminishes the presence of the divine in the church (with the Spirit's presence of primary importance). What he does do is confuse the divine and the human, for the Spirit makes the church only during the performance of particular human sacraments.

Barth, in contrast, recognizes the church as "the men assembled in it who are thereto elected by the Lord, called by His Word and constituted by His Spirit: just so many, no more and no less, these men and no other."[49] According to Carter, "Barth would have us accept as a Christian anyone who is willing to profess faith in Christ and to leave judgement in the hands of God."[50] While the emphasis is on the church's Christward orientation, the requirement for Christotelic momentum is certainly not absent.[51] For example, significant portions of *Church Dogmatics* IV/3.2 discuss particular ministry practices.[52] So one cannot here justifiably accuse Barth of ecclesial Docetism. It is perhaps fair, though, to criticize Barth for trending toward an ecclesial *Spirit*-Docetism. With regard to recognizing a church, this excess again validates both Christward

49. Ibid.

50. Carter, "Karl Barth's Revision of Protestant Ecclesiology," 37.

51. For example, John Webster comments that Barth "has a rather slender account of the moral processes of common life." John Webster, *Karl Barth* (London: Continuum, 2000), 161.

52. See in particular Barth, *Church Dogmatics*, IV/3.2, esp. pp. 864–901.

orientation and Christotelic momentum, but it excessively separates the two, seeing them as side-by-side activities, rather than intrinsically connected. As discussed in the previous chapter, this is an error some perceive in Barth's ecclesiology, and which was argued to be derived from a tendency to subsume the Spirit's ecclesial role into the Son's. Gunton, for example, writes that Barth's focus is on Christ "bringing home to the believer his past work,"[53] and "the miraculous transfer of what happened *then* to ourselves *now*"[54] rather than to the present transformative work of the Spirit and the current relationship to Christ so enabled. [55] He would prefer that Barth spoke of *participation* in the body of Christ rather than merely *encountering* another history. Bender similarly comments that "Barth often speaks of a parallelism of action, rather than an embodied action."[56]

The question that naturally arises here is that if the church's action is "embodied" and not merely paralleled; if the church "participates" in Christ's life and does not merely encounter it, then how does that "embodiment" or "participation" happen? What does the church actually do, and how does it go about doing it? This is the final ecclesiological question for this chapter.

6.4 What Does the Church Do?

Looking through the lens of the Spirit from the vantage point of Christology has afforded a view of the church as tripartite in nature, indivisible in constitution, unique in context, Christ-centered in orientation, and having a Christotelic momentum. Examining the question of "what does the church do?" or more specifically "how does the church 'embody' or 'participate in' the life of Christ?" enables

53. Colin Gunton, "Salvation," in *The Cambridge Companion to Karl Barth*, ed. John Webster (Cambridge: Cambridge University Press, 2000), 153–54.
54. Ibid., 152.
55. See ibid., 152–53.
56. Bender, *Karl Barth's Christological Ecclesiology*, 282.

the church to be characterized as *cruciform in shape*, *missional in purpose*, *narrative in character*, and *relational in identity*. While each of these characteristics is pivotal, some will be discussed in detail later, and others lie beyond the scope of this research as they primarily address what the church is for the world rather than what the church is in itself.[57] The following comments are indicative.

In regard to the church being *cruciform in shape*, the analogy between Christ and the church gives significant insight. Just as Christ "became who he was" through his obedient suffering, so the church grows increasingly to become a true reflection of Christ as it suffers in obedience. The church's Christotelic momentum, then, is a consequence of its cruciform shape. A crucial note at this point is that the church's suffering, however, is not as Christ's was, for the church suffers for Christ and serves him. In Christ, the servant form and authority coincide, for when Christ was at his weakest on the cross, his authority as the Son of God was most clearly evident. But in the church the servant form points to an outward authority, that of Christ. As such, Torrance writes that "[t]he Church follows its Lord in His servant form and by participating in His authoritative ministry, but the servant form and the authority are not identical in the person of the Church, for here the servant form is given authority precisely as the person of the Church is through self-denial and crucifixion displaced by the Person of Christ."[58] Moreover, it is as the church follows Christ in his suffering and obedience that Christ is most clearly seen through the church, and its *missional purpose* is most completely fulfilled. The pneumatological insights into the church's

57. Not that these two ecclesial aspects can be existentially distinguished. See the discussion in section 11.2.

58. Thomas F. Torrance, "Atonement and the Oneness of the Church," *Scottish Journal of Theology* 7, no. 3 (1954): 261.

missionary role are pivotal but beyond the scope of this research project.[59]

The analogy of Christ's human nature also gives significant insight into the church being *narrative in character*. In contrast to both Zizioulas and Barth's "from time to time" understanding of ecclesial existence, the pneumatological perspective suggests a narratival and developmental understanding. The Spirit's presence enables the hard rigidity of these formulations to be softened, so that just as the human nature of Christ is seen to develop over time, so the ecclesial nature of the church develops. The church, as the sequel to the incarnation, has a story in which it not only is at the present time the body of Christ and thus united to him, but it is also the bride of Christ, being prepared and perfected by the Spirit for the coming Kingdom when that unity will be fully realized. The pneumatological insights into the church's narrative character as it is transformed toward the eschaton are best viewed from the vantage point of eschatology, a topic introduced in section 11.2.

The final characteristic of the church to arise from this Christological vantage point is arguably the most significant. The church is *relational in identity*, for we participate in the Son's filial relationship with the Father. Just as God is intrinsically relational, so also is the church constituted relationally as we participate in Christ's Sonship. As has been noted, the Christological vantage point enables a view of the church as a single entity, which communes as this single identity with the Father, as we are all together in Christ. But this perspective leads to two significant and related questions. First, how do we participate in Christ's relationship with the Father? Second, how does our constitution in relationship affect our relationships with one another? In short, what does it mean that the church is not just a

59. See the brief discussion of next steps in section 11.2.

unity but a community? Not just one, but many? Partly due to Jesus' individuality, it is difficult to answer these questions directly from the vantage point of Christology. And so part three develops a *Trinitarian* Third Article Ecclesiology—viewing *the church as participant in the inner life of the Trinity*—to complement the Christological Third Article Ecclesiology developed in part two.

PART III

The Church as Participant in Trinitarian Life

In "The Church on Earth: The Roots of Community," Colin Gunton argues that in the Trinity, the church developed "a distinctively Christian ontology" but notes with regret that "its insights were for the most part not extended into ecclesiology."[1] Gunton goes on to describe how he believes a Trinitarian ecclesiology can and should be constructed. Initially recognizing the historical importance of the link between Christ and the church, he immediately notes that "Christology's tendency . . . to universalise"[2] often results in a static and authoritarian ecclesial understanding. To counteract this tendency he suggests the Spirit's role in Christ's life must be recognized and prioritized, so that ecclesiology is derived from Jesus' humanity rather than just his divinity. Gunton's comments here are very pertinent, presaging the approach taken in part two of

1. Colin Gunton, "The Church on Earth: The Roots of Community," in *On Being the Church*, ed. C. Gunton and D. Hardy (Edinburgh: T. & T. Clark, 1989), 53. Whether Gunton's sweeping claim here is justified is immaterial to the substance of the argument in this part of the research, however.
2. Ibid., 59–60.

this research. By recognizing the analogical continuities between the Spirit's role in Christ and the church, part two developed an ecclesiology conditioned by a balanced recognition of Christ's humanity.

But Gunton goes further. He comments,

> Christology is only the starting point, because it is so closely related to the question of the status of the events from which the Church originated. If we wish to say something of what kind of sociality the Church is we must move from a discussion of the relation of Christology to pneumatology to an enquiry into what it is that makes the Church what it is: and that necessitates a move from the economic to the immanent Trinity; or from the ontic to the ontological.[3]

Matching this intent, the purpose of part three is to view ecclesiology from a Trinitarian vantage point through the lens of pneumatology. In short, part two examined a direct comparison between the work of the economic Trinity and the church; part three deals with a less direct analogy between the immanent Trinity and ecclesiology. Two key reasons make this immanent Trinitarian analogical link more challenging than the previous Christological connection. First, the Christological connection to ecclesiology is more explicitly biblical than the Trinitarian connection. While not absent, references analogically linking the Trinity and the church are much less common than Christological connections.[4] Second, and more pertinently, in comparing Christ and the church, the two entities being discussed both "include" divinity and humanity. In comparing the Trinity and the church, this similarity no longer holds. One entity is entirely divine and the other is partially (and perhaps predominantly) human. As such, care must be taken that the clear distinction between Creator and creature is not minimized.

3. Ibid., 65.
4. See John 17:20–23 for a particularly clear example.

Miroslav Volf notes three clear distinctions[5] between the Trinity and the church.[6] The first distinction is between what the immanent Trinity is, and our apprehension of it. The second distinction is between our Trinitarian apprehension and ecclesiology. Terms like "*perichoresis*" or "communion" cannot be used in precisely the same way of both God and humanity, and ecclesial participation in the life of the Trinity must be understood as creaturely in order that pantheism be avoided.[7] The third distinction is between an eschatological (or optimal) ecclesiology and historical reality. As Volf recognizes, the church is "moving between the historical minimum and the eschatological maximum. For a sojourning church, only a dynamic understanding of its correspondence to the Trinity is meaningful."[8]

These distinctions mean that any simplistic, direct equivalence between the Trinity and the church is more than likely mistaken. Gunton recognizes this when he writes that "the temptation must be resisted to draw conclusions of a logicising kind: appealing directly to the unity of the three as one God as a model for a unified church; or conversely . . . arguing from the distinctions of the persons for an ecclesiology of diversity."[9] It would be a mistake to conclude, however, that there is no analogical correlation at all between the

5. Note that Volf uses the term "mediations" rather than distinctions. See Miroslav Volf, *After Our Likeness: The Church as the Image of the Trinity* (Grand Rapids: Eerdmans, 1998), 198–200.
6. While Volf's recognition and analysis of these three distinctions (or mediations) is accurate, his handling of them (particularly the second) is less so. Husbands for example writes, "Although Volf seeks to qualify the way in which Trinitarian categories such as divine 'persons,' 'relation,' or 'perichoresis' are too quickly transferred to human persons, his vigilance remains in place only for a moment." Mark Husbands, "The Trinity Is *Not* Our Social Program," in *Trinitarian Theology for the Church: Scripture, Community, Worship*, ed. David Lauber and Daniel J. Treier (Downers Grove, IL: InterVarsity, 2009), 122–23. See further section 8.1.
7. See for example Neil Ormerod, *The Trinity: Retrieving the Western Tradition* (Milwaukee: Marquette University Press, 2005), 31.
8. Volf, *After Our Likeness*, 199. For further discussion on this third distinction see the eschatological discussion in section 11.2.
9. Gunton, "The Church on Earth," 66.

Trinity and ecclesiology. Certainly there is no direct *logical* connection. There is, however, a personal and pneumatological link, for we participate "by the Spirit in the Son's communion with the Father."[10] Gunton again:

> The doctrine of the Trinity replaces a logical conception of the relation between God and the world with a personal one. . . . Such relation as there is is personal, not logical, the product of the free and personal action of the triune God. The world is therefore contingent, finite and what it is only by virtue of its continuing dynamic dependence upon its creator; or, to say the same thing in another way, by the free action of the Spirit on and towards it.[11]

The question that arises is precisely what analogical connection can be made between the Trinity and the church—in what way does the life of the church participate in the life of the Trinity? This is the key question that part three of this research addresses. Before it can be answered, however, there is a prior question: Which Trinity does the church participate in? Not that there are many Trinities, but there are many doctrines of the Trinity, as evidenced for example by the disagreements over the *filioque*.[12] As such, in determining how the church is analogically connected with the Trinity the route

10. James B. Torrance, *Worship, Community and the Triune God of Grace* (Downers Grove, IL: IVP Academic, 1996), 31.

11. Gunton, "The Church on Earth," 67. While Gunton's characterization of the link between the Trinity and the church as "personal" and "pneumatological" is accurate, his outworking of it is less so. In the referenced article, Gunton uses the abstract bridge term of "relationality" to link the two doctrines. In a similarly themed chapter, he refers to the church as a "temporal echo of the eternal community." Colin Gunton, *The Promise of Trinitarian Theology* (Edinburgh: T. & T. Clark, 1997), 79. In both examples, Gunton uses a more direct connection than his initial "personal" and "pneumatological" characterization suggests is acceptable. For further detail see Uche Anizor, "A Spirited Humanity: The Trinitarian Ecclesiology of Colin Gunton," *Themelios* 36, no. 1 (2011): 27–31. Also, Roland Chia, "Trinity and Ontology: Colin Gunton's Ecclesiology," *International Journal of Systematic Theology* 9, no. 4 (2007): 452–68. As discussed further in chapter 8, this discrepancy between Gunton's ecclesial outworking and its initial characterization is the reason his work is not used more extensively in part three.

12. See for example Thomas H. McCall, *Which Trinity? Whose Monotheism?* (Grand Rapids: Eerdmans, 2010), 1–126.

taken must follow Volf's distinctions. Step one is to determine the conception of the immanent Trinity that is most responsible to the biblical revelation. Step two determines the analogical implications of that understanding for the church in its sojourning between its historical minimum and its eschatological maximum. The discussion in part three proceeds in these steps, as outlined below.

Chapter 7 traverses the route from the economic to the immanent Trinity, from God's revelation to God's being. Recognizing the inherent risks arising from starting with God's unity and "solving" his diversity (or the reverse), this chapter focuses on that aspect of the revelation where the unity and diversity of the Godhead is clearly and simultaneously evident: Spirit Christology. As Coffey has noted: "Spirit Christology provides our best mode of access to the theology of the Trinity."[13] The recent attempts of Coffey, Moltmann, and Habets to trace this path are considered. Applying the Spirit Christological analysis in chapter 2, the first two attempts are categorized as Spirit-priority and Son-Spirit-separation proposals respectively. In contrast, Habets's argument that a coherent Spirit Christology implies a "reconceived" understanding of the Trinity where the Father eternally begets the Son by the Spirit and the Son returns the love of the Father by the Spirit not only maintains a close connection between the economic and immanent Trinity (contra Moltmann) but also enables a clear personal role for the Holy Spirit within the Godhead (contra Coffey). Consequently, this "reconceived" Trinitarian understanding will be used analogically to determine a coherent Trinitarian Third Article Ecclesiology.[14]

13. David Coffey, "Spirit Christology and the Trinity," in *Advents of the Spirit: An Introduction to the Current Study of Pneumatology*, ed. Bradford E. Hinze and D. Lyle Dabney (Milwaukee: Marquette University Press, 2005), 315.

14. There are minor points of difference between Habets's presentation of a "reconceived" understanding of the Trinity and the one developed in section 7.3.

Chapter 8 constructs a viable analogical link between the immanent Trinity and the church. Initially Miroslav Volf's characterization of the church as the image of the Trinity is considered.[15] While recognizing its many positive features, it is argued that the analogical connection between the Trinity and ecclesiology is not "reflective" but pneumatological. More specifically, the church participates not *with* the Trinity, as a "reflective" methodology espouses, but *in* its very life, joining "by the Spirit in Jesus's communion with the Father."[16] These concerns are further illuminated through Kathryn Tanner's work, which critiques those who, like Volf, draw direct and logical comparisons between the Trinity and the church. The question is raised regarding whether Tanner's concerns apply equally to the methodology of Third Article Theology. It is argued that a pneumatologically enabled but Christologically conditioned approach *can* be used to construct a viable analogical link between the Trinity and the church, as exemplified in the work of Heribert Mühlen. Mühlen contends that in both the Trinity and the church the Holy Spirit is "one person in many persons," and that through the Spirit, Christ and the church together form a single corporate personality—a "Great-I." His work demonstrates that a Third Article Theology approach can provide a viable bridge between the two loci. Without undermining this key methodological point, it is also noted that Mühlen's work suffers from a "speculative" Trinitarian starting point that is insufficiently grounded in the biblical witness.

The main aim of part three, then, is to draw an analogical link between a "reconceived" understanding of the Trinity and the ontology and life of the church, using a pneumatologically enabled but Christologically conditioned approach. Using Wolterstorff's

15. Volf, *After Our Likeness*.

16. Torrance, *Worship, Community and the Triune God of Grace*, 31.

terminology, the "reconceived" Trinity is the *control* belief, ecclesiology is the *data* belief, and Scripture and the creeds form the *background* beliefs. If we join the Son's Trinitarian life through the Spirit, then how does this genuine participation impact our understanding and practice of ecclesial life? How does the church participate in Christ's filial relationship with the Father? And how, consequently, does our constitution in relationship affect the relationships of those individuals within the overall church? In short, how do the extra- and intra-ecclesial relationships function? The straightforward reality that Christ is only one person means that these questions are difficult to answer from the isolated vantage point of Christology, but the perspective gained from a "reconceived" doctrine of the Trinity provides an ideal perspective from which to observe these ecclesiological characteristics.

Chapter 9 argues that the immanent Trinitarian identities of the Son and the Spirit are reprised (with inevitable continuities and discontinuities) on a series of expanding stages: Christologically in the hypostatic union, soteriologically in the mystical union, and most pertinently ecclesiologically in the union between individual church members. In each of these unions the salient features of the "reconceived" Trinity are repeated: (a) the Son and the Spirit are logically distinct but completely inseparable; (b) the Spirit repeatedly acts as the "personing person" and the Son as the "personed person" who is variously begotten, incarnated, united, or formed in each of the unions respectively; and (c) the outward and inward movement of the Son and the Spirit from and to the Father (which the church joins) is ongoing and eternal. While this application of the "reconceived" Trinitarian understanding to Christology and soteriology has already been (briefly) developed,[17] it has not yet been extended to

17. See particularly Kathryn Tanner, *Christ the Key* (Cambridge: Cambridge University Press, 2010), 195–206. Tanner's work in these areas is extended in chapter 9 of this research.

ecclesiology. By doing so, a *Trinitarian* Third Article Ecclesiology emerges that characterizes the church as existing in *any and all relationships where, by the Spirit, the love of Christ is offered and returned*.[18]

This Trinitarian Third Article Ecclesiology is explored in chapter 10 first by comparing it positively with the constituent ecclesiological features emerging in a recent engagement Komonchak and Dadosky have had with an initial article from Balthasar.[19] There are clear points of overlap, such as the church's intrinsically relational nature, the foundational role of the Spirit, the Spirit-inspired intersubjectivity between individuals, and the transformation of individual consciousness. But in addition a Trinitarian Third Article Ecclesiology extends this discussion by noting the intrinsically relational (as opposed to individual) presence of the Spirit, the sacramental nature of fellowship, a nuanced understanding of catholicity, and the malleable or "liquid" nature of church structures. Perhaps the key result emerging is that the Spirit "releases and reconciles the tension between the fellowship and the individual in the concept of the Church."[20] Chapter 10 also contrasts this Trinitarian Third Article Ecclesiology with those that emerge from alternative Trinitarian starting points. It notes the different analogical methodologies adopted, contrasting interpretations of the ecclesial

18. While such a characterization is entirely complementary with the ecclesial characteristics derived in part two of this work, it is premature to integrate this *Trinitarian* Third Article Ecclesiology with the *Christological* Third Article Ecclesiology already developed. As discussed in chapter 11, it makes more sense to also examine ecclesiology from the vantage points of eschatology and the world in order that a comprehensive Third Article Ecclesiology that takes into account all these perspectives can be constructed.

19. Hans Urs von Balthasar, *Explorations in Theology: Spouse of the Word*, trans. A. V. Littledale, vol. 2 (San Francisco: Ignatius, 1991), 143–92; Joseph A. Komonchak, *Who Are the Church?* (Milwaukee: Marquette University Press, 2008); John D. Dadosky, "Who/What Is/Are the Church(es)?," *The Heythrop Journal* 52, no. 5 (2011): 785–801.

20. Wolfhart Pannenberg, *Systematic Theology*, trans. G. W. Bromiley, 3 vols. (Eerdmans: Grand Rapids, 1991, 1997), 3:130. See also Veli-Matti Kärkkäinen, *An Introduction to Ecclesiology: Ecumenical, Historical and Global Perspectives* (Downers Grove, IL: IVP Academic, 2002), 123.

marks, and implications for the church's understanding and practice of prayer (an application where the consequences of adopting different Trinitarian starting points are particularly clearly illuminated). Through these comparisons the consistency, balance, and applicability of using a "reconceived" model of the Trinity and a pneumatologically enabled and Christologically conditioned analogical link between the Trinity and the church become clearly apparent.

7

From the Economic to the Immanent Trinity

The link between the economic and the immanent Trinity has been a major theme of twentieth-century theology. Consider for example the near "ubiquity" of Rahner's Rule or *grundaxiom*, originally published in 1967: that "the 'economic' Trinity is the 'immanent' Trinity and the 'immanent' Trinity is the 'economic' Trinity."[1] Walter Kasper writes a mere fifteen years later that "[w]hat K. Rahner sets down as a basic principle reflects a broad consensus among the theologians of the various churches."[2] Stanley Grenz comments, "So standard has his terminological and methodological proposal become that it routinely appears in theological works without its source being cited."[3]

1. Karl Rahner, *The Trinity*, trans. Joseph Donceel (Tunbridge Wells, UK: Burns & Oates, 1997), 22.
2. Walter Kasper, *The God of Jesus Christ*, trans. Joseph Donceel (New York: Crossroad, 1984), 274.
3. Stanley J. Grenz, *Rediscovering the Triune God: The Trinity in Contemporary Theology* (Minneapolis: Fortress Press, 2004), 57.

While Rahner's *grundaxiom* may be "ubiquitous" and reflect a "consensus" in its specific wording, there is no shortage of differing opinions and implications for which it is used. Indeed, Neil Ormerod comments: "It is not at all clear that Rahner would be happy with the multiple paths Trinitarian theology has taken from the starting point he suggested."[4] Perhaps it is not surprising that when a theological concept is squeezed to fit on a bumper sticker, it becomes easily misconstrued and even more easily misappropriated.[5] In this research, the *grundaxiom* is interpreted as affirming that the way we know of God is through his revelation ("the immanent Trinity is the economic Trinity"), and that this epistemological knowledge gained is the truth about God ("the economic Trinity is the immanent Trinity"). The first phrase is primarily exclusive. It affirms that the *only* knowledge to be gained about God is through his revelation, and that accurate conclusions about the Godhead cannot be obtained through abstract philosophical reasoning isolated from this revelation. The second phrase is primarily reiterative. It affirms that God is not malicious or capricious, and what he reveals of himself is the truth of who he is.[6] This second "vice versa" clause can become problematic if the identity between the economic and immanent Trinity is overemphasized. The fact that God reveals the truth about himself should not be extended into the assertion that the revelation exhausts the reality of God in himself,[7] or that it restricts his freedom.[8]

4. Neil Ormerod, *The Trinity: Retrieving the Western Tradition* (Milwaukee: Marquette University Press, 2005), 140. For further discussion of various expressions and limitations of Rahner's Rule, see Scott Harrower, *Trinitarian Self and Salvation: An Evangelical Engagement with Rahner's Rule* (Eugene, OR: Pickwick, 2012). Also, Chung-Hyun Baik, *The Holy Trinity—God for God and God for Us: Seven Positions on the Immanent-Economic Trinity Relation in Contemporary Theology* (Eugene, OR: Pickwick, 2011).
5. Not that Rahner is responsible for those who have misinterpreted his *grundaxiom*.
6. Note that this reseach is adopting the epistemological position of critical realism. See the previous discussion in section 3.2.
7. For an example of a theologian claiming a complete identity between the economic and immanent Trinity see C. M. Lacugna, *God for Us: The Trinity and Christian Life* (San Francisco:

Attempts to determine the nature of the immanent Trinity from the economic are often divided into two broad categories—those that start from God's revealed unity and make his diversity the issue to be solved, and those that do the reverse.[9] The first approach runs the risk of modalism, as if there is one real God "behind" the three persons revealed in the economy. In some cases, such as the Christological and Trinitarian proposals of Hendrikus Berkhof and Marcellus of Ancyra examined in chapter 2, God's unity is clearly overemphasized.[10] The second group runs the opposite risk of tritheism, as if there are three separate Gods, who are only incidentally (and sometimes eschatologically) united. Jürgen Moltmann's Christological and Trinitarian understandings clearly trend in this direction, as discussed in chapter 2 and discussed further below.

In an attempt to avoid such errors, one alternative methodology focuses on those aspects of revelation where the triunity of the

Harper, 1991). And for a refutation of it see Thomas Weinandy, "The Immanent and Economic Trinity," *The Thomist* 57 (1993): 655–66.

8. For a spirited defense of divine freedom, see Paul D. Molnar, *Divine Freedom and the Doctrine of the Immanent Trinity* (London: T. & T. Clark, 2002).

9. Often these approaches are categorized as traditional, with the western church prioritizing God's unity, and the eastern church prioritizing God's diversity. Recent historical analysis argues convincingly that such categorization is unjustified. See for example Lewis Ayres, *Nicaea and Its Legacy: An Approach to Fourth-Century Trinitarian Theology* (Oxford: Oxford University Press, 2004), 384–429, particularly p. 384n3. It is ironic, perhaps, that such a categorization can be more justly used to label contemporary theologians. As Hart writes, "The notion that, from the patristic period to the present, the Trinitarian theologies of the Eastern and Western catholic traditions have obeyed contrary logics and have in consequence arrived at conclusions inimical each to the other—a particularly tedious, persistent, and pernicious falsehood—will no doubt one day fade away from want of documentary evidence. At present, however, it serves too many interests for theological scholarship to dispense with it too casually." David Bentley Hart, "The Mirror of the Infinite: Gregory of Nyssa on the Vestigia Trinitatis," *Modern Theology* 18, no. 4 (2002): 541. See also Stephen R. Holmes, *The Quest for the Trinity: The Doctrine of God in Scripture, History and Modernity* (Downers Grove, IL: IVP Academic, 2012). For an overview of the link between the Trinity and the church in the early church see Finbarr Clancy, "*Ecclesia de Trinitate* in the Latin Fathers: Inspirational Source for Congar's Ecclesiology," in *The Mystery of the Holy Trinity in the Fathers of the Church*, ed. D. Vincent Twomy and Lewis Ayres (Dublin: Four Courts, 2007), 161–93.

10. See section 2.2.

Godhead is immediately apparent—where the unity and diversity of the Trinity are observed simultaneously. For this reason, the relationship between Spirit Christology and the Trinity is a prominent area of current research.[11] Gary Badcock comments, "What is required is a developed and integrated pneumatological Christology and Christological pneumatology that can be taken up in their reciprocity into trinitarian theology."[12] Ralph Del Colle similarly makes a significant methodological claim that "Spirit Christology in contrast to Logos Christology is more thoroughly Trinitarian."[13] He consequently argues that "the task remains to negotiate the desired Trinitarianism via the newly worked Spirit Christology."[14]

Chapter 2's discussion of Spirit Christology noted its close relationship with the immanent Trinity, concluding that a coherent Spirit-Christology makes the following two affirmations. First, Jesus Christ our Lord is fully and uniquely the person of the Son and fully and uniquely anointed by the Spirit. Second, within the incarnation the identity and missions of the Son and the Spirit are logically and chronologically synchronous (without priority), distinct (without confusion), and interdependent (without separation). This chapter's objective is to determine the implications of these two affirmations for the immanent Trinity.

11. See the collection of articles in Bradford E. Hinze and D. Lyle Dabney, eds., *Advents of the Spirit: An Introduction to the Current Study of Pneumatology* (Milwaukee: Marquette University Press, 2001), 302–46.

12. Gary D. Badcock, *Light of Truth and Fire of Love: A Theology of the Holy Spirit* (Grand Rapids: Eerdmans, 1997), 232.

13. Ralph Del Colle, "A Response to Jürgen Moltmann and David Coffey," in *Advents of the Spirit: An Introduction to the Current Study of Pneumatology*, ed. Bradford E. Hinze and D. Lyle Dabney (Milwaukee: Marquette University Press, 2005), 339.

14. Ibid. See also Philip J. Rosato, "Spirit Christology as Access to Trinitarian Theology," in *God's Life in Trinity*, ed. Miroslav Volf and Michael Welker (Minneapolis: Fortress Press, 2006), 172–76.

The initial stages of the path to be traced are similar to those outlined by Gary Badcock toward the end of *Light of Truth and Fire of Love*.[15] Badcock suggests that the reciprocal relations observed between the Son and the Spirit in a developed Spirit Christology be taken into an understanding of the immanent Trinity. Badcock examines three conceptions of inner-Trinitarian reciprocity, namely Balthasar's "Trinitarian inversion" model, *energeia*, and *perichoresis*. He concludes, "[T]he doctrine of *perichoresis* must assume new importance if the idea of inner-trinitarian reciprocity is to be developed . . . into a broadly social doctrine of the Trinity."[16] Recognizing the contribution of Richard of St. Victor, who argues that because God is love, he must necessarily be triune community, Badcock explores the nature of such a relational Trinitarian ontology.[17]

Badcock notes that in the economy the relationships between the Son and the Spirit are not identical. For example, the Spirit anoints the Son, but the Son does not anoint the Spirit. Taking this insight into the immanent Trinity means that the relationships between the persons of the Trinity can be given specific content. And this includes not only the relationship between the Son and the Spirit, but also each person's relationship with the Father.[18] For

15. Badcock, *Light of Truth and Fire of Love*, 212–56.

16. Ibid., 243. Given later discussions, note here that Badcock immediately clarifies this comment: "It is questionable, however, whether the doctrine of *perichoresis* itself can bear all the weight necessary for the development of the idea of reciprocity in the inner-trinitarian sense, since it was not originally developed with this problem in mind." This clarification is directed toward Moltmann's Trinitarian understanding, about which Badcock comments that Moltmann relies "on *perichoresis* as the *sole* principle of Trinitarian unity" (ibid., 243). Note also that while Badcock uses the terminology of social Trinitarianism, there is no implication of tritheism, as has recently become a more common way of interpreting this phrase. Badcock is expressing a preference for what is termed in this research a *relational ontology*. For a detailed explanation of this term see section 7.3.

17. Badcock has reservations about Richard's work, however, particularly the lack of an economic grounding where the Spirit and Son's reciprocity are evidenced (ibid., 246–52). See also Richard of St. Victor, *On the Trinity*, trans. Ruben Angelici (Eugene, OR: Cascade, 2011).

18. Badcock, *Light of Truth and Fire of Love*, 254–55.

any relation of the Spirit to the Son, for example, whether active or passive, is a relationship of the Spirit to the "Son of the Father." The relationship between the Son and the Spirit is thus inclusive of the Father as well. In such a way, Badcock argues that the nature of the relationships as evidenced in the economy can be applied (with careful qualifications)[19] to the relationships within the immanent Trinity. The missions reveal something of the processions. The question of exactly what is the resulting picture of God *in se* when the reality of the economic relationships is applied to the immanent Trinity is a question that Badcock leaves tantalizingly unanswered. He finishes on a constructive note, though, claiming "the reorientation of the doctrine of the Trinity to the concrete content of the economy of salvation undoubtedly provides a fruitful basis for theological reflection."[20]

Accepting the validity of Badcock's approach, the following discussion will describe and evaluate three recent and explicit attempts to boldly apply the insights of Spirit Christology to the development of not just general Trinitarian insights, but a clearer understanding of God's intrinsic nature. First, there is the proposal of David Coffey, who argues that the biblical text requires two models of the Trinity. The traditional procession model is enveloped into a "comprehensive" model where the Holy Spirit is the mutual love shared between the Father and the Son. Following the analysis and terminology of chapter 2, I shall argue that this understanding is

19. Badcock notes an important "kenotic qualification." The terms Father, Son, and Spirit together with filiation and spiration are all analogies, so caution is required in applying them from human experience to the reality of God in himself, lest what we mean by such terms is overly conditioned by our human context. Reckless conclusions ought to be avoided (ibid., 255–56). While Badcock's caution here is vitally important, it should also be recognized that while still analogies, the names Father, Son, and Spirit deserve special preference as divinely revealed names for the persons of the Godhead. See for example Alvin Kimel, ed., *Speaking the Christian God: The Holy Trinity and the Challenge of Feminism* (Grand Rapids: Eerdmans, 1992).

20. Badcock, *Light of Truth and Fire of Love*, 256.

based on a Spirit-priority Christology, that it separates God's being and becoming, and that it diminishes the full personhood of the Holy Spirit. In contrast, Jürgen Moltmann's characterization of the Trinitarian implications of Spirit Christology fully identifies the Spirit's personhood, but does so by excessively separating the economic from the immanent Trinity and each of the members of the Trinity from each other. Finally, Myk Habets argues that a coherent Spirit Christology implies a "reconceived" understanding of the Trinity similar to that developed by Thomas Weinandy, where the Father begets the Son by the Spirit. This "relational ontology," it is argued, not only maintains a close connection between the economic and immanent Trinity (contra Moltmann) but also enables a clear personal role for the Holy Spirit within the Godhead (contra Coffey). Consequently, it is this understanding of the Trinity (with a few necessary clarifications and correctives) that shall be used analogically to determine a coherent Trinitarian Third Article Ecclesiology.

7.1 A Mutual-Love Model—David Coffey

David Coffey is an Australian Roman Catholic theologian who trained under Karl Rahner and Michael Schmaus at the University of Munich. He spent much of his academic life at the Australian Catholic Institute in Sydney, although the final ten years were at Marquette University. While his work is relatively unknown, it is highly suggestive and worthy of greater attention than it has received.[21]

21. See particularly David Coffey, *Deus Trinitas: The Doctrine of the Triune God* (New York: Oxford University Press, 1999). As Kelly notes, although this book is the "culmination of the author's previous writings" it has not turned out to be the "last word" in Coffey's theology, which has been added to and clarified in the following years. See Tony Kelly, "Deus Trinitatis (Review)," *The Australasian Catholic Record* 77 (2000): 365. Note also O'Byrne's monograph-length study of Coffey's understanding of the relationship between Spirit Christology and the Trinity.

An analysis of Coffey's work begins with his recasting of Rahner's *grundaxiom*. Recognizing its possibility for misconstrual, Coffey posits instead a three-stage system of epistemological enquiry, following Lonergan's analysis of human cognition: data, understanding, and judgment.[22] The first stage is the biblical Trinity: employing the best biblical research tools to gather *data* regarding the full Trinitarian picture painted within the Scriptures. The second stage is the immanent Trinity: analyzing the biblical data to "impart form to material which would otherwise remain relatively unordered."[23] This stage goes beyond data to *understanding*, and concludes with an affirmation that the results present a genuine (although potentially incomplete) picture of God's reality. The final stage is the economic Trinity: determining how the immanent Trinity is present and active in salvation history. O'Byrne comments, "This third stage is where the Trinitarian understanding, acquired in thinking about the 'immanent' Trinity, is brought to bear on soteriology, on the themes of grace, of ecclesiology, of the sacraments, and to the question of the work of the Spirit in other religions."[24] As discussed in chapter 3, there are significant overlaps between Coffey's epistemological approach and the "Wolterstorffian" methodology adopted in this research.[25]

Given this epistemological approach, what understanding of the immanent Trinity does Coffey derive? First, he notes two biblical

Declan O'Byrne, *Spirit Christology and Trinity in the Theology of David Coffey* (Oxford: Peter Lang, 2010).

22. Lonergan, beyond this, is not a key influence on Coffey. See O'Byrne, *Spirit Christology and Trinity in the Theology of David Coffey*, 174n47.
23. David Coffey, *Grace: The Gift of the Holy Spirit* (Milwaukee: Marquette University Press, 2011), 18.
24. O'Byrne, *Spirit Christology and Trinity in the Theology of David Coffey*, 192.
25. O'Byrne gives a detailed analysis of the points of divergence and similarity between Rahner's *grundaxiom* and Coffey's methodology, and makes a case for the latter's superiority. See ibid., 155–84. For a discussion comparing and contrasting Coffey's approach with a "Wolterstorffian" approach, see section 3.2.

schemas. "Classical" theology primarily focuses on Logos Christology, and derives its understanding of the immanent Trinity from this starting point. This is what Coffey terms a "descending" theology or the "mission scheme," in which the Father sends the Son who sends the Spirit. He suggests that "classical" theology has traditionally neglected the other "return scheme" or "ascending" theology, which speaks of a "return" of Jesus by the Spirit to the Father. While the biblical data focuses on the mission scheme (unsurprisingly given the Scriptures' *pro nobis* emphasis), the "return scheme" is certainly not absent, being "fleshed out in the Gospel by the Incarnation, life, redemptive death, Resurrection, and Ascension of Jesus, Word of God and Son of Man."[26]

Coffey's proposal is that the two biblical schemas lead naturally to two immanent Trinitarian understandings. The first mission schema corresponds to the "classical" western understanding of the Trinity, which Coffey terms the "procession model," where the Son is *begotten* by the Father and the Spirit *proceeds* from the Father and the Son (*filioque*). The second return schema corresponds to a "mutual love model" of the Trinity where the Spirit exists as the mutual love of the Father and the Son. As Coffey writes in a programmatic overview, "If Jesus is brought into being as the divine Son in humanity through the Father's radical bestowal of love on him, which love is the Holy Spirit, and if the response of Jesus is a love for the Father which ultimately is a return of this same Spirit, then in the immanent Trinity itself the Holy Spirit exists as the mutual love of the Father and the Son."[27]

26. Coffey, *Deus Trinitas*, 36.

27. David Coffey, "The 'Incarnation' of the Holy Spirit in Christ," *Theological Studies* 45 (1984): 479–80. This sentence is used again in David Coffey, "A Proper Mission of the Holy Spirit," *Theological Studies* 47, no. 2 (1986): 234. It is also used as the basis of the first three chapters of O'Byrne's book: O'Byrne, *Spirit Christology and Trinity in the Theology of David Coffey*, 24.

Coffey's mutual-love model is thus developed from the basis of a Spirit Christology. Although Coffey views Spirit Christology as complementary to traditional Logos Christology, there are several key areas where his understanding differs. First, whereas a Logos Christology has the hypostatic union as prior, followed (sometimes) by the Spirit's anointing, Coffey reverses this order and begins with Jesus' anointing as logically (but not chronologically) prior to the hypostatic union.[28] Second, a traditional Logos Christology has Jesus substantially the Son through the hypostatic union. Without diminishing this truth, Coffey notes that biblically there is equally a sense in which Jesus *becomes the Son* in his humanity, so that his Sonship is achieved as well as given.[29] Third, the human love with which Jesus loves the Father is itself the Holy Spirit, so that the Holy Spirit is "incarnated" in humanity.[30]

Coffey uses the two biblical schemas analogously to address questions about the diversity and unity within the inner life of the Godhead. So, the procession model, developed in analogy from the "outward" or "sending" missions of the Son and the Spirit, answers the question of how God is three. Coffey argues that the Father, who is the "source" of the Trinity, begets the Son out of "common

28. Consider this illustrative quote, for example: "But the bestowal of the Holy Spirit of which we speak in the Incarnation is an utterly radical one, the giving of the Spirit 'without measure.' We should not be surprised, therefore, that it is radically creative and radically assimilative. Thus in one act it calls the humanity of Jesus into existence and assimilates it to its divine source by sanctifying it with the fullness of sanctifying grace and drawing it into hypostatic union with that divine person who in the Trinity is the sole object of this love, viz. the Son. The love that *rests on* the Son in the Trinity *draws into union* with the Son when directed beyond the Trinity." David Coffey, "Spirit Christology and the Trinity," in *Advents of the Spirit: An Introduction to the Current Study of Pneumatology*, ed. Bradford E. Hinze and D. Lyle Dabney (Milwaukee: Marquette University Press, 2005), 326–27. This key quotation and the priority of the Spirit that it purports will be discussed further below.

29. Again, consider the following quote, also discussed below: "In Synoptic theology the divine Sonship of Jesus is actualised in his perfect obedience to God's special will for him, along which path he is guided by the empowering Spirit to his unique destiny." David Coffey, "The Holy Spirit as the Mutual Love of the Father and the Son," *Theological Studies* 51, no. 2 (1990): 202.

30. See section 5.1.

love"—the self-love of God.[31] It cannot be out of mutual love, for there is as yet no "other" to love, and it cannot be the Holy Spirit, because the traditional *taxis* states that the Son must come before the Holy Spirit.[32] The Son in response "loves" the Father, thus enabling a "mutual" love shared by Father and Son. It is from this "mutual" love that the Holy Spirit proceeds.[33] These affirmations can, according to Coffey, be accommodated within a "classical" Trinitarian understanding.

But Coffey goes further, by claiming that the second "mutual love" model of the immanent Trinity, developed in analogy from the "inward" or "returning" missions of the Son and Spirit to the Father, answers the question of how the three are one. Starting with the three persons that arise out of the procession model, Coffey asserts that they are unified because the Father and the Son love one another and their mutual love is the Holy Spirit. O'Byrne comments: "Although Coffey does not spell it out, this Trinitarian unity is presumably to be understood in terms of a perichoretic and ek-static love by which the Father and Son are made one by the *vinculum amoris* (the Holy Spirit)."[34] Coffey sees these two models as completely compatible, just as the mission and return schemas are completely compatible, but notes that the mutual-love model transcends the procession model as the properly "Trinitarian" model, as sending does not imply a return, but return does imply and incorporate sending.[35] It is quite evident that Coffey's objective in developing

31. Coffey (like many other theologians) distinguishes between common love (the generic love of God, which can include self-love) and mutual love (the love of one for another). See Coffey, "The Holy Spirit as the Mutual Love of the Father and the Son," 198.
32. Note that in this discussion time-based terminology is used, but it does not imply a chronological sequence. The language used is analogical. This unfortunate limitation of language is a feature of all discussions of begetting and procession within the Godhead.
33. For a detailed analysis of Coffey's use of the mutual-love model see Steven M. Studebaker, *The Trinitarian Vision of Jonathan Edwards and David Coffey* (New York: Cambria, 2011), 113–66.
34. O'Byrne, *Spirit Christology and Trinity in the Theology of David Coffey*, 212.
35. Coffey, "Spirit Christology and the Trinity," 325.

these theological proposals is to not only retain the classical western Trinitarian tradition, but to complement it with the understanding arising from a Spirit Christology, which he perceives as neglected biblical data. To do this requires a more complicated understanding of the immanent Trinity, that moves *first* from one to three, and *then* from three to one.

Coffey's work represents perhaps the first attempt to reconcile the recently developed Spirit Christology with Trinitarian dogma,[36] and as such it is certainly not without critics. Two theologians in particular have devoted sustained attention to it: Paul Molnar (as a Barthian scholar) and Neil Ormerod (from a classical western perspective). Both of these fellow Catholic theologians critique Coffey's baseline Spirit Christological position, his immanent Trinitarian conclusions, and his theological approach. The following analysis uses some of their critiques to examine Coffey's proposals.

Molnar accuses Coffey of having an adoptionist Christology. Initially it is generously labeled a "persistent appearance,"[37] but despite Coffey's protests,[38] Molnar is convinced Coffey's "thinking remains adoptionistic."[39] Coffey, in response,acknowledges that Spirit Christologies are "vulnerable to the charge of adoptionism," and need to explain clearly how they avoid this error. Nevertheless, Coffey maintains (with more than a hint of frustration) that adoptionism is avoided through his "reiterated, painstakingly explained basic thesis that, according to synoptic theology, the Holy Spirit in a single act created the sacred humanity of Jesus, sanctified it, and united it hypostatically to the pre-existent divine Word suffices for this

36. For an overview of other attempts see Myk Habets, *The Anointed Son: A Trinitarian Spirit Christology* (Eugene, OR: Pickwick, 2010), 188–220.

37. Paul D. Molnar, "Deus Trinitas: Some Dogmatic Implications of David Coffey's Biblical Approach to the Trinity," *Irish Theological Quarterly* 67, no. 1 (2002): 36.

38. For example, Coffey, *Deus Trinitas*, 62.

39. Paul D. Molnar, "Response to David Coffey," *Irish Theological Quarterly* 68, no. 1 (2003): 65.

purpose."[40] While there is significant miscommunication between Molnar and Coffey, reading *both* authors' work through a "hermeneutics of hospitality,"[41] the latter's critique points to some valid concerns. On the one hand, Molnar's labeling of Coffey's Christology as adoptionist cannot be justified. As O'Byrne fairly comments, the "term 'adoptionism' is too blunt an instrument to deal with Coffey's largely unprecedented theological proposals."[42] Coffey consistently maintains that there is no chronological point where Christ's humanity existed without being hypostatically united with the Logos. On the other hand, Coffey so emphasizes and prioritizes the role of the Spirit in the incarnation's facilitation and realization that he is definitely at risk of denying the Son's full personhood within Jesus. As such, the Spirit Christological analysis introduced in chapter 2 provides a "sharper instrument" (or a more nuanced approach) to label Coffey's understanding as a "Spirit-priority" Christological proposal.

Consider the three points distinguishing Coffey's position from a logos Christology. First, Coffey makes the hypostatic union a consequence of the anointing Spirit. Even though this does not imply a chronological ordering, problems remain. For even logically, how can the humanity of Christ exist without the person of the Son. As Weinandy explains: "It is not possible for the Holy Spirit to sanctify the humanity of Jesus prior to the union, for the humanity never exists separate or apart from the Son. Even on the level of logical priority, it is through the grace of union that the Holy Spirit sanctifies the humanity."[43] By giving priority to the Spirit in the incarnation,

40. David Coffey, "In Response to Paul Molnar," *Irish Theological Quarterly* 67, no. 4 (2002): 378.

41. Regarding the "hermeneutics of hospitality," see Thomas R. Thompson, "*Interpretatio in bonem partem*: Jürgen Moltmann on the Immanent Trinity," in *Theology as Conversation: The Significance of Dialogue in Historical and Contemporary Theology: A Festschrift for Daniel L. Migliore*, ed. Bruce L. McCormack and Kimlyn J. Bender (Grand Rapids: Eerdmans, 2009), 159.

42. O'Byrne, *Spirit Christology and Trinity in the Theology of David Coffey*, 105.

Coffey denies the fullness of the Son's personhood and this point alone justifies labeling his proposal a Spirit-priority Christology.[44]

Second, consider Coffey's assertion that Jesus' Sonship is *achieved* as well as given. There are some indications that Coffey is simply affirming that as the humanity of Jesus grows and develops, the Logos' inherent divinity becomes increasingly apparent and reveals itself more completely through Jesus' humanity. He writes, "The important thing to realize is that the 'theandric' Sonship is not a substitute for the Incarnation of the divine Word, but rather its concrete effect on the sacred humanity."[45] But such clear statements notwithstanding, the language is misleading—Sonship is experienced or displayed, it isn't *achieved*—and there are certainly many sustained passages where Coffey's arguments point in the opposite direction. To illustrate with just one example, when interacting with James Dunn's work, Coffey notes the distinction between the *experience* of Sonship (which Dunn comments on) and the *objective reality* of Sonship (which Coffey is affirming), and asserts: "Through the power of the Spirit the child is created, and so made holy, or sanctified, that he is the Son of God."[46] One would rather expect an affirmation that through the Spirit the Son of God *is* made human, and as a human he increasingly displays the reality of his incarnate Sonship through the Spirit. The problem, of course, is that if Sonship is gradually realized

43. Thomas Weinandy, "Christ and the Spirit (Book Review)," *The Thomist* 59, no. 4 (1995): 658. In Del Colle's book, there is an extended explanation of Coffey's Spirit Christology. Ralph Del Colle, *Christ and the Spirit: Spirit Christology in Trinitarian Perspective* (Oxford: Oxford University Press, 1993), 91–140. In this review, Weinandy comments that Del Colle interprets Coffey's position as chronologically sequential, in that the Spirit "first creates, then sanctifies (habitual grace) and then unites (grace of union)" (ibid., 123). Interpreted this way, Weinandy rightly claims that Coffey's position is either Nestorian or adoptionist. But Weinandy, again accurately, questions whether Coffey would agree with Del Colle's chronological characterization. One may similarly question whether Weinandy's interpretation of Del Colle's characterization of Coffey's position as chronologically sequential is entirely justified.

44. See section 2.2.

45. Coffey, "In Response to Paul Molnar," 376.

46. Coffey, "The Holy Spirit as the Mutual Love of the Father and the Son," 203–4.

or achieved in Jesus' humanity (and this language is not ambiguously referring to Sonship being experienced, but to an ontological reality), then Coffey is affirming that there are times when Jesus is less than the full Son—the very definition of a Spirit-priority Christology.[47]

The third distinction is Coffey's arguing that the Spirit is "incarnate." By this term, Coffey asserts that just as Jesus realized his divine Sonship to the full human extent, the love of Jesus for the Father—the Spirit—also reached its full human measure. Molnar's response quite rightly points out that the Spirit wasn't incarnate,[48] although it is doubtful that Coffey intended both uses to be identical. Labeling the Spirit "incarnate," even within quotation marks, is decidedly unusual terminology however, and again suggests an overemphasis on the Spirit. Such impressions are reinforced when Coffey talks about the "divinity" of Jesus' human nature, for overemphasizing the Spirit's communing role leads directly to the confusion of divinity and humanity. For example, Coffey writes that "[t]he divinity of Christ is the supreme actualisation of humanity under grace, of his individual human nature under the unique grace of the incarnation."[49] And again, "[T]he divinity of Christ is not something different from his humanity; it is the humanity, i.e. human nature at the peak of its possibility."[50] O'Byrne argues that Coffey's language is simply expressing an observable divinity, and that "human" divinity needs to be sharply distinguished from God's inherent divinity.[51] If so, one wonders why Coffey would choose terminology that so clearly invites the accusation of confusing the two natures. Ormerod suggests an alternative explanation, which

47. See section 2.2.
48. Molnar, "Deus Trinitas: Some Dogmatic Implications of David Coffey's Biblical Approach to the Trinity," 50n81.
49. Coffey, *Deus Trinitas*, 162.
50. Coffey, "The 'Incarnation' of the Holy Spirit in Christ," 467.
51. O'Byrne, *Spirit Christology and Trinity in the Theology of David Coffey*, 106.

is that Coffey is confusing humanity and divinity because he has confused nature and person.[52] He asks, "What is implied when it is stated that the divinity of Christ is not ontologically something different from his humanity? If the divinity refers to the divine nature, then clearly there is a significant ontological difference. If it refers to the divine person of the Logos, then we find confusion between the categories of person and nature at work."[53]

I would argue along similar lines that Coffey has a compositional understanding of the hypostatic union. Consider this comment: "Christ had a concrete human nature, which was 'theandric' in this sense: it achieved the full potential of humanity for divinity."[54] The picture that Coffey paints, coarsely, is that of the eternal Son pouring himself into the Spirit-created humanity of Christ. But as in all such understandings, the Son's divinity must be restricted to "fit" into the constraints of humanity. The much-preferred alternative to such Spirit-priority proposals that limit the full personhood of the Son is to make a logical but not existential distinction between the nature and person of the Son.[55] With this strategy, adopted by the early church fathers, the hypostatic union need not imply that the divine nature becomes human or the human nature divine, with the consequent raising of one or lowering of the other.

Summarizing, Coffey's Christology logically prioritizes the Spirit over the Son. As a direct result, Coffey prioritizes Spirit Christology

52. Ormerod finds many flaws within Coffey's proposals. The above analysis does not own all of Ormerod's critiques, merely noting some points of agreement. See particularly Ormerod, *The Trinity*; Neil Ormerod, "What Is the Goal of Systematic Theology?," *Irish Theological Quarterly* 74, no. 1 (2009): 38–52; and Neil Ormerod, "Two Points or Four?—Rahner and Lonergan on Trinity, Incarnation, Grace and Beatific Vision," *Theological Studies* 68, no. 3 (2007): 661–73.

53. Ormerod, *The Trinity*, 129.

54. David Coffey, "Response to Neil Ormerod, and Beyond," *Theological Studies* 68, no. 4 (2007): 911. See also David Coffey, "The Theandric Nature of Christ," *Theological Studies* 60, no. 3 (1999): 405–31. In this article Coffey develops the position outlined in the quote above.

55. As mentioned, see section 2.2 for a fuller discussion of Spirit-priority proposals and compositional understandings of the incarnation.

over Logos Christology, and the mutual-love model over the procession model of the immanent Trinity. While Coffey would most likely dispute the first point, the second and third he explicitly owns. Coffey argues that Spirit Christology is superior to Logos Christology because the former can incorporate the latter,[56] and that an immanent Trinitarian understanding based on return texts (the mutual-love model) is "comprehensive," while a model based on mission texts (the procession model) is partial.[57] Because the mutual-love model is "comprehensive," all the useful truth within the procession model can be incorporated within it.

Coffey illustrates this in several ways. First he notes that the traditional *taxis* of the procession model (Father→Son→Spirit) is retained in the "memory" of the mutual-love model, just as human relationships retain a memory of the original initiator and the beloved, even if they exist presently as perfectly symmetrical. Second, he comments that when the mutual love of the Father and Son (which is the Holy Spirit) is extended beyond the Trinity, it draws into union with the Son as the Son is the entelechy of the Spirit, which explains the inversion of the traditional *taxis* in the incarnation with the Son being humanly hypostatized through the Spirit.[58] Third, Coffey argues that when the Son sends the Holy Spirit to the church, this is simply the inseparable other component of his human love for God, for (following Rahner) love of God and neighbor are anthropologically inseparable.[59] For Coffey, then, the two models don't need to be harmonized; they are "two irreducible Trinitarian data."[60] Rather the procession model is taken up within and eclipsed

56. Coffey, "Spirit Christology and the Trinity," 317–18.
57. Ibid., 325.
58. Ibid., 327.
59. See particularly Coffey, "The 'Incarnation' of the Holy Spirit in Christ," 476–78. See also Coffey, "Spirit Christology and the Trinity," 327. Note that this particular insight was discussed in section 5.1.
60. Coffey, "A Proper Mission of the Holy Spirit," 235.

by the mutual-love model. As Coffey notes, "[W]hat I intend is a state of affairs [the mutual-love model] into which its necessary preconditions [the procession model] are integrated."[61]

There is certainly significant insight in these observations, which has already been and will be further used in this research.[62] But Coffey's immanent Trinitarian understanding has underlying problems. To begin, the mutual-love model is not "comprehensive," at least not in the way the word is usually understood. If it were comprehensive, then two models wouldn't be needed. While Coffey has ingeniously inserted some of the procession model's content into the mutual-love model, two features restrict the latter's comprehensiveness. First, the substantive information inserted (e.g., the *filioque*) is sourced from the procession model, and doesn't arise naturally out of the latter model. Second, the procession model contains information that cannot be incorporated into the mutual-love model. For example, the derivation of God's diversity cannot be inserted into the "comprehensive" mutual-love model, for God's diversity is its starting point.

Ormerod suggests this lack of synthesis "could reflect a Kantian assumption that our interpretations are simply projections onto the reality of God, not genuine meanings which find their ground in reality,"[63] but this goes significantly too far. The nature of analogy does not require that a single model be developed.[64] It does require, however, that if multiple models are used to describe a single reality, then it must be clear which aspect of reality is informed by each model.[65] To achieve such clarity, Coffey posits two states to God's

61. Coffey, "Spirit Christology and the Trinity," 331.

62. The reason for this is that the "mutual love" model is not dissimilar from Weinandy's "reconceived" model, which (it is argued below) is the understanding of the immanent Trinity that most closely aligns with the biblical data.

63. Ormerod, *The Trinity*, 91.

64. See for example Coffey's response to Ormerod on this point. Coffey, "Response to Neil Ormerod, and Beyond," 907–8.

existence, which he refers to as the Trinity *in fieri* (in the state of becoming) and *in facto esse* (in the state of constituted being). Questions about the former are answered in the procession model, and questions about the latter in the mutual-love model. Coffey makes no suggestion that these are temporal states, but rather a logical order within the Godhead. And Coffey is well aware of the problem arising from such a distinction. He writes, "Immediately there arises an objection on the grounds that the eternity and perfection of the Trinity rule out any consideration of it *in fieri*. However, while readily granting the grounds of the objection, I have to say that the distinction itself remains unavoidable, because it is imposed by the Monarchy of the Father and the consequent *taxis*."[66]

But surely the distinction is not unavoidable. The monarchy of the Father does not necessarily imply two states within the Trinity, because the monarchy of the Father, together with the begetting of the Son and the procession of the Spirit can all be considered as eternally occurring. If the Father is eternally begetting the Son, then the *in fieri* Trinity *is exactly identified* with the *in facto esse* Trinity, and the distinction becomes meaningless. This is, I believe, the key challenge with Coffey's proposal, and gets to the heart of his understanding. In order to accommodate the "new" Spirit Christological texts *and* to retain the monarchy, Coffey believes he must posit two Trinities, with the first encapsulated and taken up into the second. While there are some aspects of the *in fieri* Trinity that can be incorporated into the *in facto esse* Trinity, there are core aspects that cannot. Even those that are incorporated are downplayed,

65. A good example is the wave-particle duality of quantum physics. By suggesting that photons sometimes act like particles and sometimes like waves, physicists use two models or analogies to explain reality. No attempt is made to make waves like particles or particles like waves, but the fact that two models are needed to explain a complex reality in no way affects the physicist's belief in the reality of the photons they are modeling.

66. Coffey, "Spirit Christology and the Trinity," 330.

because they do not naturally arise out of the *in facto esse* Trinitarian model. The result is that in essence Coffey has been selective in choosing which aspects of the biblical Trinity (as he terms it) to extrapolate into the immanent Trinity. Specifically, the diversity of the Trinity is essentially taken as its starting point, and its intrinsic or foundational unity is diminished.

Another flaw with Coffey's immanent Trinitarian understanding is that it doesn't adequately acknowledge the personhood of the Holy Spirit, who has no distinctly personal activity within the Trinity's inner life. Weinandy comments:

> Firstly, the Holy Spirit still remains passive within the Trinitarian life. He is merely the love that the Father and the Son bestow upon one another. Secondly, because of this passivity it is difficult to see why the Holy Spirit should be designated a "person"—a distinct subject—along with the Father and the Son. This has been a traditional problem within the whole history of Trinitarian development. I believe that the Holy Spirit will only be properly recognised as a distinct person or subject when his singular activity within the Trinity is perceived.[67]

Is it possible to develop an understanding of the immanent Trinity that incorporates both the Spirit Christological "return" texts *and* the "mission" texts, that is, a model that more adequately coordinates the processions and missions of God, while also giving the Holy Spirit an active role within the inner life of the Trinity, thus ensuring the Spirit's genuine personhood? This is precisely what Moltmann attempts. Although, as becomes clear in the following discussion, to do so requires him to make unacceptable compromises.

7.2 A Hard Social Model—Jürgen Moltmann

Chapter 2 introduced the relationship between Moltmann's Christological and Trinitarian understandings, and recognized his

67. Weinandy, "Christ and the Spirit (Book Review)," 657.

tendency to excessively separate the persons and work of the Son and the Spirit. It was noted in that discussion that two features of Moltmann's understanding—panentheism and a form of *perichoretic* unity—are common features of Son-Spirit-separation proposals, and that both have significant biblical and logical inconsistencies. The following builds on this previous discussion.

The analysis begins with Moltmann's recasting of Rahner's *grundaxiom*. Moltmann recognizes four conceptions of the Trinity, the first three of which could (with some qualifications) be termed "economic" Trinities, and the last an "immanent" Trinity. The first "Monarchical Trinity" refers specifically to the revelation of God to humanity. In this model the Son is God's self-communication and the Spirit is specifically the Spirit of the Son: the "revealedness," God's efficacious presence in the world. Moltmann claims that according to the *grundaxiom*, only this model is equated with the immanent Trinity meaning that "we can only reach the 'God for us' and can recognise nothing of 'God in Godself.'"[68] Consequently, Moltmann argues that the immanent Trinity collapses into the economic such that "there is no 'immanent Trinity' in the theologies of Karl Barth and Karl Rahner."[69] Moltmann also notes that in the Monarchical Trinity the Holy Spirit has no independent personhood. It is always and only God's efficacious presence, and never its own activity source. The second "Historical Trinity" articulates the intrinsically eschatological and evolving nature of Moltmann's Trinitarian formulation in which "the economic Trinity not only reveals the immanent Trinity; it also has a retroactive effect on it."[70] The third

68. Jürgen Moltmann, "The Trinitarian Personhood of the Holy Spirit," in *Advents of the Spirit: An Introduction to the Current Study of Pneumatology*, trans. D. Lyle Dabney, ed. Bradford E. Hinze and D. Lyle Dabney (Milwaukee: Marquette University Press, 2005), 305.
69. Ibid.
70. Jürgen Moltmann, *The Trinity and the Kingdom: The Doctrine of God* (Minneapolis: Fortress Press, 1981), 160.

"Eucharistic Trinity" is the reversal of the Monarchical Trinity, with internal dynamics derived as "the energies of the Spirit flow back to the Son and to the Father."[71] Moltmann develops this model from those "Spirit Christological" texts that talk of the Son's human return to the Father by the Spirit.

The final "Doxological Trinity" views God as he is in himself.[72] As such, it transcends and completes the revelation of the previous economic Trinities. Moltmann consequently does not see a perfect identification between the economic and immanent Trinities, but rather a lack of discrepancy. He writes: "Statements about the immanent Trinity must not contradict statements about the economic Trinity. Statements about the economic Trinity must correspond to doxological statements about the immanent Trinity."[73] This less stringent requirement enables Moltmann significant flexibility in his description of the immanent Godhead, picturing the Trinity essentially as an egalitarian society—a society of equals who all initiate action and are similarly acted upon, but with no preconceived or "normal" *taxis*. Moltmann writes, "To love and praise God as God is in himself means to see God in his perfection: the perfect Being, the perfect Community. . . . The immanent Trinity is the community of perfect love and shows the structure of perfect Community."[74]

71. Moltmann, "The Trinitarian Personhood of the Holy Spirit," 308.
72. Note however, that the very idea of a doxological Trinity "is based, not on the difference between the essential nature and the activity of God *ad extra*, but rather in the consciousness of the intending subject and in the nature of his or her linguistic acts." Badcock, *Light of Truth and Fire of Love*, 207. Despite Moltmann never directly referencing this distinction between subjective experience and ontological reality, it is difficult to perceive how you can praise God in himself without the prior belief that there is a God in himself, separate to his economic acts, that exists and therefore can be praised. Badcock, again: "Does not the entire scheme in fact depend upon a presupposed, and perhaps hidden, ontological distinction underlying the linguistic distinction?" (ibid., 208). The following discussion assumes that a metaphysics of the immanent Trinity is implicitly acknowledged by Moltmann, even though he explicitly rejects the classical distinction. See Moltmann, *The Trinity and the Kingdom*, 151–54.
73. Moltmann, *The Trinity and the Kingdom*, 154.

While differences exist, there are overlaps here with Coffey's theological proposals. Moltmann's Monarchical Trinity aligns with Coffey's procession model. Both are based on the "mission" texts of God's self-communication, and reference the traditional western Trinitarian understanding. Similarly, Moltmann's Eucharistic Trinity aligns with Coffey's "return" model. Both are based on the Spirit Christological texts of humanity's participation in Christ through the Spirit, and Christ and humanity being drawn into the Trinitarian life.[75] But where Coffey's rigorous identification between the biblical and immanent Trinity leads him to the conclusion that the immanent Trinity is best explained by a "mutual love" model, Moltmann's more flexible link enables him to posit the immanent Trinity as a perichoretic community with independent persons and no pre-set patterns. As Badcock explains, "The Father, the Son and the Holy Spirit have a history of mutual relations that are variable rather than eternally unchanging."[76]

One significant advantage of this approach over Coffey's is that it fully recognizes the Spirit's personhood. In terms reminiscent of Weinandy's comments about Coffey above, Moltmann writes:

> If one wants to maintain the full divine personhood of the Holy Spirit . . . one should say: the Holy Spirit "ek-sists" in the mutual love of the Father and the Son, but is not this love itself, because this mutual love is already there in the mutual relationships of the Father and the Son. . . . The Spirit is not only the "Spirit of the Father" and not only the "Spirit of the Son" and not only the "Spirit of the Father and the Son" but God

74. Moltmann, "The Trinitarian Personhood of the Holy Spirit," 311.
75. Del Colle insightfully recognizes the similarities between Coffey's and Moltmann's understandings of the Trinity. See Ralph Del Colle, "A Response to Jürgen Moltmann and David Coffey," in *Advents of the Spirit: An Introduction to the Current Study of Pneumatology*, ed. Bradford E. Hinze and D. Lyle Dabney (Milwaukee: Marquette University Press, 2005), 341. Del Colle also suggests that Moltmann's "doxological model is best lined up (although we may have an argument here) with Coffey's mutual-love model" (ibid.). This discussion argues (in contrast) that the different understandings the two theologians take to revising Rahner's *grundaxiom* lead to significantly different understandings of the "immanent" Trinity.
76. Badcock, *Light of Truth and Fire of Love*, 202.

> in Godself and in his Godhead, a divine Person in different relationships to the Father and to the Son.[77]

It also enables Moltmann to explain why Pentecost follows Calvary. Through his eschatological understanding, the Trinitarian relations genuinely change through the Godhead's interaction with creation. As such, it is only after the cross that the Spirit becomes the Spirit of Christ, so that *Christ* can send the Spirit to the church.[78]

Moltmann's proposals are certainly suggestive, but they have disadvantages beyond those already discussed.[79] First, there are issues surrounding the eschatological and evolving nature of Moltmann's Trinity. Badcock and Olson both note that if the immanent Trinity is in process and is genuinely affected by his interactions with creation, then there is no coherence behind the concept of a revealer underlying the revelation. God is simply reduced to his actions *ad extra*.[80] Given that Moltmann *defines* God as the one who embraces death and suffering, Hill similarly questions how such a God can continue to exist after suffering is overcome. Badcock concludes: "Moltmann's Trinitarianism may well be consistent with the idea of an eternally and infinitely unfolding process, but not, it would seem, with biblical eschatological ideas, in which the consummation will finally be realised."[81]

77. Moltmann, "The Trinitarian Personhood of the Holy Spirit," 313. See also Moltmann, *The Trinity and the Kingdom*, 125–26, 142–43.
78. John 16:7. See also Moltmann, *The Trinity and the Kingdom*, 122–28. As noted later in this chapter, although Moltmann's explanation at this point is useful and coherent, it requires a separation between the persons and the economic and the immanent Trinity that is neither orthodox nor adopted within this research.
79. See section 2.2.
80. See Badcock, *Light of Truth and Fire of Love*, 209–10. Also, Roger Olson, "Trinity and Eschatology: The Historical Being of God in Jürgen Moltmann and Wolfhart Pannenberg," *Scottish Journal of Theology* 36, no. 2 (1983): 221.
81. Badcock, *Light of Truth and Fire of Love*, 211. See also William J. Hill, *The Three-Personed God: The Trinity as a Mystery of Salvation* (Washington, DC: Catholic University of America Press, 1982), 175.

Second, there are challenges reconciling Moltmann's egalitarian, perichoretic Trinitarian community with more orthodox requirements. These come into sharpest relief when Moltmann talks of the Father's monarchy. He writes:

> It is true that the Trinity is constituted with the Father as starting point, inasmuch as he is understood as being "the origin of the Godhead." But this "monarchy of the Father" only applies to the constitution of the Trinity. It has no validity within the eternal circulation of the divine life, and none in the perichoretic unity of the Trinity. Here the three Persons are all equal; they live and are manifested in one another and through one another.[82]

Moltmann faces a conundrum here. Orthodoxy recognizes the Father's monarchy.[83] But an egalitarian Trinity can have no monarch. Moltmann thus posits two parts to God's being—existence and relationality. In Trinitarian existence, the Father is primary and source. In Trinitarian relationship, there is not even a first among equals. Clearly there are similarities here with Coffey's distinction between God *in fieri* and God *in facto esse*. And all the same problems arise.[84] On what basis can one suggest that "existence" and "relations" are so distinct? Surely God's being is constituted in relationship, and to posit otherwise is to abandon God's simple, perfect, and eternal

82. Moltmann, *The Trinity and the Kingdom*, 175.

83. It is worth noting here that a number of contemporary theologians locate the monarchy in the entire Godhead and not merely with the person of the Father. Perhaps this would have been a more satisfactory solution to Moltmann's conundrum. See for example Thomas F. Torrance, *Trinitarian Perspectives: Toward Doctrinal Agreement* (Edinburgh: T. & T. Clark, 1994), 120. See also Joseph A. Bracken, "Trinitarian Spirit Christologies: In Need of a New Metaphysics?" *Theological Studies* 72, no. 4 (2011): 750–67; and Myk Habets, "Getting Beyond the *Filioque* with Third Article Theology," in *Ecumenical Perspectives on the Filioque for the 21st Century*, ed. Myk Habets (London: Bloomsbury / T. & T. Clark, 2014), 211–30.

84. Even sympathetic commentators to Moltmann's work find this move puzzling. Bauckham comments: "It is true that, at one of the points where Moltmann is slavishly and unnecessarily faithful to features of traditional Trinitarian theology, he does retain the traditional idea of the Father as sole source of Godhead (the so-called monarchy of the Father)." Richard Bauckham, "Jürgen Moltmann's *The Trinity and the Kingdom of God* and the Question of Pluralism," in *The Trinity in a Pluralistic Age*, ed. Kevin J. Vanhoozer (Grand Rapids: Eerdmans, 1997), 158.

nature. Moreover, such a flattening of the *taxis* of the immanent Trinity doesn't accurately reflect the economic revelation.[85]

Third, the minimal requirement that the immanent Trinity should not "contradict" the economic Trinities provides significant flexibility. But with such latitude, how can we ever be certain that our conception of the immanent Trinity is genuine? The risk here is that we will simply fashion the Trinity into what we wish it to be. Moltmann uses this latitude to its full extent, positing a Trinity where all possible permutations of different relationships can and do occur, but that nevertheless maintains an egalitarian equality. The realization that Moltmann's Trinitarian conception corresponds so closely to a modern western image of an ideal society greatly elevates the concern that such a "projectionist" error has been made. If God is a genuine reality and not merely the figment of our doxological imaginations, then what we say of him must correspond to that reality in order to be genuinely true. But the key points of Moltmann's immanent Trinity—the egalitarian and inherently flexible nature of the Trinitarian relationships—are not and cannot be constructed from the data of the economic Trinities he has used. The characteristics of Moltmann's immanent Trinitarian understanding are not contradicted, but neither are they well illustrated. If the particularities of the economy are merely particularities and not exemplars, then any attempt to generalize them is futile. Such generalizations may be useful for solving modern social problems, but whether they accurately reflect God's immanent nature is highly questionable.[86]

85. Of course, Moltmann's scheme does not require a perfect correspondence between the economic and immanent Trinity. It is interesting to note here that Moltmann's understanding of the *in fieri* Trinity is quite similar to Weinandy's "reconceived" Trinity. See for example Thomas Weinandy, *The Father's Spirit of Sonship: Reconceiving the Trinity* (Edinburgh: T. & T. Clark, 1995), 71n32.

86. The comments of C. S. Lewis (obviously independent and prior) are perhaps too emphatic as a response to Moltmann's work: "What makes some theological works like sawdust to me is

Both Moltmann and Coffey attempt to determine the implications Spirit Christology has on our understanding of the immanent Trinity. Moltmann finds a place for the genuine personhood of the Holy Spirit in a hard social model, but at the expense of removing the strong identity between the economic and immanent Trinity, and so reducing our knowledge of God to supposition. Coffey, in contrast, maintains a strong link between the economic and immanent Trinities in developing a mutual-love model, but his inadequate Spirit Christology leads to an impersonal characterization of the Spirit's immanent identity. Both understandings also require a distinction between the Trinity's becoming and present existence, which compromises the perfection and simplicity of the Godhead. Is there an immanent Trinitarian model that equates God's being and becoming, maintains a strong link between the immanent and economic Trinity while also simultaneously positing an active personal role for the Holy Spirit within the Trinity's inner life? The next section argues that Weinandy's "reconceived" understanding of the immanent Trinity, and its link to Spirit Christology as developed by Habets, has precisely these features.

7.3 A "Reconceived" Model—Weinandy and Habets

The "reconceived" understanding of the immanent Trinity proposed by Weinandy and endorsed by Habets is described as follows:

> [T]he Father begets the Son in or by the Holy Spirit. The Son is begotten by the Father in the Spirit and thus the Spirit simultaneously proceeds from the Father as the one in whom the Son is begotten. The

the way authors can go on discussing how far certain positions are adjustable to contemporary thought, or beneficial in relation to social problems, or 'have a future' before them, but never squarely ask what grounds we have for supposing them to be true accounts of any objective reality. As if we were trying to make rather than to learn. Have we no Other to reckon with?" C. S. Lewis, *Prayer: Letters to Malcolm* (London: Fount, 1964), 106.

> Son, being begotten in the Spirit, simultaneously loves the Father in the same Spirit by which he himself is begotten (is Loved).[87]

This section explains how this model emerges from a coherent Spirit Christology, and demonstrates that it fulfills the criteria mentioned above.

Weinandy and Habets arrive at a similar understanding of the immanent Trinity, although they approach it from different (but overlapping) perspectives. Weinandy uses a wide range of biblical and traditional sources, and motivated particularly by his observations of recent ecumenical efforts, argues that the "trinitarian tradition, of both the East and the West, was converging on something like my thesis."[88] Habets, in contrast, develops a coherent Spirit Christology in which the Son and Spirit are distinct but inseparable, and then (following a survey of existing Catholic and Protestant formulations) concludes that Weinandy's understanding of the Trinity is "compatible with the Spirit Christology I am developing."[89] Both formulations adopt a similar set of presuppositions. First, they both critically accept Rahner's *grundaxiom*, although Habets has reservations about the "vice versa," noting a necessary "apophatic" reticence.[90] For Habets, the economic Trinity is metaphysically identified with the immanent Trinity, but there is no suggestion that the entire identity of God is revealed in salvation history.[91] Second, both formulations recognize that while the Bible speaks functionally, it is acceptable and necessary to translate these patterns into an ontological understanding. In other words, the way the triune

87. Weinandy, *The Father's Spirit of Sonship*, 17. See also Habets, *The Anointed Son*, 224. Habets has also extended his formulation of Weinandy's understanding. See Myk Habets, "*Filioque? Nein*: A Proposal for Coherent Coinherence," in *Trinitarian Theology after Barth*, ed. Myk Habets and Phillip Tolliday (Eugene, OR: Pickwick, 2011), 161–202.
88. Weinandy, *The Father's Spirit of Sonship*, 18.
89. Habets, *The Anointed Son*, 223.
90. See ibid., 220. See also Weinandy, *The Father's Spirit of Sonship*, 22.
91. See Habets, *The Anointed Son*, 220. Weinandy, *The Father's Spirit of Sonship*, 22.

God acts in salvation history accurately reveals who God actually is. Both thus share a commitment to divine simplicity, where God's being is his act. In addition to Scripture, Weinandy reaches and works out this position using Roman Catholic sources, most notably Thomas Aquinas, while Habets uses Reformed resources, particularly Thomas Torrance.

Following Habets's Spirit Christological development, the first step is to notice the recurrent scriptural pattern where the Father incarnates (or alternatively sends, or names, or acts through) the Son/Logos by the Spirit, and the Son responds to the Father by precisely the same Spirit through which he is incarnated (or alternatively sent, or named, or acted through). Habets discusses five gospel "disclosure episodes" or "messianic *kairoi*"[92] in the synoptic gospels[93] as exemplars of this pattern.[94] First, the conception, where the Father incarnates the Son by the Spirit (cf. Luke 1:35).[95] Weinandy significantly comments that "[t]he Father begetting his Son in the womb of Mary by the Holy Spirit becomes, I believe, a temporal icon of his eternally begetting the Son by the Holy Spirit."[96] Second, the baptism of Jesus, where the Father declares Jesus as his Son by the Spirit (cf. Matt. 3:16).[97] Third, Jesus' ministry broadly conceived, where he is revealed as the Son through the Spirit's anointing of his words and works (cf. Luke 4:16-19).[98] For example, Habets comments on Jesus' Nazareth Manifesto that "Luke is clearly presenting Jesus' relationship with

92. Habets has recently changed the term he uses to refer to these episodes to more accurately reflect the Spirit-Christological features of the texts. Habets, "Getting Beyond the *Filioque* with Third Article Theology," 211–30.

93. He also notes how the same pattern recurs in John's Gospel and the epistles.

94. Habets actually references six episodes. However, the sixth—Christ's exaltation—does not clearly exemplify the pattern noted above, as the exalted Christ sends the Spirit. This is discussed further below.

95. Habets, *The Anointed Son*, 123–31. Habets provides a much more comprehensive analysis. These verses are merely exemplars.

96. Weinandy, *The Father's Spirit of Sonship*, 42.

97. Habets, *The Anointed Son*, 131–44.

98. Ibid., 144–60.

the Spirit as the power of his ministry and thus a key to a correct understanding of his identity."[99] Fourth, Jesus' passion, where it is by the Spirit that Jesus offers himself to God (cf. Heb. 9:14).[100] Weinandy comments that "if 'Abba' can only be spoken in the Spirit (see Gal 4:6; Rom 8:15) then it is in the crucifixion that we witness most clearly that eternal bond of love forged in the Spirit between the Father and the Son."[101] Fifth, Jesus' resurrection, where it was by the Spirit that Jesus was raised and declared to be the Son of God with power (cf. Rom. 8:11).[102]

In addition to these five *gospel* "messianic kairoi," the same pattern can be observed both prior to and following the incarnation. Prior, the world was created by the Father speaking the Word through the Spirit (cf. Gen. 1:1-3; John 1:3; etc.) and God's Word was spoken to and through the prophets by God's Spirit (cf. Zech. 7:11-12).[103] Following the incarnation, Weinandy notes that Christian conversion follows the same pattern, where we have died with Christ and been raised with him, and now, it is *by the Spirit* that we are identified as sons and daughters of the Father (Rom. 8:14-16; Gal. 4:6-7). Weinandy writes, "The Holy Spirit, the Spirit of sonship, transforms us into the glorious image of God that is Christ fashioning us into sons of God."[104]

Turning from the economic to the immanent Trinity, and employing the presupposition that functional patterns in Scripture reveal ontological reality, Habets and Weinandy argue that the regular appearance of this pattern within time implies that the Father *eternally* begets the Son in or by the Spirit. For example, Weinandy

99. Ibid., 147.
100. Ibid., 160–70.
101. Weinandy, *The Father's Spirit of Sonship*, 29. See further ibid., 29–31.
102. Habets, *The Anointed Son*, 170–76. Although Habets clearly recognizes the Son was not passive in his resurrection.
103. The pattern is perhaps more "read into" the OT than evidently obvious within it *a priori*.
104. Weinandy, *The Father's Spirit of Sonship*, 35. For the overall discussion see ibid., 33–38.

writes: "It is inconceivable, especially if we assume that the persons of the Trinity reveal themselves as they are in themselves . . . thus acting *ad extra* as they act *ad intra*, that we would become sons and daughters of the Father in a manner different from that in which the eternal Son becomes Son."[105] And again, "If the Father incarnates the Son through the Holy Spirit—the Spirit of Sonship—then should not the Father also, within the immanent Trinity, beget the Son in the Holy Spirit?"[106] In this understanding, what the Father gives to the Son in the act of begetting him is precisely the Spirit of Sonship by which he returns love to the Father. Thus the begetting and the response are chronologically and logically synchronous. "All three persons, logically and ontologically, spring forth in one simultaneous, nonsequential eternal act in which each person of the Trinity subsistently defines, and equally, is subsistently defined by the other persons."[107]

What is being proposed by Weinandy and Habets is a "reconceived" understanding of the Trinity that is intrinsically and eternally dynamic. There is simultaneously an outward movement, where the Son and the Spirit are begotten and spirated by the Father, and an inward movement, where the Son returns the love of the Father by the Spirit given to him. As in both western and eastern Trinitarian understandings, the Father is the "originating person," the source of the Trinity, and the Son is the "personed person," begotten as the image of the Father. The key contrast with the west (where the Spirit proceeds from the Father *and the Son*) and the east (where the Spirit proceeds from the Father alone, or through the Son) is the role of the Spirit. The "reconceived" Trinity characterizes the Spirit as the "personing person." The Spirit proceeds from the Father as the

105. Ibid., 36.
106. Weinandy, "Christ and the Spirit (Book Review)," 658.
107. Habets, *The Anointed Son*, 223. See also Weinandy, *The Father's Spirit of Sonship*, 14–15.

one in whom the Son is begotten or personed, and at the same time is the Spirit of Sonship by which the Son returns love to the Father, and so "persons" the Father as Father. In short, the "originating person" (the Father) persons the "personed person" (the Son), in or by the "personing person" (the Spirit). The Spirit is the "personing person" not only for the Son but for the Father as well, because the Father is personed as the Father only through the response of love that the Son offers by the Spirit of Sonship given to him.[108]

This "reconceived" Trinitarian model has a number of advantages. First (contra Moltmann), it maintains a strong identity between the economic and immanent Trinity. To choose one pivotal example, it has already been noted that in a coherent Spirit Christology the identity and missions of the Son and the Spirit must be logically and chronologically synchronous, inseparable, and distinguishable. These characteristics are directly reflected in the "reconceived" Trinity, for just as in speaking Breath and Word emerge together as two synchronous, inseparable, but logically distinguishable parts of the one act, so the Son and Spirit are derived from the one begetting/spirating act of the Father.[109] As Habets writes, "As the Word of God, the Father breathes forth the Son which implies impulse and motion. This impulse or motion is the breath of God, the *pneuma*, hence

108. I am unaware of any precedents for the specific terminology used (originating person, personed person, personing person). There are, however, certainly precedents for using such labeling in Trinitarian analysis. Choosing just two of many examples, the utilization bears some similarities with Barth's famous Trinitarian terminology of *revealer, revealed, revealedness*. Karl Barth, *Church Dogmatics*, trans. G. W. Bromiley (Peabody, MA: Hendrickson, 2010), I/1, 348–83. More recently Grenz argued for an attribution of *naming, being named, name sharing*. Stanley J. Grenz, *The Named God and the Question of Being: A Trinitarian Theo-Ontology* (Louisville: Westminster John Knox, 2005), 290. Perhaps the closest example is Mühlen's designation of the Spirit as *one person in two persons*, discussed in section 8.3.

109. Similarly, and in contrast to the traditional understanding, knowing and loving can be considered as simultaneous. "While in human beings something must first be known before it is loved, in God the knowing and loving are simultaneous—the begetting and spirating come forth from the Father as distinct, but concurrent, acts." Weinandy, *The Father's Spirit of Sonship*, 71–72.

Word and Spirit together go out from the Father in a mutual, co-inhering relationship with each other."[110]

Second (contra Coffey), it enables the personhood of the Holy Spirit to be fully recognized. The Holy Spirit is not merely the mutual love of the Father and Son, and thus passive and impersonal, but "is given an active role within the Trinity that guarantees him a personal distinction."[111] This enables a new and profound understanding of *perichoresis* as action. *Perichoresis*, in this Trinitarian understanding, comes not *as a result* of the begetting or spirating within the Godhead—a secondary activity—but is the process of begetting and spirating *in itself*. So *perichoresis* is both *circumincessio* (active penetration) and *circuminsessio* (passive coinherence). Further, this mutual *perichoresis* (or begetting, spirating, return, etc.) is the very activity that characterizes all three persons as persons. "While the Son and Holy Spirit come forth from the Father, yet in the coming forth all three persons become who they are, and they do so precisely in reciprocally interacting upon one another, simultaneously fashioning one another to be who they are and so becoming who they are in themselves."[112] So the Father is the "originating person," in his begetting of the Son, and also is actively determined to be the *Father* as by the Spirit the Son responds to him in love. Similarly the Son is the "personed person" in his begottenness by the Father, and also is actively determined to be the *Son* by the Spirit of Sonship through whom he responds in filial love to the Father. And not just the Father and the Son but the Spirit too is personed in a unique subsisting relation. The Spirit is the "personing person," because he "subsists precisely as the one in whom the Father and the Son are named and thus personed and simultaneously the Spirit is named

110. Habets, *The Anointed Son*, 226.
111. Ibid., 225.
112. Weinandy, *The Father's Spirit of Sonship*, 78–79.

and personed."[113] As Weinandy summarizes, "The persons themselves are the co-inhering acts."[114] All three persons exist in subsistent relationship to one another through active interpenetration.

Third (contra both Coffey and Moltmann), there is no distinction between God's being and becoming, between the Trinity *in fieri* and *in facto esse*. God always exists in the Father's eternal and ongoing begetting of the Son by the Holy Spirit. As such, God's simplicity and eternality is maintained and affirmed. This gives an insightful understanding of the freedom of God. Zizioulas, for example, defines a "person" as someone who is completely free—no limitations, no boundaries. But humans cannot be free in this sense because their existence is conditional. They do not choose to exist.[115] But in a "reconceived" Trinitarian understanding, God is both uncreated and exists moment by moment in a perichoretic, subsistent relationship. Further, the logical simultaneity of the model locates this choice not with the Father exclusively (as Zizioulas incorrectly does using a strict monopatrist theology),[116] nor in some abstract *ousia* but in the entirety of the triune Godhead. God *is love* (1 John 4:8), for God exists in, by, and through love. God's being and personhood is in communion, and without this communion God would not be.

Broadly then, this "reconceived" understanding of the immanent Trinity can be categorized as a relational Trinitarian ontology, that is, an ontology where God's being is constituted by his internal relationships, one in which God's essence cannot be abstracted from or reduced to these dynamic relationships.[117] Such an ontology is characterized by relationships that are permanent, unchanging,

113. Habets, "*Filioque? Nein*," 196.
114. Weinandy, *The Father's Spirit of Sonship*, 80.
115. John Zizioulas, *Being as Communion: Studies in Personhood and the Church* (Crestwood, NY: St. Vladimir's Seminary Press, 1985), 42–49.
116. See section 4.2.
117. See particularly Habets, "Getting Beyond the *Filioque* with Third Article Theology," 211–30.

eternal,[118] and fully mutual.[119] While such a relational ontology and the "reconceived" Trinitarian understanding it underlies has significant strengths,[120] there are two critiques that need to be addressed.

The first concerns a traditional understanding of the divine *taxis*. While the "reconceived" model recognizes the Father's *monarchia*,[121] questions exist regarding the order of the Son and the Spirit. Coffey claims that Weinandy "changes the *taxis* in the immanent Trinity, placing the Holy Spirit before the Son,"[122] and goes on to argue that "[i]f the Father begets the Son 'in' the Holy Spirit, this can only mean that the Son comes forth from the Father and the Holy Spirit (*Spirituque*). . . . The infinity and perfection of the divine persons dictate that any use in their regard of prepositions denoting activity can only signify that they are coprinciples of other divine persons."[123] Responding to this critique requires recognizing the model's simultaneity. *Spirituque* is a technically accurate (though misleading) Trinitarian descriptor, for the Spirit is actively involved in begetting the Son. But *filioque* (and even *patreque*) is also technically accurate,

118. These characteristics contrast with Bracken's proposal, for example, who suggests that a process metaphysics fits better with Third Article Theology. See Bracken, "Trinitarian Spirit Christologies: In Need of a New Metaphysics?" 750–67. For a refutation, see Habets, "Getting Beyond the *Filioque* with Third Article Theology," 211–30.

119. Fully mutual relationships contrast with Coffey's characterization of the Spirit as passive, merely receiving from the Father and Son but not contributing to them.

120. It is puzzling why Weinandy's proposal has received relatively little scholarly attention. One possible reason is its positioning as a potential resolution of the East/West divisions. Ayres comments perceptively that it is "hard to believe that finding some sort of compromise solution to the questions of the *filioque* will actually solve the theological disputes between East and West." Lewis Ayres, "The Father's Spirit of Sonship (Review)," *The Journal of Theological Studies* 50, no. 1 (1999). Farrow alternatively suggests that "Weinandy's programme has merit but the product is too sketchy to be fully convincing." Douglas Farrow, "The Father's Spirit of Sonship (Review)," *Expository Times* 107, no. 7 (1996): 220.

121. Without any accompanying subordinationist tendencies, or what Weinandy calls Neoplatonic emanationism. See Weinandy, *The Father's Spirit of Sonship*, 55–56.

122. Coffey, "Spirit Christology and the Trinity," 335.

123. Ibid. For similar critiques see O'Byrne, *Spirit Christology and Trinity in the Theology of David Coffey*, 200; and Studebaker, *From Pentecost to the Triune God*, 145–46.

for the Spirit exists through the act of the Father's begetting the Son and the Son's pneumatologically enabled response of love.[124] Habets summarizes this simultaneity by cautiously owning Leonardo Boff's statement: "Everything in God is triadic, everything is *Patreque*, *Filioque*, and *Spirituque*."[125] Similarly, Weinandy notes that the begetting/spirating of the Son/Spirit are "simultaneous but distinct acts."[126]

Nevertheless, there is some validity in Coffey's critique that the "reconceived" model denies the traditional *taxis*. Certainly the Father remains monarchially first in any ordering, although by first there is no implication of sequence, which Weinandy is concerned to remove altogether.[127] The monarchy is inherent in the Father's fatherhood: his eternal begetting of the Son by the Spirit. He is and remains begetter, sender, and source. The ordering of the Son over the Spirit,

124. Habets has an intriguing extension of the "reconceived" model that assigns origin not only to the Son and the Spirit but to the Father as well. In this understanding the Father "comes to be" by the Son and the Spirit. See Habets, "*Filioque? Nein*," 161–202. While this proposal diverges from tradition, it seems a natural extension of the "reconceived" understanding and as such is worthy of further consideration. It is, however, neither necessary nor adopted for the Trinitarian analysis and application in this research.

125. Ibid., 194. Habets also rightly argues that Boff's Trinitarian characterization "risks flattening out the *taxis* of the three divine persons, if not negating them completely" (ibid., 194–95).

126. Weinandy, *The Father's Spirit of Sonship*, 71n32. Here, Weinandy is taking issue with Durrwell's understanding of the Trinity (which aligns closely with Coffey's misunderstanding of Weinandy's model) that the Spirit "is the begetting" (ibid.). Studebaker makes the same error, arguing that in Weinandy's understanding the Spirit is "instrumental" in the Father begetting the Son, and then reducing the Spirit to being a mere "instrument," and consequently not personal. Studebaker, *From Pentecost to the Triune God*, 140–43. Using such logic, one could just as plausibly argue that in the "reconceived" Trinity the Son is "instrumental" in spirating the Spirit, and therefore not personal! The point being missed is that the Spirit is not "merely" instrumental. Spiration is the necessary counterpart to begetting, logically distinct but existentially inseparable from it.

127. Personal communication with Father Weinandy confirms this understanding (Washington, DC, November 26, 2012). In a recent article on the *filioque*, Weinandy comments, "While there must be an order among the persons of the Trinity, there must not be a sequence among the persons of the Trinity. Order is far different from sequence, but the traditions of the East and West have yet to fully appreciate this distinction." Thomas Weinandy, "The *Filioque*: Beyond Athanasius and Thomas Aquinas: An Ecumenical Proposal," in *Ecumenical Perspectives on the Filioque for the 21st Century*, ed. Myk Habets (London: Bloomsbury / T. & T. Clark, 2014), 194–95.

however, present in both western and eastern conceptions, is replaced with a logical simultaneity. The *taxis* reflected in Weinandy's Trinity is thus (contra both Coffey's and O'Byrne's understandings above) the Father as first (by virtue of the *monarchia*) and the Son and Spirit as equally and simultaneously second. Certainly this is different from the traditional *taxis* of Father→Son→Spirit, and this difference needs to be acknowledged. But the key question is whether such a *taxis* contradicts the biblical revelation in the economy. The central argument of a coherent Spirit Christology is that it simply doesn't. Virtually all of God's dealings with humanity demonstrate not the traditional *taxis* of the Son's priority over the Spirit, but a logical and chronological synchronicity between the two. Kathryn Tanner, for example, argues precisely this point:

> In sum, Son and Spirit come forth together from the Father and return together in mutually involving ways that bind one to the other. There are not two separable comings out of Son and Spirit and then two separable returns of the one and the other, but in each case of coming out or return a single three-person movement in which they both come out or go back together in complex dependence upon what the other has from and gives back to the Father.[128]

And again:

> The pattern of coming out and going back can be talked about as either F>sp>S>sp>F (with an emphasis on the Son) or F>s>SP>s>F (with an emphasis on the Spirit), because it is both at once.[129]

Weinandy and Habets, to my knowledge, do not explicitly state the distinction between the traditional and the revised *taxis* implicit in their understanding. However, they both regularly comment on the correspondence the "reconceived" Trinity has with the *biblical* or

128. Kathryn Tanner, *Christ the Key* (Cambridge: Cambridge University Press, 2010), 177.
129. Ibid., 195.

economic taxis. For example Habets writes, "By utilising this model of the Trinity . . . we are also able to account meaningfully for the *taxis* that so clearly is present within intra-Trinitarian relations and expressed in the economy."[130] If, following Irenaeus, we accept the analogy that the Son and the Spirit are the two "hands of God,"[131] then combining a coherent Spirit Christology with a "reconceived" model of the Trinity informs the important affirmation that *God is not right-handed*. There is no chronological or logical priority given to the Son over the Spirit, or the Spirit over the Son in God's ambidextrous action in the world, or indeed within God himself.

But there is a further concern here, which leads to the second area of critique. It was asserted above that "*[v]irtually* all of God's dealings with humanity demonstrate . . . a logical and chronological synchronicity" (italics added). But what of the Son's *sending* of the Spirit *to the church*? How does this "reconceived" understanding of the Trinity, in which the Son and Spirit are logically synchronous, account for such a clear biblical ordering? Rather surprisingly, I am unaware of any place where Weinandy or Habets directly address the apparent contradiction between the *economic* ordering of Christ *sending* the Spirit, and the *immanent* simultaneity of the Son and Spirit within the Trinitarian formulation. Habets, for example, rigorously examines the economic reversal where Jesus goes from being the servant to Lord of the Spirit. It forms his sixth and final episode (or messianic *kairoi*) within Christ's life.[132] He writes, "[T]he exaltation and enthronement [of Christ] . . . [acted] as a final chapter to his earthly history and the opening chapter of his new relationship to his kingdom as Lord of the Spirit."[133] But when Habets turns to the

130. Habets, *The Anointed Son*, 224.

131. Irenaeus, "Against Heresies," in *The Ante-Nicene Fathers: Translations of the Fathers down to A.D. 325*, ed. Alexander Roberts and James Donaldson (Peabody, MA: Hendrickson, 1996), 3.6.1, 1:531.

132. Habets, *The Anointed Son*, 176–86.

ontological implications of his Spirit Christological understanding, this sixth episode and the change in relationship doesn't get mentioned. Weinandy's analysis is even more perplexing, for at no point within *The Father's Spirit of Sonship* does he mention the Son's sending of the Spirit. Why are the immanent, ontological implications of such an important economic *kairoi* not considered?

At this point, the second critique of the "reconceived" Trinity appears to be a valid criticism. But the criticism can only be applied to Habets's and Weinandy's *presentation* of the Trinitarian conception, and not its inherent features.[134] For a resolution readily presents itself through an examination of the interaction of the Spirit and Christ's humanity. Two points discussed in chapter 5 are pertinent.[135] First, the Spirit's sending to the church is uniquely defined by Christ's

133. Ibid., 178.

134. Interestingly, Studebaker critiques not just Habets's presentation but the inherent features of his Spirit Christology at precisely this point. Steven M. Studebaker, *From Pentecost to the Triune God: A Pentecostal Trinitarian Theology* (Grand Rapids: Eerdmans, 2012), 177–82. Affirming the determinative role of the Spirit developed in the first five *kairoi*, Studebaker takes issue with Habets's argument in the sixth that Christ becomes the "determining subject of the Spirit." Habets, *The Anointed Son*, 173. Studebaker argues that in Habets's presentation, the "Spirit's identity and work morph into Christology." Studebaker, *From Pentecost to the Triune God*, 180. Recognizing and affirming Habets's argument that the Spirit (together with the Son) is determinative of Christ, Studebaker argues that after the resurrection Habets "abandons this insight and returns to a Christocentric theology" (ibid., 181). I argue in contrast that no such abandonment occurs, and that despite Habets's appearing at times to suggest an ontological change in ordering, his ultimate proposal is for a mutual simultaneity between the Son and the Spirit in the economy. The strongest evidence for this is Habets's conclusion that Weinandy's "reconceived" Trinity, with its clearly evident simultaneity between Son and Spirit, is "compatible with the Spirit Christology I am developing." Habets, *The Anointed Son*, 223. There are two errors to avoid here. Emphasizing the Spirit too strongly reduces Christ to a "mere" conduit by which the Spirit enters humanity and minimizes Christ's ongoing personhood. Studebaker's presentation trends in this direction. Attempting to avoid this, Habets strongly emphasizes Christ's role in sending and conditioning the Spirit, which opens his presentation to the (ultimately unsustainable) critique that pneumatology becomes subordinate to Christology. A better approach which clearly avoids both errors is to not contrast Christology and pneumatology, but rather the Spirit and the Son, who can and should be seen as mutually determinative of not just Christology but ecclesiology, logically distinct but existentially inseparable in all their immanent and economic activity. See further the discussion of Christocentric and pneumacentric theologies in section 11.1.

135. See section 5.1.

humanity and its relation to the human nature of the church. Second, it is an "experienced" Holy Spirit—who has "learned" what it means to unite divinity and humanity in the person of the (now exalted) Jesus Christ—that is sent to the church to unite it with Jesus. The conclusion is that the Son should *not* be understood as the sender of the Spirit, if by sender the implication is "initiator," or "controller," or "Lord." Rather, he should be understood as the mediator through which the Holy Spirit enters the life of the church. In the former sense, the *Father* is the Spirit's sender, as explicitly stated in John's Gospel: "When the Advocate comes, whom I will send to you *from the Father*—the Spirit of truth *who goes out from the Father*—he will testify about me" (John 15:26, italics mine). Christ is not passive—a *mere* mediator or conduit, however, for the Spirit's role in coming to the church through Christ is to unite the church to Christ. Indeed, Christ comes to the church in the Spirit (e.g., 1 Cor. 15:45), or analogically applying the Trinitarian language above to the mystical union, Christ is "personed" in the church by the Spirit.[136] The biblical expression of the Son sending the Spirit, when examined in depth, is consequently another example of the Son and Spirit's simultaneity. The Father sends the Spirit through Christ, and in sending the Spirit to us, Christ himself is present.[137]

136. As argued in chapter 9, the Trinitarian union is reprised (with continuities and discontinuities) in the economy. So in the mystical union between Christ and the church, the Spirit "persons" the Son in his body: the church.

137. Two verses often used to argue that Christ sends the Spirit in the sense of "initiator" or "Lord" are 1 Cor. 15:45 and 2 Cor. 3:17. A detailed reading clearly demonstrates that neither do so. The former verse refers to Christ becoming "the life-giving Spirit." The point being made here is not that Christ initiates the sending of the Spirit, but rather that Christ's human resurrection is the basis for the Spirit's gift to believers and their consequent future resurrection. As Gordon Fee comments, "The language 'life-giving' repeats the verb used of Christ in the Adam-Christ analogy in verse 22, indicating decisively, it would seem, that the interest here is . . . in his resurrection as the ground of ours." Gordon Fee, *The First Epistle to the Corinthians*, ed. Ned B. Stonehouse et al. (Grand Rapids: Eerdmans, 1987), 789. The latter verse states "the Lord is Spirit." Rather than ontologically identifying the Spirit with Christ (see section 2.2), or affirming that the Spirit is directed by Christ, this statement simply identifies the Spirit with the divine identity. Fee asserts that "this is . . . a pneumatological passage, not a Christological one."

To conclude this chapter, consider two key episodes in salvation history: the incarnation (in which the Father sends the Son by the Spirit) and Pentecost (in which the Father sends the Spirit by the Son). How do these differing economic patterns impact our understanding of God's immanent reality? Option 1 (Coffey) argues that there are two Trinitarian models. Option 2 (Moltmann) argues that the divine *taxis* can and does change both economically and immanently. Option 3 (Weinandy and Habets) argues that an accurate theological understanding of both episodes reveals a logical and chronological simultaneity between the Son and the Spirit. Certainly each of these options has advantages. Each one embraces the full revelation of God, including the Spirit Christological texts. Further, they all attempt to bring a dynamism and personalism to the Trinity. But the first two options gain these advantages through unacceptable compromises. Coffey's model suffers chiefly in its preference for his second Trinitarian model over the first, so that the biblical data used to create the first is either neglected or minimized. Moltmann's model, in contrast, suffers from the distance it places between the economic and immanent Trinity. Both conceptions also sacrifice God's simplicity and eternality. The third option is a "reconceived" understanding of the Trinity, which in contrast maintains a close link between the economic and immanent Trinity, and doesn't explicitly or implicitly neglect any biblical data. Further it recognizes the full personhood of each member of the Trinity, and logically identifies God's being and becoming, providing as a result a profoundly enriched understanding of *perichoresis* as being-in-action, or act-in-being.

Fee, *God's Empowering Presence*, 311n91. Barnett concurs: "One turns to the Lord, the Lord is the Spirit; therefore one turns to the Spirit." Paul Barnett, *The Second Epistle to the Corinthians*, ed. Stonehouse et al. (Grand Rapids: Eerdmans, 1997), 200.

Given that our Trinitarian understanding is being enriched over time,[138] no human conception of the immanent Trinity can ever be considered complete. As such, a distinction must be made between God in himself, and how we understand him. Mystery remains. But mystery is no excuse not to delve as deeply as humanly possible into God's immanent being. The argument above is that a "reconceived" understanding of the Trinity provides a responsible contemporary understanding of God's immanent being, gained as it is from a Spirit Christological vantage point. This chapter began with the question: In which human conception of the Trinity does the church participate? It closes with an affirmation that a "reconceived" understanding provides a Trinitarian starting point that is faithful to the biblical witness.

While their work invites such exploration, neither Weinandy nor Habets have yet examined the implications of this "reconceived" Trinitarian understanding in other areas of theology, nor yet the specific implications it has for ecclesiology.[139] Chapter 9 examines this subject in detail, viewing the link between the "reconceived" Trinity and the church through a pneumatological lens. But prior to addressing that crucial topic, it is necessary to determine a coherent means of analogically linking the Trinity and ecclesiology. Chapter 8 initially critiques Volf's "reflective" Trinitarian ecclesiology before turning to a more general discussion of how the two doctrines can be analogically related.

138. See section 1.3 (v).

139. Habets has developed the beginnings of a Third Article Soteriology and anthropology (see Habets, *The Anointed Son*, 243–56). While these developments are *consistent* with a "reconceived" Trinity, they do not explicitly begin from this Trinitarian vantage point. To my knowledge, the only theologian to pursue this path is Kathryn Tanner in her application of a "reconceived" Trinitarian understanding to soteriology and the mystical union. Tanner, *Christ the Key*, 192–206.

8

From the Immanent Trinity to Ecclesiology

Given how regularly the church is characterized as an image or icon of the Trinity, it is remarkable how little systematic effort links the two theological doctrines in detail. In his 1998 monograph *After Our Likeness* Volf comments, "[I]t is surprising that no one has carefully examined just where such correspondences [between Trinitarian and ecclesial communion] are to be found, nor expended much effort determining where ecclesial communion reaches the limits of its capacity for such analogy."[1] While this comment is perhaps less true now than it was a decade and a half ago, it is probably accurate that (Volf's work aside) there is still a lack of *systematic* and *detailed* analysis of the analogical link between the Trinity and the church. Such scarcity may be caused, in part, by the deep reservations emerging about whether the church can actually be viewed as an "image" of the Trinity. For example, Kathryn Tanner argues that "it would be better to steer attention away from Trinitarian relations when

1. Miroslav Volf, *After Our Likeness: The Church as the Image of the Trinity* (Grand Rapids: Eerdmans, 1998).

making judgments about the proper character of human ones in Christian terms."[2] The question thus arises: Is there a valid analogical connection that can be drawn between the Trinity and the church? And if so, what insight does it give us about the church's nature and activity?

This chapter argues that there is such an analogical bridge, but that it is qualitatively different from the "reflective" method adopted by Volf and others who reason similarly. The church is not "like" the Trinity, nor is it "the image" of the Trinity. Rather the church is "in" the Trinity, participating in its very life because of the indwelling Holy Spirit and Christ's priestly mediation. Consequently, a pneumatological lens enables a real but limited analogical connection to be drawn between the immanent Trinity and ecclesiology.[3] The Spirit's mission in the church corresponds with the Spirit's immanent Trinitarian identity. Further, through the Spirit the church is united to the incarnate Son and joins his filial relationship to the Father, so that our participation in the Trinity corresponds with Christ's Trinitarian identity.

The argument divides into three sections. First, Volf's efforts to characterize the church as the image of the Trinity are critiqued, noting concerns with his methodology, consistency, and comprehensiveness. Volf's underlying assumption that the church reflects or "images" the Trinity is questioned. Second, Tanner's concerns about all "reflective" links between the Trinity and the church are evaluated. These concerns are recognized as valid when applied to Volf's reflective approach, but it is argued that they are less applicable to the analogical approach of Third Article Theology—an

2. Kathryn Tanner, *Christ the Key* (Cambridge: Cambridge University Press, 2010), 207–8.

3. Drawing an analogical connection between the immanent Trinity and ecclesiology raises the question of what connection exists between the economic Trinity and the church. As mentioned in the introduction to part three, this was precisely the subject of part two, which explored ecclesiology from the vantage point of Spirit Christology.

approach that is pneumatologically enabled but Christologically conditioned. Roman Catholic scholar Heribert Mühlen uses such an analogical link by arguing that in both the Trinity and the church "the Holy Spirit is one person in many persons."[4] Given this, the third section examines whether Mühlen's work avoids Tanner's concerns. While several weaknesses of Mühlen's theological position are identified, each is traced back to his speculative Trinitarian starting point rather than his methodological approach. This reveals the potential (worked out in the following chapters) to develop a pneumatologically enabled but Christologically conditioned analogical link between a "reconceived" understanding of the Trinity and the church, thus enabling the construction of a coherent Trinitarian Third Article Ecclesiology.

8.1 Reflective Imaging

As previously noted, attempts to link the economic and immanent Trinity are often divided into those that assume divine unity and then consider God's diversity (running the risk of modalism), and those that do the reverse (running the risk of tritheism). Related problems emerge when such approaches are extended to ecclesiology, with the former tending toward a hierarchical ecclesiology, and the latter a modernist individualism.

Volf's characterization of his dialogue partners provides exemplars of the first grouping. Volf argues, for example, that Joseph Ratzinger's (now Benedict XVI, Pope emeritus) "Augustinian" Trinitarianism emphasizes the one *ousia* with the *hypostases* being "pure relations." The result is that in the Trinity *and the church*, the one is structurally

4. Heribert Mühlen, *Una Mystica Persona. Die Kirche als das Mysterium der heilsgeschichtlichen Identität des Heiligen Geistes in Christus und den Christen: Eine Person in vielen Personen* (Paderborn: Ferdinand Schöningh, 1967), 63. As quoted in and translated by Wolfgang Vondey, *Heribert Mühlen: His Theology and Praxis* (Dallas: University Press of America, 2004), 105.

decisive. "In Ratzinger, we encounter an (almost completely) one-sided relation of the whole and the one to its concrete realisations."[5] Consequently, the church is seen as a single subject, with the universal church given priority over the local. "Because Ratzinger understands the Church from the perspective of the whole, that is, from that of the one subject of the church, relations . . . must necessarily be structured *hierarchically*."[6] The (over)emphasis on oneness means bishops outrank congregations, and the pope outranks the bishops.[7] Volf concludes, "Ratzinger . . . understand[s] the Trinity hierarchically, and ground[s] the hierarchical relations within the church in part on this basis."[8] While some (justifiably) question whether Volf accurately portrays and critiques Ratzinger's views,[9] his characterization illustrates well the tendency for a "unity to diversity" Trinitarian understanding to lead to a hierarchical ecclesiology.

Volf's own proposal trends in the opposite direction. In constructing an alternative, explicitly Free Church ecclesiology, Volf follows Moltmann's hard social model of the Trinity, and concludes that a church should be "characterized by symmetrical and decentralized distribution of power and freely affirmed interaction."[10] In the following, Volf's logical or "reflective" connection between the Trinity and the church is outlined and then critiqued.

Volf understands the Christian initiation process as an essentially Trinitarian event.[11] Through faith, we come into communion with

5. Volf, *After Our Likeness*, 123.
6. Ibid., 72.
7. Ibid., 214, 236.
8. Ibid., 236. Volf draws a similar conclusion about Zizioulas's Trinitarian ecclesiology. See section 4.2.
9. The counterargument that Ratzinger's ecclesiology is influenced more directly by Christology than the Trinity has significant merit, for example. See Kevin J. Bidwell, *"The Church as the Image of the Trinity": A Critical Evaluation of Miroslav Volf's Ecclesial Model* (Eugene, OR: Wipf & Stock, 2011), 114–22. See also Ralph Del Colle, "Communion and Trinity: The Free Church Ecclesiology of Miroslav Volf—A Catholic Response," *Pneuma* 22, no. 2 (2000): 303–27.
10. Volf, *After Our Likeness*, 236.

God, and *simultaneously* into communion with others who trust God. This horizontal communion is second ontologically but not chronologically.[12] Faith is "a simultaneous incorporation into both Trinitarian and ecclesial communion."[13] Again, "To experience faith means to become an ecclesial being."[14] Indeed, following Matt. 18:20 Volf argues the presence of Christ is promised firstly to the entire congregation, and only *through* this to the individual.[15] "It is precisely as the congregation assembling together in the name of Christ that the church is an image of the Trinity."[16]

For Volf, the church reflects the Trinity in its relationships. Just as individual divine *hypostases* do not exist in isolation from the Trinitarian community, individual Christians do not live in isolation from the ecclesial community. This is in strong distinction to *human beings*, who can live in isolation and even mutual hatred. As Christians, however, individuals within the church affirm their ecclesial personhood through mutual giving and receiving—through fellowship with other believers.[17] However, the analogy is not perfect. First, because the church's communion is held together by a covenant of will, while the communion of God is self-existent. Essentially, Volf argues, God *doesn't* exist without communion, whereas individuals within the church *choose* to be in communion. The possibility of noncommunion remains.[18] Second, church members' mutual love reflects the love between the persons of the

11. Or at least he claims to. See ibid., 197. It doesn't seem to be explicitly worked out as such though, as noted below.
12. Ibid., 173.
13. Ibid., 197.
14. Ibid., 174.
15. Ibid., 162. Although Volf makes this point initially, at various later stages in his argument (noted below) the reverse appears to be the case.
16. Ibid., 197.
17. Ibid., 206.
18. Ibid., 207.

Godhead only in a broken fashion, as we journey toward the new creation.[19]

Volf also claims that the church reflects the Trinity in its mutual indwelling. Here though, the similarity is more limited. In terms of the church's mutual indwelling of God, the Spirit indwells church members as one subject indwelling another (*true perichoresis*) but in the reverse direction church members merely indwell the "*life-giving ambience of the Spirit*" and not the Spirit as subject.[20] In terms of church members' indwelling each other, Volf argues that while the Trinitarian *hypostases* indwell each other perichoretically, ecclesial persons indwell each other through the "interiority of personal characteristics."[21] To validate this, Volf notes the Johannine phrase "as you, Father, are in me and I am in you" is continued not by "may they also be in each other," but rather "may they also be in us."[22] Thus human *perichoresis* is qualitatively different from divine *perichoresis*—church members are open to each other only through the Spirit as they are located in Christ.

Volf locates both the *catholicity* and the *unity* of the church in the Spirit's interiority. In Jesus, humanity sees the Father (Spirit) because the Father (Spirit) indwell(s) the Son. The Son thus carries the *essence* of the Godhead, and in that sense is *catholic*—representing the entire Godhead through a single person. But similarly in each ecclesial person, through the Spirit, "we give to each other a piece of ourselves, something of that which we have made of ourselves in communion with others; and from others we take not only something, but also a piece of them."[23] According to Volf, this "mutual internalization of personal characteristics"[24] makes each person *catholic*, as each unique

19. Ibid.
20. As opposed to indwelling the "person" of the Spirit (ibid., 211).
21. Ibid.
22. John 17:21. Ibid., 212.
23. Ibid., 211.

person individually represents the entire church.[25] The *unity* of the church flows not from a believer's *perichoresis*, but from the interiority of the Spirit, as the same Son indwells all Christians through this Spirit.[26] Consequently, Volf argues, the church is an "intimate communion of independent persons,"[27] and exists wherever the Spirit "is present in its ecclesially constitutive activity."[28] It is in this way that two or three gathered together image the Trinity and create an instance of the one true church. But not just any gathering constitutes a church. Volf outlines several criteria. They must assemble "*in the name of Christ*" (Matt. 18:20).[29] They must publicly profess their faith in him, including through baptism and the Lord's Supper.[30] And they must be open to other churches.[31]

Given the church's limited imaging, which Trinitarian aspects ought to be reflected in ecclesial structures? Volf follows Moltmann in distinguishing between the constitution and relations of the Trinitarian persons. While the Father is the ontological ground of the Son and the Spirit, in his relations with them he is merely "one among others."[32] Because of this, ecclesial unity should not be conceived in one person representing Christ for—or over—others (as per Ratzinger), but rather in the correspondence of the entire

24. Ibid.
25. Ibid., 211–12. By using the word "catholic" here Volf presumably means that we each individually represent the entirety of the church. But the environment, creature, and Creator are also internal to this individual, making them even more broadly representative or "catholic."
26. Ibid., 212–13.
27. Ibid., 213.
28. Ibid., 129. By "ecclesially constitutive" Volf is referring to the way the Spirit unites the gathered congregation to God and into the church throughout history.
29. Ibid., 145. This is the first of several examples where Volf appears to be using this verse in the reverse manner to his original claim.
30. In confessing faith in Jesus, "cognitive specification and personal identification coincide" (ibid., 148).
31. As the same Spirit "that makes each local Church 'independent' of the other Churches simultaneously connects them with one another" (ibid., 155).
32. Ibid., 217. Moltmann's theological move here was critiqued in section 7.2. Volf's similar move is critiqued in Stephen R. Holmes, *The Quest for the Trinity: The Doctrine of God in Scripture, History and Modernity* (Downers Grove, IL: IVP Academic, 2012), 26–28.

church to the Trinity.[33] For Volf, this "Free" Church understanding interprets the unity of Christ and church not as identical subject (again, as per Ratzinger) but as bride and groom become one while remaining distinct subjects.[34] Volf argues that the church is not a single subject, and so its unity cannot be represented by a single person. Rather it is a polycentric community,[35] where the Spirit constitutes the church through the calling and charismatic gifting of each of the mutually serving members. The *charismata* are universally distributed, fundamentally interdependent, and synchronically and diachronically varied. They form the institutions of the church. Consequently ordination should be viewed as merely another *charismata*, one that ensures all the other *charismata* are functioning effectively. The offices are for the well-being (*bene esse*) of a church, but don't constitute its being (*esse*).[36]

Putting all this together, what is Volf's ecclesiology? He summarizes:

> Every congregation that assembles around the one Jesus Christ as Savior and Lord in order to profess faith in him publicly in pluriform fashion, including through baptism and the Lord's Supper, and which is open to all churches of God and to all human beings, is a Church in the full sense of the word, since Christ promised to be present in it through his Spirit as the first fruits of the gathering of the whole people of God in the eschatological reign of God. Such a congregation is a holy, catholic and apostolic Church.[37]

33. Volf, *After Our Likeness*, 218.
34. Ibid., 142.
35. Ibid., 224.
36. Ibid., 152.
37. Ibid., 158.

Volf's work has (mostly) been received with critical acclaim.[38] It is not without its critics, however. The following lists some concerns, from the least to the most significant. The critiques are overarching, although illustrative examples are noted.

First, Volf argues that the inadequacies of Roman Catholic and Eastern Orthodox church structures parallel their misunderstandings of the nature of the Trinity. The underlying rationale is that mistaken theology leads to inadequate ecclesiology. But the situation is obviously more complex. Social realities within denominations weren't created in a logical, top-down fashion from initially abstracted theological understanding. Indeed it could just as confidently be claimed that churches first develop particular structures (based on pragmatism, culture, or necessity), and then *post facto* look to (and perhaps even subtly alter) their theologies to justify the developed structure.[39] While theology *should* drive practice, the reverse often occurs. Although never stated explicitly,[40] Volf is well aware of this dual, interconnected development of structure and theology. His entire analysis of Ratzinger and Zizioulas can be understood broadly as a critique of their traditions allowing the structural tail to wag the theological dog.

But is not Volf's work similarly tainted? As an explicit defense of Free Church ecclesiology, Volf is naturally drawn to those theological understandings and perspectives that justify the nature and structure of Free Church ecclesiology. And this ecclesiology, just like that of the Catholic or Orthodox Church, has been derived through factors that are not just theological but pragmatic, cultural,

38. See for example John W. Stewart, "After Our Likeness (Review)," *The Christian Century* 115, no. 16 (1998): 541; and Natalie K. Watson, "After Our Likeness (Review)," *Anglican Theological Review* 81, no. 4 (1999): 745.

39. Kenneson states this explicitly: "Ecclesial traditions justify their ecclesiologies theologically after the fact." Philip D. Kenneson, "After Our Likeness (Review)," *Modern Theology* 15, no. 3 (1999): 374.

40. Although see Volf, *After Our Likeness*, 215n103.

and of necessity. To what extent has Volf's *a priori* ecclesiology driven his theological choices? For example, why should Volf choose to model Moltmann's understanding of the Trinity, as opposed to that of Augustine or Palamas? No detailed theological justification is given, beyond the recognition that Moltmann's hard social Trinitarianism parallels existing egalitarian, nonhierarchical Free Church structures. Similarly, why should Volf choose to interpret the relation between Christ and the church as a relational unity akin to husband and wife as opposed to the (more traditional) closer identification of head and body? Volf's justification is that as a "polycentric community,"[41] the church cannot be characterized as a single subject. The fact that Volf's theological choices are specifically those that justify an existing ecclesiology does not make them intrinsically wrong. But it does raise questions about his theological method. To what extent is Volf's Free Church tail wagging his Trinitarian dog?

Second, applying Moltmann's egalitarian Trinity consistently to ecclesiology implies that any distinction between "office" and "laity" should be abolished. But Volf does not do this.[42] Rather, Volf aims to "ground the institution of office and ordination theologically."[43] He develops the concept of "office" as merely one type of *charismata*, and then attempts to minimize the distinction between it and other giftings: "There can be no difference in principle between officeholders and other members."[44] But if there is no difference, why are some "office" holders and others not? Why not remove the

41. Ibid., 224–25.
42. As many reviewers note. For example, "Volf never really overcomes the clergy/laity bipolarity." Howard A. Snyder, "After Our Likeness (Review)," *Asbury Journal* 60, no. 2 (2005): 131. Even those who broadly affirm Volf's Trinitarian ecclesiology critique this point. For example, Robert A. Muthiah, *The Priesthood of All Believers in the Twenty-First Century: Living Faithfully as the Whole People of God in a Postmodern Context* (Eugene, OR: Pickwick, 2009), 78–80.
43. Volf, *After Our Likeness*, 245.
44. Ibid., 246.

status of officeholders altogether? Volf presumably recognizes that in churches a difference in function necessarily implies a difference in title or status. This does not imply one is "over" or "better" and the other "lower" or "subordinate," just that doing different jobs means being given different positions and titles. But why can this recognition not also be applied to the life of the Trinity? And how can Volf theologically justify a status distinction within a church when he has deliberately eliminated all traces of it within the Godhead, particularly when his ecclesiology is built explicitly upon a purely Trinitarian reflection?

Third, Volf's ecclesiology suffers from the lack of an explicitly Christological perspective. At the end of an exhaustive study, Bidwell concludes: "In all of the enthusiasm to recover the much neglected doctrine of the Trinity, Volf provides a timely and valuable caution because he loses sight of Christology in his pursuit of a church to reflect the Trinity."[45] Essentially, because Volf overemphasizes what the church *will be* (eschatologically as a reflection of the Trinity) he minimizes what it *already is* (Christologically). Volf's Trinitarian focus means the "eschatological maximum" is clearly visible; the absence of a complementary Christological determination causes the "historical minimum" to be lost in the shadows.[46] As Dulles comments, "Volf finds that Zizioulas falls into an excessively realized eschatology—a criticism that has also been voiced from a Catholic point of view. But does not Volf go to the opposite extreme? What is the correct balance between the 'already' and the 'not yet'?"[47]

45. Bidwell, *"The Church as the Image of the Trinity"*, 240.

46. Note Volf's previously mentioned comments on the church sojourning between a historical minimum and an eschatological maximum in part three's introduction. Volf, *After Our Likeness*, 199.

47. Avery Dulles, "After Our Likeness (Review)," *First Things: A Monthly Journal of Religion and Public Life*, no. 87 (1998): 52.

Volf mentions three distinctions restricting the correlation between the Trinity and the church. These are not wrong, merely incomplete without Christological corrective.[48] The first distinction between God's self-revelation and Trinitarian doctrine is required because of humanity's imperfect understanding. But in Jesus Christ it is *truly* God that has been *fully* revealed to us—revelation is true. The second distinction between a human doctrine of the Trinity and an "optimal" eschatological ecclesiology is required because creatures reflect God imperfectly. But by being united with Jesus Christ believers genuinely become part of the life of God—participation is real. The third distinction between eschatological and historical ecclesiology is required because the church is journeying toward fulfillment. But in Jesus Christ God became flesh, and inaugurated his Kingdom here in this space and time—the Kingdom has come. As creatures, we are limited, which Volf's Trinitarian perspective makes clear. But without an explicit Christology balancing the eschatological and Trinitarian factors, theologians can allow (as Volf has) the "historical minimum" of the church to be excessively characterized by mere anthropocentric functionality.

One potential effect of this unbalanced eschatological force is that Volf's Trinitarian ecclesiology primarily addresses questions of church structure. Structures are necessary and important, but Volf's emphasis on them is imbalanced. What about context?[49] What about prayer? What about liturgical practice? What about mission? Volf is forced to emphasize structure as it forms the major distinction between Free and other churches. But should an ecclesiology in general, and a Trinitarian ecclesiology in particular, be structurally focused?[50] Perhaps alternative questions such as how the church can

48. As noted earlier, Volf uses the word "mediations" rather than "distinctions."

49. As Stewart writes, Volf "neglects to consider the theological dilemmas associated with locating a congregation . . . in specific and variegated social contexts." Stewart, "After Our Likeness (Review)," 4.

live in but not be of the world or how God can be evidenced through our ecclesial life are other significant issues that a sublime subject like Trinitarian ecclesiology should also be wrestling with. Could an overemphasis on the church's limitations have led to a lack of trust in the church and the Spirit within it to deal with variegated situations in variegated ways?

Volf's work represents perhaps the most systematic attempt to correlate the Trinity and the church, but its results are not convincing. Concerns exist with *methodology*: Volf's *a priori* decision to defend a Free Church understanding has influenced his Trinitarian and theological choices; with *consistency*: Volf simultaneously maintains both a perfectly flat Trinity and an ecclesiological status distinction between clergy and laity; and with *comprehensiveness*: Volf's lack of an explicitly Christological perspective results in an underrealized ecclesiology. All of these issues could be corrected. Perhaps a revised methodology (with a more justifiable Trinitarian starting point), improved consistency (which uniformly reflects Trinitarian insights in ecclesial practice), and a more comprehensive approach (through including both Christological and other correctives) would result in an entirely justifiable picture of the church as an "image" of the Trinity. Even with such hypothetical improvements, however, a number of theologians are voicing the opinion that Volf's approach is fundamentally flawed. They argue that a "reflective" model cannot work because the church is not an image of the Trinity at all. For example, Brad Green writes, "The move from Trinitarian relationships to human relationships is, in the end, a difficult one to make."[51] Kathryn Tanner is more

50. See for example Hunt's interesting article comparing how the Trinity is used to justify a broad and conflicting range of ecclesial structures. She argues convincingly that the link from the Trinity to ecclesial structures is therefore ultimately untenable. Anne Hunt, "The Trinity and the Church: Explorations in Ecclesiology from a Trinitarian Perspective," *Irish Theological Quarterly* 70, no. 3 (2005): 215–35.

definitive, arguing that "it would be better to steer attention away from Trinitarian relations when making judgments about the proper character of human ones in Christian terms."[52] The next section examines the critiques of Tanner and others, in order to determine if their concerns are justified, and whether they can be more broadly applied to all analogical approaches linking the Trinity and the church, particularly the pneumatological approach adopted by a Third Article Theology.

8.2 Analogical Connection

The previous section raised significant concerns regarding Volf's "reflective" analogical link between the Trinity and ecclesiology. Many theologians have noted similar issues with not just Volf's work, but with a number of similar contemporary attempts to draw an analogical link between the Trinity and human activity. Keith E. Johnson, for example, describes theologians who draw flawed analogies between the Trinity and ecclesiology (Gunton),[53]

51. Brad Green, "After Our Likeness (Review)," *Evangelical Review of Theology* 26, no. 1 (2002): 92–93.
52. Tanner, *Christ the Key*, 207–8.
53. For example, Johnson critiques Gunton's claim that "the church is what it is by virtue of being called to be a temporal echo of the eternal community that God is." Colin Gunton, *The Promise of Trinitarian Theology* (Edinburgh: T. & T. Clark, 1997), 79. While not discounting Gunton's entire ecclesial framework, Johnson argues that his reference to the Trinity as *justification* for the being or character of the church is fundamentally flawed. See for example the discussion in Keith E. Johnson, "*Imitatio Trinitatis*: How Should We Imitate the Trinity?" *Westminster Theological Journal* 75 (2013): 318. As previously mentioned, I distinguish between how Gunton *characterizes* the analogical link between the Trinity and the church as "personal" or "pneumatological" and how he then *utilizes* "relationality" to directly link the two. Webster fairly critiques Gunton here by arguing that "deploying 'relation' (or more abstractly, 'relationality') as a bridge term between God and creatures can prove precarious, effecting the passage from God to church too comfortably, without securing an adequate sense of the unqualified gratuity of the church's created existence and of its difference from God who is the uncreated source of its life." John Webster, "In the Society of God: Some Principles of Ecclesiology," in *Perspectives on Ecclesiology and Ethnography*, ed. Pete Ward (Grand Rapids: Eerdmans, 2012), 206. For a more detailed treatment that points to similar issues, see Bernhard Nausner, "The Failure of a Laudable Project: Gunton, the Trinity and Human Self-Understanding," *Scottish Journal of Theology* 64, no. 4 (2009). Given this discrepancy, the

teamwork (Cladis), mission (Bjork), societal relations (Boff), politics (Moltmann), marriage (Grudem), and parenting (Kroening).[54] Given that so many analogical links between the Trinity and human activity appear mistaken, the immediate question arising is whether *all* analogical comparisons between the Trinity and human activity are invalid. Particularly pertinent for this research is whether a viable analogical link between the Trinity and ecclesiology can be constructed. Some theologians caution against such an approach. For example, John Webster argues (without detailed explanation) that "[t]he connection of theology proper and ecclesiology is best explicated not by setting out two terms of an analogy but by describing a sequence of divine acts both in terms of their ground in the immanent divine being and in terms of their creaturely fruits."[55] Can arguments against specific Trinitarian analogies be universally generalized?

The most persuasive argument against specific analogical connections between Trinitarian and human relations is Kathryn Tanner's essay on "Politics."[56] While admirably broad in its

following analysis does not use the details of Gunton's Trinitarian ecclesiology beyond noting its initial characterization and intent.

54. Keith E. Johnson, "*Imitatio Trinitatis*," 318–21. For a similar argument, see Keith E. Johnson, *Rethinking the Trinity and Religious Pluralism: An Augustinian Assessment* (Downers Grove, IL: IVP Academic, 2011), 195–209.

55. Webster, "In the Society of God," 206. Webster's mistake in this assertion is his implication that the two contrasting methodologies are mutually exclusive. As argued in this chapter, and evidenced in the next, this is simply not the case. It is only because of the "sequence of divine acts" that the analogy between the Trinity and the Church has validity. Our life is akin in some way to the life of the Trinity only because the Godhead lives in and through us via the temporal missions of the Son and the Spirit. The analogy follows the participation. Webster's critique is certainly justified against what we have termed "reflective" or "direct" analogical links, but not against the pneumatologically enabled, Christologically conditioned approach being proposed here.

56. Tanner, *Christ the Key*, 207–46. As noted on p. xi of *Christ the Key*, this chapter covers similar ground to Kathryn Tanner, "Trinity," in *The Blackwell Companion to Political Theology*, ed. Peter Scott and William T. Cavanaugh (Malden, MA: Blackwell, 2007), 319–32. Several other articles make similar arguments, although most focus more narrowly on one theologian's work. See Mark Husbands, "The Trinity Is *Not* Our Social Program," in *Trinitarian Theology for the Church: Scripture, Community, Worship*, ed. David Lauber and Daniel J. Treier (Downers Grove,

application, it is important to note that in this pivotal essay Tanner *does not* argue against *all* analogical connections between the Trinity and the church *universally*,[57] but rather takes explicit aim at the likes of Volf, Moltmann, Zizioulas, Boff, and LaCugna who make a direct, logical, or what this research has termed a "reflective" connection between the two theological loci.[58] She nevertheless raises several significant concerns with existing efforts to correlate ecclesial and Trinitarian life. This section argues that Tanner's concerns are entirely valid when addressing "reflective" analogical approaches like Volf's, and probes whether they are equally convincing when applied to an alternative pneumatologically enabled analogical approach.

Tanner's first concern surrounds the inflated claims made for the Trinity's application to human relationships.[59] She questions the maxim that monotheism is intrinsically linked with authoritarianism, and argues that monotheism could just as easily be used as an argument against hierarchy, given that there is no lord apart from

IL: InterVarsity, 2009), 120–41; Richard Bauckham, "Jürgen Moltmann's *The Trinity and the Kingdom of God* and the Question of Pluralism," in *The Trinity in a Pluralistic Age*, ed. Kevin J. Vanhoozer (Grand Rapids: Eerdmans, 1997), 155–64; Alastair McFadyen, "The Trinity and Human Individuality," *Theology* 95 (1992): 10–18; Ted Peters, *God as Trinity: Relationality and Temporality in Divine Life* (Louisville: Westminster John Knox, 1993); John Behr, "The Trinitarian Being of the Church," *St. Vladimir's Theological Quarterly* 48, no. 1 (3003): 67–71; and Johnson, *Rethinking the Trinity*, 195–209.

57. Personal correspondence confirms that although Johnson rules out all analogies that imply a "platonic reflection of God's inner life" (email, November 23, 2013), he does not exclude *all* analogical correspondence: "We do analogically imitate the immanent (and economic) Trinity." He comments constructively, however, that such analogical imitation is "directed towards the communicable attributes of the Trinity," and that any analogical reflection between God's immanent being and ecclesiology happens through "a mediating term (God's relation to us) and a mediating power/presence (Son/Spirit)" (email, November 28, 2013). This viewpoint bears quite some similarity with the pneumatologically enabled and Christologically conditioned analogical connection developed in the remainder of chapter 8, and worked out in chapter 9.
58. Tanner, *Christ the Key*, 207. Interestingly, Tanner does not include Mühlen in this list. Mühlen's pneumatologically enabled analogical link between the Trinity and ecclesiology will be examined in section 8.3 as an example of an approach that avoids Tanner's concerns.
59. On this point, see also Alister E. McGrath, "The Doctrine of the Trinity: An Evangelical Reflection," in *God the Holy Trinity: Reflections on Faith and Practice*, ed. Timothy George (Grand Rapids: Baker Academic, 2006), 30–32.

God. Certainly the OT Scriptures paint the two notions as contradictory (cf. 1 Sam. 8:7). Correspondingly, Tanner notes that the sociopolitical potential of Trinitarian theology is decidedly ambiguous. For example, the fact that Trinitarian persons are defined by their relationship could imply that people are to be defined by their (often demeaning) social roles. Order in the Trinity could be used to justify an oppressive hierarchy. Gendered Trinitarian language has the possibility of rendering women as second-class citizens. Overall, Tanner notes, Trinitarianism has to be interpreted quite narrowly for it to be maintained as politically progressive. Such a narrow Trinitarian interpretation is certainly evident in Volf's work,[60] while the direct link that Volf's *Doktorvater* Moltmann draws between monotheism and authoritarianism is not just unproven, but also highly questionable.[61]

Tanner's second concern is that making the Trinity socially applicable to human relationships involves unjustified theological moves. She gives several examples. First, she notes that the perfectly reciprocal *perichoresis* that is assumed to exist in the immanent Trinity remains to be reconciled with the economic reality, where Jesus acts in a nonmutual relation of obedience and subordination to the Father. Second, she recognizes the importance of the distinctions between the persons of the Trinity in any social application, but also the lack of any explanation for how they came to exist as different from each other. Third, in order to have social applicability the term "person" must be understood similarly for both divinity and humanity. This means that rather than being merely a means to

60. See particularly Miroslav Volf, ""The Trinity Is Our Social Program": The Doctrine of the Trinity and the Shape of Social Engagement," *Modern Theology* 14, no. 3 (1998): 407–12.

61. See particularly Moltmann, *The Trinity and the Kingdom*, 129–50. Perhaps the term "monotheism" is unwisely chosen by Moltmann, which may slightly lessen the severity of Tanner's critique. Bauckham suggests that perhaps Moltmann's meaning is closer to "unitarianism." Bauckham, "Jürgen Moltmann's *The Trinity and the Kingdom*," 156–57.

highlight the Trinitarian person's constitutive relationality, as is more traditional, the term "person" is given a much more substantive definition. Essentially, says Tanner, to be applicable, the Trinity must be considered as a close analogy to a society of human persons, with the clear implication of tritheism.[62] Certainly this critique can be applied effectively to Volf's work. As noted above, there is no detailed justification given by Volf for choosing Moltmann's hard social model for the Trinity, except that it matches his egalitarian understanding of a Free Church.[63] And more than one commentator has labeled Moltmann's Trinitarian understanding as tritheistic.[64]

Following these two pointed critiques, Tanner's subsequent concerns are more general. Her third concern centers upon human knowledge of the Trinity's inner workings being too limited to effectively apply to human relationships. "We do not understand very well what we mean when using ordinary language to speak of the Trinity."[65] How are the persons of the Trinity "in" one another; how are they "equal" to one another; how do they "relate" to one another? These are all questions that according to Tanner we do not have very good answers to, except by comparing them to our human experience. This leads to the fanciful scenario, well documented by Karen Kilby in the case of *perichoresis*, where something unknown in the Trinity is "filled out" from human experience, only then to be presented as a resource for guiding human experience.[66] Tanner

62. See also Bauckham, "Jürgen Moltmann's *The Trinity and the Kingdom*," 160–61. And Husbands, "The Trinity Is *Not* Our Social Program," 122–23.
63. On this point, see particularly Bidwell, *"The Church as the Image of the Trinity"*, 194–95.
64. See for example Paul S. Fiddes, *Participating in God: A Pastoral Doctrine of the Trinity* (London: Darton, Longman & Todd, 2000), 47. See also the discussion on Moltmann and Christological proposals that excessively separate the Son from the Spirit in section 2.2.
65. Tanner, *Christ the Key*, 222.
66. Karen Kilby, "Perichoresis and Projection: Problems with Social Doctrines of the Trinity," *New Blackfriars* 81, no. 957 (2000): 432–45. In a discussion of recent Trinitarian ecclesiologies, Anne Hunt raises similar concerns, but also notes that "a certain circularity is justified given our understanding of the human person's and the Church's real participation in—and not just imitation of—the Trinity, through baptism and grace." Hunt, "The Trinity and the Church,"

notes similarly that often the move "down" from the Trinity to social relations is complemented by a move "up" where we determine to what degree we can imitate the Trinity by observing human reality. But then the Trinitarian analogy "fails to do any work; it does not tell one anything one did not already know."[67]

Once again, this critique can be fairly applied to Volf's methodology. Consider his analysis of human *perichoresis*. For Volf the persons of the Godhead indwell each other as subjects, where by contrast, it is only by the interiority of personal characteristics that humans indwell one another. By this, I presume Volf to mean that I take into my character a small portion of my ecclesial sister's thankfulness, or my brother's courage. But if personal characteristics are the closest correlation between God's perichoretic life and ours that Volf can manage, what need for the Spirit?[68] Non-Christians as well as Christians take on others' personal characteristics. Long-married couples often reflect each other's mannerisms, patterns, and character, for both good and ill. What is left that is unique, miraculous, or supernatural in our ecclesial connection? The overly separated nature of the persons in Moltmann's tritheistic Godhead is mimicked in the overly independent nature of the persons in Volf's polycentric church. The Trinitarian reflection adds nothing more to our knowledge of human relationships than was already obvious from our own personal experience.

Tanner's fourth concern notes that because of humanity's finitude and sinfulness, much Trinitarian truth cannot be directly applied to humans. Consider first the limitations of human finiteness. We cannot dwell "in" one another like the persons of the Trinity do.

233. This distinction between imitation and participation is pertinent and will be used further in this and the following chapters.

67. Tanner, *Christ the Key*, 230.

68. Or perhaps better, what distinction is there between the role of the Spirit in Christians and those who are not?

We must distinguish between our existence and our character, while for the Trinitarian persons those qualities coincide. Indeed, according to Tanner, giving to others often involves loss to ourselves, whereas the persons of the Trinity are *constituted* by giving to the other. Tanner notes that the strategy of using the economic Trinity to bridge the "finite/infinite" gap is fruitless. In the economy there is a dialogical fellowship of love and mutual service between the Father and the Son, but this fellowship is derived directly from the Word becoming flesh, and is not intrinsic to the Trinity itself. In the Trinity there is only one will and therefore no dialogical fellowship for us to imitate. Compounding our finiteness is our fallen condition. Human society is full of suffering, sin, and corruption. Tanner thus comments, "Turned into a recommendation for social relations, the trinity seems unrealistic, hopelessly naïve, and, for that reason, perhaps even politically dangerous."[69] Most theologians consequently reduce the Trinity to a societal "utopian goal."[70] Tanner again notes that the economic Trinity does not assist in bridging the "perfect/fallen" gap. For the economic Trinity encountered our suffering world by embracing our reality: a suffering father and a crucified son. Having descended so far, the Trinity gives no new information on human society than what we already knew.

Tanner outlines a significant conundrum here: to the degree that the Trinity either is or becomes like humanity, it can teach us nothing about human society, for we already know from experience what it means to be human. But to the degree that the Trinity remains distinct from humanity, we are inevitably powerless to imitate it. And certainly her concerns at this point (as in each of the others) are borne out by the above analysis. For if, like Volf, we

69. Tanner, *Christ the Key*, 228.
70. Volf certainly understands the Trinitarian image this way. See Volf, *After Our Likeness*, 198–200.

understand the church as merely the reflective image of the Trinity, then what hubris to claim we reflect the Godhead? But we can (and must!) claim a much closer correlation. Through the Spirit we are united with Christ, and participate in his filial relationship of Sonship with the Father. So our imaging of the Godhead is not arbitrary reflection—it is God living in us and us living in God; we join the Trinitarian life.[71] Volf begins this way, by claiming an ontological connection between Trinitarian and ecclesial life,[72] but in detailing this connection he reverts to purely reflective language.[73] Rather than examining how God actually *is* seen in ecclesial experience, he examines how the church can be *like* the Trinity.[74] With such distance between divinity and humanity, a "reflective" methodology makes the exercise of determining continuities and discontinuities highly subjective, allowing scattered results. Indeed, Tanner regards viewing human society as a reflection of the Trinity as a mostly pointless exercise. She does, however, offer an alternative.

Tanner finds a model for human society not in the Trinity but in the incarnation. According to Tanner, the infinite/finite or perfect/fallen gap is closed through two very different things, that remain very different, being joined together in Christ. Thus, hope for human

71. References such as this to believers living in God should not be interpreted generically, but through the doctrine of *union with Christ*. Only as we are united to Christ through the Spirit do we participate in the Trinitarian life. See for example J. Todd Billings, "Union with Christ and the Double Grace: Calvin's Theology and Its Early Reception," in *Calvin's Theology and Its Reception*, ed. J. Todd Billings and I. John Hesselink (Louisville: Westminster John Knox, 2012), 49–71. Also, Marcus Johnson, "'The Highest Degree of Importance': Union with Christ and Soteriology," in *Evangelical Calvinism*, ed. Myk Habets and Bobby Grow (Eugene, OR: Pickwick, 2012), 222–52.
72. Volf, *After Our Likeness*, 197.
73. For example, Husbands writes, "Reminding us that 'human beings can correspond to the uncreated God only in a creaturely way,' he quickly proceeds to depict the goal of salvation as restored human community corresponding to the mutual self-offering of the triune God." Husbands, "The Trinity Is *Not* Our Social Program," 123.
74. Paul Fiddes sees the tendency of "reflective" methodologies to observe and then replicate the Trinity as a consequence of an Enlightenment split between subject and object. Fiddes, *Participating in God*, 11–56.

society comes not from how similar the Trinity is to humanity, but from how different it is. It is not brought down; we are raised up. We do not imitate Trinitarian life; through Christ we participate in it. Along these lines, Tanner comments, "Why think we will relate to other humans . . . in anything like the way we relate to Father or Spirit?"[75] Or, she could have added, in anything like the way the Father, Son, and Spirit relate to each other. She argues that our relationships primarily image Christ's relationships and not intra-Trinitarian relationships. As we "take on his shape in relations with other human beings, we are to form the citizens or members of a new kingdom or community with Christ as both the director and forerunner of the sort of new lives we are to lead together."[76] The incarnation is thus a much better analogy for a human community to aspire toward. For Tanner, then, the idea that the church should be modeled on Trinitarian relationships needs to be replaced with the idea that we share in Trinitarian life, as humans through grace are made one with Jesus who participates in the Trinity by nature. Jesus' relations with the Father and with others are what ours are to be like. There are obviously some points of discontinuity, given that Jesus is both human *and divine* and lived a tempted *and sinless* life. But even with this limitation, Tanner argues that a Christological analogy provides much greater practical insight into human relationships.

Consider how the problems listed above quickly fall away when using a Christological approach. Our lack of knowledge of the immanent Trinity is of no hindrance, for we look rather to the character of Jesus' human relationships to see how the Trinity applies to human life directly. And our finiteness similarly is resolved, for Jesus models perfectly for us how a finite human is to relate to both God and others. We remain in a sin-scarred world, but our grand

75. Tanner, *Christ the Key*, 237.
76. Ibid., 241.

hope is that this too will pass away when we are fully united to Christ in the eschaton. No longer do we need to make the theologically unjustified moves that a close correspondence between the Trinity and human society requires, but rather we can fully recognize the impact of Jesus' humanity on his relationship with the Father, and the distinctions that exist between it and the inner life of the Trinity. And finally, the recognition that Jesus responded to different people in different ways releases us from the fear that the resulting political recommendations will be either unrealistic or uncritically complacent.

Applied specifically to the "reflective" approach of Volf and others, Tanner's argument is very persuasive. But even fully acknowledging her concerns, the argument she presents does not remove in intent or outcome any possibility of an analogical link between the Trinity and the church. What of an alternative approach that complements a Christological methodology (as developed in part two of this research) by considering the implications for the church participating "in" the life of the Trinity? Such an analogical link would focus not on "reflective" imaging but on pneumatological participation. In Gunton's words, it would "replace a *logical* conception of the relation between God and the world with a *personal* one."[77] What if the similarities between divine and human relationships come not because humans are somewhat like divinity, but because they are personally indwelt by the divine Spirit, and therefore united with the human Christ? If this approach is adopted, then the continuities between the Spirit's immanent identity and his ecclesial role could be used to inform our ecclesial understanding. And believers' pneumatological union with Christ would enable comparison between his Sonship and our participatory role in the Trinity. Do

77. Colin Gunton, "The Church on Earth: The Roots of Community," in *On Being the Church*, ed. C. Gunton and D. Hardy (Edinburgh: T. & T. Clark, 1989), 67.

Tanner's concerns hold equal weight when applied to this quite different, less direct, and more nuanced analogical approach?

Their weight may well be significantly diminished. Tanner's first concern can certainly be neglected. No inflated claims regarding the Trinity's intrinsic application to human relationships are made in such an approach. No denigration of monotheism as autocracy, or ecclesiologically motivated selective interpretation of Trinitarianism is being applied. Her second concern is similarly diminished. While there is still a need for a relational Trinitarian ontology, none of the "heavy lifting" done by the concept of *perichoresis*, the excessive differentiation of the Trinitarian persons within a "hard" social Trinity, or the accused implication of tritheism are required. Indeed, in this approach, it is only once the understanding of the Trinity deemed most faithful to the biblical witness has been determined, that the life of the immanent Trinity, and in particular the Spirit's Trinitarian identity is compared with the Spirit's ecclesial role.

Tanner's third concern regarding our limited knowledge of the Trinity retains some applicability. It is unwise to claim too great a knowledge of the Trinity's inner workings. But similarly it is unnecessary to claim too limited a knowledge of them, an error that Tanner perhaps veers toward in her critique.[78] Consider an overall methodology that moves from the economic Trinity (and particularly Spirit Christology) to the immanent Trinity, and then from the immanent Trinity to the church. At the very least, such an approach avoids Kilby's accusation of circular reasoning.[79] Tanner's fourth concern notes the inapplicability of Trinitarian insights to human relationships due to our finitude and sinfulness. While these differences must be acknowledged, the counterpoint must also be

78. While Tanner understandably emphasizes humanity's lack of Trinitarian knowledge in her "political" critique, she also uses and applies a specific Trinitarian understanding in other work. Her critical comments need to be regarded in this light. See further section 9.1.

79. Kilby, "Perichoresis and Projection," 432–45.

recognized. For there are also similarities that derive not from the fact that humans apart from God are a little like him (a spurious argument indeed) but from believers' participation in God's Trinitarian life. The immanent Trinitarian Spirit also dwells within believers, and this Spirit unites us to Christ the Son, enabling believers to share his filial relationship with the Father.

When making judgments about ecclesial relationships, Tanner argues for a Christological approach over a "reflective" Trinitarian methodology.[80] Taken to an extreme—one of which presumably Tanner would not approve—her argument can imply that the immanent Trinitarian identity has nothing constructive to say about inter- or intra-church relationships.[81] And such a broad claim is unjustified. While significant insights into the church's being and mission can be derived from directly observing Jesus' identity and mission, a Trinitarian analogy enables further illumination. A pneumatologically enabled and Christologically conditioned analogical approach between the Trinity and the church is coherent and viable, because the immanent identities of the Son and the Spirit are revealed throughout all aspects of the economy. There are continuities between the immanent identity of the Son and the Spirit in the Trinitarian union and the hypostatic union (Christology), the mystical union (soteriology), and the ecclesial union (ecclesiology). It is difficult, however, to pursue this discussion in such abstract terms. So the argument turns now to the work of Heribert Mühlen, who uses a pneumatologically enabled but Christologically conditioned approach to maintain that "the Holy Spirit is one person in many persons,"[82] a Trinitarian insight he applies to the life of the church.

80. While agreeing with Tanner, I would add that this incarnational analogy is pneumatologically enabled. As argued in part two, the church only reflects Jesus *through the Spirit*.

81. As such, part three of this research is not intended to contradict Tanner's work (in chapter 5 of *Christ the Key*) but rather to extend her work in chapter 4 of the same book, to an area (ecclesiology) that neither Tanner, Weinandy, nor Habets has yet explored in detail.

8.3 Pneumatological Participation

This chapter has outlined concerns not just with Volf's characterization of the church as a Trinitarian "image," but with "reflective" methodologies in general. These concerns raise the question of whether not just "reflective" but all analogical comparisons between the two doctrines are misguided. Particularly, can a viable analogical connection be constructed that uses a pneumatological lens? This section examines one theologian's use of such a Third Article Theology approach, comparing the identity and role of the Holy Spirit in the Trinity, in Christ, and in Christians. It will be argued that Heribert Mühlen's work provides a coherent example for how insights about the immanent Trinity can be analogically applied to the life of the church. Without undermining this key methodological point, it is also noted that Mühlen's "speculative" Trinitarian starting point and *a priori* acceptance of the *filioque* is insufficiently grounded in the biblical revelation, and as such leads to misguided conclusions. The recognition that Mühlen's pneumatological methodology is valid even if his starting point is mistaken encourages exploring the analogical implications of the "reconceived" Trinity for the anointed church through such an approach.

Heribert Mühlen was a Roman Catholic from Germany, who (like David Coffey) trained under Karl Rahner and Michael Schmaus, spending his academic life at the Theology Faculty Paderborn. Pope Paul VI appointed him as a theological expert during the Second Vatican Council. Mühlen's work is well known among Catholic scholars, but is perhaps less prevalent in Protestant scholarship.[83] His theological work examined here is contained in *Der Heilige Geist als*

82. Mühlen, *Una Mystica Persona*, 63. As quoted in and translated by Vondey, *Heribert Mühlen*, 105.
83. Particularly his early publications, which are the subject of this analysis.

Person[84] and its sequel *Una Mystica Persona*.[85] Mühlen presents the best example of a contemporary theologian who makes an explicit link between the Spirit's immanent identity and his ecclesial role.[86] The following discussion examines and then critiques Mühlen's analogical methodology.

Basing his understanding on both Scripture and tradition,[87] Mühlen argues that the Holy Spirit should be identified as the "we" in person, the inner-Trinitarian we-relation.[88] His argument begins by developing a Trinitarian analogy using personal pronouns, designating the Father as "I" (emphasizing his self-derivation), and the Son as "Thou" (emphasizing his unique filial relationship). Mühlen rejects the conception that the Holy Spirit can be *identically* understood as the mutual love (or I-Thou relation) of the Father and Son on both scriptural and logical grounds,[89] but rather characterizes the Spirit through considering the traditional formula "two persons spirating nevertheless one spirator." Focusing on the "two persons spirating," the emphasis is on the Spirit proceeding from the reciprocal love of the Father and the Son. Mühlen illustrates this by picturing a father and mother together being independent but

84. Heribert Mühlen, *Der Heilige Geist als Person. Beitrag zur Frage nach der dem Heiligen Geiste eigentümlichen Funktion in der Trinität, bei der Inkarnation und im Gnadenbund* (Münster: Aschendorff, 1963).

85. Mühlen, *Una Mystica Persona*.

86. Given that Mühlen's work is being used here simply as an example, the following description is excessively brief. A more comprehensive examination of Mühlen's work is both profitable and justified. See particularly Vondey, *Heribert Mühlen*, 49–160.

87. Particularly Augustine, Thomas Aquinas, and Richard of St. Victor.

88. Mühlen, *Der Heilige Geist als Person*, 157. As translated by and quoted in Vondey, *Heribert Mühlen*, 78. This unusual terminology will be explained below.

89. Regarding the former, Mühlen notes that when Scripture talks of the love of the Father for the Son, or the Son for the Father, the Holy Spirit is not mentioned as if it were that love. Regarding the latter, Mühlen uses Richard of St. Victor's claim that there are two types of love within the Godhead: reciprocal and common love. The Holy Spirit cannot exist as the reciprocal love of Father and Son because then there would be no common love. The Father and Son in their action of love to each other act separately and not together—by definition there is no commonality to their mutual love.

necessary "principles" in the proceeding of a child. The "one spirator" puts the emphasis on the numerically single divine nature, and thus the common act performed together by the two persons. Again using the marriage illustration, "the reciprocal 'yes' of the two spouses already anticipated a we-union . . . [with the resulting] child as the concretization of this common 'we' in person."[90] Just as the Father is constituted in relation to his Son (by active generation) and the Son is constituted in relation to his Father (by passive generation), so the Father and the Son together constitute the Holy Spirit in their common we-act (which is active spiration) and the person of the Holy Spirit is constituted in relation to the Father *and* the Son by the associated *passive* spiration. Mühlen concludes: "In a way comparable to saying that the Son is the subsisting act of knowledge of the Father (which includes love) one can likewise say that the Holy Spirit is the subsisting we-act between the Father and the Son, he is the 'we' in person, that is, the inner-Trinitarian we-relation."[91] Summarizing, Mühlen characterizes the Trinity as I-Thou-We relations, noting specifically that for the Spirit "the union of the I and the thou 'becomes' person,"[92] and is thus the personification of the relating community: "one person in two persons."[93] It is this understanding of the Spirit that Mühlen applies to the church.

Mühlen characterizes the church using the traditional formula: *una mystica persona*. He argues that the Bible implicitly uses the notion of "corporate personality," which fluidly transitions from the individual to the community and back. Introducing the terminology of the "Great-I," which stands between the "I" of the individual and the

90. Vondey, *Heribert Mühlen*, 77.

91. Mühlen, *Der Heilige Geist als Person*, 157. As quoted in and translated by Vondey, *Heribert Mühlen*, 78.

92. Vondey, *Heribert Mühlen*, 78.

93. Mühlen, *Der Heilige Geist als Person*, 157. As quoted in and translated by Vondey, *Heribert Mühlen*, 78.

"we" of community,[94] Mühlen uses the biblical metaphors of the church as the body and the "fullness" of Christ to argue that Christ and the church together form a "Great-I." Further, Mühlen notes that the "potency" through which Christ unites himself with the church as the "Great-I" is the Spirit: the "absolute mystery that in this plurality of human persons one uncreated person operates as the final principle of union."[95] Just as in the Trinity the Spirit is the "we" in person between the Father and the Son, one person in two persons, so in the church the Spirit is the "we" in person between Christ and Christians, one person in many persons. In ecclesiology, as in the Trinity, it is "the proper function of the Holy Spirit to relate persons"[96] and consequently the church can "be understood as the mystery of the presence of the Holy Spirit in Christ and in Christians."[97]

From this basis, Mühlen addresses the twin questions of how the Holy Spirit is present in Christ and the church. Regarding the former, Mühlen's presuppositional acceptance of the *filioque* leads to the implication that the hypostatic union logically precedes the anointing. Consequently, the habitual graces, which are enabled by the indwelling Holy Spirit, are logically dependent on the grace of union, which is enabled by the divine Son. And from this Christologically conditioned insight he deduces the general rule: "grace presupposes a person."[98] Mühlen also improves upon the traditional scholastic understanding by providing a distinct role for the Spirit in the growth and development of Jesus' humanity.[99] Badcock comments: "Mühlen is able to argue that the Spirit created in Jesus such graces as were required for his messianic office and that,

94. The Great-I occurs when a community is "represented" by an individual. For example, Moses, Abraham, or Israel (i.e., Jacob) himself with the Israelite nation.
95. Mühlen, *Una Mystica Persona*, 63. As quoted in and translated by Vondey, *Heribert Mühlen*, 105.
96. Vondey, *Heribert Mühlen*, 115.
97. Ibid.
98. Ibid., 120.
99. As noted in section 2.2.

through time, these graces increased and developed in his personal history."[100] While these graces depend directly on the Spirit, they find their ultimate cause in the divine presence of the Son, as the Spirit's presence is dependent on the hypostatic union.

Regarding the latter ecclesial anointing, Mühlen argues that the church is not a continuation of the hypostatic union (a unique historical event) but rather a continuation of Jesus' *anointing*.[101] He speaks of the "uncreated grace" of the Holy Spirit, which is numerically identical in both Christ and the church, and contrasts it with "created grace" (i.e., the effects of the self-communication of God within human persons), which differs between Christ and the church. He writes: "The church is the mystery of the identity (union) of the uncreated grace (of the Holy Spirit) and the simultaneous non-identity (differentiation) of the created grace in Christ and us."[102] Mühlen unpacks this ecclesiological formulation by exploring how the Holy Spirit is "one person in many persons" in the church. Focusing first on the "one in many" aspect, he contrasts Jesus' temporary earthly presence with the Spirit's ongoing presence. Mühlen argues that as one person in many persons the Spirit continues Christ's work through history, making his sacrifice present through and beyond time. The Holy Spirit transcends the distinctions of time and space, and does so both within and beyond history. The Spirit therefore relates us as the historical church not just to the glorified and eternal Son but also to the historical Jesus. Both the covenant and the "Great-I" have their continuity ensured by the

100. Gary D. Badcock, *Light of Truth and Fire of Love: A Theology of the Holy Spirit* (Grand Rapids: Eerdmans, 1997), 151.

101. For example, see the discussion in Bradford E. Hinze, "Releasing the Power of the Spirit in a Trinitarian Ecclesiology," in *Advents of the Spirit: An Introduction to the Current Study of Pneumatology*, ed. Bradford E. Hinze and D. Lyle Dabney (Milwaukee: Marquette University Press, 2005), 355–57.

102. Mühlen, *Una Mystica Persona*, 211. As quoted in and translated by Vondey, *Heribert Mühlen*, 122.

Holy Spirit. "The Holy Spirit as the 'we' in person . . . is himself the continuity between the historical and glorified Christ and the Church."[103] The second aspect of Mühlen's investigation is on the Holy Spirit as "one *person* in many *persons*" in the Trinity and the church; that is, the analogy's *personal* aspect. Mühlen finds here an understanding of the covenant between God and humanity, with Christ acting on both sides. As divine, Christ is the cause of the sending of the Holy Spirit and in this gives himself fully to humanity. As human, Christ enters into a relationship with humanity through the Spirit that intensifies believers' ability to respond in obedience. The Holy Spirit thus comes from Christ, and through uniting us with him continues Christ's anointing in the church.

Summarizing, Mühlen applies the Spirit's immanent Trinitarian identity as "one person in many persons" horizontally and vertically to the life of the church. Horizontally, Jesus' salvation is passed on through the Spirit's presence, who unlike Jesus is present at all places and times within and beyond history.[104] Vertically, the reception of the Spirit gives individual Christians access to the Father through Christ. Mühlen concludes: "The Church is the visible and tangible form of the invisible Holy Spirit and therefore the grace of God and Christ. This, however, is possible only because the Holy Spirit is numerically one and the same in the Father, in the Son, and in the whole Church."[105]

In reflecting on Mühlen's analysis, two overarching points can be made. First, and positively, Mühlen's work succeeds in avoiding Tanner's four concerns for analogically linking the Trinity and

103. Mühlen, *Una Mystica Persona*, 284–85. As quoted in and translated by Vondey, *Heribert Mühlen*, 125.

104. It is of course true to say that Jesus is omnipresent through the Spirit, but this is only true *through the Spirit*. Viewed from the limitations of his incarnate humanity, Jesus is localized. He is restricted to being at one place at one time, as are all spacetime-bound creatures.

105. Mühlen, *Una Mystica Persona*, 358. As quoted in and translated by Vondey, *Heribert Mühlen*, 131.

ecclesiology. Second, and negatively, each troubling affirmation in Mühlen's work can be traced back to his speculative Trinitarian starting point. Considering first the positive aspect, I argue in the following that not only does Mühlen's work avoid Tanner's concerns, but it clearly demonstrates that a Trinitarian perspective is needed to complement and enhance the Christological vantage point Tanner commends.

Tanner's first two concerns are easily avoided. Regarding the first—that inflated claims are made about the Trinity's application to human relationships—Mühlen is not taking an abstract, communal, Trinitarian quality such as diversity or equality as his point of comparison between the Trinity and the church, but rather the personal presence and working of the Spirit. Consequently he makes no assumptions that a Trinitarian understanding corresponds to any human social structure. Regarding the second—that unjustifiable theological moves have been made in order to correlate Trinitarian and human community—Mühlen's Trinitarian understanding is heavily derived from traditional and scriptural sources, and not based on an *a priori* ecclesiology. While Mühlen extends the tradition in describing the Holy Spirit as one person in two persons, this does not make the Trinity more human but rather more distinct from humanity. A *human* personification of a "we" relation is virtually inconceivable. God's interpenetrating divinity is the only thing that makes such a concept plausible. While Mühlen's mutual-love understanding certainly requires a relational ontology, his Trinitarian conception is easily distinguished from tritheism.[106]

106. Mühlen's key defense against the charge of tritheism is that the pronouns used are not merely expressions of self-consciousness but also incommunicable existence, and it is those particular aspects that are conveyed in assigning pronouns to the divine persons. Hughson writes that "I and thou express human subsisting both in its intrinsically interpersonal and in its solitary, incommunicable aspects." Donald Thomas Hughson, "I-Thou-We: A Critical Study of the Analogy Central to the Pneumatology of Heribert Mühlen" (Ph.D. diss., Toronto: University

The issue underlying Tanner's third concern is that human qualities are getting implicitly mapped onto Trinitarian relationships. Tanner asserts that in view of this, applying Trinitarian insights to human relationships is fruitless. Such a logical path cannot be overextended, though. If there is nothing "Trinitarian" about the church, then not only is the church not the *image* of the Trinity, it does not participate in Trinitarian life. Removing all traces of the Trinity means removing all traces of the divine, an equally undesirable result. Certainly we have a limited knowledge of the Trinity. But if that is all we have, then that is what we must work with. Insight into how the church is divine simply cannot be gained by studying the natural characteristics of human society. Mühlen's methodology takes that person of the Trinity that dwells within the church and asserts that the Spirit's ecclesial role matches to some extent his immanent identity. He argues that the Spirit unites us with Christ as the "Great-I," and so enables us to participate in his Trinitarian Sonship. Examined in detail, Mühlen's approach is actually the direct opposite of Tanner's underlying concern that human qualities are being mapped onto Trinitarian relationships. The question is precisely how (following Christ our prototype, and in Christ as our "Great-I") human relationships can participate in the divine life through the presence of the Spirit, while still remaining fully human. Mühlen's approach thus explicitly aims to answer how ecclesial relationships within the church are more than merely anthropological, and in such a pursuit making the Trinity more like humanity is evidently pointless.

Tanner's fourth concern is that much of what is said about the Trinity is not directly applicable to humans, because of humanity's finitude and sinfulness. And while she is undoubtedly correct in

of Saint Michael's College, 1981), 93. For more detail see ibid., 83–93. See also Vondey, *Heribert Mühlen*, xxiii.

this, there is certainly one Trinitarian reality that is applicable to humanity: the Spirit's presence. And as the cross demonstrates, this Spirit dwells within humanity even in the midst of our finitude and present sinfulness. It is precisely the presence of the Spirit that enables the conundrum outlined by Tanner to be resolved.[107] Humanity does not need to become "like" the Trinity for an analogy between the two to be of theological value to us, for the third person of the Trinity dwells within us, as he dwells within the Trinity, and as he dwells within the incarnate Christ. And this Spirit unites us to Christ, enabling us to participate in Christ's Trinitarian Sonship. Herein lies the beauty of a Third Article Theology approach. For just as Tanner urges, this methodology points us first and foremost to Christ. The Spirit in Christ becomes the primary means by which we initially understand the role of the Spirit in the church. Much understanding can be gained regarding the ontology and action of the church by observing it from a Christological perspective, enabled through a pneumatological lens. This was precisely the purpose of part two, which concluded with a picture of the church as a single entity, which communes as this single entity with the Father through the Spirit, as we all together are united to Christ in the Spirit.

But, recognizing this, it is not necessary or fruitful to reject all analogical insights between the Trinity and the church in favor of purely Christological insights. The use of analogy does not need to be restricted to Christology, but merely conditioned by it. There remain significant ecclesiological questions that are not well illustrated through a purely Christological analogical approach. In part, this is because the Christological analogy leans toward Jesus' earthly incarnation, and not a broader Christological horizon. As Webster

107. The conundrum, mentioned earlier, is that to the extent the Trinity's relationships are like human relationships we don't need to know of them, while to the extent they are unlike human relationships we cannot imitate them.

comments, "Ecclesiology tends to be preoccupied with the question: What kind of continuity is there between the incarnate and the ecclesial body? The very form of the question narrows the range in which the relations and differences between Christ and the church may be understood."[108] Webster argues that we need to consider not just the incarnation, but the eternal deity and exaltation of the Son in comparing Christ and the church. An emphasis on these (often neglected) aspects of Christology and their implications for ecclesiology is encouraged in a *Trinitarian* Third Article Theology.

A Trinitarian vantage point encourages other questions to be examined, such as: How do we participate in Christ's relationship with the Father? How does our constitution in relationship with Christ affect our relationships with one another? In short, what does it mean that the church is not just a unity but a community? Not just united with Christ, but participants in a community with him? Not just one, but many? Mühlen's work demonstrates that viewing the church from the perspective of the Trinity enables a clearer vantage point from which to view the answers to such questions. For example, when his insight that the Spirit's Trinitarian role as one person in many people is applied to the church it reveals how the salvation of Jesus is extended to the whole church through the presence of the one Spirit. This insight is not gained from a Christological analogy, but a Trinitarian one that is then applied to soteriology and ecclesiology. It thus demonstrates just one example of the validity of Mühlen's methodology to analogically relate the Trinity and the church through the lens of the Spirit. And it prompts the question of what other insights could be gained through such an approach.

108. Webster, "In the Society of God," 209.

While the above analysis of Mühlen's work demonstrates the validity of using a Christologically conditioned pneumatological lens to examine the analogies between the Trinity and the church, gaining accurate ecclesial insights will require a different Trinitarian starting point. Mühlen's methodology is coherent, but his analysis and conclusions need to be refined. The following argument examines several critiques of Mühlen's Trinitarian, Christological, and ecclesiological analysis, noting that in each area his misguided conclusions are derived from his "speculative" Trinitarian starting point being insufficiently grounded in the biblical witness.

First, there is criticism of Mühlen's "I-Thou-We" Trinitarian analogy. Hughson notes that no consistent name is found for the Holy Spirit, who in the overall analogy is the we-in-person, but becomes a "thou" in active relation to the Father and the Son (which is characterized as a we-thou relation) and an "I" in passive relation to the Father and the Son (which is characterized as an I-you [plural] relation). For Hughson, this triple naming suggests that the pronoun-based analogy breaks down in categorizing the personhood of the Holy Spirit.[109] Coffey similarly criticizes Mühlen's pronominalization, by arguing that the "we" is the principle from which the Holy Spirit proceeds, rather than the Holy Spirit in person. According to Coffey, the pronoun "we" can only be used for the Father and the Son together, but not for the Holy Spirit, which is distinct from and in a relation of opposition to them.[110] Bracken's critique further notes that the Holy Spirit as the "subsistent we relation" can never address the Father or Son individually, but only together.[111] Together, these arguments point to the overall

109. Hughson, "I-Thou-We," 202–10.

110. See David Coffey, *Deus Trinitas: The Doctrine of the Triune God* (New York: Oxford University Press, 1999), 134–35. For Coffey's overall critique of Mühlen see David Coffey, *Grace: The Gift of the Holy Spirit* (Milwaukee: Marquette University Press, 2011), 119–50.

conclusion that Mühlen's Trinitarian understanding insufficiently recognizes the Spirit's personhood.

Regarding Mühlen's Christology, Coffey argues insightfully that in separating the anointing from the hypostatic union, Mühlen artificially separates Christ's person from his office.[112] Further, making Christ's anointing dependent on the hypostatic union contradicts the biblical account of the Spirit's facilitation of the incarnation. One could perceptively question Mühlen on this point: If the Spirit has a vital role in the Son's increasing graces, how can he be absent from the original grace of union? Marino similarly notes that for Mühlen there is "a certain 'dependency' of the Holy Spirit on the Logos, so that the proper function of the Holy Spirit is seen only in the work of Christ."[113] Together with Gwan-Hee Kim, he argues that this comes from Mühlen's overdependence on a western Logos Christology and neglect of Spirit Christology.[114] Utilizing the Spirit Christological analysis of chapter 2, Mühlen's Christology can be accurately categorized as a Son-priority proposal.[115]

Mühlen's ecclesiological conclusions can also be questioned. The church's continuity with Jesus' anointing but discontinuity with the hypostatic union is argued by Czaja to neglect "the significant consideration, [of] how Christians participate in the 'being' of

111. See Joseph A. Bracken, "The Holy Trinity as a Community of Divine Persons, II. Person and Nature in the Doctrine of God," *The Heythrop Journal* 5, no. 15 (1974): 257–70, particularly pp. 263–68. Bracken argues for seeing the Trinitarian "we" as the cumulative working of all three Trinitarian persons. See for example Joseph A. Bracken, Robert Thomas Sears, and Richard Hill, "Trinity and World Process," *Proceedings of the Annual Convention of the Catholic Theological Society of America* 33 (1978): 203–20.

112. For this and Coffey's following critiques, see Coffey, *Grace*, 91–119. Also, David Coffey, "A Proper Mission of the Holy Spirit," *Theological Studies* 47, no. 2 (1986): 237–43.

113. This is Vondey's summary of Marino's argument. Vondey, *Heribert Mühlen*, xxxiv. See also Francesco Marino, "L'ecclesiologia di Heribert Mühlen: La chiesa nel mistero dello Spirito di Christo e del Padre" (S.T.D. diss., Pontificia Facoltà Teologica dell'Italia Meridionale Sezione S. Luigi, Naples, 1998), 226–33.

114. See the discussion in Vondey, *Heribert Mühlen*, xxxiv–xxxv.

115. See section 2.2.

Jesus."[116] Further, there appears to be an inconsistency of logical order. In both the Trinity and the hypostatic union, first there is the union and then logically subsequent to it, the Holy Spirit is spirated or dwells. But with the mystical union, it is through the Spirit that believers are united with Christ (e.g., 1 Cor. 6:17). In the former two situations the Spirit is the consequence of the union, in the latter the Spirit is the cause of the union. There is thus a crucial point of discontinuity between the immanent identity of the Spirit and his role in the economy. Mühlen's general rule that "grace presupposes a person" heightens the severity of this critique. According to Mühlen's understanding of the Trinity, the union of equals spirates the Spirit. But between Christ and humanity, there is no union of equals. Do we not need to be "personed" before such a "union of persons" can be formed? And how can we be "personed" apart from the grace of the Holy Spirit?

In all three doctrinal areas—Trinity, Christology, ecclesiology—Mühlen's work faces significant challenges. But these challenges are not grounded in his analogical methodology, but rather his speculative Trinitarian understanding. In particular, they result from his *a priori* assumption of the *filioque*. In ecclesiology, Mühlen's problematic assertion that grace presupposes a person is sourced directly back to the *filioque*, for in the Trinity the generation of the Son logically occurs "before" the spiration of the Spirit. Mühlen's Son-priority Christology is also sourced from his commitment to the *filioque*, which affirms the Son is logically prior to the Spirit. And in the Trinity, it is the *filioque* that (in part) causes Mühlen's speculative identification of the Spirit as the "we" of the Father and the Son, thereby minimizing the Spirit's personhood.

116. As described in ibid., xxxi.

Interestingly, the Indonesian-born scholar Johannes Baptist Banawiratma, realizing these problems are all rooted in Mühlen's speculative Trinitarian starting point, suggests Mühlen's methodology be reversed, starting with the economy and concluding with a Trinitarian understanding. He writes, "If the theological 'entrance' is taken at the historical manifestation of the church—not at the eternal and trans-historical structures of the Trinitarian life of God—then there emerges from the beginning more strongly the significance of the life and historical sending of Jesus as well as the participation of the Church in it."[117] Vondey notes, however, that "Banawiratma's re-visioning of Mühlen's theology did not find great support among scholars."[118]

A different methodology has been adopted in part three of this research. Rather than Banawiratma's (or Rahner's) single directional route from the economy to the immanent Trinity, it has used a "Wolterstorffian" approach.[119] Recognizing Spirit Christology as the economic reality that most clearly illumines God's triune nature, a route was traced upwards to gain a biblically responsible understanding of the immanent Trinity. The analysis concluded that Weinandy's "reconceived" conception of the Trinity (where the Father begets the Son by the Holy Spirit) provides such a model. The relation between the immanent Trinity and ecclesiology was then considered. Rejecting the "reflective" approach adopted by Volf and validly critiqued by Tanner, it was argued that a pneumatologically enabled, but Christologically conditioned methodology provides a coherent and viable link between the Trinity and the church. This Third Article Theology approach maintains that the church

117. Johannes Baptist Banawiratma, *Der Heilige Geist in der Theologie von Heribert Mühlen. Versuch einer Darstellung und Würdigung* (Frankfurt: Peter Lang, 1981), 235. As quoted in and translated by Vondey, *Heribert Mühlen*, xxx.

118. Vondey, *Heribert Mühlen*, xxx.

119. See section 3.2.

participates in the life of the Trinity because of the indwelling Spirit who unites us to Christ, enabling our participation in his Trinitarian Sonship. Mühlen's characterization of the Holy Spirit as "one person in many people" in the Trinity, Christ, and the church provided an excellent example that such an analogical link is both plausible and profitable. Without invalidating this important methodological point, several concerns were noted with Mühlen's conclusions, all of which were traced back to Mühlen's speculative Trinitarian starting point, and particularly his presuppositional acceptance of the *filioque*. This leads to the final step in our analogical methodology, which is to employ a pneumatologically enabled, Christologically conditioned approach to view the anointed church from the vantage point of the "reconceived" Trinity, thus fashioning a coherent *Trinitarian* Third Article Ecclesiology. It is this final step that is the focus of the next chapter.

9

Ecclesial Communion in the Trinity

The objective of part three of this research and this chapter in particular is to examine the church through the lens of the Spirit from the vantage point of the Trinity. Following the preparation of chapter 7, which argued that a "reconceived" Trinitarian understanding was faithful to the biblical witness, and chapter 8, which argued that the approach of Third Article Theology can coherently establish an analogical connection between the Trinity and the church, this chapter examines the ontology and activity of the church through a pneumatologically enabled but Christologically conditioned analogical link with the "reconceived" Trinity. In Wolterstorff's terms the "reconceived" Trinity is the *control belief*, ecclesiology is the *data belief*, and Scripture and the creeds form the *background beliefs*.[1] Two relational aspects of the church's existence are seen clearly from this vantage point. First, its inter-ecclesial relational aspects: the Spirit unites the church with Christ, and the church then

1. See section 3.2.

shares Christ's filial relationship with the Father. In J. B. Torrance's succinct expression (which the titles of both part three and this chapter refer to), the church participates "by the Spirit in Jesus's communion with the Father."[2] It is not just believers as separated individuals who participate in Jesus' communion, however, but the united church. There is *one* relationship, which the *many* participate in together as we are united in Christ and to each other. Section 9.1 examines the dynamics of this communal Trinitarian worship and service.

Second, the intra-ecclesial relational aspects: the Spirit unites us not just to Christ (*as* the church) but to each other (*within* the church). Evidentially the church is not one, but many. It is many in a biological sense (consisting of many individuals), a geographical sense (existing in many different localities), and in a sociological sense (exhibiting many different contextual expressions). How can this diversity be resolved with the church's oneness in Christ? And how do we share in each other's diversity? In other words, what does it mean that the church is catholic, with each a part of the other, and each a part of the whole? In what way are believers connected, while remaining distinct? Section 9.2 examines the dynamics of these intra-ecclesial relationships.

9.1 Inter-Ecclesial Relationships

The following discussion argues that ecclesial worship and service happen as together we participate in Jesus' communion with and sending from the Father through the Spirit, as (again, together) we are in Christ and in the Spirit.[3] More concisely, church life occurs as

2. James B. Torrance, *Worship, Community and the Triune God of Grace* (Downers Grove, IL: IVP Academic, 1996), 31.
3. Through the Spirit, the church participates not just in the Son's communion, but also in his mission to the world. While a natural extension of this research, the exploration of the church's

we participate in Trinitarian life. Such an understanding is not new.[4] In recent decades, it has been particularly associated with the Scottish theologian J. B. Torrance,[5] emerging also in Kathryn Tanner's work,[6] among others. Tanner, for example, notes that both the church's worship and service (as upward and downward moves to and from the Father with Christ in the Spirit) are participations in Trinitarian life. She pictures this ecclesial participation as simultaneous ascents and descents, noting that "just as they did in the life of the Trinity itself, the two movements should properly coincide."[7] The following discussion explores the parallels between Christ's Trinitarian life and that of the church's communal life as it is united with Christ, by examining how the immanent identities of the Son and Spirit are reprised (with continuities and discontinuities) in the hypostatic union and the mystical union.

The Trinitarian Union

The "reconceived" understanding of the Trinity developed and affirmed in section 7.3 is a relational ontology where the Father begets the Son in the Spirit, and the Son simultaneously loves the Father in the same Spirit by which he was begotten. The begetting of the Son and the proceeding of the Spirit are thus logically distinct

participation in the Son's mission to the world is beyond the scope of this research. See the discussion of next steps in section 11.2.

4. The notion of ecclesial participation in God's life is at least as old as Eastern Orthodoxy. On a related note, theotic themes may be compatible with the research direction pursued here, but they are not an essential part of it. The intentionally chosen language here speaks of *participation* rather than *theosis*.
5. See Torrance, *Worship, Community and the Triune God of Grace*. Also James B. Torrance, "The Vicarious Humanity of Christ," in *The Incarnation: Ecumenical Studies in the Nicene-Constantinopolitan Creed A.D. 381*, ed. Thomas F. Torrance (Edinburgh: Handsell, 1981); and James B. Torrance, "The Trinity and Worship (Lecture)" (Auckland: St. John's College, 1989).
6. Kathryn Tanner, *Christ the Key* (Cambridge: Cambridge University Press, 2010), 140–206. These pages refer to the complete article, although it is only in pp. 196–206 that Tanner explicitly applies this to Christian life.
7. Ibid., 206.

but existentially inseparable. The understanding is dynamic and continuous—an outward motion of fatherly begetting and love is accompanied by a simultaneous inward motion of filial response and love. And the Spirit is the person through which both "movements" occur; thus he is the Spirit of Sonship and the Spirit of Fatherhood. Three distinctive features of this inner-Trinitarian dynamism were noted and are recalled briefly here.

First, the Son and the Spirit do not exist or act sequentially but are logically and chronologically synchronous. The Father begets the Son and spirates the Spirit in one single action, and the Son returns love to the Father by the Spirit in a single action, simultaneous with the first. Just as in human speech, breath and word are logically distinguishable but completely inseparable, so too is the Father's "Breathing" of the "Word." Second, each of the persons is active and constitutive within the Trinity. As such, Trinitarian *perichoresis* comes not as a *result* of begetting or spirating, but is *identified* as the continuing or eternal action by which the members of the Trinity beget/spirate/person one another. The "originating person" (the Father) continually persons the "personed person" (the Son) in or by the "personing person" (the Spirit), and the Father is similarly personed through the Son's Spirit-enabled continual loving response. Third, the Trinity *in fieri* is identical to the Trinity *in facto esse*. This dynamic, perichoretic movement of Father, Son, and Spirit through which the Trinity is constituted is not a once-only occurrence but eternally occurring. God exists moment by moment as this relational, communal being. In every instant of eternity, the Godhead is constituted and subsists through the Father begetting the Son in the Spirit, and the Son returning the love of the Father through the Spirit of Sonship given to him.

The Hypostatic Union

This understanding of the immanent Trinity is now applied to the economic reality of the Son becoming incarnate, with the inevitable limitations and alterations that space, time, and humanity bring to the dynamic, eternal Trinitarian identity.[8] The eternal Son performs all actions jointly with the Father and the Spirit; he is an agent of creation, judge, redeemer, and receiver of worship. But in taking on humanity Jesus is simultaneously a created man, a judged man (for *our* sins), the prototype of our redemption, and the one true worshipper, our great High Priest. So the relational ontology of the immanent Trinity is reprised on a new stage. The Father sends the Son to become incarnate by the Spirit (analogous to the Father begetting the Son by the Spirit). Jesus vicariously suffered our humanity, and learned obedience through what he suffered (Heb. 5:8). The Father by the Spirit conceived and empowered Jesus, who by this Spirit saw, listened to, obeyed, and was (willingly) utterly dependent on the Father. Jesus in his incarnation always had the status of Sonship, but rather than directly using the power inherent in his divine nature, he relied on the Spirit through whom the Father enabled the human Jesus both to be and to act as the true Son of the Father.

But the "gift" of Sonship Jesus received from the Father by the Spirit, which enables Jesus to become who he is (in his humanity) and act as he does (as a human), is turned immediately back to the Father. Jesus prays to and worships the Father, and all that he is and has is given to the Father by the Spirit as a loving response. This is the second, *ascending* aspect of Trinitarian life worked out in space, time, and in Jesus' humanity. By the Spirit, the Son *as a human* responds to the Father in love through the Spirit of Sonship given to him *in his humanity* by the Father. The simultaneous nature

8. Note that this subsection concisely traverses in reverse the argument traced in section 7.3.

of the immanent identity is inevitably elongated and spread, for the limitations of space, time, and Jesus' changing and growing humanity bring to it an intrinsically sequential component. Jesus must grow and develop as a human in order to increasingly experience in an actualized relationship the Sonship which is his by nature.[9] But even with this elongation, the overall dynamic shape of the immanent identity remains. Throughout the incarnation, and now in glory, Jesus' relationship with the Father was and is one of intimate communion. Not just originally, but continually being given the gift of Sonship in his humanity by the Spirit from the Father, Jesus returns the love of the Father by the Spirit in a continuous act of human worship.

So on creation's stage, in the hypostatic union, the three features of the immanent Trinity noted above are retained, but with modifications derived from the intrinsically limited reality of space, time, and human nature. First, the Son and the Spirit *together* are sent out from and return to the Father. In the hypostatic union, there is no Jesus (the Son) without the Spirit, and no Spirit without Jesus (the Son). Second, the Father continually indwells Jesus in his humanity and Jesus continually indwells the Father (John 17:21) and both these indwellings happen by the Spirit. While it is probably wise to hesitate in calling this human indwelling *perichoresis*,[10] in a similar "perichoretic" sense, the Son is only the incarnate Christ by means of the indwelling Spirit given from the Father, through whom the hypostastic union is originally enabled and continuously sustained. In this sense, in the hypostatic union the Spirit enables

9. See for example Thomas Weinandy, "Jesus' Filial Vision of the Father," *Pro Ecclesia* 13, no. 2 (2004): 189–201.

10. The reticence in terming this mutual indwelling of the Father and the human Christ as *perichoresis* stems in part from ontological necessity no longer being the case. While the incarnate Son is sustained through the continued gift of the Spirit from the Father, the Father is not sustained through the human love of Christ. The Father is perichoretically indwelled by Christ's person (identified as the Son) but not by Christ's impersonal human nature.

the Son to be embodied as human, paralleling his *personing* of the immanent Son in eternity. So in the incarnation, the immanent identities are reprised: the Father is the "originating person," the Spirit the "personing person" (as the Son's "incarnator"), and the Son the "personed person" (as incarnate). Third, while the human growth and development of Jesus means his filial relationship with the Father through the Spirit is only gradually and increasingly experienced, Jesus' status of Sonship nevertheless remains constant. Given the restrictions of space, time, and human nature, there is a distinction needed here between the status and experience of Sonship in the human life of Jesus. Following the dyothelite doctrine that Christ has a divine and human will, his status is constant (derived as it is from the continuing gift of the Spirit to the Son from the Father), while his experience is changing and developing (dependent as it is on the changing and developing capacities of Jesus' human will).

The Mystical Union

In the mystical union the dynamic, relational nature of the immanent Trinity expands again into new territory. For as the incarnate Son loves and worships the Father by the Spirit, believers join Christ's vicarious humanity, participating in his filial relationship. The church joins Jesus' acceptable response of love and worship to the Father. But how does this happen? How does the church participate in Christ's worship? How do we attain the status of sonship, and how do we appropriate that status in a growing, but genuinely intimate experience of fellowship and communion with the Father?[11]

11. Clearly the argument at this point is verging on key soteriological questions, which go well beyond the scope of this research. In the following, the reality of union with Christ and his vicarious humanity is affirmed and assumed rather than argued for, with a primary focus being on working out its ecclesiological implications. A detailed soteriological examination from the basis of a Third Article Theology is a nontrivial, necessary, and future examination that is not pursued here. A good starting point though is Myk Habets, *The Anointed Son: A Trinitarian*

Obviously the church participates in Christ's communion *through* Christ himself. Jesus is the sole mediator between God and humanity (John 14:26; Matt. 11:27). The Epistle to the Hebrews presents Jesus as the perfection of the priesthood that "represented" the Israelites before God.[12] He has become human like us, and so we have confidence through Jesus' blood to enter the Most Holy Place where God resides (Heb. 10:19). We enjoy the status of sonship because Jesus the Son in his vicarious humanity has responded to God on behalf of humans.[13] We are drawn into a relationship with the Father as we share in Jesus' response—our participation in his perfect response. But how is that status appropriated in a reality of fellowship, an active experiential relationship?[14] Paul explains that "because [we] are sons [i.e., our status], God sends the Spirit of his Son into our hearts, the Spirit who calls out 'Abba, Father' [i.e., our relationship]" (Gal. 4:6). So we appropriate our relationship through the Spirit. We participate in the intimate communion between the Father and the Son, calling the Father "Father" because the Spirit testifies to us that we are actually children of God (Rom. 8:16). We remain in active fellowship with the Father through the Spirit, as we are united to the incarnate Son.

The immanent identities of the Son and the Spirit are thus reprised in this mystical union. Just as the Son was begotten in eternity *through the Spirit*; just as Christ was hypostatically united in the incarnation *through the Spirit*; so the church is adopted as sons and daughters of

Spirit Christology (Eugene, OR: Pickwick, 2010), 243–57. See also Tanner, *Christ the Key*, 58–139; J. Todd Billings, *Union with Christ: Reframing Theology and Ministry for the Church* (Grand Rapids: Baker Academic, 2011), 222–52; Marcus Johnson, "'The Highest Degree of Importance': Union with Christ and Soteriology," in *Evangelical Calvinism*, ed. Myk Habets and Bobby Grow (Eugene, OR: Pickwick, 2012), 222–52; and Marcus Johnson, *Christ in You, the Hope of Glory: A Theology of Union with Christ* (Wheaton: Crossway, 2013).

12. For a detailed description, see Torrance, *Worship, Community and the Triune God of Grace*, 46–50.
13. See Torrance, "The Vicarious Humanity of Christ," 127–47.
14. See the similar discussion in section 5.2.

God in Christ *through the Spirit*. The Spirit continues to do what he has always done and will always continue to do—*person* sons and daughters of God in Christ. Recognizing necessary discontinuities, there are also significant continuities between the unions: what the Spirit does in eternity is what the Spirit does in the incarnation is what the Spirit does in the church. As Calvin asserts: "We are the sons of God because we have received the same Spirit as his only Son."[15] And the Son too reprises his immanent identity in the mystical union. So the Son who is eternally begotten, who is incarnated in creation, is embodied in the church which consequently becomes his mystical body. Again, recognizing necessary discontinuities, there are significant continuities between the Son being *personed* in the Trinity, *personed* in the hypostatic union, and most pertinently here, *personed in the church*.[16] So now it is Christ who lives his life through us (e.g., Gal 2:20). Calvin again: "[W]e are *one* with the Son of God not because he conveys his substance to us, but because, by the power of the Spirit, he imparts to us his life and all the blessings which he has received from the Father."[17]

Tanner, here, makes the natural link between baptism and our initial participation in Jesus' return to the Father by the Spirit:

> Our initial ascent to the Father with Christ requires us to be joined to Christ, to become Christ's own, through the power of the Spirit; and is therefore associated with baptism. The Spirit ministers to us at our baptisms in order to make us one with Christ, according to the Father's will. United in baptism to Christ, before we fully manifest that unity in the sort of lives we lead, and simply for that reason moving along with him in his return to the Father, we ascend to the Father by being

15. John Calvin, *Calvin's Commentaries*, trans. John Pringle, 23 vols. (Grand Rapids: Baker, 2009), Gal. 4:6, 23:120.
16. Note that it is the same "person" being personed in each of these cases. So the "person" embodied in the church is identified as the person of Christ, who is identified as the person of the Son.
17. Calvin, *Calvin's Commentaries*, John 17:21, 18:184.

> brought back as sinners before him, into his very presence just as we are with all our faults, to be found favorable in the Father's sight because of the company we keep.[18]

The discussion so far has only considered one side of the reprised immanent identities. Through the Spirit, the church participates in Jesus' perfect offering of love and worship to the Father, but what of her service and sending with him? To explain, consider first Jesus' one perfect sacrifice through his death and resurrection (Heb. 10:10). As believers are in Christ, what is true of him becomes true of us—we join Jesus in his sacrificial death. We have died and been raised with him through our baptism "in Christ Jesus" (Rom. 6:3, 6–7). This is the return journey, where we participate in Christ's response of love to the Father. But the journey does not terminate there. Together with Christ and the Spirit believers are sent out again, just as Christ and the Spirit were originally sent. The immanent identity of outward and inward movement, sending and return, continues on this new stage of ecclesial humanity. Having died with Jesus, having been raised with him, believers continue to live with him, presenting our bodies as *living* sacrifices, holy and pleasing to God as our spiritual act of worship (Rom. 12:1), thus following the lead of Jesus, the one true High Priest and perfect sacrifice. And Christ is not just with us but in us, living his life through the church. As Purves comments:

> Through union with Christ, which is the principal work of the Holy Spirit, we participate in Christ's ministry, attesting with thanksgiving what he did two thousand years ago, bearing witness in power to what he does today and anticipating in hope his future ministry . . . every pastoral event is constrained by the ministry of Jesus Christ.[19]

18. Tanner, *Christ the Key*, 198.
19. Andrew Purves, *The Crucifixion of Ministry* (Downers Grove, IL: IVP, 2007), 127.

So to focus only on believers' participation in Christ's response of love to the Father is to present a one-sided picture. Alone, it can imply that we bumble around mumbling inconsequential and meaningless prayers and performing useless sacrifices of worship, which Jesus modifies in both content and intent when conveying them to the Father. But the church does not come to the Father only *through* Christ, but *in* Christ. The life of the church joins the life of the Trinity not just through what Christ has done for us, but because Christ indwells his body the church in the mystical union. Jesus not only makes it possible for us to pray, he teaches us what to pray (cf. Luke 6:9–14). Jesus not only presents our worship, he directs our worship. As J. B. Torrance writes, "The real agent in worship, in a New Testament understanding, is Jesus Christ who leads us in our praises and prayers. . . . He is the High Priest who, by his one offering of himself for us on the cross, now leads us into the Holy of Holies, the holy presence of the Father, in holy communion."[20]

But again, what good are Jesus' teachings if we cannot hear them? What good is Jesus' lead if we cannot follow it? Being "in the Spirit" not only enables us to experience our status in an active fellowship where we pray to and worship the Father; it allows us to hear the words of Jesus as he guides us. The Spirit speaks only what he hears (John 16:13). He takes what is Jesus' and makes it known to us (John 16:15). He teaches us all things (John 14:26), convicts us of sin (John 16:8), guides us into truth (John 16:13), and reveals the mind of Christ to us (1 Cor. 2:16). Through being in the Spirit—open to his guidance and aware of his presence—Christ tells us what to pray for and leads us in worship and service.[21] So when we pray, we do so "in the Spirit" (Jude 21; John 4:24), listening for Jesus' directions

20. Torrance, *Worship, Community and the Triune God of Grace*, 23.

21. Note here that Christ only leads and directs us as the Father directs him, for the Son does only what he sees the Father doing (John 5:19), and says only what the Father tells him to say (John 12:49).

from the Father, just as Jesus listened to the Father in the Spirit. As we obey Jesus' directions, we actively participate in the perfect response of love and worship that Jesus gives the Father. Jesus gives directions through the Spirit "into our unclean mouths that we may pray through him and with him and in him [by the Spirit] to the Father, and be received by the Father in him."[22] What this means is that the expansion of the immanent Trinitarian identity into creation does not result in a single dynamic cycle, where believers participate in Jesus' response and the process is then complete. Rather there are many revolutions continually repeated in time, just as there are in eternity. Not only do believers participate in the Son's worship of the Father through the Spirit, we are also sent into the world as Christ's mystical body, with him leading the church and living in us and through us in our service for God.

This pattern is modeled and enacted in the Eucharist, as Tanner notes:

> The Eucharistic service, moreover, repeats in miniature the whole movement of ascent and descent, going to the Father and receiving from him, through Christ in the power of the Spirit. . . . We are offered ourselves as the bread and wine are offered to the Father so that all are made over into Christ's Spirit-filled humanity. The good things of the earth in forms that nourish our bodies—bread and wine—are first offered up in thanksgiving by us to the Father in Christ's own movement to him, and then received back from the Father as new Spirit-filled nourishment for new life in the form of Christ's own body and blood, through the power of the Spirit that makes those elements one with them.[23]

Reviewing, then, the church participates in the Son's communion with the Father not just *through* Jesus (joining his response to the Father) and *through* the Spirit (uniting us to Jesus), but *in* Jesus

22. Thomas F. Torrance, *The Mediation of Christ* (Edinburgh: T. & T. Clark, 1992), 87–88.
23. Tanner, *Christ the Key*, 200.

(participating in his ongoing ministry), and *in* the Spirit (enabling us to hear his words and follow his lead). The immanent Trinitarian identities are thus expanded not only into Jesus' incarnate body through the hypostatic union, but even further into the human community of the church through the mystical union. And in this expansion, the same three features reoccur. First, the Son and the Spirit are breathed out from the Father and return to the Father in a logically synchronous way. Their activity is logically distinct, but their ecclesial work is inseparable. In the church, as in Christ and the Trinity, there is no Spirit without the Son and no Son without the Spirit. Second, the Spirit again acts as the "personing person" and the Son as the "personed person." It is by the Spirit that the church is "personed" as the mystical body of Christ, or similarly in reverse, Christ is "embodied" in the church by the Spirit. Third, the church's participation in the Trinitarian life is not a once-off activity, but a continuously repeating cycle. As Tanner comments, "Son and Spirit are sent out to us in order to enable our return to the Father. But returned to the Father we are sent out with Son and Spirit again to do the Father's work of service to the world. The return brings with it another going out because in returning we are incorporated into the dynamic Trinitarian outflow of God's own life for the world."[24]

This ecclesial participation in Trinitarian life is illustrated not just in ecclesial practices (as noted), but also in the broad pattern of Christian life. As believers come together to worship through all manner of outward expressions, we participate in Christ's loving response to the Father by the Spirit. But "at the end of worship comes the benediction and we are then sent out like Christ into the world to do the Father's business in the power of the Spirit."[25] So our participation in the Son's worship has an implicit sending

24. Ibid., 205.
25. Ibid., 206.

within it. Our coming to the Father turns us to the world. But our sending to the world also has within it an intrinsic return to the Father, for by the Spirit we join the Son's missional role, uniting all things together in Christ, so they may be presented to the Father (Eph. 1:10). Sent from the Father, we "gather the world" in order to present it to the Father in Christ through the Spirit (1 Cor. 15:24–28). So our mission to the world intrinsically turns us to the Father, just as our coming to the Father turns us to the world. In this way, the perichoretic nature of the immanent Trinity is reprised and worked out in ecclesial practice.[26]

While the above discussion outlines clear and significant continuities between the Son and Spirit's immanent identities and their roles in the mystical union, there are discontinuities as well. In terms of experience, the perfectness of the church's discernment, obedience, worship, and service is limited by our finiteness, humanness, and fallenness. The church is still growing into Christ, and so we often have neither the capacity to understand nor the language to express what Christ speaks to us through the Spirit, nor even the present humility and ability to follow where Christ leads us. Moreover, though we are enabled by the Spirit, all too often we choose not to follow Christ's lead. Recognizing this discontinuity, the distinction between status and experience outlined in the hypostatic union becomes significant. The church, like the incarnate Son but even more obviously so, is in a staggered process of growth and development. So its experience as a participant in the life of the Trinity is often marred and flawed. In terms of status, though, the church's participation in Trinitarian life is undeniable and sure, rooted in the asymmetry of the correspondence. The church *is* the

26. Although it is not outworked further here, this understanding clearly runs counter to Yong's proposal of prioritizing pneumatology over Christology in mission. See Amos Yong, *Beyond the Impasse: Toward a Pneumatological Theology of Religions* (Grand Rapids: Baker, 2003).

church precisely because of Christ and the Spirit. It is Christ who is "personed" or "embodied" in the mystical body of the church through the Spirit. It is *their* return to the Father in which we participate, and not merely ours. The church's security and salvation thus rest in Christ and the Spirit, which gives us great cause for confidence, even when its actions give us pause. As Canlis asserts: "God's love is not a message for us to believe, but a divine reality to which we are united. . . . When the Spirit enables us to cry, 'Abba,' this is the remarkable sign that we are relating to God from the transformed reality of *adoptive sonship*. Our cry of 'Abba' is not cerebral but pneumatological."[27]

Before turning from the subject of inter-ecclesial relationships to that of intra-ecclesial relationships, consider again the intrinsically communal nature of ecclesial participation in the Trinitarian life. Note first pragmatically that as individual children of God, we receive common guidance. Other individuals within the church are in Christ, just as we are. All the instructions and leading about prayer, worship, and service come from the same source, namely from the Father through Christ and the Spirit, and consequently have the same goal. In the Spirit and in Christ, then, we become *one in purpose*. Second, as intrinsically limited humans, no individual has the ability alone to completely discern how we should worship and serve. As a community we gain confidence in our discernment through the confirmation of others, and in community we learn from and teach each other how to be more completely in the Spirit (able to discern God's guidance), and in Christ (willing to obey God's guidance). In this, we are *one in need*. Third (as discussed below), we are one not just pragmatically but ontologically. In Christ, we are new creations (2 Cor. 5:17), each defined by our relationship with Christ in the

27. Julie Canlis, "Union with Christ in the Reformed Tradition: Critical Issues" (paper presented at the American Academy of Religion, Chicago, 2012), 5.

Spirit, and consequently, by our relationship with each other in Christ and in the Spirit. As the immanent Trinitarian dynamism extends to the incarnation and to the church, and we become caught up within it, we become one in nature, need, and purpose—one in Christ, just as Jesus prayed (John 17:20-24). Our union with Christ happens communally, and cannot be considered in an exclusively individualistic way.

9.2 Intra-Ecclesial Relationships

The previous section described an immanent Trinitarian dynamism that gets reprised on a series of expanding stages. In the Trinitarian union, the Father begets the Son by the Spirit, who then returns the love of the Father by the very Spirit of Sonship in which he was begotten. In the hypostatic union, the Father sends the Son to become incarnate by the Spirit, and Jesus returns (human) love to the Father by the same Spirit in which he was conceived and is sustained. In the mystical union, the Spirit is sent by the Father through Christ to unite the church to Christ, and the church then participates in Christ's filial relationship by this same Spirit. While there are distinctions between each of these unions, there are significant continuities as well. Most crucially, in each the Son is "personed" by the Spirit. That is, the Spirit (the "personing person") is repeatedly the means by which the new reality is brought into being. And the Son (the "personed person") is repeatedly identified as or with the new reality that is begotten, created, or embodied. Further, in each case the new reality responds to the Father (the "originating person") by the Spirit through which they have been begotten, created, or embodied. It is this Spirit-enabled response that makes the Trinitarian, hypostatic, and mystical unions truly complete.

A natural question is whether this reprising can be extended one step further. Do these immanent identities also get reprised in the ecclesial union of one individual believer to another? The following discussion argues that this "reconceived" Trinitarian dynamism *can* be analogically applied to intra-ecclesial relationships, but (as with its application to the hypostatic and mystical unions) only if the analogy is pneumatologically enabled and Christologically conditioned. The argument proceeds in two stages.

First, the relationship between Christ and each individual believer is examined. The Father sends the Spirit to believers through the mediation of Christ our great High Priest, and by this Spirit believers are reborn as individuals united to Christ—ecclesial persons who participate in Christ's Sonship. Both Spirit and Son reprise their immanent identities. By the Spirit (the "personing person") we are reborn as more than human individuals, becoming ecclesial persons. And Christ is formed in each believer (or lives in them, or is "personed" in them) as we respond by the Spirit given to us by the Father through Christ. It is this "personing" in Christ through the Spirit that binds us together as the church—a united mystical body.

Second, it is argued that the relationship believers have with other believers analogically reflects the relationship Christ has with individual believers. Christ uniquely is our great High Priest, but in him we become a Kingdom of priests. As such, each of us *participates* in his mediatorial role, offering the gift of Christ's Spirit to each other as members of a united priesthood. Believers are thus united to Christ not just directly but also *through other believers*. It is primarily through Christ that the Spirit is given and believers are personed, but secondarily and in a participatory manner, believers are also personed as we offer Christ's love to each other by the Spirit, and respond by the Spirit given to us. This leads to a simple but profound characterization of the church (viewed from this Trinitarian vantage point) as constituted in any and all relationships where by the Spirit the love of Christ is offered and returned.

The Ecclesial Union (between Christ and Individual Believers)

The route traced in discussing the ecclesial union between Christ and individual believers begins with the affirmation that Christ and the Spirit together (and not one or the other in isolation) form the sum total of grace. Grace is not a quality, a status, or a power, but rather a relationship. As Tanner puts it, "The strong sense here in which we participate or share in what we are not could simply be called grace."[28] All of salvation's benefits can be summed up in and flow from this one key reality—that through Christ the Father sends us his Spirit to unite us to Christ. To establish this, we place the work of Jonathan Edwards and David Coffey in dialogue with T. F. Torrance.[29]

Jonathan Edwards critiqued the existing Reformed Protestant tradition where Christ achieves salvation and the Spirit applies the benefits of salvation to humanity as introducing an imbalance. According to Edwards, this paradigm subordinates the Spirit's work to that of the Son. Further, the gift of righteousness is not commensurate with the cost of Christ's suffering. Edwards argues in contrast that "[t]he end of the Father in electing is the Spirit. He elects to a possession of this benefit. His end in giving the Son [is] to purchase this. The end of the Son in all his suffering is to obtain this, to purchase this. This was the great precious thing to which all that the other two do is subordinated."[30] Studebaker explains Edwards's understanding as "the Holy Spirit does not apply the benefit of

28. Tanner, *Christ the Key*, 58.

29. The following two paragraphs briefly summarize the trend of the argument in Steven M. Studebaker, *The Trinitarian Vision of Jonathan Edwards and David Coffey* (New York: Cambria, 2011), 113–41. Studebaker particularly notes the similarities between the end points of both Edwards's and Coffey's arguments.

Christ's work, but rather the Holy Spirit is the benefit of Christ's work."[31] The gift of salvation is precisely the Spirit, a gift equal to the cost of Christ's suffering. Edwards thus views redemption in a primarily relational and not a juridical light. The Spirit brings the saints into union with Christ and fellowship with God. God is thus both the cause and content of salvation.[32]

David Coffey's Roman Catholic tradition requires him to approach the question from a different starting point, but his conclusion is very similar. Coffey begins with the scholastic doctrine of appropriations, where a given economic work is designated to a particular person of the Trinity, in order to acknowledge their respective roles, but still preserving the truth that in his actions toward the world God is undivided. While some scholars recognize a proper mission that is unique to the Son, the Spirit is not normally granted a similarly unique role in sanctification. Consequently, the believer relates with God but not specifically with the Trinitarian hypostases. Coffey critiques this view by suggesting in contrast that both the Son and the Spirit have a proper mission—the Son in the incarnation, and the Spirit in grace.[33] It is the Spirit that conforms and brings a person into relationship with God. Whereas Roman Catholics tend to describe grace through the effect that it has on the soul, Coffey argues that grace is fundamentally the union of a person with the Spirit, and these other effects are consequences of this spiritual union. Technically, Coffey argues (contra Rahner) that rather than being the role of the entire Godhead, it is specifically and only the *Spirit's* activity in grace that is quasi-formal. The "formal" quality refers to the fact that the

30. Jonathan Edwards, *The Works of Jonathan Edwards*, ed. Sang Hyun Lee, 25 vols. (New Haven: Yale University Press, 2003), 21:146–47.
31. Studebaker, *The Trinitarian Vision*, 128.
32. See also Edwards, *The Works of Jonathan Edwards*, 17:207–10.
33. This research argues in contrast that both Spirit and Son have logically distinct but existentially inseparable missions in the incarnation and "in grace" (identified below as the pneumatically enabled union between Christ and the believer).

Spirit acts in humanity as he does in the Trinity, drawing human persons into a loving relation. The "quasi" quality is that humans do not become personally identical with the Holy Spirit.[34]

In contrast, Torrance argued in his published dissertation that *Christ* should be seen as the content of grace. "Grace is in fact identical with Jesus Christ in person and word and deed."[35] And again: "It would be safe to say that Paul never speaks of grace, except as grounded in the self-giving of God in the person and death of Jesus, and in every instance it is the objective side of its content that predominates."[36] Torrance argues that the primary failing of the Apostolic Fathers was that grace became separated from the objective reality of Jesus Christ, and was reduced to a power enabling Christians to live a holy life. He comments negatively: "Grace was now regarded as Pneumatic."[37] Torrance's concern, however, is not a simplistic overemphasis on the pneumatological aspect of grace. Rather, he is critiquing an inadequate view of the Spirit which is divorced from Christ. Torrance bemoans "a parallel change in the understanding of the Holy Spirit, which by this time had largely lost the inseparable attachment it has to Christ . . . and came to be thought of as pneumatic power."[38] Indeed, despite his bold Christological statements, Torrance recognizes and validates the important role of the Spirit in a Pauline understanding of grace. "The objective deed of God in Christ for men while they are yet sinners, and the presence of Christ to men through the Spirit form the content of the Pauline *charis*."[39] His primary goal in using Christological language is to

34. See particularly David Coffey, "A Proper Mission of the Holy Spirit," *Theological Studies* 47, no. 2 (1986): 227–50; and David Coffey, *Grace: The Gift of the Holy Spirit* (Milwaukee: Marquette University Press, 2011).
35. Thomas F. Torrance, *The Doctrine of Grace in the Apostolic Fathers* (Eugene, OR: Wipf & Stock, 1996), 21. See further pp. 20–35.
36. Ibid., 28–29.
37. Ibid., 139.
38. Ibid., 140.

affirm that grace is God- and not human-centered; grace is primarily about God's lavish giving and only secondarily about human reception.

Placing these accounts side by side enables some clear conclusions. First, despite the differences in terminology and starting points, there are deep similarities between Edwards's and Coffey's identification of the Spirit as the content of God's grace, with Christ as the means. Torrance, in contrast, sees Christ as the content of God's grace, with the Spirit as the means. The problem with the former position is the tendency to divorce pneumatological grace from Christ, a direction in which Coffey's presentation perhaps trends.[40] The problem with the latter position is the tendency to divorce Christological grace from the Spirit. For not just our relational union with Christ, but even Christ's incarnation is pneumatologically enabled, a point Torrance often glosses over.[41] Recognizing validity and challenges with both positions, this research affirms that Christ and the Spirit together (and not one or the other in isolation) form the sum total of grace. Pneumatological grace cannot be divorced from Christ, and Christological grace cannot be divorced from the Spirit. This shared affirmation is a key recognition that will be particularly important in the development of the following argument. Grace should be identified relationally as the Spirit-enabled union of believers with Christ. While objective forgiveness came through the cross, the subjective experience of forgiveness does not precede relationship, but logically follows it. The experience of forgiveness is thus not the prerequisite of union with Christ but its consequence. Indeed, all salvation's benefits can be summed up in and flow from this one key

39. Ibid., 30.

40. See for example Coffey, *Grace*, 17–19.

41. See for example Stanley S. Maclean, *Resurrection, Apocalypse, and the Kingdom of Christ: The Eschatology of Thomas F. Torrance* (Eugene, OR: Pickwick, 2012), 169.

reality—that through Christ, the Father sends us his Spirit to unite us to Christ. Christ and the Spirit together form the sum total of grace.

Interestingly, Pentecostal scholar Steven Studebaker argues that Edwards and Coffey have additional similarities: they both recognize that "the Holy Spirit's role in redemption reflects the Spirit's immanent personal identity"[42] and they "both utilize the mutual love model of the Trinity"[43] to understand the Spirit's immanent identity. The Third Article Theology being developed here agrees with the first point (and indeed extends it beyond redemption into ecclesiology)[44] but disagrees with the second.[45] Recognizing that both the giver and the gift of grace are identifiable as both Christ and the Spirit, who in their redemptive activity (as in their immanent identity) are existentially inseparable but logically distinct, consider the Spirit-enabled union between Christ and each believer. While the comments above regarding the mystical union were concerned with the relationship between Christ and the church as a single community, similar comments can clearly be made regarding the relationship between Christ and each individual believer.[46] From the

42. Studebaker, *The Trinitarian Vision*, 142.

43. Ibid. It should be noted that much of Edwards's language is at such a level of generality that it can be incorporated into either the mutual-love model or the "reconceived" model. While Edwards begins with the mutual-love model, his eventual understanding transcends it. Some thus see Studebaker's characterization of Edwards as narrow. See for example Kyle C. Strobel, *Jonathan Edwards's Theology: A Reinterpretation* (London: Bloomsbury, 2013), particularly pp. 50, 65–71. Also, Myk Habets, "The Surprising Third Article Theology of Jonathan Edwards," in *The Ecumenical Edwards: Jonathan Edwards and the Theologians*, ed. Kyle Strobel (Farnham, UK: Ashgate, forthcoming), n.p. Whether Studebaker accurately characterizes Edwards is immaterial for the purposes of this argument.

44. This extension of the Spirit's immanent role in redemption to his role in the church is also seen in the work of Edwards. Such an extension also fits with Coffey's overall theological methodology, although he never explicitly applies the mutual-love model's pneumatology to intra-ecclesial relationships. See the discussion in section 3.2.

45. Reasons for rejecting the mutual-love model as a comprehensive Trinitarian understanding were discussed in section 7.1. The inadequacy of this model's applicability to ecclesiology is addressed in section 10.2.

46. One assumes this is the reason that Kathryn Tanner and J. B. Torrance are not specific regarding whether it was as individuals or as a community that we participate in Christ's worship of the Father.

Father, through Christ, each believer is given the Spirit to unite them with Christ and to participate in his filial Sonship. As noted in Studebaker's analysis of Edwards and Coffey, the Spirit's role reflects his immanent identity, but unlike Studebaker's second point it is God's "*reconceived*" and not his "mutual love" Trinitarian identity that is in evidence.

This "reconceived" Trinitarian identity's reprisal is observable through the working out of its three key features in the relationship between Christ and each individual believer. First, for each individual, as in the church, there is no Son without the Spirit and no Spirit without the Son—as discussed above, their work of grace is logically distinct but inseparable. Second, it is by the Spirit uniting us to Christ that we are constituted as ecclesial persons. While our individual consciousness is not overridden or removed, we join a collective ecclesial consciousness, participating in the "mind of Christ" (1 Cor. 2:16).[47] So (unlike the mutual-love model) the Spirit is the "personing person," and Christ is the "personed person," who lives in and through us.[48] And third, this gift of the Spirit to unite each of us to Christ is not a once-off action but a continuing activity. It is precisely because of this continuing activity, and not because of some past event, that we are "personed" as ecclesial beings and remain alive in Christ. As Paul says, "In him, we live and move and have our being" (Acts 17:28), and again, "It is no longer I that lives, but Christ that lives in me" (Gal. 2:20). Just as the Spirit

47. The terms "ecclesial consciousness" and "mind of Christ" are viewed as virtual synonyms. Note also that sharing in the mind of Christ or a collective "ecclesial consciousness" should be seen to imply more than just a noetic understanding but a profound ontological union. See for example Paul D. Molnar, "The Eucharist and the Mind of Christ: Some Trinitarian Implications from Thomas Torrance's Theology," in *Trinitarian Soundings in Systematic Theology*, ed. Paul Louis Metzger (London: T. & T. Clark, 2005), 175–88, particularly pp. 180–81.

48. It is wise (again) to hesitate in terming Christ's union with individual believers as *perichoresis*. Although a viable argument for this is contained in James D. Gifford Jr., *Perichoretic Salvation: The Believer's Union with Christ as a Third Type of Perichoresis* (Eugene, OR: Wipf & Stock, 2011).

continually persons Christ eternally, so the Spirit continually acts as the "personing person" in each individual believer as a new creation in Christ, forming or "personing" Christ in us. Sent from the Father through Christ's humanity, both the Son and the Spirit act in our individual lives in a manner analogous to their "reconceived" immanent identities within the Trinity.

Perhaps the key image by which this mediatorial reality is conveyed in the New Testament is the picture of Jesus as our great High Priest. The logic of priesthood is precisely that of mediation. "Priests stood in the middle, between God on the one hand and all the rest of the people on the other. In that intermediate position, priests had a twofold task, a job that meant working in both directions."[49] The very language and nature of priesthood implies three parties: the mediator (or priest), the one who is being mediated on behalf of, and the one to whom access is being gained. As J. B. Torrance outlines, both Christ's ministry and the role of the High Priest on the Day of Atonement should be understood together in this way.[50] Just as the High Priest stood *with* the people as their appointed representative before God, so Jesus stands with us as our divinely appointed representative, bone of our bone and flesh of our flesh. Just as the High Priest consecrated himself through liturgical cleansing, so Jesus sanctifies himself for our sake (John 17:19; Heb. 2:11). Just as the High Priest places his hand on a sacrificial animal, confessing and laying on it the sins of Israel, Jesus offers not an animal but himself as

49. Christopher J. H. Wright, *The Mission of God's People: A Biblical Theology of the Church's Mission* (Grand Rapids: Zondervan, 2010), 120. Wright writes in more detail: "The priesthood was thus a two-directional representational or mediatory task between God and the rest of the Israelites, bringing the knowledge of God to the people and bringing the sacrifices of the people to God. In addition to these twin tasks, it was of course a prime privilege and responsibility of the priests to *bless the people* in the name of YHWH (Num 6:22-27)." Christopher J. H. Wright, *The Mission of God: Unlocking the Bible's Grand Narrative* (Downers Grove, IL: IVP Academic, 2006), 331.

50. See Torrance, *Worship, Community and the Triune God of Grace*, 43–67, particularly pp. 46–49.

the Lamb of God to take on the sins of the world. Just as the High Priest takes the blood of the slain animal to the holy of holies, to vicariously intercede for Israel to God, so Jesus ascends bodily to the Father after his sacrificial death to personally intercede for us (John 20:17). And just as the High Priest returns to the waiting people to offer them peace from God in the form of the Aaronic blessing (Num. 6:24-26), Christ returns and offers us peace from the Father (John 20:19-22).

Jesus, then, is our great High Priest, and through his life, death, and resurrection he has made the way open for us to walk boldly with him into the throne room of God: he has offered us the grace of God. And the grace he offers us in this High Priestly mediation (as was argued above) is precisely union with him through the Spirit. J. B. Torrance concludes his discussion of Jesus' High Priesthood in just this way: "It is the return of the High Priest who now gives the gift of the Spirit."[51] O'Collins and Jones, toward the end of an exhaustive study on Christ's priesthood, affirm similarly, if more comprehensively and in terms that echo the third "continuous" feature of a "reconceived" Trinity that:

> The priesthood of Christ continues forever, since he eternally intercedes for the world and blesses the world, offers himself through the Holy Spirit to the Father, continues to pour out the Holy Spirit upon the Church and the world, acts on earth as primary minister in all the Church's preaching and sacramental life, and in heaven remains for ever the Mediator through whom the blessed enjoy the vision of God and the risen glory of life.[52]

51. Ibid., 49. This is only the first half of the quote, though. See the subsection below for the quote's completion. J. B.'s brother T. F. Torrance writes similarly and in more detail: "The very Spirit through whom He offered Himself eternally to the Father He has sent down on us in His high priestly blessing, fulfilling in the life of His Church on earth that which He has fulfilled on our behalf in the heavenlies." Torrance, *Royal Priesthood*, 15.
52. Gerald O'Collins and Michael Keenan Jones, *Jesus Our Priest: A Christian Approach to the Priesthood of Christ* (Oxford: Oxford University Press, 2010), 265. While agreeing with the substance of this quote, it does imply that Christ initiates sending the Spirit to the church, a

In conclusion then, all the benefits of salvation that come to us both as the church and as individual Christians flow from the logically prior reality of our union with Christ in the Spirit. In this both Christ and the Spirit reprise their "reconceived" immanent identities. So, in the language of C. S. Lewis, it is the Spirit that gives us faces, so that we can look on God face to face.[53] The "face" the Spirit gives us, both collectively and individually, is Christ's face. In the language of persons used above, the Spirit is the "personing person" who enables a personal relationship with God. And the "ecclesial person" we become, both collectively and individually, is the person of Christ. The church joins Jesus' filial relationship, participating in his offering of an acceptable sacrifice of praise and worship to the Father. And in Johannine language, by the Spirit believers are "born again" (John 3:5–8) as children of the Father, participating in the life of Christ both collectively and individually as his ecclesial body: "This is how we know that we live in him and he in us: He has given us of his Spirit" (1 John 4:13). And in response to this extraordinary truth, how can we not exclaim joyfully, "See what great love the Father has lavished on us, that we should be called children of God! And that is what we are" (1 John 3:1).

The Ecclesial Union (between Individual Believers)

The New Testament does not merely speak of *Christ* as the great High Priest, but each believer individually as a priest, together forming a kingdom of priests, or a royal priesthood. Because we are united to Christ we share in his priestly identity. To complete the J. B. Torrance quotation above: "It is the return of the high priest who now gives the gift of the Spirit that they [i.e., Christ's disciples, or

position that was nuanced from sequentiality to simultaneity in an earlier discussion. See section 7.3.

53. C. S. Lewis, "Till We Have Faces," in *Selected Readings* (London: HarperCollins, 2002), 615.

by extension the church] might share with him the apostolic mission to the world (see also Heb. 3:1) as a royal priesthood with the word of forgiveness."[54] O'Collins and Jones comment similarly: "While the priesthood of Christ is unique, it is also participated in, albeit differently, by all the baptized."[55] If each of us (individually) are priests and members of a royal priesthood, and priesthood intrinsically is a mediatory activity that involves three parties, then who are the other two parties involved? Given that we participate in the life of Christ the Son, one party must be the Father. The second is other people, both those who are united with Christ (other church members, who are also priests) and those who are not.[56] Recalling that Christ's priestly gift of grace is the gift of union with him through the Spirit, then our participatory role as priests leads to the conclusion that we too offer others grace as we participate in Christ. Each believer's union with Christ goes not just directly through the Spirit, but also through other believers! Believers are "personed" not just by Christ's relationship with them through the Spirit, but by other believers' relationships with them as well. Not only is Christ formed or "personed" in each believer directly through Christ's gift of the Spirit, but also in a participatory way other believers person each other. In this manner the Spirit plays a similar role in the church to his immanent reality, and the dynamic nature of the Trinity is extended not just *to* the church, but *within* it to the intra-ecclesial union existing between two or more individual church members.

This ecclesial union can be characterized as follows: as believers participate in Christ's life, they offer his love to other believers by the Spirit, and these other believers, by this very Spirit given to them, return the love of Christ to the one who originally offered it. In this

54. Torrance, *Worship, Community and the Triune God of Grace*, 49.
55. O'Collins and Jones, *Jesus Our Priest*, 271.
56. This offer of the Spirit to the world through the church will be discussed more fully in chapter 10.

union, the Spirit acts (again) as the "personing person," constituting others as ecclesial persons in Christ through their receipt and response of love. And the respondent is intrinsically identified with Christ (the "personed person"), for it is in his or her response of love enabled by the offered Spirit that he or she participates in Christ's life. In other words, it is through their Spirit-enabled positive response that Christ is formed in them. Consider the three key features of the "reconceived" Trinitarian understanding, and how they analogously work themselves out in these intra-ecclesial unions. First, the work of the Son and the Spirit are inseparable but logically distinct from each other. It is only as we participate in the life of Christ that we can offer his love by the Spirit, and it is only as this love is received and returned by the Spirit that Christ is "personed" in the receiver. Second, in the very act of reaching out with the love of Christ by the Spirit, both the one receiving the love and the one giving it are constituted as ecclesial persons in Christ. While, again, we should hesitate to call this *perichoresis* in a Trinitarian sense, there are significant analogical similarities. For example, while an individual is not permanently constituted as an ecclesial person by any single instance of this giving from one ecclesial person to another, their existence as an *ecclesial* person *is* completely constituted through the cumulative total of Christ and others' gift of the Spirit to them, and their return of it to Christ and others. Third, this gift of the Spirit from one to another is not a single activity that is once done and then complete, but a continuing action. We are continually "personed" in Christ as he offers us the gift of the Holy Spirit and we return that love to him by the very Holy Spirit continually given to us, *and* we are continually personing each other in Christ as we offer the Spirit to others, and as they receive and return the love offered by the very Spirit continually given to them.

This understanding of ecclesiology, derived from the perspective of the Trinity through the methodology of Third Article Theology enables a clear characterization of the church as existing in *any and all relationships where, by the Spirit, the love of Christ is offered and returned*. The following chapter explores this *Trinitarian* Third Article Ecclesiology. Initially, a positive comparison is made with the ecclesiology emerging from a recent interaction with Balthasar's work by Roman Catholic scholars Komonchak and Dadosky. Then, a negative comparison is made with those ecclesiologies that emerge from different Trinitarian starting points, and that use "reflective" mechanisms to analogically connect the Trinity with the church.

10

A Trinitarian Third Article Ecclesiology

It is to everyone's loss that many churchgoers neglect Trinitarian doctrine as merely a metaphysical problem, rather than delighting in its mystery. A metaphysical problem aims for solution; the mystery of the Trinity is inexhaustible. A metaphysical problem "can be held at arm's length; [the] mystery [of the Trinity] encompasses us and will not let us keep at a safe distance."[1] A metaphysical problem is abstract and theoretical; the mystery of the Trinity is practical and unavoidable. The metaphysical problem of the Trinity (i.e., How can God exist as three and one?) is of minor interest; the mystery of the Trinity (i.e., How can we know, worship, and experience the God revealed to us through the Spirit in Jesus Christ?) is central to our understanding and practice of Christian worship and service. The main objective of part three of this research is to draw an analogical link between the Trinity and the church—to view the church as a participant in the inner life of the Trinity. The overarching logic is

1. Daniel L. Migliore, *Faith Seeking Understanding: An Introduction to Christian Theology* (Grand Rapids: Eerdmans, 1991), 3.

that if the church participates in God's life, then our church life must in some way reflect Trinitarian life. What ecclesial insights can be drawn from such participatory involvement?

The working out of this overarching logic follows a "Wolterstorffian" trajectory.[2] The first question addressed was to which understanding of the Trinity the church is analogously related. Building on the biblical insights of Spirit Christology led to a "reconceived" understanding of the Trinity where the Father begets the Son by the Spirit. This Trinitarian understanding maintains a close connection between the economic and immanent Trinity, while enabling an active personal role for the Holy Spirit. The second question was the construction of a viable analogical link between the Trinity and the church. It was argued that Volf's "reflective" approach didn't "preserve an ontological distinction between God and humanity."[3] An alternative pneumatological approach, based on believers' genuine participation in (and not just with) Trinitarian life through the Spirit, was found to avoid this and related errors. Such a pneumatological approach explores the Son and Spirit's reprised immanent roles in the hypostatic union, the mystical union, and most pertinently in the ecclesial union between individual church members, enabling an understanding of the church as existing in *any and all relationships where, by the Spirit, the love of Christ is offered and returned*. This chapter first discusses some of the constituent features of this Trinitarian Third Article Ecclesiology, and then contrasts it with ecclesiological understandings that emerge from alternative Trinitarian starting points.

2. See section 3.2.

3. Mark Husbands, "The Trinity Is *Not* Our Social Program," in *Trinitarian Theology for the Church: Scripture, Community, Worship*, ed. David Lauber and Daniel J. Treier (Downers Grove, IL: InterVarsity, 2009), 121.

10.1 Constituent Features

There are clear resonances between a Trinitarian Third Article Ecclesiology and many constituent features emerging from a recent interaction with Balthasar's work by two other Roman Catholic theologians Komonchak and Dadosky (both of whom are particularly influenced by Lonergan's methodological work).[4] The following discussion outlines the major themes of this dialogue, followed by an explanation of how these themes overlap with and are extended by a Trinitarian Third Article Ecclesiology. The dialogue's starting point was an essay contained in Balthasar's book *Spouse of the Word*, titled "Who Is the Church?" Balthasar answers the question in the essay's title with the affirmation that the church is Christ's bride, and goes on to explore the intimate (and intrinsically feminine) relations that arise from this image.[5]

Komonchak's major objection is that Balthasar characterizes the church as a single person.[6] He counters that the key question is not "Who is" but "*Who are* the Church?" (italics mine), which becomes the title of his essay. He comments, "I wish to be clear from beginning to end that the church is a social phenomenon, and that any question about the referent of the word will always refer to us as a group of people, to 'real subjects.'"[7] The church's identity is thus "the community of disciples of Jesus Christ."[8] According to Komonchak, this characterization is not a first-order "image" (such as the ninety-six biblical ecclesial images outlined by Paul Minear),[9]

4. Bernard Lonergan, *Method in Theology* (Toronto: University of Toronto Press, 1990). The other references are noted below.

5. Hans Urs von Balthasar, *Explorations in Theology: Spouse of the Word*, trans. A. V. Littledale, vol. 2 (San Francisco: Ignatius, 1991), 143–92.

6. It is questionable whether this characterization is altogether fair, as Balthasar's essay clearly recognizes and even emphasizes at times the individual components of the church.

7. Joseph A. Komonchak, *Who Are the Church?* (Milwaukee: Marquette University Press, 2008), 15.

8. Ibid., 30.

nor a second-order "model" (such as the five, or more recently six, church models outlined by Avery Dulles),[10] but rather a "primary notion, both sociologically and theologically,"[11] to which all images and models refer. "To say the Church is the Mystical Body of Christ is to say that the assembly of believers is the Mystical Body of Christ; if the Church is the Bride of Christ, the assembly of believers is the Bride of Christ."[12] What sort of entity, then, is the church—this community of disciples? Komonchak initially follows Lonergan in describing it as an entity "constituted by meaning and motivated by value."[13] Avoiding the temptation to reify the church, he concludes:

> All of the initiative lies with God, out of his freedom; but what this free initiative enables and effects is the liberation of our freedom by the common love, hope, and faith that constitute and distinguish the Church. The ontological reality of the Church consists of the common intentional acts of meaning and value of her members. The Church is an event of intersubjectivity.[14]

Komonchak also characterizes the church as an event of *ongoing self-constitution*,[15] being simultaneously gathered and gathering. Rescuing the matriarchal image of the church from its more authoritative associations, he argues that every believer is both mother and mothered, both giving and receiving, both gathering and being gathered.[16]

Dadosky's discussion of these two essays, wittily titled "Who/What Is/Are the Church(es)?" labels Komonchak's description of the church

9. Paul Minear, *Images of the Church in the New Testament* (Philadelphia: Westminster, 1961).
10. See Avery Dulles, *Models of the Church*, expanded edition (New York: Doubleday, 2002). Dulles comments that "the number of models may be varied almost at will" (ibid., 3).
11. Komonchak, *Who Are the Church?*, 31.
12. Ibid., 32.
13. Ibid., 34.
14. Ibid., 39.
15. Ibid., 43.
16. Ibid., 46–50.

as a community of disciples a third-order definition (or what Lonergan terms a critical exigence).[17] As Dadosky explains, "Clarification of this third order definition is pertinent to systematic theology in that it guides the use of first and second order definitions in theology."[18] It is at this level, which Lonergan labels "Judgment," that something can be characterized as "real," precisely the terminology that Komanchak also utilizes. But Dadosky takes the application of Lonergan's framework to Komonchak's analysis one step further, beyond first-order "experience" (the biblical images of the church), second-order "understanding" (intelligible models of the church), and third-order "judgment" (the definition of the church as "the followers of Jesus Christ"), to fourth-order "decision," which he refers to as "the foundational ecclesial reality wrought through conversion of being in love with God that establishes the faith of true believers."[19] Referring to *Lumen Gentium*, Dadosky describes this foundational "decision" or "conversion" as being "those 'possessing the Spirit of Christ' and the habit of charity."[20] Dadosky recognizes that Komonchak also places foundational significance on *Spiritum Christi habentes* (possessing the Spirit of Christ),[21] but in explaining the ecclesial implications of this fourth level he turns to a phrase from Balthasar's original essay: *anima ecclesiastica* (ecclesial soul).[22]

Using Mary and then the apostle Paul as case studies or even prototypes, Balthasar comments on a new consciousness attained by the individual upon becoming a believer, where the "newness

17. John D. Dadosky, "Who/What Is/Are the Church(es)?," *The Heythrop Journal* 52, no. 5 (2011): 787–88. See also Lonergan, *Method in Theology*, xi.
18. Dadosky, "Who/What Is/Are the Church(es)?" 789.
19. Ibid.
20. Ibid., 788.
21. Ibid., 792.
22. While the term *anima ecclesiatica*, or ecclesial soul, can and has historically been used in a variety of ways, its use in this research is restricted specifically to consciousness as per its description in Balthasar's essay: "the 'ecclesiasticizing' of individual consciousness." Balthasar, *Spouse of the Word*, 166.

in question consists not in a diminution, still less an extinction of personal consciousness, but in its being taken along in faith into the consciousness of Christ."[23] This is an "*'ecclesiasticizing' of the individual consciousness.*"[24] Dadosky quotes Balthasar at some length, regarding the transformation or "ecclesiasticizing" of Paul's individual consciousness: "It is the 'I' of Christ's mission, the 'I' transformed into the servant of Christ, from flesh become spirit. It is ecclesiastical, and manifests itself—brings out its own anatomy before the eyes of all—only because it is a paradigm of the mission, the functional side of the Church, of membership in the body of Christ."[25] He then generalizes by explaining that "[t]he personal 'I' indicates the new person possessing the Spirit of Christ in one's innermost being and also becomes an extension of Christ's mission in the Church—to the 'we' of the Church."[26] Referring to Komonchak's characterization of the church as an event of intersubjectivity, Dadosky posits that this intersubjectivity arises directly from an individual's rebirth in Christ, and consequent expansion into the ecclesial consciousness. He thus argues that conversion has an intrinsically horizontal as well as vertical dimension, and "demand[s] an orientation towards others."[27] Dadosky concludes as follows:

> Anima ecclesiastica provides a special theological category for clarifying what Lonergan outlined more generally in *Method in Theology* as the *dynamic state of being in love in an unrestricted manner*. The ecclesial soul provides a language for the particular Christian responsible to a community, insofar as private consciousness becomes ecclesial public consciousness.[28]

23. Ibid., 166–67.
24. Ibid., 166 (italics in original).
25. Ibid., 168. See also Dadosky, "Who/What Is/Are the Church(es)?" 798.
26. Dadosky, "Who/What Is/Are the Church(es)?" 798.
27. Ibid., 799.
28. Ibid., 798.

There are clear resonances between some key ecclesial aspects discussed in this dialogue and a Trinitarian Third Article Ecclesiology characterized as *any and all relationships where, by the Spirit, the love of Christ is offered and returned.* The first resonance is the church's intrinsically relational nature. All three Catholic theologians classify the church in personal terms—each identifies its identity as a "who" and not a "what." The Trinitarian Third Article Ecclesiology developed above similarly posits that the church is defined relationally: both a vertical relationship as by the Spirit the church participates in Christ's filial worship and service (where the church is viewed singly), and multiple horizontal relationships between Christ and individual ecclesial persons (with the church viewed as plural). The church exists as a confluence of multiple relationships between ecclesial persons and cannot be understood or abstracted apart from these (for example, to a set of principles, a subset or hierarchy).

Second, Komonchak characterizes the church as an event of *intersubjectivity*, whose ontological reality exists through "intentional acts of meaning" among her members. A Trinitarian Third Article Ecclesiology is similarly characterized. Indeed, it is not just any relationships or acts of meaning, but specifically the *love of Christ* offered and returned that ontologically constitutes the church. Third, Komonchak also notes that it is through intersubjectivity that individuals are drawn into the church. Ecclesial persons are not only embraced within the church but embrace others. There is thus mutual giving and receiving—in Komonchak's language each believer is both mother and mothered. A similar understanding emerges in a Trinitarian Third Article Ecclesiology, where each member of the church "persons" others through offering the love of Christ by the Spirit, but also is personed themselves by receiving this gift from others. By the Spirit, the love of Christ is offered *and returned*. And only when the process is happening in both directions is the "mind of Christ" formed in and among us.

Fourth, and significantly, the dialogue pointed to the role of the Spirit as the foundational ecclesial reality. What Komonchak hints at, Dadosky makes explicit: that a person's being possessed by the Spirit of Christ in their innermost being enables this mutual giving and receiving—these intentional acts of meaning that ontologically constitute the church. A Trinitarian Third Article Ecclesiology similarly finds a central place for the Holy Spirit as the enabler and sustainer of the church, although (as noted below) it revises talk of the Spirit as being an individual's possession. Fifth, Dadosky reengaged Balthasar's use of *anima ecclesiastica* as a means to clarify the "ecclesiasticizing" of an individual consciousness through participation in the intersubjectivity within the church. While certainly not accepting all the historic appellations associated with this Latin phrase, the expanding of individual consciousness described by Balthasar and Dadosky closely matches the "ecclesial person" concept developed in a Trinitarian Third Article Ecclesiology. Both *anima ecclesiastica* and "ecclesial person" are faltering human phrases that attempt to describe the transformational change that occurs when, by the gift of the Spirit from Christ and others and the "intersubjectivity" that follows, Christ is "personed" or made alive in the consciousness of both the individual and the community.

Finally, it is pertinent to note that this understanding of the role of the Spirit resolves the question from which this dialogue started, that is, whether the church should be described singly ("Who is the church?") or in plural ("Who are the church?"). For it is clearly both. The Spirit, reprising his immanent role as "personing person," persons Christ in *both* the individual and the community, so that individuals, without losing or diminishing their own consciousness, participate in Christ's consciousness. This leads to an all-important ecclesiological principle that "the work of the Spirit releases and reconciles the tension between the fellowship and the individual in the concept of the church, and hence, the underlying anthropological tension between society and individual freedom."[29]

The discussion above demonstrates that there are significant overlaps between recent Catholic theology and a Trinitarian Third Article Ecclesiology. But there are also differences or (better) extensions to aspects of the dialogue. First, the Spirit, rather than being the "possession" of an individual, is identified as dwelling *between* one believer and the next. Using an imperfect physical analogy, the Spirit is more akin to a photon than an electron, being never at rest. An "individualized" Spirit is as inconceivable as a stationary photon. In the immanent Trinity, the Spirit is never merely the Father's Spirit or the Son's Spirit, but is rather the Spirit by which the Father persons the Son, and by which the Son persons the Father. As such, in the "reconceived" model the Spirit is *continually* given from the Father to the Son and *continually* returned. It is in this *continual* giving and returning that the Godhead is eternally constituted. It is only as the Father gives the Spirit, and only as he receives the Spirit in return from the Son, that he has the Spirit. Similarly in the church, the Spirit is never an individual's possession, but one who indwells the relational intersubjectivity between persons. In ecclesial contexts, as in the Trinity, it is only as believers are giving and being given the Spirit—personing others and being personed by others through offering and returning the love of Christ

29. Wolfhart Pannenberg, *Systematic Theology*, trans. G. W. Bromiley, 3 vols. (Grand Rapids: Eerdmans, 1991, 1997), 3:130. See also Veli-Matti Kärkkäinen, *An Introduction to Ecclesiology: Ecumenical, Historical and Global Perspectives* (Downers Grove, IL: IVP Academic, 2002), 123; and Veli-Matti Kärkkäinen, *Toward a Pneumatological Theology: Pentecostal and Ecumenical Perspectives on Ecclesiology, Soteriology, and Theology of Mission* (Lanham, MD: University Press of America, 2002), 89. Note that while Pannenberg is undoubtedly correct in making this bold pneumato-ecclesial statement, its use here does not imply that the author accepts *in toto* his other ecclesiological affirmations that lead to or from this statement.

by the Spirit—that believers have the Spirit. This is not to suggest that the Spirit leaves believers, or that he comes and goes, for there always exists a relationship between Christ and the individual believer which the Spirit indwells, even when the relations between one believer and another are suboptimal or even nonexistent. But the key point of distinction is that the Spirit indwells the relationship, and is not localized as an individual's possession.

A second point of extension is the sacramental nature of fellowship. It is through fellowship, both with Christ and with others, that Christ is "personed" or formed in believers. It is in offering Christ's love to others by the Spirit that believers share his mind and become ecclesial persons (cf. Matt. 18:20). This leads to an important clarification of the Protestant doctrine of the priesthood of all believers. In contrast to the commonly (mis)understood application of this phrase to imply that believers all have their own individual access to God and consequently are not subject to another's authority, or dependent on another's involvement, a Trinitarian Third Article Ecclesiology suggests in contrast that believers' access to God is not just through Christ, but through other believers as they participate in Christ's life and share his priestly role. The mind of Christ is formed through genuine fellowship. So the phrase "priesthood of all believers" does not mean that all believers have individual and unmediated access to God. In contrast, all believers "stand in the gap." All believers mediate God's presence to each other.

This leads directly to a third point, which is a nuanced understanding of catholicity. If believers are personed not just by Christ, but by other believers, then each believer has a role in constituting other believers as ecclesial persons. This personing happens as believers offer the love of Christ to each other by the Spirit, enabling the mind of Christ to be formed in them. Two implications arise. Initially, since there is just one Spirit and one

Christ being personed in each individual and community, even the smallest gathering of ecclesial persons—at the most remote geographical location and in extreme sociological isolation—is intimately connected to each of the others. In Christ through the Spirit, we are all connected to each other, as one universal, *catholic* church. This catholicity is not organizational but organic, not physical but spiritual. It is because the Spirit connects every believer to Christ that we are connected to one another, across the vastness of distance and difference. This first aspect of catholicity is complete and unchangeable, secure in the church's pneumatological union with Christ. But the church is not only catholic, but *being catholicized.* Our intrinsic catholicity has to be increasingly realized for the life of Christ to be more fully formed. Geographic barriers need to be crossed, sociological differences need to be bridged, separate ecclesial gatherings need to genuinely interact, and this needs to happen precisely so that by the Spirit, the love of Christ can be offered and returned, in order that the mind of Christ be more fully formed in individual believers and corporate communities. This is no small or simple task, for the distances are vast and the differences are great, but the church is nevertheless called to become who we are. We *are* catholic through the Son and the Spirit; and so we must be increasingly catholicized in both practice and form.

A fourth point of extension is the notion of return and its implications.[30] It was noted above that as priests, ecclesial persons mediate between God and both other ecclesial persons and others in the world. The distinction between the two is not in the giving of the Spirit. The church as a kingdom of priests represents the world to God, and by the Spirit offers the love of Christ to all without discrimination.[31] Other ecclesial persons return the love of Christ

30. This notion could be considered as implicit in the concept of intersubjectivity, though, and perhaps should be considered as much an overlap as an extension.

when it is offered to them. But those who are not ecclesial persons choose not to return it. They make this choice, even though they are enabled to return this love, being empowered by the very gift of the Spirit offered to them through Christ and through others. This understanding of the Spirit as always being given but not always received or returned has two important consequences. First, it provides a natural boundary line for where the church ends and the rest of the world begins. The church boundary exists where the love of Christ is offered by the Spirit but not returned. Put simply, mission occurs wherever the love of Christ is offered by the Spirit; church occurs wherever that love is returned (by the same Spirit). An exploration of this boundary leads to the topic of the church's mission and place in the world, which is beyond the scope of this research, beyond briefly noting that it does appear to run counter to those missional understandings that prioritize pneumatology over Christology.[32]

Second, it characterizes the ecclesial persons of the church as truly free. As noted in section 4.2, Zizioulas argues that God's freedom resides in his choice to exist moment by moment, which he labels as personhood.[33] In a Trinitarian Third Article Ecclesiology, enabled as we are by the Spirit to respond to others with Christ's love, we similarly affirm moment by moment our existence as *ecclesial persons*. In an analogous manner to God affirming his existence through the Father's continual begetting of the Son by the Spirit and the Son's continual return of love to the Father by the Spirit of Sonship given

31. In this the church continues the priesthood of the Israelite nation mediating between God and the world (Exod. 19:6). See for example Christopher J. H. Wright, *The Mission of God's People: A Biblical Theology of the Church's Mission* (Grand Rapids: Zondervan, 2010), 120–26.
32. For example Amos Yong, *Beyond the Impasse: Toward a Pneumatological Theology of Religions* (Grand Rapids: Baker, 2003). See section 11.2 for further discussion together with a justification of this scope restriction.
33. See section 4.3. Also John Zizioulas, *Being as Communion: Studies in Personhood and the Church* (Crestwood, NY: St. Vladimir's Seminary Press, 1985), 43–49.

to him, we affirm our *ecclesial* personhood by offering and returning the love of Christ to others by the Spirit. The Spirit as the "personing person" gives us the freedom to become and to remain as ecclesial persons (2 Cor. 3:17).

A final point of extension is that a Trinitarian Third Article Ecclesiology allows and even encourages various ecclesial structures depending on various internal and external circumstances. There is no one definitive structure that a Trinitarian Third Article Ecclesiology can be said to endorse. A useful explanatory image here is viewing the church as liquid. The liquid metaphor needs to be distinguished from other uses though. Zygmunt Bauman, for example, coined the phrase "liquid modernity" to describe the regular individual identity reconstruction occurring in contemporary western society.[34] Similarly, in a popular exposition of church leadership titled *AquaChurch*, Leonard Sweet suggests techniques to pilot a church in today's "fluid" western culture.[35] In both cases, however, liquidity is a cultural and not an ecclesial mark, except perhaps responsively. The image of the church as liquid used here is not intended responsively (as something we flow with) but intrinsically (as something we are). So the church is not solid: ecclesial persons arrayed in static, unvarying patterns. Nor is it gaseous: ecclesial persons loosely connected and predominantly independent. Rather, the church is liquid, with connections made and broken based primarily on proximity. This liquidity (or plasticity or malleability) does not involve the reconstructing of individual identities (as in Bauman's portrayal of modern individualism) nor is it a pragmatic response to a movable culture (as in Sweet's management techniques),

34. Zygmunt Bauman, *Liquid Modernity* (Malden, MA: Blackwell, 2000); and Zygmunt Bauman, *The Individualized Society* (Malden, MA: Blackwell, 2001). I am very grateful to Andrew Picard for introducing me to the seminal work of Zygmunt Bauman.

35. Leonard Sweet, *AquaChurch: Essential Leadership Arts for Piloting Your Church in a Fluid Culture* (Loveland, CO: Group Publishing, 1999).

but the church adopts different forms and shapes in response to external and internal situations, with each form reflecting a common underlying identity, form, and symmetry.[36]

The key to the liquid metaphor is that individual components (or molecules) of the liquid are connected to all others they are in proximity with, and on being removed from these and placed in proximity with others, quickly attach bonds. While ecclesial form and structure is malleable dependent on external circumstances, it retains its central properties with consistency and permanence.[37] This malleable characteristic is why this discussion has resisted the direction of many other Trinitarian ecclesiologies to justify a particular structure. A recent analysis by Anne Hunt endorses such reticence. Hunt explores several recent connections between the Trinity and the church made by various theologians and notes that they

> vary dramatically in their conclusions regarding Church structure and organization and would seem to be as varied as the theologians themselves. Indeed, the supposed Trinitarian-inspired structures bear such close correspondence to the ecclesial traditions from which the theologians themselves come that one must doubt that the Trinity really is the determining feature.[38]

She concludes, "[O]ur understanding of the mystery of the Trinity does not and in fact cannot serve to legitimate particular social or ecclesial structures."[39]

36. See for example Andrew Walls's "indigenizing principle" and "pilgrim principle," noting the changing face of the church structures across the centuries. Andrew F. Walls, "The Gospel as Prisoner and Liberator of Culture," in *The Missionary Movement in Christian History* (Maryknoll, NY: Orbis, 1996), 2–7.
37. The image of liquid here is that whether it is in a cup or pouring from a tap, water is still water both at an individual atomic and an atomic interactional level.
38. Anne Hunt, "The Trinity and the Church: Explorations in Ecclesiology from a Trinitarian Perspective," *Irish Theological Quarterly* 70, no. 3 (2005): 215–16. See also the discussion in section 8.2.
39. Ibid., 234.

10.2 Other Trinitarian Ecclesiologies

The features of a Trinitarian Third Article Ecclesiology outlined above are some of the clear implications of analogically applying a "reconceived" understanding of the Trinity to ecclesiology through the lens of pneumatology. While not exhaustive, they demonstrate well the viability and value of such an analogical approach, and suggest that continued reflection on a pneumatologically enabled but Christologically conditioned analogical link between the Trinity and the church will provide greater ecclesiological insight. Employing a Wolterstorffian methodology, a logical next step would involve a detailed study of the biblical text from the perspective of these new insights to rigorously determine whether they match and reinforce the biblical revelation, and indeed to observe what new *biblical* insights emerge through examining the text from the vantage point of these Trinitarian Third Article Ecclesiology insights. Rather than pursuing either of these options (i.e., leveraging the Trinitarian analogy to the point of exhaustiveness, or testing and verifying the ecclesial insights gained through a detailed scriptural analysis), this final section turns instead to a comparison between a Trinitarian Third Article Ecclesiology and other Trinitarian ecclesiologies. The comparison is made as straightforward as possible by clustering the various models and ecclesiologies considered in the previous chapters into three (inevitably loose) groupings: an "egalitarian" grouping that accentuates the egalitarianism of both the Trinity and the church (notably Moltmann and Volf); a "mutual love" grouping that uses a mutual-love Trinitarian model with a necessary emphasis upon the *filioque* (including Coffey, Mühlen, and, to a lesser extent, Edwards); and finally, a "reconceived" grouping that uses a "reconceived" Trinitarian model that is reprised Christologically, soteriologically, and ecclesiologically (including Weinandy, Tanner, and Habets).[40]

For each grouping, the initial Trinitarian understanding, the method of analogical linking, and the resultant ecclesiology are considered and compared, concluding with a final application of each to Christian prayer, an example that illustrates the practical differences of adopting different Trinitarian starting points and analogical linking mechanisms to a central and defining practice of the church. This comparison serves as both a summary of the material covered in part three, and a final argument for the advantages of a "reconceived" understanding of the Trinity and a Trinitarian Third Article Ecclesiology.

Other Trinities

Consider first the Trinitarian understanding adopted by each of these groupings. The "egalitarian" grouping understands the Trinity as an ideal society of equals who both initiate action and are acted upon with no predisposed order. As Moltmann writes: "The immanent Trinity is the community of perfect love and shows the structure of perfect community."[41] The key challenge this understanding faces is the distance it places between the economic and immanent Trinity, with the latter "not contradicting" the former. How can such distance rise above projectionism, and enable true knowledge of the God we worship? The "mutual love" grouping understands the Trinity as the Father begetting the Son, with the Holy Spirit either arising from or being directly identified with the mutual love they share. The dual challenge faced by this understanding is first its minimization of the Spirit's personhood, who has no singular activity within the inner Trinitarian life, and second the inadequate biblical basis for

40. This research fits within and extends this third category.
41. Jürgen Moltmann, "The Trinitarian Personhood of the Holy Spirit," in *Advents of the Spirit: An Introduction to the Current Study of Pneumatology*, trans. D. Lyle Dabney, ed. Bradford E. Hinze and D. Lyle Dabney (Milwaukee: Marquette University Press, 2005), 311.

preferencing a mutual-love model, with its justification being either assumed (Edwards),[42] selective (Coffey),[43] or speculative (Mühlen).[44] In contrast, a "reconceived" understanding of the Trinity maintains a close link between the immanent and economic Trinity, recognizes the full personhood of the Holy Spirit, and responsibly acknowledges all significant biblical data. In so doing it develops a Trinitarian model where the Son is breathed out from and then responds to the Father in the Spirit, and this Son/Spirit movement from and to the Father continues eternally.

Other Trinitarian Analogies

Turning to the link between the Trinity and the church, the overarching point is that the analogical connection is driven to a great extent by the Trinitarian model adopted. For the "egalitarian" grouping, the nondifferentiated nature of the immanent Trinitarian relationships leads to a nondifferentiated relationship that humanity has with each of the Trinitarian persons. We do not participate *in* the life of the Trinity but only share characteristics and fellowship *with* them, enabling and in fact demanding a "reflective" rather than an intrinsically personal link. To explain in more detail, the "egalitarian" understanding flattens the distinctions between the members of the Trinity, and holds that for the Trinity *in facto esse*, the relationships between the Trinitarian persons are changeable and incidental. Relations between Trinitarian persons can alter in a similar way to

42. This characterization is a little harsh, given that Edwards's context did not require the specificity evidenced in the modern theologies of Coffey and Mühlen, and that the weight of modern scholarship seems to be pointing to Edwards transcending a simple mutual-love model. See Kyle C. Strobel, *Jonathan Edwards's Theology: A Reinterpretation* (London: Bloomsbury, 2013). Nevertheless Studebaker comments, "Edwards used the framework of the mutual love model . . . but he left outstanding its explanation . . . he assumed the mutual love model and its assimilative characteristic." Steven M. Studebaker, *The Trinitarian Vision of Jonathan Edwards and David Coffey* (New York: Cambria, 2011), 142.

43. See section 7.1

44. See section 8.3.

relations between human persons, so that Trinitarian persons cannot be distinguished on the basis of their relations. But if Trinitarian persons' relationships with each other are nondifferentiated and their distinctive characteristics flattened, then ultimately, so are our relationships with them. Human participation in Trinitarian life is not determined through clear, permanent, and unique relationships with individual members of the Trinity, but rather we join them *as a community*.

Bauckham insightfully argues that the twin ideas of the church participating in the Trinitarian life and the Trinity being a model for the church (both of which are adopted by this "egalitarian" grouping) are compatible if we "think of the Trinity as simply like a group of three friends who include us in their friendship as yet more friends."[45] This means that "the kind of relationship (friendship) enjoyed by the original group of three friends is the kind of relationship the new members of the circle have with each other, since what has happened is that the friendship circle has been expanded."[46] Essentially, the church's transformation is to participation *with* the Trinity (which the "egalitarian" grouping affirms), rather than participation *in* it (which is the position argued by this research). For Moltmann and Volf, we take on Trinitarian characteristics, but we cannot indwell their life. The challenge is that this logical consequence of the "egalitarian" grouping's assumptions runs counter to the reality that human relationships with the Trinitarian persons *are* uniquely and permanently differentiated. Indeed, Moltmann at times acknowledges these distinctions, recognizing that flattening them is a key risk of social Trinitarianism that should be avoided.[47] But in

45. Richard Bauckham, "Jürgen Moltmann's *The Trinity and the Kingdom of God* and the Question of Pluralism," in *The Trinity in a Pluralistic Age*, ed. Kevin J. Vanhoozer (Grand Rapids: Eerdmans, 1997), 160.
46. Ibid., 160–61. See also Paul S. Fiddes, *Participating in God: A Pastoral Doctrine of the Trinity* (London: Darton, Longman & Todd, 2000), 46–49.

applying the concept of the church as an "image" of the Trinity, he and the others in this "egalitarian" grouping implicitly remove the distinctive relational content by which the Trinitarian persons are characterized. As Bauckham concludes: "The concept of the Trinity as a society on which human society can be modelled flattens these trinitarian differences and reduces our sense of the otherness of God, which precisely the doctrine of the Trinity should heighten."[48]

The pneumatological link utilized by the second, "mutual love" grouping enables participation in the inner Trinitarian life as we are bound to the Trinity through the Spirit as the mutual bond of love, but requires an ambiguous and unworkable redesignation of the Spirit's role. To explain, in the mutual-love model, the Holy Spirit proceeds from the community of the Father and the Son, with the Spirit either identified as or arising from the bond of love between them. The key insight that is repeatedly applied is that "whatever the Spirit is in the immanent Trinity, the Spirit is in the economy of redemption."[49] Christology becomes the definitive demonstration of this principle, but it is applied also in soteriology and ecclesiology. The challenge arising is the logical ordering of the Son and the Spirit. For the "mutual love" grouping, the Spirit's immanent proceeding follows the Son's begetting (*filioque*) as a *consequence*. In the soteriological outworking, however, the Spirit is the *means* by which the union is enabled.[50] The intermediate Christological result is a point of divergence, where Coffey maintains the Spirit's priority and Mühlen the Son's priority. But, in either case, the immanent role of

47. See for example Jürgen Moltmann, *The Trinity and the Kingdom: The Doctrine of God* (Minneapolis: Fortress Press, 1981), 189–90.

48. Bauckham, "Jürgen Moltmann's *The Trinity and the Kingdom*," 162.

49. Studebaker, *The Trinitarian Vision*, 142.

50. Coffey has not extended his Trinitarian understanding into its ecclesiological implications, although he affirms that such an extension is possible. He certainly has applied his theological understanding to soteriology, however. See David Coffey, *Grace: The Gift of the Holy Spirit* (Milwaukee: Marquette University Press, 2011).

the Spirit as a *consequence* changes to an economic (or at least ecclesial) role as a *means*. Such a change is necessitated by human limitations. As Studebaker comments:

> Mutual love is reciprocal; it requires the return of love by an equal. ... The saints' reciprocation of love is not sufficient because regardless of the height it reaches, it still pales in comparison to the divine communication of love to them. Just as the immanent trinitarian expression of love requires two divine persons, so also the economic manifestation of divine love calls for an offer and return between two divine persons.[51]

Reconciling the Spirit's immanent identity as consequence (due to the *filioque*) with the Spirit's economic role as means (due to human limitations) takes quite some theological ingenuity.

Coffey certainly attempts to rise to the challenge, by using and extending two of Rahner's concepts: first, the inseparable unity of human love of God and neighbor,[52] and second, the concept of entelechy.[53] Coffey argues that when the Son becomes incarnate, his love for the Father (as Spirit) intrinsically includes his love for humans (again as Spirit). But the Spirit's primary entelechy is to rest upon the Son (because the Father's love for the Son is logically prior to the Son's love for the Father). So the Spirit sent from Christ, following its entelechy draws humans into union with the Son, making them sons and daughters of the Father in the Son. Certainly, this is an ingenious solution, but not altogether convincing. Among the most immediate problems are whether love of God and humanity are

51. Studebaker, *The Trinitarian Vision*, 154. This comment occurs in a critique of Edwards's application of the overall pneumatological principle.
52. See particularly Coffey, *Grace*, 149–55.
53. Entelechy: an intrinsic principle driving someone toward their destiny. See David Coffey, "The Spirit of Christ as Entelechy," *Philosophy and Theology* 13 (2001): 363–98; and David Coffey, *"Did You Receive the Holy Spirit When You Believed?" Some Basic Questions for Pneumatology* (Milwaukee: Marquette University Press, 2005), 76, 102–3. For a summary of Coffey's argument here see Studebaker, *The Trinitarian Vision*, 163.

actually identical. Molnar, for example, argues against their unity, while maintaining a close similarity.[54] Second, and more critically, the solution requires an abandoning of the "mutual" nature of the Spirit which is this grouping's presuppositional starting point. Surely, if the mutual-love model is to be accepted, the Father is just as strong a candidate for the entelechy of the Spirit as the Son. More importantly, picking either one over the other introduces an intrinsic directionalism to the Spirit's supposed mutuality. While the overall logic that the Spirit's role in the economy reflects his immanent identity is sound, the "mutual love" Trinitarian model adopted demands a highly questionable redesignation of the Spirit's role in the economy from consequence to means.

The third grouping solves this problem by adopting a "reconceived" understanding of the Trinity, where the *immanent* personal role for the Spirit is recognized as a means and not just a consequence. The overall logic for the analogical link between the Trinity and the church is similar to the previous "mutual love" grouping, being pneumatologically enabled but Christologically conditioned; however, a different Trinitarian starting point means the Spirit's immanent identity can be reprised more consistently in the economy. In fact, both the Spirit and Son's immanent identities are reprised Christologically, soteriologically, and ecclesiologically. The first expansion is into creation, with the addition/limitation of space, time, and growth. In this Christological outworking, the Father sends the Son to become incarnate by the Spirit, and he returns human love to the Father by this Spirit. As a human who changes and grows, a distinction is needed between Jesus' status as Son (which is constant) and his human experience of Sonship (which changes and grows). The second expansion is into humanity, with

54. Paul D. Molnar, "Love of God and Love of Neighbor in the Theology of Karl Rahner and Karl Barth," *Modern Theology* 20, no. 4 (2004): 567–99.

the addition/limitation being the intrinsic *plurality* of human beings. In this soteriological outworking, the Father sends the Spirit through Christ to unite us with the Son, and united with him we join in his Trinitarian life as he returns love to the Father by the Spirit. The final expansion is our joining the Son and the Spirit as they are sent out by the Father, with the addition/limitation being our *participation* in Christ and the Spirit's sending. In this ecclesiological (and missional) outworking, believers offer the love of Christ to others (and to the world) by the Spirit, and they respond in love by the very Spirit offered to them through believers and through Christ. By this mutual giving and receiving Christ is "personed" or formed among believers both individually and communally, by the "personing person": the Spirit. This return and sending with Christ and the Spirit is not a once-off event, but rather an ongoing dynamic activity. In Christ and in the Spirit, believers are continually returning to the Father in worship and being sent by him in fellowship and mission, thus participating together in time and space with the eternal, dynamic activity of the immanent Trinity.

Other Trinitarian Ecclesiologies

Having considered the immanent Trinitarian understanding of the three groupings, and the way this understanding interacts with and to a large extent drives the analogical link between the Trinity and the church, the discussion turns to the Trinitarian ecclesiologies that emerge from each approach.[55] The following discussion outlines three key points of distinction between the ecclesiologies, centered in turn on their understanding of the church as one, holy, and catholic.[56]

55. Note that while the "egalitarian" grouping has a systematically developed ecclesiology in Volf's work, the variety existing in the "mutual love" grouping makes it more difficult to isolate a definitive ecclesiology. Given that Coffey hasn't extended his Trinitarian understanding to ecclesiology, and Edwards's ecclesiological outworking tends to be more incidental than systematic, the examination here concentrates mostly on Mühlen's ecclesiology.

First, regarding the church as one, all three ecclesiologies acknowledge and reconcile unity and diversity within the church, but do so in quite different ways. So for the "egalitarian" grouping, unity in diversity emerges because each independent person (individually) has the same Spirit. As Volf comments,

> Because the Son indwells human beings through the Spirit, however, *the unity of the church is grounded in the interiority of the Spirit*—and with the Spirit also in the interiority of the other divine persons—*in Christians*. . . . Just as God constitutes human beings through their social and natural relations as independent persons, so also does the Holy Spirit indwelling them constitute them through ecclesial relations as an intimate communion of independent persons.[57]

The logic here is that we are *first* individual Christians with the gift of the Spirit, who *then* come together because of the common Spirit we share as a united community. Diversity precedes unity. For the "mutual love" grouping, and focusing particularly on Mühlen's ecclesiology, unity in diversity emerges because the numerically same Holy Spirit that was in Christ is in the church as a whole, which as we come together in mutual love enables the different effects of the self-communication of God (or created grace) within different persons. Mühlen writes, "The church is the mystery of the identity (union) of

56. The mark of apostolicity is not included here as it is not in dispute. Differing Trinitarian ecclesiologies all acknowledge the foundation of the prophets and the apostles on which the church is built. They do, however, view the other marks of unity, holiness, and catholicity in differing ways. Regarding the mark of apostilicity, Peterson interestingly suggests that using a Third Article Theology approach requires a reinterpretation of the term to mean not just "founded on the apostles and prophets" but missional. She writes, "When we hear 'apostolic' we should think 'missional.' . . . It is the Holy Spirit who serves as the church's 'mission director,' turning disciples into apostles, so that the gospel may be proclaimed to the ends of the earth." Cheryl M. Peterson, *Who Is the Church? An Ecclesiology for the Twenty-First Century* (Minneapolis: Fortress Press, 2013), 133. Given that this deals with the interaction between the church and the world, it is beyond the scope of this investigation, but see the discussion of next steps in section 11.2.

57. Miroslav Volf, *After Our Likeness: The Church as the Image of the Trinity* (Grand Rapids: Eerdmans, 1998), 213. (Italics are Volf's.)

the uncreated grace (of the Holy Spirit) and the simultaneous non-identity (differentiation) of the created grace in Christ and us."[58] The logic in this case is that the Holy Spirit is given to the church first. As we enter into a covenant relationship with Christ in the church we then participate in the Holy Spirit as the one person in many, which enables us to receive the benefits of salvation as persons. Unity precedes diversity.[59]

The "reconceived" ecclesiological understanding is different again, and rather than having unity precede diversity or diversity precede unity, argues that unity is embraced diversity, from Christ and from believers. We are not one as a church because all individual Christians "have" the same Spirit, for the Spirit is not an individual possession, but intrinsically relational. Each of us has the Spirit only as we give and receive the Spirit. Nor are we one as a church because the Spirit is "one person in many persons" who dwells in us as we come together. Rather, we are one because as we participate in Christ by the Spirit, offering and returning his love to other ecclesial persons by the Spirit, the one Christ is "personed" in us. The necessary distinction must be made here between status and experience, given our timebound existence. The church is one, because we are (together) united in Christ by the Spirit. The Father offers us the Spirit through Christ, and all those that respond by this Spirit are in Christ by the Spirit and are one. But our experience of this unity grows as we participate more fully in Christ by the Spirit, offering his love to others by the Spirit. In this way Christ is more completely "personed" in us communally and individually—Christ is formed in us. We experience

58. Heribert Mühlen, *Una Mystica Persona. Die Kirche als das Mysterium der heilsgeschichtlichen Identität des Heiligen Geistes in Christus und den Christen: Eine Person in vielen Personen* (Paderborn: Ferdinand Schöningh, 1967), 211. As quoted in and translated by Wolfgang Vondey, *Heribert Mühlen: His Theology and Praxis* (Dallas: University Press of America, 2004), 122.

59. Note the previously mentioned tendency for "unity to diversity" understandings of the Trinity to lead to hierarchical ecclesiologies. See the discussion at the beginning of section 8.1.

unity as we embrace our diversity, by participating in Christ's love of others by the Spirit.

Catholicity is closely related to unity, and so similarly while all three ecclesiologies affirm the catholic nature of the church, each treats the concept slightly differently. The "egalitarian" grouping sees catholicity as an individual property commonly shared by each ecclesial person. Through the Spirit we take on (or interiorize) others' personal characteristics, and each "takes up others into himself or herself."[60] Catholicity is that the entirety of the church is (in a limited way) represented in each individual, in an analogous understanding to the entirety of the Godhead dwelling in the Son (Col. 2:9). The "mutual love" grouping understands catholicity differently, not as an individual but a collective property rightly attributable only to the entire church, in which the Holy Spirit dwells as the "one person in many persons." Specifically for Mühlen, the Holy Spirit is the continuing of the anointing of Christ in the church, and ensures the historical continuity between the two. As such, the church's catholicity refers to the reality that the salvation of Jesus is passed on by the presence of the Holy Spirit uniquely in the church.

The "reconceived" understanding adopts an alternative view. Rather than seeing the catholicity of the church as residing primarily in the individual Christian, or in the entire (institutional) church, it posits an understanding where the church's catholicity is situated primarily in the Spirit-enabled relationships of love that exist between ecclesial persons. In this understanding believers are personed in Christ not just directly from Christ through the Spirit, but also by the love of Christ offered from others to the believer by the Spirit. It is in our Spirit-empowered relationships in Christ with one another that we make the church what it is as a mutually conditioned organism.

60. Volf, *After Our Likeness*, 211.

Once again, a necessary distinction between status and experience is required. As there is just one Christ being "personed" by one Spirit, we are all connected through this one Christ and one Spirit to each other. Sharing the one ecclesial consciousness—the mind of Christ—no matter how divided geographically, sociologically, or even emotionally the church is, each grouping is nevertheless connected with all others. Our unchangeable status is universal—a truly *catholic* church. But because of this reality there is a calling, impetus, and an empowering through the Spirit to become increasingly *catholicized* in experience, bridging the geographic, sociological, and emotional distances between us to offer the love of Christ to others by the Spirit, so that the mind of Christ may be more fully formed in us both communally and individually.

A consideration of the mark of holiness recognizes similar distinctions between the three ecclesiological groupings. The "egalitarian" grouping sees holiness as predominantly located in the individual: "the commitment of those assembled to allow their own lives to be determined by Jesus Christ."[61] The "mutual love" grouping, and Mühlen specifically, sees it as communal, particularly the gift of "consecrating grace" evidenced in the sacraments of ordination, baptism, and confirmation that maintain the historical continuity between Christ and the church.[62] A Trinitarian Third Article Ecclesiology understands holiness, in contrast, as both a status and a growing experience. The status comes through our union with Christ by the Spirit, which we have responded to by the gift of the Spirit given, and in so doing have been set apart as distinct from the rest of the world: ecclesial persons. But similarly Christ is formed in us as we reach out to others with the love of Christ by the Spirit, enabling us as a community and as individuals not just to be his,

61. Ibid., 147.
62. See the discussion in section 8.3.

but to reflect his character and actions. In a Trinitarian Third Article Ecclesiology, holiness (similarly to oneness and catholicity) is thus not understood individually or collectively but relationally.

While rejecting the suggestion that the "reconceived" Trinity and a Third Article Trinitarian ecclesiology are Hegelian syntheses of the "mutual love" and "egalitarian" understandings, there is nevertheless some indication from this discussion that they do integrate the best of both alternatives, combining the collectiveness of one with the individuality of the other in an intrinsically relational understanding. Noting also that "egalitarian" proponents are mostly Free Church advocates, "mutual love" proponents are mostly Roman Catholic, while those advancing a "reconceived" Trinity have a relatively diverse set of denominational loyalties,[63] this may justify a cautious optimism about Third Article Theology's ecumenical potential. It is naïve, of course, to imagine that a "reconceived" ecclesiology will easily span between vastly different understandings and traditions. Nevertheless, there is hope perhaps that a Third Article Ecclesiology, and Third Article Theology in general, may prove to be a useful ecumenical resource.

Prayer: An Application

While it is not possible within the scope of this research to apply an understanding of these Trinitarian ecclesiologies to every aspect of the church's life, one application of a more practical nature is illustrative and may be helpful. The final discussion thus turns to the example of prayer. How do these differing Trinitarian ecclesiologies impact the way believers understand and go about approaching God in prayer? Consider first the "egalitarian" grouping. If, rather than participating in the Trinitarian life, we *reflect* it as if, in Bauckham's

63. Weinandy is Roman Catholic, Tanner is Anglican, and Habets is Baptist and Reformed.

critical assessment, we are joining a group of friends, then prayer is fundamentally a task *we* do. It is offered to the persons of the Trinity, certainly, and the Trinitarian persons may help, but ultimately it is sourced from ourselves as individuals. It cannot be *sourced* from the Trinitarian persons, because it is *offered* to them, and we cannot have differentiated relationships with them, for they do not have differentiated relationships with each other. Del Colle notes precisely this issue:

> Out of deep respect for Professor Moltmann I implore him to consider that the divine unity is indeed a perichoretic tri-*unity* (as he so strongly affirms), but that this tri-*unity* manifests now and in glory the constitutive distinction of persons without which our participation in the divine nature could not occur, for our very persons are birthed anew by the Spirit to manifest the Son to the glory of the Father.[64]

Thus, although the "egalitarian" understanding is intentionally Trinitarian, the effect on the prayer life of the church is not dissimilar to that of the "Unitarian" model critiqued by J. B. Torrance. "No doubt we need God's help to do it [i.e., pray and worship]. We do it because Jesus taught us to do it and left us an example of how to do it. But worship is what *we* do before God."[65] The "egalitarian" understanding does not provide any practical assistance or insight to our prayer life beyond throwing us back on our own individual initiative. It is, at the very least, indicative that while Volf's monograph mentions prayer when discussing Ratzinger's and Zizioulas's ecclesiologies, in his own explication of Trinitarian ecclesiology prayer does not merit a single mention.[66] The "egalitarian" model may give insight into ecclesial structures,[67] but

64. Ralph Del Colle, "A Response to Jürgen Moltmann and David Coffey," in *Advents of the Spirit: An Introduction to the Current Study of Pneumatology*, ed. Bradford E. Hinze and D. Lyle Dabney (Milwaukee: Marquette University Press, 2005), 346.
65. James B. Torrance, *Worship, Community and the Triune God of Grace* (Downers Grove, IL: IVP Academic, 1996), 20.

even its protagonists have little to say about its impact on the church's prayer life.

The second, "mutual love" grouping is more fruitful. Using Mühlen's ecclesiology, the Spirit is one person in many persons who (unlike Christ) is extended in time and space. As we come together as the church, through the past work of Christ, the Spirit takes us together into the throne room of the Father. The advantage of this understanding over the former approach is the communal nature of our prayer. As Sarot comments:

> By making prayer . . . into a community task, through which individual believers train themselves to be valuable members of the community and accept that disposition and attention may follow upon rather than precede a prayer, one takes away some of the pressure of praying . . . a certain division of labour becomes visible . . . Thus this view, while upholding a high ideal, does not require the nearly impossible.[68]

The disadvantage is that it is still we who are praying (albeit enabled by the Spirit) and not the glorified Christ with or through us. For in the mutual-love model, the Spirit cannot address the Son and Father separately, but only together. So in this understanding, united with the Holy Spirit, we relate to the glorified Christ and the Father together. More specifically, in Mühlen's understanding the Holy Spirit continues Christ's anointing in the church but it is discontinuous with the hypostatic union. Thus the Spirit makes Christ's sacrifice present, and (in reverse) we participate in the life of the historical Christ. So communally, the Spirit leads us into the presence of the Father and the Son, but we do not participate in the

66. According to the index: see Volf, *After Our Likeness*, 312. It is recognized that the argument from absence is the weakest of arguments. So while an indicative data point, this is a long distance from an irrefutable proof.
67. Although, as has already been noted, these insights are questionable. See Hunt, "The Trinity and the Church," 215–35.
68. Marcel Sarot, "Trinity and Church: Trinitarian Perspectives on the Identity of the Christian Community," *International Journal of Systematic Theology* 12, no. 1 (2010): 41.

present Sonship of Christ, the glorified Jesus' filial relationship. We thus only pray *to* Christ, not *with* Christ.[69] The overall problem is that the discontinuity with the hypostatic union has a "neglect of the significant consideration, [of] how Christians participate in the being of Jesus."[70] Not only is such a picture contrary to the biblical witness (e.g., Heb. 10:21), it is decidedly inadequate in practice. Even with access granted, even with the enabling of the Spirit, even joined together as a community, how can we pray as we ought if Jesus does not pray with (and in) us?

In contrast to both previous options, the "reconceived" understanding of the Trinity sees prayer simply as believers joining the dynamic immanent Trinitarian life, with all three persons actively and intimately involved. It is initiated by the Father, who through the Spirit directs Christ as to how we should pray, and Christ in turn directs us as we are in him (opening our lives to his reign in us) and in the Spirit (enabled to hear him guiding us). Then, because of our union with Christ, as we obediently follow the guiding of the Spirit, the Father accepts our prayers as if they were from Jesus. Essentially, Jesus takes our prayers and gives them to the Father as if they were his. It is him who prays, and we pray only in him. Sarot's comments accurately characterize this understanding: "We do not pray *to God*, but *in God*. It is only because the Christian community in prayer is the body of the Son that it has *through the Spirit* access *to* the Fatherhood *of the Father*."[71] In this "reconceived" understanding

69. It could be justifiably argued that a different interpretation of *Mühlen*'s ecclesiology, or more specifically Coffey's understanding, does not have this limitation, and that for example introducing the concept of entelechy means that the Spirit unites us to Christ first, after which we participate in his relationship of Sonship with the Father. While this is a much more satisfactory understanding, the issue is its consistency with the overall Trinitarian understanding. To make such an argument requires a relaxing (at the least) of the mutual nature of the Spirit's immanent and economic identity, and thus runs counter to the overall direction posited by this "mutual" Trinitarian understanding.

70. Vondey, *Heribert Mühlen*, xxxi. Vondey is summarizing the work of Czaja in this comment.

of the Trinity and its analogical application to ecclesiology, prayer is something of a soliloquy with God as source, life, and object.[72] The wonder is that he chooses us as intermediaries and participants. C.S. Lewis, who himself espoused a robust doctrine of Trinitarian participation,[73] expresses this well:

> They tell me, Lord that when I seem
> To be in speech with you
> Since but one voice is heard, it's all a dream,
> One talker aping two.
> Sometimes it is, yet not as they
> Conceive it, Rather I
> Seek in myself the things I hoped to say,
> But lo! The wells are dry.
> Then seeing me empty, you forsake
> The listener's role and through
> My dumb lips breathe and into utterance wake
> The thoughts I never knew.
> And thus you neither need reply
> Nor can; thus while we seem
> Two talkers, thou art One forever, and I
> No dreamer, but thy dream.[74]

71. Sarot, "Trinity and Church," 44 (italics in original). Note that Sarot does not distinguish between different Trinitarian models or Trinitarian ecclesiologies in formulating this characterization of prayer.

72. Not that human agency is denied, but it is a participating, corresponding agency. As Vincent Brümmer comments: "In this Trinitarian way, however, God's agency is not coercive but enabling and motivating and therefore does not deny the freedom, responsibility and personal integrity of the human agent through whose action God realizes his will. On the contrary, it is still up to human agents to do God's will . . ." Vincent Brümmer, *What Are We Doing When We Pray?On Prayer and the Nature of Faith* (Burlington, VT: Ashgate, 2008), 75.

73. See Myk Habets, "Walking in *mirabilibus supra me*: How C. S. Lewis Transposes Theosis," *Evangelical Quarterly* 82, no. 1 (2010): 15–27. "For Lewis, all people are bound for immortality, not the sloughing off of human nature but a participation in the triune Godhead" (ibid., 20).

74. C. S. Lewis, *Prayer: Letters to Malcolm* (London: Fount, 1964), 71. Note that Lewis believes (accurately) that the word "dream" in the last line is too pantheistic.

11

Conclusion

The foregoing chapters have established the value of applying the approach of Third Article Theology to ecclesiology. Just as Spirit Christology supplies insight into the person and life of Christ through using a pneumatological lens, this research has demonstrated that similar benefits result from observing the church through the lens of the Spirit. This concluding chapter first summarizes the approach used and some key insights gained, then outlines potential steps for extending this research into a comprehensive Third Article Ecclesiology.

11.1 Summary

The phrase Third Article Theology is used in two senses: first as a theological methodology; and second as the theological understanding that emerges from using this method. In terms of methodology, its two major distinguishing features are that (1) it starts with the Spirit, and (2) it looks through rather than at the Spirit.[1] While such a theological approach is often characterized by its differentiating features (e.g., from First and Second Article Theologies), it is better understood within the context of the modern Trinitarian renaissance. Just as a renewed Trinitarian focus has led to examining other doctrines in the light of the Trinity, a renewed pneumatological focus is leading to an examination of other doctrines through the lens of the Spirit.

To date, Third Article Theology has focused mostly on the person and work of Jesus. Perhaps the fundamental Spirit Christological recognition to emerge is that the Spirit and not just the Logos is foundational in understanding Jesus' identity and mission: "[W]ho Jesus is and the salvation that he brings proceeds from a basic pneumatological orientation."[2] From a positive perspective, exploring this recognition enabled two insights to be affirmed. First, that our Lord Jesus Christ is fully and uniquely the person of the Son and fully and uniquely anointed by the Spirit. Second, that within the incarnation the identity and missions of the Son and the Spirit are logically and chronologically synchronous (without priority), distinct (without confusion), and interdependent (without separation). From a negative standpoint, six categories of Spirit Christological errors were identified: those that denied or underemphasized the Son's personhood in Christ, those that denied or underemphasized Christ's anointing by the Spirit, and those that either excessively confused or excessively separated the Son and the Spirit's identity in Christ. These insights have proved to be of immense value as Third Article Theology turns from Christology to ecclesiology.

Looking through the lens of the Spirit at ecclesiology, it became clear that this doctrine cannot be treated in isolation. Consequently, a Third Article Theology approach was constructed that examined

1. For further methodological criteria see section 1.3.
2. Ralph Del Colle, "Spirit-Christology: Dogmatic Foundations for Pentecostal-Charismatic Spirituality," *Journal of Pentecostal Theology* 3 (1993): 95–96. See further chapter 2.

ecclesiology through the lens of the Spirit from the vantage point of other theological doctrines.[3] This research used two vantage points: Christology and the Trinity. Regarding the former, it is the Spirit that makes the church the body of Christ, meaning that Christology is pneumatologically connected with ecclesiology. Regarding the latter, it is the Spirit that enables the church to participate in Trinitarian life, similarly linking Trinity and ecclesiology through a pneumatological lens. Other theological loci could also have been used as vantage points, as discussed in section 11.2 below. The following summary outlines the logical process used and key implications arising through viewing Third Article Ecclesiology from each of these vantage points, noting for each an ecclesial sacrament, an ecclesial mark, and a practical implication.

The Vantage Point of Christology

The view of ecclesiology afforded from Christology was explored through two key premises. First, that significant insight into the ontology of the church can be gained through comparison with the ontology of Jesus Christ. Second, that the correspondence between Christ and the church cannot be adequately examined without giving prominence to the Spirit. The first premise was unpacked through examining the ecclesiologies of Barth and Zizioulas.[4] While acknowledging significant strengths in both formulations, it was argued that Barth overemphasizes the divine and human aspects of ecclesiology being "without confusion," while Zizioulas overemphasizes them being "without separation." The root cause of both was argued to be what was termed an ecclesial Spirit-Eutychianism: both theologians too greatly merge and confuse the Son and the Spirit's involvement in the life of the church. For Barth,

3. For further discussion see chapter 3.
4. See chapter 4.

this is evidenced in a slight tendency to subsume the Spirit's work into the Son's (which was termed an ecclesial Spirit-Docetism), while for Zizioulas the Son's work is significantly subsumed into the Spirit's (ecclesial Spirit-Ebionism). In a conclusion reminiscent of the earlier Spirit Christological insight, it was argued that an ecclesiology that adequately recognizes both the humanity and divinity of the church requires both the Son and Spirit's ecclesial roles to be logically distinguished without being existentially separated.

This led to paralleling the Spirit's involvement in Christ and the church. As Kärkkäinen asserts, "[T]he only way to construe a viable pneumatological ecclesiology is to reflect very carefully on the relationship between Christ and the Spirit on the one hand, and on the relation of the Spirit to the church on the other hand, and then try and see these three as mutual entities that inform each other."[5] Five pneumatologically inspired parallels between Christ and the church were noted: (1) The Spirit conceives (Christ and the church); (2) The Spirit sustains the communion (of Christ and the church); (3) The Spirit conforms (Christ and the church); (4) The Spirit directs and empowers (Christ and the church); and (5) The Spirit is displayed and mediated (by Christ and the church).[6] Following Barth's notion of correspondence, it was recognized that these parallels have continuities, discontinuities, and asymmetries. Exploring these aspects enabled an ecclesial understanding to emerge as viewed from the vantage point of Christology through the lens of the Spirit: a *Christological* Third Article Ecclesiology. Key features arising from this perspective were that the church is tripartite in nature, indivisible in constitution, unique in context, Christ-centered in orientation

5. Veli-Matti Kärkkäinen, *Toward a Pneumatological Theology: Pentecostal and Ecumenical Perspectives on Ecclesiology, Soteriology, and Theology of Mission* (Lanham, MD: University Press of America, 2002), 93.
6. See chapter 5.

with a Christotelic momentum, cruciform in shape, narrative in character, and relational in identity.

The benefit of such a Christological Third Article Ecclesiology is that it not only avoids the twin errors of ecclesial Docetism and ecclesial Ebionism (which overemphasize either the church's divinity or humanity), but also avoids the errors of ecclesial Spirit-Docetism and ecclesial Spirit-Ebionism (which respectively minimize or overemphasize the Spirit's ecclesial role and consequently the connection between Christ and the church). Ecclesial Spirit-Docetism leads to an excessive separation between Christ and the church (evidenced to a degree in Barth's ecclesiology), while ecclesial Spirit-Ebionism confuses and sometimes even melds them (as evidenced in Zizioulas's ecclesiology).

The most obvious implication of a Christological Third Article Ecclesiology is the mark of ecclesial indivisibility: the historical church is one. It is insufficient, though, to say that the historical church is one merely because of Christ or merely because of the Spirit. One Christ without the ontologically establishing presence of the Spirit within the present state of fallen humanity leads inexorably to a logically and practically divided church. One Spirit without the separate otherness of Christ as eschatological goal requires a present perfection that simply doesn't exist. The historical church is one because there is one Christ *and* one Spirit, by which we as one church participate in Christ's one relationship of Sonship with his one Father.[7]

In terms of practical implication, the key insight of a Christological Third Article Ecclesiology is the church's unique context: having a relationship with Jesus and being a part of the church cannot be distinguished. The argument here was not for precedence but

7. See further section 6.1.

for equivalency. When a person is united to Christ by the Spirit, then that uniquely occurs through the transformation of that person into the church, the body and bride of Christ. As Gunton puts it, "[T]he Spirit works in the church: his is a churchly rather than an individual sphere of activity."[8] The church consists of individuals who are pneumatologically united to Christ.

To express this differently, the church is precisely identifiable as the human community of the baptized, those who have been baptized into Christ's body by the Spirit, leading to union both with Christ and with other believers. Consequently, baptism is the ecclesial sacrament most clearly illuminated in a Christological Third Article Ecclesiology.[9] Using a pneumatological lens, baptism refers to both that of Spirit and water. Third Article Theology illuminates their complementarity. Beyond simply not emphasizing water-baptism over Spirit-baptism or vice versa, a Christological Third Article Ecclesiology also balances two other tendencies. First, it avoids ecclesial Spirit-Ebionism, which merges Spirit- and water-baptism and consequently regards baptism as dangerously magical, essentially putting the church in control of the Spirit. Second, it avoids the opposite error of ecclesial Spirit-Docetism, which values both Spirit- and water-baptism, but views them as separate and (more importantly) separable. Through the Spirit, water-baptism becomes the analogy of Spirit-baptism, the human counterpart of a divine action.

The Vantage Point of the Trinity

Gaining a view of ecclesiology from a Trinitarian perspective was significantly more challenging. The first question was which

8. Colin Gunton, "Baptism: Baptism and the Christian Community," in *Father, Son and Holy Spirit: Toward a Trinitarian Theology* (London: T. & T. Clark, 2003), 213.
9. See further section 6.2.

Trinitarian vantage point to utilize. Even though Coffey, Moltmann, and Habets each correctly follow the reasoning that "Spirit Christology provides our best mode of access to the theology of the Trinity,"[10] they nevertheless derive significantly different Trinitarian understandings. It was argued that only the third of these maintains a close link between the immanent and economic Trinities (contra Moltmann's hard social model) and between the Trinity *in fieri* and *in facto esse* (contra Coffey's dual models). Consequently, this research concluded with Habets that Spirit Christology leads to a Trinitarian understanding compatible with that proposed in Weinandy's *The Father's Spirit of Sonship*, where the Father begets the Son in or by the Holy Spirit, and the Son loves the Father in or by the Spirit given to him from the Father.[11] Three key features of this Trinitarian understanding were noted: (a) the Son and the Spirit are logically distinct but inseparable in their activity; (b) the Spirit is the "personing person" and the Son the "personed person" begotten in the Trinitarian union; and (c) the outward and inward movement of the Son and the Spirit from and to the Father is simultaneous, ongoing, and eternal. It is this Trinitarian understanding that was used in constructing a Trinitarian Third Article Ecclesiology.

The second question was how to construct an analogical link between the Trinity and the church that does not minimize the creator/creature distinction. Volf's well-known use of a "reflective" analogical method was considered, but it was argued that the church should not be viewed as an "image" of the Trinity: the church does not participate *with* the Trinity (sharing its characteristics) but *in* it (enjoying its very life). An alternative pneumatologically enabled

10. David Coffey, "Spirit Christology and the Trinity," in *Advents of the Spirit: An Introduction to the Current Study of Pneumatology*, ed. Bradford E. Hinze and D. Lyle Dabney (Milwaukee: Marquette University Press, 2005), 315.
11. See further section 7.3.

and Christologically conditioned approach for analogically linking the two doctrines was proposed.[12] The underlying logic is that the Spirit's immanent identity (as "personing person") and consequently the Son's immanent identity (as "personed person") are reprised economically on a series of expanding stages: Christologically in the hypostatic union between Christ's human and divine natures, soteriologically in the mystical union between Christ and the church, and ecclesiologically in the union between Christ and each individual church member, and in a related manner in the union between individual church members.[13] In the hypostatic union, the Son is the personed person and the Spirit is the means by which the Son is personed as a human: the Son is incarnated as Christ by the Spirit. In the mystical union, the church is "personed" as Christ's mystical body by the Spirit: Christ is embodied in the church by the Spirit. And most pertinently here in the ecclesial union, the Spirit constitutes believers as "ecclesial persons" by enabling them to share in Christ's ecclesial consciousness: Christ is formed in each believer through the Spirit. While the parallels are not exact, there are clear continuities between each of these unions, continuities that derive from the reprising of the Spirit and Son's immanent identities. The key result arising from this Trinitarian Third Article Ecclesiology is consequently a characterization of the church as existing in any and all relationships where, by the Spirit, the love of Christ is offered and returned.

Perhaps the most immediate implication is the sacramental nature of fellowship.[14] It is through pneumatologically enabled fellowship, both with Christ and with others, that Christ is "personed" or formed in each believer. It is in offering Christ's love to others by the Spirit

12. See chapter 8.
13. See the outworking in chapter 9.
14. See section 10.1.

that we share his mind and become ecclesial persons. This leads to an important clarification of the Reformation doctrine of the priesthood of all believers. In contrast to the (mis)understanding that interprets this phrase as believers all having their own individual access to God, Trinitarian Third Article Ecclesiology argues that our means of approaching the Father is not merely through Christ but also through each other. The mind of Christ is formed in us as we genuinely fellowship together, so that rather than having *no one* "stand in the gap," it asserts that participating in Christ, *all believers* "stand in the gap" mediating God to each other.

A related implication is a nuanced understanding of catholicity.[15] Given that believers are personed not just by Christ alone, but by Christ through others, then each of these has a role in constituting other believers as an ecclesial person in Christ. Two implications arise. First, given there is one mind of Christ that we share by the Spirit, each person, however isolated, is intimately connected with others as one universal, *catholic* church. This catholicity is secure and unchangeable, rooted in the church's pneumatological union with Christ. But the church is not just catholic, but being *catholicized*. Our intrinsic catholicity has to be increasingly realized for the mind of Christ to be fully formed in us. Geographic barriers need to be crossed, sociological differences need to be bridged, separate ecclesial gatherings need to genuinely interact, and this needs to happen precisely so that by the Spirit, the love of Christ can be offered and returned, in order that the mind of Christ be more fully formed in us. We are catholic through the Son and the Spirit, and so we must be increasingly catholicized in both practice and form.

One practical application of Trinitarian Third Article Ecclesiology is our understanding of prayer, particularly how prayer differs from

15. See section 10.1.

ecclesiologies derived from other Trinitarian vantage points.[16] By employing a pneumatological lens and looking from the vantage point of Weinandy's "reconceived" Trinitarian model, prayer is clearly illuminated as something we do *in* God, and not something we merely do *to* God. Other Trinitarian ecclesiologies characterize prayer as derived from our initiative. Using Moltmann's hard social model, for example, the Trinitarian persons do not have differentiated relationships with one another, so believers cannot have differentiated relationships with them. We join with them as one friend joining an already-existing group of friends, participating *with* them, but not *in* their life. In Coffey's mutual-love model, the Holy Spirit draws us to the Father and the Son together, for in this understanding the Spirit cannot address the Father and Son separately. Hence we do not participate in the Son's relationship with the Father, as the Holy Spirit takes us to both simultaneously. In contrast to these options, starting from Weinandy's "reconceived" Trinitarian model, it is "only because the Christian community in prayer is the body of the Son that it has *through the Spirit* access *to* the Fatherhood *of the Father*."[17]

Discussion

Before turning to how this research may be extended toward a comprehensive Third Article Ecclesiology, this discussion addresses two key concerns theologians have raised regarding Third Article Theology, and particularly its extension beyond Christology.

First, perhaps the fundamental concern raised about Third Article Theology—both by those supportive of it or otherwise—is an intrinsic tendency to subordinate Christ to the Spirit. Just as Spirit Christology has an inbuilt vulnerability to the charge of

16. See section 10.2.

17. Marcel Sarot, "Trinity and Church: Trinitarian Perspectives on the Identity of the Christian Community," *International Journal of Systematic Theology* 12, no. 1 (2010): 44.

adoptionism,[18] there is a similar and related anxiety that Third Article Theology's extension into other loci will lurch reactively from Christomonism too far in the direction of pneumatomonism. For example, in a response to Dabney, Kärkkäinen says,

> I have concerns, however, about whether pneumatology should play such a leading role in the theological program of Pentecostalism, let alone that of other traditions. I am sure that Dabney doesn't want his article to be read as giving undue emphasis to the Spirit to the detriment of Christology, but I fear that this might be the case with the approach of the theology of the third article.[19]

Given that Third Article Theology's extension beyond Christology is a new and not-yet well-established theological approach, it is difficult to comment definitively on whether such concern is justified. While in some cases there may be a trend in this direction,[20] I contend that this research does not succumb to pneumatomonism, nor does it give undue emphasis on the Spirit at the expense of Christology. As such, it demonstrates that Christological subordination is not a necessary consequence of Third Article Theology.

Consider the central role of Christology in each part of this work. First, in part one, not just adoptionism, but any Christology that prioritized the Spirit over the Son was explicitly rejected. It was argued that both the Son and the Spirit's logically distinct but existentially inseparable reality in Christ was required for a coherent understanding of Jesus' ontology. In part two, ecclesiology was observed primarily from a Christological perspective. Our

18. See for example Coffey, "In Response to Paul Molnar," *Irish Theological Quarterly* 67, no. 4 (2002): 378.

19. Veli-Matti Kärkkäinen, "David's Sling: The Promise and the Problem of Pentecostal Theology Today: A Response to D. Lyle Dabney," *Pneuma* 23, no. 1 (2001): 151.

20. Some Pentecostal scholarship can trend this way. See for example Steven M. Studebaker, *From Pentecost to the Triune God: A Pentecostal Trinitarian Theology* (Grand Rapids: Eerdmans, 2012). Also, Amos Yong, *Beyond the Impasse: Toward a Pneumatological Theology of Religions* (Grand Rapids: Baker, 2003).

understanding of Christ was the vantage point, and the lens used was the Spirit. Again in this part, ecclesiological positions that overemphasized the role of the Spirit in the church were explicitly noted and avoided. In part three, the starting point was not Christology but the Trinity. However, this Trinitarian vantage point was gained through first examining how both the Son and the Spirit were in Christ. And the connection constructed between the Trinity and the church was explicitly noted as Christologically conditioned, with analogical linking mechanisms that skipped a Christological constraint (e.g., Volf's approach) explicitly rejected. Both implicitly and explicitly, in each part of this research, a Third Article Theology approach has not drawn attention away from Christology but toward it. In Third Article Theology, as developed in this research, Christ remains central.

Other theologians suggest, in contrast, that many proponents of Third Article Theology do not go far enough in prioritizing the Spirit. Noting the common tendency for theologians to define the Spirit through Christ, while neglecting the Spirit's constitutional role in personing Christ,[21] Studebaker (rather unusually) uses the term "Christocentrism" to characterize those who subordinate the Spirit to Christ, which he defines as follows: "Christocentrism correctly emphasizes the importance of the revelation of God in Jesus Christ, but neglects the significance of pneumatology for understanding the Trinitarian God."[22] He then goes on to critique several theologians who have explored this area—Pannenberg, Gunton, Weinandy, Moltmann, Habets—as having what he terms "Christocentric" tendencies,[23] arguing for example that Habets "retains a subordination of pneumatology to Christology."[24] His overall

21. See for example Gordon Fee, *God's Empowering Presence: The Holy Spirit in the Letters of Paul* (Peabody, MA: Hendrickson, 1994), 837.
22. Studebaker, *From Pentecost to the Triune God*, 82–83.
23. See for example ibid., 83, 96, 120, 177–82.

purpose in this categorization is "not to replace Christocentrism with pneumacentrism . . . [but] to overcome the implicit subordination of the Spirit to Christ in traditional Trinitarian theologies."[25] Whether or not Studebaker is correct in his assessment of other Third Article Theologies, the question arises as to whether the Third Article Ecclesiology developed in this research subordinates the Spirit to Christ. I would argue that it evidently does not. All the insights in the above paragraph regarding the central role of Christology in each part of this research could be duplicated with regard to the Spirit, which is both explicitly and implicitly just as primary to the theological moves made in this research as Christology has been. The Third Article Ecclesiology developed in this research clearly prioritizes pneumatology in its content and not just in its title.

I would argue further that these concerns regarding whether Christology has been subordinated to pneumatology or vice versa are in themselves misleading, and they are so for two reasons. The first problem is that the assumption underlying them is that Christ and the Spirit somehow make up a zero-sum game, so that more of Christ means less of the Spirit, and more of the Spirit means less of Christ. Clearly this is not the case, either Christologically or ecclesiologically. The second, and following, problem is that the comparison between pneumatocentrism and Christocentrism (to use Studebaker's terminology) is not even. The former refers to the Spirit, who is one of three divine hypostases. The latter refers to Christ, who is divine *and* human, and (as argued in chapter 2) whose ontological identity depends foundationally on both the enhypostatic personhood of the Son and the full anointing of the Spirit. Consequently, a fairer comparison would be between pneumatocentrism and logocentrism. Certainly either the Spirit or

24. Ibid., 177. This particular concern was briefly addressed in Section 8.3.
25. Ibid., 166.

the Son can be overemphasized in both Christology and in ecclesiology, as this research has amply demonstrated, but there is also no necessity for them to be. The position adopted in this research is that the immanent identities and economic missions of the Son and the Spirit are logically distinct but existentially inseparable, with their economic roles being reprisals of the immanent identities where they are (or at least should be considered as) both united and distinct. The question of whether the Son is subordinate to the Spirit or the Spirit to the Son thus reduces ultimately not to a question of theological approach, but rather to the underlying Trinitarian model adopted. As has been argued earlier, an "ambidextrous" Trinitarian understanding that preferences neither hand of God is a natural outworking of a Third Article Theology.

11.2 Further Extensions

Christology and the Trinity were chosen as the vantage points from which to examine ecclesiology in this research project not just because to date, they are the furthest-developed doctrines within Third Article Theology, but also because the relationship between each and ecclesiology is intrinsically and clearly pneumatological. Regarding Christology, it is the Spirit that forms the church as the body of Christ. Regarding the Trinity, it is by the Spirit that the church joins in the life of the Trinity. There are, of course, other perspectives from which ecclesiology can be examined. The following discussion examines the vantage points of eschatology (the church as anticipation of the coming Kingdom) and the world (the church as witness to God's work in the world), before discussing how all four perspectives can be integrated to form a comprehensive Third Article Ecclesiology.

The Vantage Point of Eschatology

While God's coming Kingdom has not yet been explicitly used in this research as a vantage point from which to view ecclesiology,[26] the interaction between the church's eternal identity and her present timebound existence has already emerged as a recurring theme. Part two's Christological perspective revealed a picture of the church as both Christ's body and his future bride, eternally united to him while also being prepared for him. Part three's Trinitarian perspective required a differentiation between ecclesial status and experience, with the implication that the church is both one and being united, both catholic and being catholicized, both holy and being sanctified. Looking from both the Christological and Trinitarian vantage points through the lens of the Spirit has led to an understanding of the church as both being and becoming, a community whose identity is defined beyond time and space, but whose present existence is both restricted to and being transformed within time.

Using the vantage point of eschatology elevates this subject from an implicit theme to an explicit investigation. Just as there is an analogical correspondence between Christ and the church (as the sequel to the incarnation), and between the Trinity and the church (as participant in the life of God), there is also a correspondence between the coming Kingdom and the church (as the Kingdom's proleptic anticipation). Such a strong connection between church and eschatology is well accepted, with the former described as the "eschatological fact *par excellence*,"[27] a "real instance of . . . something future already present."[28] Explicitly observing this eschatological link

26. Christology and the Trinity are constitutive for a Third Article Ecclesiology, while eschatology is illustrative. The eschatological perspective is thus a helpful corroboration of the case being made, but does not necessarily form a major section of this research. However, it is necessary to explore the eschatological perspective *en route* to a comprehensive Third Article Ecclesiology.
27. Karl Barth, *Church Dogmatics*, trans. G. W. Bromiley (Peabody, MA: Hendrickson, 2010), IV/3.1, 321.

enables the temporal nature of the church as a "being transformed" institution to be explicitly illuminated and examined.

Analyzing the analogous relationship between the Kingdom and the church is expedited (at least initially) because it somewhat parallels the possible relationships between Christ and the church. Just as a continuum of possible correlations exist, ranging from the church being an extension of the incarnation through to Christ and the church being merely metaphorically similar, a closely related continuum of correlations exists between the church and the Kingdom. At one end is the virtual equivalency of church and Kingdom, a position held, for example, by the Roman Catholic Church prior to Vatican II.[29] At the other end of the continuum is the not-uncommon Protestant position that views the church and Kingdom as entirely separate entities, with the church impoverished as merely a present "holding pen" for believers, strongly distinguished from the Kingdom which awaits her.[30] The close correlation or excessive distinction between church and Kingdom is often associated respectively with the correlation or distinction between church and Christ. Similarly to the possible Christological correlations examined in part two, though, neither end of the continuum does justice to the nuanced relationship between church and Kingdom pictured in the Scriptures, where both significant continuities and necessary discontinuities clearly exist. This paralleling of the Christological vantage point leads to the suggestion of a "Chalcedonian" relationship. Perhaps, in a manner analogous to Christology, the Kingdom and the church are related "inconfusedly, unchangeably, indivisibly, inseparably."[31] Such a "Chalcedonian"

28. Wolfhart Pannenberg, *Metaphysics and the Idea of God*, trans. P. Clayton (Grand Rapids: Eerdmans, 1990), 96.
29. John Haughey, "Church and Kingdom: Ecclesiology in the Light of Eschatology," *Theological Studies* 29, no. 1 (1968): 73.
30. Ibid., 74.

eschatology and the understanding of time undergirding it is the approach adopted by the likes of Karl Barth and T. F. Torrance. These theologians argue that a "Chalcedonian" analogy can be applied between the church and the Kingdom because eschatology can and should be characterized Christologically. As Torrance explains, "[E]schatology is nothing but a thorough going expression of the doctrine of grace as it concerns history, so that the important word is not *eschaton* (the last event) but *Eschatos* (the last one)."[32] Or similarly, "Eschatology properly speaking is the application of Christology to the Kingdom of Christ and to the work of the Church in history."[33]

The insights gained through this understanding are significant. Perhaps the primary eschatological insight of the twentieth century is Barth's realization that the Word became not just flesh but time.[34] The implication is that there are three "times" to be considered: "old" time (what humans currently experience), eternity (God's time), and "new" time (redeemed, community time in reconciliation and union with eternity). To express the relation between these three positively, Torrance turns to Chalcedon:

> Just as in Christ God and man are united in such a way that there is neither fusion on the one hand nor yet separation on the other, without any diminishing of the completeness or perfection of deity or of humanity, so here too we may think of there having taken place in the Incarnation as it were a hypostatic union between the eternal and the temporal in the form of new time.[35]

The incarnational analogy is not sufficient alone, though.

31. Jaroslav Pelikan and Valerie Hotchkiss, eds., *Creeds and Confessions of Faith in the Christian Tradition: Early, Eastern and Medieval* (New Haven: Yale University Press, 2003), 181.
32. Thomas F. Torrance, *Incarnation: The Person and Life of Christ*, ed. Robert T. Walker (Downers Grove, IL: InterVarsity, 2008), 309.
33. Thomas F. Torrance, *Royal Priesthood: A Theology of Ordained Ministry* (Edinburgh: T. & T. Clark, 1993), 43.
34. See for example Barth, *Church Dogmatics*, III/2, 437–42.

> We must go a step beyond Chalcedon, and . . . carry the hypostatic union in our thought through the Cross to its perfection in the Resurrection. We must think . . . of fallen time as having perfected itself through the Cross and resurrection into the abiding triumph of a perfection in God which both consummates the original purposes of creation and crowns it with glory.[36]

The implication is that there are two tensions to be considered, an "eschatological" tension between "new" and "old" time, and an ultimate "teleological" tension between the eternal and temporal. For Torrance, the first is equivalent to the tension between the new creation and the fallen world, while the second is equivalent to the holiness/sinfulness tension.[37]

Perhaps the clearest ecclesial outworking of this "Chalcedonian" eschatology is in the sacraments. Torrance sees the twin sacraments of baptism and the Eucharist as corresponding to the "eschatological" and "teleological" tensions respectively.[38] Baptism signifies that we are "in Christ," and it is through baptism that we become a "bodily church," incorporated once and for all into Christ as part of the new creation. For this reason it is a once-only, unrepeatable action. The Eucharist in contrast is repeatable, grounded in the flow of time, and thus corresponds to the teleological tension between time and eternity. It emphasizes the incorporation of the church into Christ as an ongoing temporal reality, focusing on the continuing reality of Christ in us. Torrance characterizes Eucharistic worship in Chalcedonian terms. So the Eucharistic offering is neither confused with Christ's offering (a "Catholic" tendency), nor separated from it

35. Thomas F. Torrance, "The Modern Eschatological Debate," *Evangelical Quarterly* 25 (1953): 224. See also Torrance, *Incarnation: The Person and Life of Christ*, 334–36; and Thomas F. Torrance, *Space, Time and Resurrection* (Edinburgh: T. & T. Clark, 1976), 98–99.
36. Torrance, "The Modern Eschatological Debate," 224–25.
37. This is because Torrance argues that Christ assumed a *fallen* human nature.
38. Thomas F. Torrance, "Eschatology and the Eucharist," in *Intercommunion*, ed. D. M. Baillie and J. Marsh (London: SCM, 1952), 312.

(a "Protestant" tendency), but is analogous to it, a "*re-actio*" to Christ's "*actio*."[39]

Despite such clear ecclesiological insights gained from an eschatological perspective, concerns remain about a "Chalcedonian" eschatology's use of pneumatology. Even sympathetic commentators on Barth and Torrance's eschatology note that the Spirit's role is not sufficiently explored. For example, Langdon critically summarizes Barth's view of ecclesial time by noting he has an "underdeveloped view of the Holy Spirit's agency. . . . [E]cclesial time as the time of the Spirit is not a major concern of Barth and therefore is insufficiently developed."[40] Such an absence is significant because, as Lemmer concludes after a detailed study of Ephesians, "the triad, eschatology, pneumatology and ecclesiology, are ineluctably and reciprocally linked; without any one of these elements, the others totally lose their significance and become non-existent."[41]

One option is to read the Spirit back into Barth's eschatology, such as occurs explicitly in Langdon's analysis.[42] Using such an approach, he suggests that for Barth the Spirit's work *ad extra* is analogically related to his work *in se*. Just as the Spirit is the bond between Father and Son, so he is the bond between Christ and his body. The Holy Spirit thus joins ecclesial time with the "new" time of Christ as a "*vinculum* of contemporaneity."[43] This may be interpreted

39. Maclean, *Resurrection, Apocalypse, and the Kingdom of Christ*, 143. See also Torrance, "Eschatology and the Eucharist," 327.

40. Adrian Langdon, *God the Eternal Contemporary: Trinity, Eternity and Time in Karl Barth* (Eugene, OR: Wipf & Stock, 2012), 185. For a similar comment regarding Torrance see Maclean, *Resurrection, Apocalypse, and the Kingdom of Christ*, 169.

41. H. R. Lemmer, "Pneumatology and Eschatology in Ephesians: The Role of the Eschatological Spirit in the Church" (Ph.D. diss., Pretoria: University of South Africa, 1988), summary. See also Emmanuel Clapsis, "The Holy Spirit in the Church," *Ecumenical Review* 41, no. 3 (1989): 341.

42. Langdon, *God the Eternal Contemporary*, 168–70. Maclean does a less explicit but similar "reading back into" with Torrance's analysis. See Maclean, *Resurrection, Apocalypse, and the Kingdom of Christ*, 101–89.

43. Langdon, *God the Eternal Contemporary*, 169.

as the Spirit's role in the "eschatological" tension. But in addition, the Holy Spirit is the perfecting cause, subjectively imparting Christ's reconciliation to believers as "the form and power in which the Son makes his completed work manifest to humanity."[44] This is the Spirit's "continuous, dynamic, particular and unifying"[45] role in the "teleological" tension.

But even with this *post facto* adjustment, concerns remain. Perhaps the most obvious oddity is that for Barth and Torrance, eschatology seems to have become virtually divorced from a study of the *last things*: resurrection, last judgment, heaven, and hell. While Torrance particularly emphasizes the need to recognize both the eschatological and the teleological tension, for both Barth and Torrance the "balance appears to tip in favour of the eschatological end."[46] Evidence for this can be found, for example, in Torrance's minimal working out of the theme of hope, which Maclean attributes to neglecting the Spirit, or in what Langdon terms Barth's tendency toward a *disembodied* church: "Barth divides the true church from the ongoing history of the community."[47] For both Barth and Torrance, the "without confusion" relationship of new and old time is emphasized much more than the "without separation" aspect, and teleology is consequently subordinated to eschatology. This issue is brought into sharpest relief in Barth's implication that time in the new creation is done away with, which creates "too much discontinuity between the present state of creation and the new creation to come."[48] Vondey perhaps exaggerates, but he locates a clear tendency in a pneumatologically underdetermined

44. Ibid., 165.
45. Ibid., 173.
46. Maclean, *Resurrection, Apocalypse, and the Kingdom of Christ*, 197.
47. Langdon, *God the Eternal Contemporary*, 47.
48. Ibid., 204.

"Chalcedonian" eschatology, by writing: "Barth can speak of the 'Spirit in history' but he does not know the 'Spirit of history.'"[49]

How can the positive insights of "Chalcedonian" eschatology and its implications for ecclesiology be retained, while its imbalances are corrected? Hütter suggests a way forward by examining pneumatological embodiment in specific ecclesial practices.[50] At this point the parallel with Christology emerges again, for in chapter 4 the next step after examining Barth's "Chalcedonian" ecclesiology from a Christological vantage point was to examine Zizioulas's Eucharistic ecclesiology and particularly its definition of the church through its sacramental practices. While not pivotal in that discussion, it was noted in passing that Zizioulas tended to collapse eschatology into sacramentology. This potential solution has an equal and opposite tendency to insufficiently separate the church and the Kingdom. After a detailed analysis of Hütter, for example, Mawson comments that

> the recognition that the church can itself be sinful implies the need for maintaining a clearer distinction between the church and the Kingdom. A deeper recognition of sin in the church implies that there can be no smooth transition (or *telos*) extending from this sinful community to the Kingdom. Against . . . Hütter, the Kingdom is not already significantly embodied and visible in the church's own communal identity and practices, or at least not in such a way that the church will bypass God's final judgement and radical negation of its current form.[51]

Gunton similarly comments that closely identifying sacrament, church, and eschatological goal "simply will not do."[52] He clarifies, "It is the narrated passion and resurrection which determine the church

49. Wolfgang Vondey, "The Holy Spirit and Time in Contemporary Catholic and Protestant Theology," *Scottish Journal of Theology* 58, no. 4 (2005): 398.

50. Reinhard Hütter, "Karl Barth's 'dialectical catholicity': Sic et Non," *Modern Theology* 16, no. 2 (2000): 149–50.

51. Michael Mawson, "The Spirit and the Community: Pneumatology and Ecclesiology in Jenson, Hütter and Bonhoeffer," *International Journal of Systematic Theology* 15, no. 4 (2013): 468.

and its worship. Therefore . . . the notion . . . that the eucharist makes the church should be rejected."[53]

While a full critique of the eschatological framework underlining Eucharistic ecclesiologies is well beyond the scope of this brief discussion, the paralleling of the Christological logic in part two suggests that there may well be significant promise in similarly using a Third Article Theology approach to view ecclesiology from the vantage point of eschatology.[54] Undergirding this is the recognition that just as the Spirit makes the church the body of Christ, it is the Spirit that makes the church the proleptic anticipation of the coming Kingdom. Using a pneumatological lens thus seems ideally suited to exploring the analogical link between church and Kingdom. Such an analysis is hindered somewhat, because a specifically Third Article Eschatology is still awaiting development. For example, Mühlen's observation in 1964—that a book on the Holy Spirit and time had not yet been written—"still holds true today."[55] The above analysis, however, suggests that investigating Third Article Eschatology and the perspective it gives on ecclesiology could profitably be developed in tandem. While this avenue of research is still to be explored, an *Eschatological* Third Article Ecclesiology should provide particular insight into the church as a "being transformed" institution, with a focus on *how* the church is transformed by the Spirit and particularly the spiritual gifts. Other features that are particularly well illuminated

52. Colin Gunton, "'Until He Comes': Towards an Eschatology of Church Membership," *International Journal of Systematic Theology* 3, no. 2 (2001): 190.

53. Ibid., 194.

54. Peterson's narrative reading of Acts through the lens of the Spirit will be particularly helpful in this task. Through such an approach, she notes the Spirit's identity in Acts as having three features: (1) an eschatological event that cleanses hearts and brings new life, (2) an empowering to share the word boldly, and (3) a drawing of those who have been renewed into deep communion with God and with each other. Cheryl M. Peterson, *Who Is the Church? An Ecclesiology for the Twenty-First Century* (Minneapolis: Fortress Press, 2013), 108–12.

55. Vondey, "The Holy Spirit and Time in Contemporary Catholic and Protestant Theology," 393. See also Mühlen, *Una Mystica Persona*, 279.

from this perspective include what it means for the church to both be and become holy (in the world but not of it [John 17:14-15]), and (following Torrance's insights) the Eucharistic sacrament.

The Vantage Point of the World

Perhaps the most obvious perspective that is not explicitly used in this research is viewing the church in terms of its place in the world. The decision to not include this perspective was a necessary (if unwelcome) one, not because the relationship between the church and the world is unimportant, but because it is so significant and complex it could not be adequately addressed within the scope of this work. The approach a Third Article Theology takes to examining this perspective differs substantially from the other three vantage points, however, because while the church is ontologically dependent on Christology, Trinity, and (in a slightly different sense) eschatology, the church is ontologically prior to the world. To explain, Henri de Lubac distinguishes between the active and passive aspects of the word *ecclesia*. The church is simultaneously "*the community called together*" and "*the community of the called together.*"[56] Dadosky extends this understanding by further distinguishing between "the nature and the mission of the church—the nature pertains to the people gathered, and its mission is to gather others."[57] Clearly, these two aspects of the church are strongly interrelated. Perhaps, with some caution regarding overlapping terminology, one aspect may be labeled as the *immanent* church: the community of the called together, what the church is *in itself* by virtue of its relationship with God; and the other the *economic* church: the community called

56. Henri de Lubac, *The Splendour of the Church*, trans. Michael Mason (London: Sheed & Ward, 1956), 69–86, particularly pp. 69–73.

57. John Dadosky, "*Ecclesia de Trinitate*: Ecclesial Foundations from Above," *New Blackfriars* 94, no. 1049 (2013): 65.

together, what the church is *for the world* by virtue of its relationship with God. And having introduced such terminology, it can also be affirmed that *the immanent church is the economic church and the economic church is the immanent church.*

A comprehensive Third Article Ecclesiology would address both of these ecclesial aspects, but the scope of the research has been intentionally limited to focus on just the first: the immanent church, what the church is *in itself* by virtue of its relationship with God. The justification for initially examining this aspect of the church as a starting point is that the church is normative and ontologically prior to the world—the world exists as the context for the church.[58] While the church is certainly affected by (and indeed totally dependent on) the world, this effect and dependence is secondary: "The influence of the Church upon the world is . . . exemplary and normative, whereas the influence of the world upon the Church is secondary and exceptional."[59] As such it makes sense to examine what the church is in itself before examining what the church is for the world, with the latter being seen as a consequence of the former.[60]

It is this insight that enables not just the prioritization used in this research, but also an analogical connection between the world and the church to be drawn. In a sense, the economic church is examined and viewed *through* an understanding of the immanent church. Not,

58. For example, Barth comments that "[o]ur only option is truly to see and understand world-occurrence as the environment of the people of God and its history, recognising that it cannot be understood or interpreted in terms of itself but only of the community, or more strictly of its vocation, or more strictly still of the Lord who calls it and of the prophetic witness which He has entrusted to it, but recognising also that when it is understood in this way it is seen for what it really is, in its truth and actuality." Barth, *Church Dogmatics*, IV/3.2, 685. Of course this does not deny that for Barth the church exists in total freedom from *and* total dependence on the world. See ibid., IV/3.2, 734.

59. As summarized in Bender, *Karl Barth's Christological Ecclesiology* (Burlington, VT: Ashgate, 2005), 241. See also de Lubac, *The Splendour of the Church*, 76–77.

60. Kline criticizes Jenson, for example, for only considering the first of these aspects. See Peter Kline, "Participation in God and the Nature of Christian Community: Robert Jenson and Eberhard Jüngel," *International Journal of Systematic Theology* 13, no. 1 (2011): 38–61.

it should be emphasized again, that the second aspect is unimportant or unrelated, as the adapted *grundaxiom* above affirms. It is by looking from the vantage points of Christology, the Trinity, and eschatology through the lens of the Spirit that we gain a view not just of what the church is in itself, but what the church is for the world. Indeed, the vantage points of both Christology and the Trinity (the theological doctrines that have formed the control beliefs of this research) and the vantage point of eschatology have significant implications for the economic as well as the immanent church.

From a Christological vantage point, it is as the church follows Christ in his suffering and obedience that Christ is most clearly seen through the church, and its missional task in and to the world is most clearly fulfilled. As Torrance explains, "[W]herever the Church shows forth His death until He comes and presents its body a living sacrifice, there the image of Christ is to be seen and His Body is to be discerned in the Church."[61] This has relevance not just for the internal transformation of the church, as discussed in part two, but also for the church's mission to the world. There is a parallel between how Christ, empowered and guided by the Spirit, both revealed God to the world and drew it to God through his obedient suffering, and how the church in adopting a cruciform shape participates in a similar role. While a necessary asymmetry needs to be recognized, consequent links can be made between the anointing of the Spirit on a community of believers and that community both being empowered in mission and embracing the neglected. A Christological vantage point, through the lens of the Spirit, thus gives a perspective not just on the "immanent" but the "economic" church. The church's pneumatologically enabled

61. Thomas F. Torrance, "Atonement and the Oneness of the Church," *Scottish Journal of Theology* 7, no. 3 (1954): 259.

missional role in the world asymmetrically parallels the missional role of Christ.

From a Trinitarian vantage point, the church participates not just in the continual return of the Son and the Spirit *to* the Father in worship, but also in their continuing mission as they are sent into the world *by* the Father. Exploring this involves extending the immanent Trinitarian identities of the Son and Spirit beyond the hypostatic union, the mystical union, and the ecclesial union, into yet another sphere. This may be termed a missional union (or perhaps better, a missional offering), for just as the church exists wherever by the Spirit the love of Christ is offered and returned, mission occurs wherever by the Spirit the love of Christ is offered, and salvation comes wherever that love is returned. A Trinitarian Third Article Ecclesiology thus also naturally extends beyond the "immanent" church to its "economic" reality and missional role.

From an eschatological vantage point, the church anticipates God's kingly reign and is empowered through the Spirit to extend it throughout the world. It is a "transforming" and not just a "being transformed" institution, creating systemic change in communities and environments through witnessing to God's work in the world. Note again the pneumatological nature of the connection, for the Spirit is the primary agent of God in the world, and the church achieves its purpose only as it joins and witnesses to the Spirit's work. One of the key investigation areas here will of course be the working of the Spirit not just through but beyond the church.[62]

An examination of the "economic" aspect of the church thus extends the perspective of the "immanent" church gained from each of these vantage points. It is hoped that both the eschatological vantage point and this complementary "economic" ecclesial aspect

62. See for example, Philip J. Rosato, "The Mission of the Spirit Within and Beyond the Church," *Ecumenical Review* 41, no. 3 (1989): 388–97.

will be addressed in upcoming Third Article Theology research, and integrated with the findings of this present research.

Conclusion: A Comprehensive Third Article Ecclesiology

A comprehensive and coherent Third Article Ecclesiology will require not just observing ecclesiology through the lens of the Spirit from each of these four vantage points (Christology, Trinity, Eschatology, World), but integrating the viewpoints gained and resolving any arising tensions. It would be idealistic to believe that the ecclesial perspectives gained from each of the vantage points will integrate with each other perfectly, given the human excesses and oversights bound to creep into all of them.[63] Nevertheless, there are grounds for hoping that the different Third Article Theology vantage points will complement each other more than they contradict.

Note, for example, that while each of the vantage points illuminate all four ecclesial marks to a degree, early investigations suggest that they each most clearly illuminate a different mark. Christology, as already noted, particularly illuminates the ecclesial mark of oneness: the church is one because by one Spirit believers participate in Christ's one relationship of Sonship with his one Father. The Trinity particularly illuminates the mark of catholicity: as suggested earlier, believers are personed not just through Christ alone but through others, as by the Spirit they offer Christ's love to each other and so share in his ecclesial consciousness. Early investigations suggest the eschatological vantage point particularly illuminates the mark of holiness: by the Spirit, believers are set apart for (and from) the future, journeying toward the eschaton and uniquely on earth carrying the

63. For example, the ecclesiology of Volf discussed in section 8.1 amply illustrated the tendency for an exclusively Trinitarian perspective to minimize the correspondence of present ecclesial reality with our eschatological hope, while similarly an exclusively Christological perspective can trend in the reverse direction.

foretaste of it within them. And finally, the vantage point of the world illuminates the ecclesial mark of apostolicity, although it is a "refined" understanding of apostolicity that "must be understood in the original New Testament sense of being sent out to bear witness to the eschatological future that has broken forth in the life, death and resurrection of Jesus Christ,"[64] a "refined" definition that Peterson notes as a natural consequence of examining ecclesiology through the lens of the Spirit. By the Spirit, we are sent into the world, following in the footsteps of those sent by Jesus.

A similar observation can be made regarding the sacraments, although again this word needs to be used in a "refined" sense as a human activity in which Christ is evidently present. Already it has been observed that the Christological perspective illuminates the sacrament of baptism and the Trinitarian perspective illuminates the "sacrament" of fellowship (Matt. 18:20). Early investigations suggest that the eschatological perspective will illuminate the Eucharistic sacrament, while the perspective from the world clearly gives insight into the "sacrament" of mission (Matt. 28:18-20). Given that an Eschatological or "Missional" Third Article Ecclesiology has not yet been developed, the observations here should be regarded as potential insights rather than rigorously evident conclusions. Nevertheless, while caution is wise, there is reason to be hopeful that integrating the perspectives gained from each of the vantage points will be both manageable and profitable.

At this point, with much research still to be done, it is of course impossible to say definitively what a truly systematic and comprehensive Third Article Ecclesiology will look like. But notwithstanding such analysis and future perception, the Christological and Trinitarian viewpoints alone have yielded

64. Peterson, *Who Is the Church?*, 133. For further discussion of this "refined" definition of apostolicity, see ibid.

significant insight into the constituent features of a Third Article Ecclesiology. If Cheryl Peterson is correct in positing that "the real crisis facing the Churches is one of identity"[65] and "to discover who the Church is . . . we ought to 'start with the Spirit,'"[66] then it is hoped that this research provides a helpful step forward in identifying the church as truly Christologically conditioned and irreducibly pneumatologically enabled: the anointed church.

65. Cheryl M. Peterson, "Who Is the Church?," *Dialog* 51, no. 1 (2012): 24.
66. Ibid., 28.

Bibliography

Anizor, Uche. "A Spirited Humanity: The Trinitarian Ecclesiology of Colin Gunton." *Themelios* 36, no. 1 (2011): 26–41.

Aquinas, Thomas. *Summa Theologica.* Translated by Fathers of the English Dominican Province. London: Burns, Oates & Washbourne, 1920.

Arendzen, John. "Marcellus of Ancyra." Volume 9, Page 191 in *The Catholic Encyclopedia.* Edited by William J. McDonald. Palatine, IL: Jack Heraty & Associates, 1967.

Augustine. *Confessions.* Translated by E. M. Blaicklock. London: Hodder & Stoughton, 1983.

Ayres, Lewis. *Nicaea and Its Legacy: An Approach to Fourth-Century Trinitarian Theology*. Oxford: Oxford University Press, 2004.

———. "The Father's Spirit of Sonship (Review)." *The Journal of Theological Studies* 50, no. 1 (1999): 430–32.

Badcock, Gary D. *Light of Truth and Fire of Love: A Theology of the Holy Spirit.* Grand Rapids: Eerdmans, 1997.

———. *The House Where God Lives: Renewing the Doctrine of the Church for Today*. Grand Rapids: Eerdmans, 2009.

Baik, Chung-Hyun. *The Holy Trinity—God for God and God for Us: Seven Positions on the Immanent-Economic Trinity Relation in Contemporary Theology*. Eugene, OR: Pickwick, 2011.

Balthasar, Hans Urs von. *Explorations in Theology: Spouse of the Word*. Translated by A. V. Littledale. Vol. 2. San Francisco: Ignatius, 1991.

———. *Theo-Drama: Theological Dramatic Theory*. Translated by G. Harrison. 5 vols. San Francisco: Ignatius, 1988.

Banawiratma, Johannes Baptist. *Der Heilige Geist in der Theologie von Heribert Mühlen. Versuch einer Darstellung und Würdigung*, European University Studies 23. Frankfurt: Peter Lang, 1981.

Barnett, Paul. *The Second Epistle to the Corinthians*. Edited by Ned B. Stonehouse, F. F. Bruce, and Gordon D. Fee, The New International Commentary on the New Testament. Grand Rapids: Eerdmans, 1997.

Barr, William R., and Rena M. Yocum. "Introduction." Pages 1–10 in *The Church in the Movement of the Spirit*. Edited by William R. Barr and Rena M. Yocum. Grand Rapids: Eerdmans, 1994.

Barth, Karl. *Church Dogmatics*. Translated by G. W. Bromiley. Peabody, MA: Hendrickson, 2010.

———. "Concluding Unscientific Postscript on Schleiermacher." Pages 261–79 in *The Theology of Schleiermacher*. Edited by D. Ritschl. Grand Rapids: Eerdmans, 1982.

———. *Karl Barth's Table Talk*. Edinburgh: Oliver & Boyd, 1963.

———. *Letters: 1961-1968*. Translated by Geoffrey W. Bromiley. Edinburgh: T. & T. Clark, 1981.

———. *The Humanity of God*. Richmond, VA: John Knox, 1972.

Bauckham, Richard. "Jürgen Moltmann's *The Trinity and the Kingdom of God* and the Question of Pluralism." Pages 155–64 in *The Trinity in a Pluralistic Age*. Edited by Kevin J. Vanhoozer. Grand Rapids: Eerdmans, 1997.

———. *The Theology of Jürgen Moltmann*. Edinburgh: T. & T. Clark, 1995.

Bauman, Zygmunt. *Liquid Modernity*. Malden, MA: Blackwell, 2000.

———. *The Individualized Society*. Malden, MA: Blackwell, 2001.

Behr, John. "The Trinitarian Being of the Church." *St. Vladimir's Theological Quarterly* 48, no. 1 (3003): 67–88.

Bender, Kimlyn J. *Karl Barth's Christological Ecclesiology*. Aldershot, UK: Ashgate, 2005.

Berkhof, Hendrikus. *Christian Faith: An Introduction to the Study of the Faith*. Grand Rapids: Eerdmans, 1979.

———. *The Doctrine of the Holy Spirit: The Annie Kinkead Warfield Lectures*. Richmond, VA: John Knox, 1964.

Berkhof, Louis. *Systematic Theology*. Edinburgh: Banner of Truth, 1939.

Bhaskar, Roy. *A Realist Theory of Science*. 2nd ed. Brighton, UK: Harvester, 1978.

———. Dialectic: The Pulse of Freedom. London: Verso, 1993.

Bidwell, Kevin J. *"The Church as the Image of the Trinity": A Critical Evaluation of Miroslav Volf's Ecclesial Model*. Eugene, OR: Wipf & Stock, 2011.

Billings, J. Todd. *Union with Christ: Reframing Theology and Ministry for the Church*. Grand Rapids: Baker Academic, 2011.

———. "Union with Christ and the Double Grace: Calvin's Theology and Its Early Reception." Pages 49–71 in *Calvin's Theology and Its Reception*. Edited by J. Todd Billings and I. John Hesselink. Louisville: Westminster John Knox, 2012.

Bloesch, Donald. *The Holy Spirit: Works and Gifts*. Downers Grove, IL: InterVarsity, 2000.

Bobrinskoy, Boris. "Holy Spirit." Pages 470–73 in *Dictionary of the Ecumenical Movement*. Edited by Nicholas Lossky, José Miguez Bonino, John S. Pobee, Tom F. Stransky, Geoffry Wainwright, and Pauline Webb. Grand Rapids: Eerdmans, 1991.

Bracken, Joseph A. "The Holy Trinity as a Community of Divine Persons, II. Person and Nature in the Doctrine of God." *The Heythrop Journal* 5, no. 15 (1974): 257–70.

———. "Trinitarian Spirit Christologies: In Need of a New Metaphysics?" *Theological Studies* 72, no. 4 (2011): 750–67.

Bracken, Joseph A., Robert Thomas Sears, and Richard Hill. "Trinity and World Process." *Proceedings of the Annual Convention of the Catholic Theological Society of America* 33 (1978): 213–28.

Brewer, David Instone. "Three Weddings and a Divorce: God's Covenant with Israel, Judah and the Church." *Tyndale Bulletin* 47, no. 1 (1996): 1–25.

Briggman, Anthony. *Irenaeus of Lyons and the Theology of the Holy Spirit.* Oxford: Oxford University Press, 2012.

Brümmer, Vincent. *What Are We Doing When We Pray? On Prayer and the Nature of Faith.* Burlington, VT: Ashgate, 2008.

Bryant, David J. "God's Body or Beloved Other? Sallie McFague and Jürgen Moltmann on God and Creation." Pages 179–93 in *Theology as Conversation: The Significance of Dialogue in Historical and Contemporary Theology: A Festschrift for Daniel L. Migliore.* Edited by Bruce L. McCormack and Kimlyn J. Bender. Grand Rapids: Eerdmans, 2009.

Calvin, John. *Calvin's Commentaries.* Translated by John Pringle. 23 vols. Grand Rapids: Baker, 2009.

———. *Institutes of the Christian Religion.* Translated by Henry Beveridge. Peabody, MA: Hendrickson, 2008.

Canlis, Julie. "Union with Christ in the Reformed Tradition: Critical Issues." Paper Presented at the American Academy of Religion. Chicago, 2012.

Carter, Craig A. "Karl Barth's Revision of Protestant Ecclesiology." *Perspectives in Religious Studies* 22, no. 1 (1995): 35–44.

Cartwright, Sophie. "The Image of God in Irenaeus, Marcellus, and Eustathius." Pages 173–82 in *Irenaeus: Life, Scripture, Legacy.* Edited by Paul Foster and Sara Parvis. Minneapolis: Fortress Press, 2012.

Chia, Roland. "Trinity and Ontology: Colin Gunton's Ecclesiology." *International Journal of Systematic Theology* 9, no. 4 (2007): 452–68.

Ciraulo, Jonathan Martin. "Sacraments and Personhood: John Zizioulas' Impasse and a Way Forward." *The Heythrop Journal* 53, no. 6 (2012): 993–1004.

Clancy, Finbarr. "*Ecclesia de Trinitate* in the Latin Fathers: Inspirational Source for Congar's Ecclesiology." Pages 161–93 in *The Mystery of the Holy Trinity in the Fathers of the Church*. Edited by D. Vincent Twomy and Lewis Ayres. Dublin: Four Courts, 2007.

Clapsis, Emmanuel. "The Holy Spirit in the Church." *Ecumenical Review* 41, no. 3 (1989): 339–47.

Coffey, David. "A Proper Mission of the Holy Spirit." *Theological Studies* 47, no. 2 (1986): 227–50.

———. *Deus Trinitas: The Doctrine of the Triune God*. New York: Oxford University Press, 1999.

———. *"Did You Receive the Holy Spirit When You Believed?" Some Basic Questions for Pneumatology*. Milwaukee: Marquette University Press, 2005.

———. *Grace: The Gift of the Holy Spirit*. Faith and Culture. Milwaukee: Marquette University Press, 2011.

———. "In Response to Paul Molnar." *Irish Theological Quarterly* 67, no. 4 (2002): 375–78.

———. "Response to Neil Ormerod, and Beyond." *Theological Studies* 68, no. 4 (2007): 900–15.

———. "Spirit Christology and the Trinity." Pages 315–38 in *Advents of the Spirit: An Introduction to the Current Study of Pneumatology*. Edited by Bradford E. Hinze and D. Lyle Dabney. Milwaukee: Marquette University Press, 2005.

———. "The Holy Spirit as the Mutual Love of the Father and the Son." *Theological Studies* 51, no. 2 (1990): 193–229.

———. "The 'Incarnation' of the Holy Spirit in Christ." *Theological Studies* 45 (1984): 466–80.

———. "The Spirit of Christ as Entelechy." *Philosophy and Theology* 13 (2001): 363–98.

———. "The Theandric Nature of Christ." *Theological Studies* 60, no. 3 (1999): 405–31.

Cook, Michael L. *Trinitarian Christology: The Power That Sets Us Free*. New York: Paulist, 2010.

Cooper, John W. *Panentheism: The Other God of the Philosophers*. Grand Rapids: Baker, 2006.

Dabney, D. Lyle. "Otherwise Engaged in the Spirit: A First Theology for a Twenty-First Century." Pages 154–63 in *The Future of Theology: Essays in Honor of Jürgen Moltmann*. Edited by Miroslav Volf, Carmen Krieg, and Thomas Kucharz. Grand Rapids: Eerdmans, 1996.

———. "Saul's Armour: The Problem and Promise of Pentecostal Theology." *Pneuma* 23, no. 1 (2001): 115–46.

———. "Starting with the Spirit: Why the Last Should Now Be First." Pages 3–27 in *Starting with the Spirit*. Edited by Stephen Pickard and Gordon Preece. Hindmarsh: Australian Theological Forum, 2001.

———. "Why Should the First Be Last? The Priority of Pneumatology in Recent Theological Discussion." Pages 240–61 in *Advents of the Spirit: An Introduction to the Current Study of Pneumatology*. Edited by Bradford E. Hinze and D. Lyle Dabney. Milwaukee: Marquette University Press, 2005.

Dadosky, John. "*Ecclesia de Trinitate*: Ecclesial Foundations from Above." *New Blackfriars* 94, no. 1049 (2013): 64–78.

———. "Who/What Is/Are the Church(es)?" *The Heythrop Journal* 52, no. 5 (2011): 785–801.

Davidson, Ivor. "Theologizing the Human Jesus: An Ancient (and Modern) Approach to Christology Reassessed." *International Journal of Systematic Theology* 3, no. 2 (2001): 129–53.

de Lubac, Henri. *The Splendour of the Church.* Translated by Michael Mason. London: Sheed & Ward, 1956.

Del Colle, Ralph. "A Response to Jürgen Moltmann and David Coffey." Pages 339–46 in *Advents of the Spirit: An Introduction to the Current Study of Pneumatology.* Edited by Bradford E. Hinze and D. Lyle Dabney. Milwaukee: Marquette University Press, 2005.

———. *Christ and the Spirit: Spirit Christology in Trinitarian Perspective.* Oxford: Oxford University Press, 1993.

———. "Communion and Trinity: The Free Church Ecclesiology of Miroslav Volf—A Catholic Response." *Pneuma* 22, no. 2 (2000): 303–27.

———. "Spirit-Christology: Dogmatic Foundations for Pentecostal-Charismatic Spirituality." *Journal of Pentecostal Theology* 3 (1993): 91–112.

———. "Spirit Christology: Dogmatic Issues." Pages 3–19 in *A Man of the Church: Honoring the Theology, Life, and Witness of Ralph Del Colle.* Edited by Michel René Barnes. Eugene, OR: Pickwick, 2013.

Dulles, Avery. "After Our Likeness (Review)." *First Things: A Monthly Journal of Religion and Public Life*, no. 87 (1998): 50+.

———. *Models of the Church.* Expanded edition. New York: Doubleday, 2002.

Edwards, Jonathan. *The Works of Jonathan Edwards.* Translated by Sang Hyun Lee. 25 vols. New Haven: Yale University Press, 2003.

Eliot, T. S. *The Complete Poems and Plays: 1909-1950.* Orlando: Harcourt Brace, 1971.

Erickson, Millard. *Christian Theology*. Grand Rapids: Baker, 1983.

Farrow, Douglas. *Ascension and Ecclesia: On the Significance of the Ascension for Ecclesiology and Christian Cosmology*. Edinburgh: T. & T. Clark, 1999.

———. "The Father's Spirit of Sonship (Review)." *Expository Times* 107, no. 7 (1996): 220.

Fee, Gordon. *God's Empowering Presence: The Holy Spirit in the Letters of Paul.* Peabody, MA: Hendrickson, 1994.

———. *The First Epistle to the Corinthians*. Edited by Ned B. Stonehouse, F. F. Bruce, and Gordon D. Fee, The New International Commentary on the New Testament. Grand Rapids: Eerdmans, 1987.

Fiddes, Paul S. *Participating in God: A Pastoral Doctrine of the Trinity*. London: Darton, Longman & Todd, 2000.

Field, Barbara. "The Discourses behind the Metaphor 'the Church is the Body of Christ' as Used by St. Paul and the 'Post Paulines'." *Asia Journal of Theology* 6, no. 1 (1992): 88–107.

Gifford Jr., James D. *Perichoretic Salvation: The Believer's Union with Christ as a Third Type of Perichoresis*. Eugene, OR: Wipf & Stock, 2011.

Giles, K. N. "The Church in the Gospel of Luke." *Scottish Journal of Theology* 34 (1981): 121–46.

Goheen, Michael. *A Light to the Nations: The Missional Church and the Biblical Story*. Grand Rapids: Baker Academic, 2011.

Gollwitzer, Helmut. "Kingdom of God and Socialism in the Theology of Karl Barth." Pages 77–120 in *Karl Barth and Radical Politics*. Edited by George Hunsinger. Philadelphia: Westminster, 1976.

Grant, Robert M. *Jesus After the Gospels: The Christ of the Second Century*. London: SCM, 1990.

Green, Brad. "After Our Likeness (Review)." *Evangelical Review of Theology* 26, no. 1 (2002): 91–93.

Grenz, Stanley J. *Rediscovering the Triune God: The Trinity in Contemporary Theology*. Minneapolis: Fortress Press, 2004.

———. *The Named God and the Question of Being: A Trinitarian Theo-Ontology*. Louisville: Westminster John Knox, 2005.

———. *The Social God and the Relational Self: A Trinitarian Theology of the Imago Dei*. Louisville: John Knox, 2001.

———. *Theology for the Community of God*. Grand Rapids: Eerdmans, 1994.

Grosso, Andrew. "Spirit Christology and the Shape of the Theological Enterprise." Pages 206–22 in *A Man of the Church: Honoring the Theology,*

Life, and Witness of Ralph Del Colle. Edited by Michel René Barnes. Eugene, OR: Pickwick, 2012.

———. "The Anointed Son (Review)." *International Journal of Systematic Theology* 14, no. 3 (2012): 365–68.

Guba, Egon G., and Yvonna S. Lincoln. "Competing Paradigms in Qualitative Research: Theories and Issues." Pages 17–38 in *Approaches to Qualitative Research: A Reader*. Edited by S. N. Hessie-Biber and P. Leavy. New York: Oxford University Press, 1976.

Gunton, Colin. "Baptism: Baptism and the Christian Community." Pages 201–15 in *Father, Son and Holy Spirit: Toward a Trinitarian Theology*. London: T. & T. Clark, 2003.

———. "John Owen and John Zizioulas on the Church." Pages 187–205 in *Theology through the Theologians: Selected Essays (1972-1995)*. London: T. & T. Clark, 1996.

———. "Persons and Particularity." Pages 97–108 in *The Theology of John Zizioulas*. Edited by Douglas H. Knight. Aldershot, UK: Ashgate, 2007.

———. "Salvation." Pages 143–58 in *The Cambridge Companion to Karl Barth*. Edited by John Webster. Cambridge: Cambridge University Press, 2000.

———. "The Church on Earth: The Roots of Community." Pages 48–80 in *On Being the Church*. Edited by C. Gunton and D. Hardy. Edinburgh: T. & T. Clark, 1989.

———. *The Promise of Trinitarian Theology*. 2nd ed. Edinburgh: T. & T. Clark, 1997.

———. *Theology through the Theologians*. London: T. & T. Clark, 1996.

———. "Two Dogma's Revisited: Edward Irving's Christology." Pages 151–68 in *Theology through the Theologians: Selected Essays (1972-1995)*. London: T. & T. Clark, 1996.

———. "'Until He Comes': Towards an Eschatology of Church Membership." *International Journal of Systematic Theology* 3, no. 2 (2001): 187–200.

———. *Yesterday and Today: A Study of Continuities in Christology*. London: Dartman, Longman & Todd, 1983.

Habets, Myk. "Developing a Retroactive Hermeneutic: Johannine Theology and Doctrinal Development." *American Theological Inquiry* 1 (2008): 77–89.

———. "*Filioque? Nein*: A Proposal for Coherent Coinherence." Pages 161–202 in *Trinitarian Theology after Barth*. Edited by Myk Habets and Phillip Tolliday. Eugene, OR: Pickwick, 2011.

———. "Getting Beyond the *Filioque* with Third Article Theology." Pages 211–30 in *Ecumenical Perspectives on the Filioque for the 21st Century*. Edited by Myk Habets. London: Bloomsbury / T. & T. Clark, 2014.

———. *The Anointed Son: A Trinitarian Spirit Christology*. Eugene, OR: Pickwick, 2010.

———. "'The Dogma Is the Drama': Dramatic Developments in Biblical Theology." *Stimulus* 16, no. 4 (2008): 2–5.

———. "The Surprising Third Article Theology of Jonathan Edwards." In *The Ecumenical Edwards: Jonathan Edwards and the Theologians*. Edited by Kyle Strobel. Farnham, UK: Ashgate, forthcoming.

———. "Theological Interpretation of Scripture in Sermonic Mode: The Case of T. F. Torrance." Pages 44–71 in *Ears That Hear: Explorations in Theological Interpretation of the Bible*. Edited by Joel Green and Tim Meadowcroft. Sheffield: Sheffield Phoenix Press, 2013.

———. *Theosis in the Theology of Thomas Torrance*. Farnham, UK: Ashgate, 2009.

———. "Walking in mirabilibus supra me: How C. S. Lewis Transposes Theosis." *Evangelical Quarterly* 82, no. 1 (2010): 15–27.

Haight, Roger. "The Case for Spirit Christology." *Theological Studies* 53 (1992): 257–87.

Hanson, R. P. C. *The Search for the Christian Doctrine of God: The Arian Controversy 318-381 AD*. Edinburgh: T. & T. Clark, 1988.

Harrower, Scott. *Trinitarian Self and Salvation: An Evangelical Engagement with Rahner's Rule*. Eugene, OR: Pickwick, 2012.

Hart, David Bentley. "The Mirror of the Infinite: Gregory of Nyssa on the Vestigia Trinitatis." *Modern Theology* 18, no. 4 (2002): 541–61.

Hauerwas, Stanley. *Christian Existence Today: Essays on Church, World and Living in Between*. Durham, NC: Labyrinth, 1988.

———. *The Peaceable Kingdom*. Notre Dame: Notre Dame University Press, 1983.

———. *With the Grain of the Universe*. London: SCM, 2002.

Haughey, John. "Church and Kingdom: Ecclesiology in the Light of Eschatology." *Theological Studies* 29, no. 1 (1968): 72–86.

Hawthorne, Gerald F. *The Presence and the Power: The Significance of the Holy Spirit in the Life and Ministry of Jesus*. Dallas: Word, 1991.

Hays, Richard. "Spirit, Church, Resurrection: The Third Article of the Creed as Hermeneutical Lens for Reading Romans." *Journal of Theological Interpretation* 5, no. 1 (2011): 35–48.

Healy, Nicholas M. *Church, World and the Christian Life: Practical-Prophetic Ecclesiology*. Cambridge: Cambridge University Press, 2000.

———. "Karl Barth's Ecclesiology Reconsidered." *Scottish Journal of Theology* 57, no. 3 (2004): 287–99.

———. "Practices and the New Ecclesiology: Misplaced Concreteness?" *International Journal of Systematic Theology* 5, no. 3 (2003): 287–308.

———. "The Logic of Karl Barth's Ecclesiology: Analysis, Assessment and Proposed Modifications." *Modern Theology* 10, no. 3 (1994): 253–70.

Helland, Roger. "The Hypostatic Union: How Did Jesus Function?" *Evangelical Quarterly* 65, no. 4 (1993): 311–27.

Hiebert, P. G. "The Category Christian in the Mission Task." Pages 107–36 in *Anthropological Reflections on Missiological Issues*. Grand Rapids: Baker, 1994.

Hill, William J. *The Three-Personed God: The Trinity as a Mystery of Salvation.* Washington, DC: Catholic University of America Press, 1982.

Hinze, Bradford E. "Releasing the Power of the Spirit in a Trinitarian Ecclesiology." Pages 347–81 in *Advents of the Spirit: An Introduction to the Current Study of Pneumatology*. Edited by Bradford E. Hinze and D. Lyle Dabney.

Hinze, Bradford E., and D. Lyle Dabney, eds. *Advents of the Spirit: An Introduction to the Current Study of Pneumatology*. Milwaukee: Marquette University Press, 2001.

Holloway, James Y., ed. *Barth, Barmen and the Confessing Church Today.* Lewiston, NY: Edwin Mellen, 1992/1995.

Holmes, Stephen R. *The Quest for the Trinity: The Doctrine of God in Scripture, History and Modernity*. Downers Grove, IL: IVP Academic, 2012.

Horgan, Thaddeus D. "Biblical Basis and Guidelines." Pages 11–28 in *The Church in the Movement of the Spirit.* Edited by William R. Barr and Rena M. Yocum. Grand Rapids: Eerdmans, 1994.

Horton, Michael S. *Covenant and Eschatology: The Divine Drama.* Louisville: Westminster John Knox, 2002.

———. *People and Place: A Covenant Ecclesiology.* Louisville: Westminster John Knox, 2008.

Hughson, Donald Thomas. "I-Thou-We: A Critical Study of the Analogy Central to the Pneumatology of Heribert Mühlen." Ph.D. diss., Toronto: University of Saint Michael's College, 1981.

Hunsinger, George. "Baptism and the Soteriology of Forgiveness." *International Journal of Systematic Theology* 2, no. 3 (2000): 247–69.

———. *Disruptive Grace: Studies in the Theology of Karl Barth.* Grand Rapids: Eerdmans, 2000.

———. *How to Read Karl Barth: The Shape of His Theology.* New York / Oxford: Oxford University Press, 1991.

———. *The Eucharist and Ecumenism*. Cambridge: Cambridge University Press, 2008.

———. "The Mediator of Communion: Karl Barth's Doctrine of the Holy Spirit." Pages 148–85 in *Disruptive Grace: Studies in the Theology of Karl Barth*. Grand Rapids: Eerdmans, 2000.

Hunt, Anne. "The Trinity and the Church: Explorations in Ecclesiology from a Trinitarian Perspective." *Irish Theological Quarterly* 70, no. 3 (2005): 215–35.

Husbands, Mark. "The Trinity Is *Not* Our Social Program." Pages 120–41 in *Trinitarian Theology for the Church: Scripture, Community, Worship*. Edited by David Lauber and Daniel J. Treier. Downers Grove, IL: InterVarsity, 2009.

Hütter, Reinhard. "Karl Barth's 'dialectical catholicity': Sic et Non." *Modern Theology* 16, no. 2 (2000): 137–57.

———. *Suffering Divine Things: Theology as Church Practice*. Translated by Doug Scott. Grand Rapids: Eerdmans, 2000.

Ignatius. *The Epistles of St. Ignatius: Bishop of Antioch*. Translated by J. H. Strawley. London: Society for Promoting Christian Knowledge, 1900.

Irenaeus. "Against Heresies" in *The Ante-Nicene Fathers: Translations of the Fathers down to A.D. 325*. Edited by Alexander Roberts and James Donaldson. Peabody, MA: Hendrickson, 1996.

Jenson, Robert. *Systematic Theology*. 2 vols. Oxford: Oxford University Press, 1997, 1999.

———. "You Wonder Where the Spirit Went." *Pro Ecclesia* 2 (1993): 296–304.

Jess-Cooke, Carolyn. *Film Sequels: Theory and Practice from Hollywood to Bollywood*. Edinburgh: Edinburgh University Press, 2009.

Johnson, Keith E. "*Imitatio Trinitatis*: How Should We Imitate the Trinity?" *Westminster Theological Journal* 75 (2013): 317–34.

———. *Rethinking the Trinity and Religious Pluralism: An Augustinian Assessment.* Downers Grove, IL: IVP Academic, 2011.

Johnson, Marcus. *Christ in You, the Hope of Glory: A Theology of Union with Christ.* Wheaton: Crossway, 2013.

———. "'The Highest Degree of Importance': Union with Christ and Soteriology." Pages 222–52 in *Evangelical Calvinism.* Edited by Myk Habets and Bobby Grow. Eugene, OR: Pickwick, 2012.

Kapic, K. M. "The Spirit as Gift: Explorations in John Owen's Pneumatology." Pages 113–40 in *The Ashgate Research Companion to John Owen's Theology.* Edited by K. M. Kapic and M. Jones. Farnham, UK: Ashgate, 2012.

Kärkkäinen, Veli-Matti. *An Introduction to Ecclesiology: Ecumenical, Historical and Global Perspectives.* Downers Grove, IL: IVP Academic, 2002.

———. *Christ and Reconciliation.* 5 vols. Vol. 1, Constructive Christian Theology for the Pluralistic World. Grand Rapids: Eerdmans, 2013.

———. "David's Sling: The Promise and the Problem of Pentecostal Theology Today: A Response to D. Lyle Dabney." *Pneuma* 23, no. 1 (2001): 147–52.

———. *The Trinity: Global Perspectives.* Louisville: Westminster John Knox, 2007.

———. *Toward a Pneumatological Theology: Pentecostal and Ecumenical Perspectives on Ecclesiology, Soteriology, and Theology of Mission.* Lanham, MD: University Press of America, 2002.

Kasper, Walter. *Jesus the Christ.* Translated by V. Green. London: Burns & Oates, 1977.

———. *The God of Jesus Christ.* Translated by Joseph Donceel. New York: Crossroad, 1984.

Kelly, Tony. "Deus Trinitatis (Review)." *The Australasian Catholic Record* 77 (2000): 365–66.

Kenneson, Philip D. "After Our Likeness (Review)." *Modern Theology* 15, no. 3 (1999): 373–75.

Kilby, Karen. "Perichoresis and Projection: Problems with Social Doctrines of the Trinity." *New Blackfriars* 81, no. 957 (2000): 432–45.

Kimel, Alvin, ed. *Speaking the Christian God: The Holy Trinity and the Challenge of Feminism*. Eerdmans: Grand Rapids, 1992.

Kline, Peter. "Participation in God and the Nature of Christian Community: Robert Jenson and Eberhard Jüngel." *International Journal of Systematic Theology* 13, no. 1 (2011): 38–61.

Komonchak, Joseph A. *Who Are the Church?* Milwaukee: Marquette University Press, 2008.

Lacugna, C. M. *God for Us: The Trinity and Christian Life*. San Francisco: Harper, 1991.

Langdon, Adrian. *God the Eternal Contemporary: Trinity, Eternity and Time in Karl Barth*. Eugene, OR: Wipf & Stock, 2012.

Lemmer, H. R. "Pneumatology and Eschatology in Ephesians: The Role of the Eschatological Spirit in the Church." Ph.D. diss., Pretoria: University of South Africa, 1988.

Lewis, C. S. *God in the Dock*. Glasgow: Fount, 1979.

———. "Meditation in a Toolshed." Pages 52–55 in *Compelling Reason: Essays on Ethics and Theology*. Edited by W. Hooper. London: Fount, 1998.

———. *Prayer: Letters to Malcolm*. London: Fount, 1964.

———. "Till We Have Faces." Pages 443–623 in *Selected Readings*. London: HarperCollins, 2002.

———. *The Screwtape Letters: Letters from a Senior to a Junior Devil*. Glasgow: Collins, 1989.

Lonergan, Bernard. *Method in Theology*. Toronto: University of Toronto Press, 1990.

López, José, and Garry Potter, eds. *After Postmodernism: An Introduction to Critical Realism*. London: Continuum, 2001.

Lossky, Vladimir. *The Mystical Theology of the Eastern Church*. London: James Clarke, 1957.

Luther, Martin. *Luther's Works*. Translated by H. J. Grimm. 55 vols. Vol. 31. Philadelphia: Fortress Press, 1957.

Maclean, Stanley S. *Resurrection, Apocalypse, and the Kingdom of Christ: The Eschatology of Thomas F. Torrance*. Eugene, OR: Pickwick, 2012.

Marino, Francesco. *L'ecclesiologia di Heribert Mühlen: La chiesa nel mistero dello Spirito di Christo e del Padre*. S.T.D. diss., Pontificia Facoltà Teologica dell'Italia Meridionale Sezione S. Luigi, Naples, 1998.

Mangina, Joseph L. "Bearing the Marks of Jesus: The Church in the Economy of Salvation in Barth and Hauerwas." *Scottish Journal of Theology* 52 (1999): 269–305.

———. "The Stranger as Sacrament: Karl Barth and the Ethics of Ecclesial Practice." *International Journal of Systematic Theology* 1, no. 3 (1999): 322–39.

Mawson, Michael. "The Spirit and the Community: Pneumatology and Ecclesiology in Jenson, Hütter and Bonhoeffer." *International Journal of Systematic Theology* 15, no. 4 (2013): 453–68.

McCall, Thomas H. *Which Trinity? Whose Monotheism?* Grand Rapids: Eerdmans, 2010.

McDonnell, Killian. "A Response to D. Lyle Dabney." Pages 262–64 in *Advents of the Spirit: An Introduction to the Current Study of Pneumatology*. Edited by Bradford E. Hinze and D. Lyle Dabney. Milwaukee: Marquette University Press, 2005.

———. "The Determinative Doctrine of the Holy Spirit." *Theology Today* 39, no. 2 (1982): 142–61.

———. "A Trinitarian Theology of the Holy Spirit." *Theological Studies* 46, no. 2 (1985): 191–227.

McFadyen, Alastair. "The Trinity and Human Individuality." *Theology* 95 (1992): 10–18.

McFarland, Ian A. "The Body of Christ: Rethinking a Classic Ecclesiological Model." *International Journal of Systematic Theology* 7, no. 3 (2005): 225–45.

McGrath, Alister E. *A Scientific Theology*. 3 vols. Grand Rapids: Eerdmans, 2001–2003.

———. *Christian Theology*. 2nd ed. Malden, MA: Blackwell, 1994.

———. "The Doctrine of the Trinity: An Evangelical Reflection." Pages 17–35 in *God the Holy Trinity: Reflections on Faith and Practice*. Edited by Timothy George. Grand Rapids: Baker Academic, 2006.

McMaken, W. Travis. *The Sign of the Gospel: Toward an Evangelical Doctrine of Infant Baptism after Karl Barth*. Minneapolis: Fortress Press, 2013.

McPartlan, Paul. *The Eucharist Makes the Church: Henri de Lubac and John Zizioulas in Dialogue*. Edinburgh: T. & T. Clark, 1993.

———. "Who Is the Church? Zizioulas and von Balthasar on the Church's Identity." *Ecclesiology* 4, no. 3 (2008): 271–88.

Migliore, Daniel L. *Faith Seeking Understanding: An Introduction to Christian Theology*. Grand Rapids: Eerdmans, 1991.

———. "Vinculum Pacis—Karl Barth's Theologie des Heiligen Geistes." *Evangelische Theologie* 6 (2000): 131–52.

Minear, Paul. *Images of the Church in the New Testament*. Philadelphia: Westminster, 1961.

Molnar, Paul. *Divine Freedom and the Doctrine of the Immanent Trinity*. London: T. & T. Clark, 2002.

———. "Deus Trinitas: Some Dogmatic Implications of David Coffey's Biblical Approach to the Trinity." *Irish Theological Quarterly* 67, no. 1 (2002): 33–54.

———. "Love of God and Love of Neighbor in the Theology of Karl Rahner and Karl Barth." *Modern Theology* 20, no. 4 (2004): 567–99.

———. "Response to David Coffey." *Irish Theological Quarterly* 68, no. 1 (2003): 61–65.

———. "The Eucharist and the Mind of Christ: Some Trinitarian Implications from Thomas Torrance's Theology." Pages 175–88 in *Trinitarian Soundings in Systematic Theology*. Edited by Paul Louis Metzger. London: T. & T. Clark, 2005.

Moltmann, Jürgen. *The Church in the Power of the Spirit: A Contribution to Messianic Ecclesiology*. New York: Harper & Row, 1977.

———. "The Trinitarian Personhood of the Holy Spirit." Pages 302–14 in *Advents of the Spirit: An Introduction to the Current Study of Pneumatology*. Translated by D. Lyle Dabney. Edited by Bradford E. Hinze and D. Lyle Dabney. Milwaukee: Marquette University Press, 2005.

———. *The Trinity and the Kingdom: The Doctrine of God*. Minneapolis: Fortress Press, 1981.

———. *The Way of Jesus Christ: Christology in Messianic Dimensions*. San Francisco: HarperCollins, 1990.

Moule, C. F. D. *The Origin of Christianity*. Cambridge: Cambridge University Press, 1977.

Mühlen, Heribert. *Der Heilige Geist als Person. Beitrag zur Frage nach der dem Heiligen Geiste eigentümlichen Funktion in der Trinität, bei der Inkarnation und im Gnadenbund*. Münster: Aschendorff, 1963.

———. *Una Mystica Persona. Die Kirche als das Mysterium der heilsgeschichtlichen Identität des Heiligen Geistes in Christus und den Christen: Eine Person in vielen Personen*. 2nd ed. Paderborn: Ferdinand Schöningh, 1967.

Muis, J. A. N. "Can Christian Talk about God Be Literal?" *Modern Theology* 27, no. 4 (2011): 582–607.

Muller, R. A. *Dictionary of Latin and Greek Theological Terms*. Grand Rapids: Baker, 1985.

Muthiah, Robert A. *The Priesthood of All Believers in the Twenty-First Century: Living Faithfully as the Whole People of God in a Postmodern Context*. Eugene, OR: Pickwick, 2009.

Nausner, Bernhard. "The Failure of a Laudable Project: Gunton, the Trinity and Human Self-Understanding." *Scottish Journal of Theology* 64, no. 4 (2009): 403–20.

Newman, Paul W. *A Spirit Christology: Recovering the Biblical Paradigm of Christian Faith*. Lanham, MD: University Press of America, 1987.

Nissiotis, N.A. "Theological Rapprochement: The Doctrine of the Holy Spirit (Review)." *Ecumenical Review* 17, no. 3 (1965): 274–76.

O'Byrne, Declan. *Spirit Christology and Trinity in the Theology of David Coffey*. Oxford: Peter Lang, 2010.

O'Collins, Gerald, and Michael Keenan Jones. *Jesus Our Priest: A Christian Approach to the Priesthood of Christ*. Oxford: Oxford University Press, 2010.

Olson, Roger. "Trinity and Eschatology: The Historical Being of God in Jürgen Moltmann and Wolfhart Pannenberg." *Scottish Journal of Theology* 36, no. 2 (1983): 213–27.

Ormerod, Neil. *The Trinity: Retrieving the Western Tradition*. Milwaukee: Marquette University Press, 2005.

———. "Two Points or Four?—Rahner and Lonergan on Trinity, Incarnation, Grace and Beatific Vision." *Theological Studies* 68, no. 3 (2007): 661–73.

———. "What Is the Goal of Systematic Theology?" *Irish Theological Quarterly* 74, no. 1 (2009): 38–52.

Otto, Randalf. "The Use and Abuse of Perichoresis." *Scottish Journal of Theology* 54, no. 3 (2001): 366–84.

Pannenberg, Wolfhart. *Metaphysics and the Idea of God*. Translated by P. Clayton. Grand Rapids: Eerdmans, 1990.

———. *Systematic Theology*. Translated by G. W. Bromiley. 3 vols. Eerdmans: Grand Rapids, 1991, 1997.

Pelikan, Jaroslav, and Valerie Hotchkiss, eds. *Creeds and Confessions of Faith in the Christian Tradition*. New Haven: Yale University Press, 2003.

Perriman, Andrew. "'His Body, Which is the Church . . .' Coming to Terms with Metaphor." *Evangelical Quarterly* 62, no. 2 (1990): 123–42.

Peters, Ted. *God as Trinity: Relationality and Temporality in Divine Life*. Louisville: Westminster John Knox, 1993.

Peterson, Cheryl M. *Who Is the Church? An Ecclesiology for the Twenty-First Century*. Minneapolis: Fortress Press, 2013.

———. "Who Is the Church?" *Dialog* 51, no. 1 (2012): 24–30.

Pickard, Stephen, and Gordon Preece, eds. *Starting with the Spirit*. Hindmarsh: Australian Theological Forum, 2001.

Pinnock, Clark H. *Flame of Love: A Theology of the Holy Spirit*. Downers Grove, IL: IVP Academic, 1996.

Polanyi, Michael. *Personal Knowledge: Towards a Post-Critical Philosophy*. London: Routledge & Kegan Paul, 1969.

Polkinghorne, John. *The Faith of a Physicist*. Minneapolis: Fortress Press, 1996.

Purves, Andrew. *The Crucifixion of Ministry*. Downers Grove, IL: IVP, 2007.

Rahner, Karl. *Karl Rahner in Dialogue: Conversations and Interviews 1965-1982*. Edited by Paul Imhof and Hubert Biallowons. Translated by Harvey D. Egan. New York: Crossroad, 1986.

———. *The Trinity*. Translated by Joseph Donceel. Tunbridge Wells, UK: Burns & Oates, 1997.

———. *Theological Investigations*. Translated by Karl-H. Kruger and Boniface Kruger. 23 vols. London: Darton, Longman & Todd, 1974.

Richard of St. Victor. *On the Trinity*. Translated by Ruben Angelici. Eugene, OR: Cascade, 2011.

Rogers, Eugene F. *After the Spirit: A Constructive Pneumatology from Resources outside the Modern West*. Grand Rapids: Eerdmans, 2005.

———. "The Mystery of the Spirit in Three Traditions: Calvin, Rahner, Florensky Or, You *Keep* Wondering Where the Spirit Went." *Modern Theology* 19, no. 2 (2003): 243–60.

Rosato, Philip J. "Called by God, in the Holy Spirit: Pneumatological Insights into Ecumenism." *Ecumenical Review* 30, no. 2 (1978): 110–26.

———. "Spirit Christology: Ambiguity and Promise." *Theological Studies* 38 (1977): 423–29.

———. "Spirit Christology as Access to Trinitarian Theology." Pages 166–76 in *God's Life in Trinity*. Edited by Miroslav Volf and Michael Welker. Minneapolis: Fortress Press, 2006.

———. "The Mission of the Spirit Within and Beyond the Church." *Ecumenical Review* 41, no. 3 (1989): 388–97.

Sarot, Marcel. "A Critical Discussion of Thomas G. Weinandy's *Does God Suffer?*" *Ars Disputandi* 1 (2001): no page numbers.

———. "Trinity and Church: Trinitarian Perspectives on the Identity of the Christian Community." *International Journal of Systematic Theology* 12, no. 1 (2010).

Schleiermacher, Friedrich. *The Christian Faith*. London: T. & T. Clark, 1999.

Sirks, G. J. "The Cinderella of Theology: The Doctrine of the Holy Spirit." *Harvard Theological Review* 50, no. 02 (1957): 77–89.

Smail, Thomas. *Like Father, Like Son: The Trinity Imaged in Our Humanity*. Grand Rapids: Eerdmans, 2006.

———. *Reflected Glory: The Spirit in Christ and Christians*. Grand Rapids: Eerdmans, 1975.

Smith, Steven G. *The Concept of the Spiritual: An Essay in First Philosophy*. Philadelphia: Temple University Press, 1988.

Snyder, Howard A. "After Our Likeness (Review)." *Asbury Journal* 60, no. 2 (2005): 127–34.

Spence, Alan. "The Significance of John Owen for Modern Christology." Pages 171–84 in *The Ashgate Research Companion to John Owen's Theology*. Edited by K. M. Kapic and M. Jones. Farnham, UK: Ashgate, 2012.

Spurgeon, Charles H. *The Treasury of David*. 6 vols. London: Passmore & Alabaster, 1888.

Stewart, John W. "After Our Likeness (Review)." *The Christian Century* 115, no. 16 (1998): 541.

Strobel, Kyle C. *Jonathan Edwards's Theology: A Reinterpretation*. London: Bloomsbury, 2013.

Studebaker, Steven M. *From Pentecost to the Triune God: A Pentecostal Trinitarian Theology*. Grand Rapids: Eerdmans, 2012.

———. "Integrating Pneumatology and Christology: A Trinitarian Modification of Clark H. Pinnock's Spirit Christology." *Pneuma* 28, no. 1 (2006): 5–20.

———. *The Trinitarian Vision of Jonathan Edwards and David Coffey*. New York: Cambria, 2011.

Sutherland, Martin. "Pine Trees and Paradigms: Rethinking Mission in the West." Pages 131–48 in *Mission Without Christendom: Exploring the Site*. Edited by Martin Sutherland. Auckland: Carey Baptist College, 2000.

Sweet, Leonard. *AquaChurch: Essential Leadership Arts for Piloting Your Church in a Fluid Culture*. Loveland, CO: Group Publishing, 1999.

Tanner, Kathryn. *Christ the Key*. Cambridge: Cambridge University Press, 2010.

———. "Trinity." Pages 319–32 in *The Blackwell Companion to Political Theology*. Edited by Peter Scott and William T. Cavanaugh. Malden, MA: Blackwell, 2007.

Thompson, John. *Modern Trinitarian Perspectives*. New York: Oxford University Press, 1994.

Thompson, Thomas R. "Interpretatio in bonem partem: Jürgen Moltmann on the Immanent Trinity." Pages 159–78 in *Theology as Conversation: The Significance of Dialogue in Historical and Contemporary Theology: A Festschrift for Daniel L. Migliore*. Edited by Bruce L. McCormack and Kimlyn J. Bender. Grand Rapids: Eerdmans, 2009.

Torrance, Alan J. *Persons in Communion: An Essay on Trinitarian Description and Human Participation*. Edinburgh: T. & T. Clark, 1996.

Torrance, James B. "The Trinity and Worship (Lecture)." Auckland: St. John's College, 1989.

———. "The Vicarious Humanity of Christ." Pages 127–47 in *The Incarnation: Ecumenical Studies in the Nicene-Constantinopolitan Creed A.D. 381*. Edited by Thomas F. Torrance. Edinburgh: Handsell, 1981.

———. *Worship, Community and the Triune God of Grace*. Downers Grove, IL: IVP Academic, 1996.

Torrance, Thomas F. "Atonement and the Oneness of the Church." *Scottish Journal of Theology* 7, no. 3 (1954): 245–69.

———. "Eschatology and the Eucharist." Pages 303–50 in *Intercommunion*. Edited by D. M. Baillie and J. Marsh. London: SCM, 1952.

———. *Incarnation: The Person and Life of Christ*. Edited by Robert T. Walker. Downers Grove, IL: InterVarsity, 2008.

———. *Karl Barth, Biblical and Evangelical Theologian*. Edinburgh: T. & T. Clark, 1990.

———. *Reality and Evangelical Theology*. 2nd ed. Downers Grove, IL: IVP, 1992.

———. Royal Priesthood: A Theology of Ordained Ministry. Edinburgh: T. & T. Clark, 1993.

———. *Space, Time and Resurrection*. Edinburgh: T. & T. Clark, 1976.

———. *The Doctrine of Grace in the Apostolic Fathers*. Eugene, OR: Wipf & Stock, 1996.

———. "The Goodness and Dignity of Man in the Christian Tradition." *Modern Theology* 4, no. 4 (1988): 309–22.

———. *The Mediation of Christ*. 2nd ed. Edinburgh: T. & T. Clark, 1992.

———. "The Modern Eschatological Debate." *Evangelical Quarterly* 25 (1953): 45–54, 94–106, 67–78, 224–32.

———. *The Trinitarian Faith: The Evangelical Theology of the Ancient Catholic Church*. Edinburgh: T. & T. Clark, 1988.

———. *Theological Science*. Oxford: Oxford University Press, 1969.

———. *Theology in Reconciliation: Essays Towards Evangelical and Catholic Unity in East and West.* London: Geoffrey Chapman, 1975.

———. *Trinitarian Perspectives: Toward Doctrinal Agreement.* Edinburgh: T. & T. Clark, 1994.

Treier, Daniel J. *Introducing Theological Interpretation of Scripture: Recovering a Christian Practice.* Grand Rapids: Baker Academic, 2008.

Twelftree, Graham H. *People of the Spirit: Exploring Luke's View of the Church.* Grand Rapids: Baker Academic, 2009.

Vanhoozer, Kevin J. *Is There a Meaning in This Text?* Leicester: Apollos, 1998.

———. *The Drama of Doctrine: A Canonical-Linguistic Approach to Christian Theology.* Louisville: Westminster John Knox, 2005.

Volf, Miroslav. *After Our Likeness: The Church as the Image of the Trinity.* Grand Rapids: Eerdmans, 1998.

———. "'The Trinity Is Our Social Program': The Doctrine of the Trinity and the Shape of Social Engagement." *Modern Theology* 14, no. 3 (1998): 403–23.

Volf, Miroslav, and Maurice Lee. "The Spirit and the Church." Pages 382–409 in *Advents of the Spirit: An Introduction to the Current Study of Pneumatology.* Edited by Bradford E. Hinze and D. Lyle Dabney. Milwaukee: Marquette University Press, 2005.

Vondey, Wolfgang. *Heribert Mühlen: His Theology and Praxis.* Dallas: University Press of America, 2004.

———. "The Holy Spirit and Time in Contemporary Catholic and Protestant Theology." *Scottish Journal of Theology* 58, no. 4 (2005): 393–409.

Walls, Andrew F. "The Gospel as Prisoner and Liberator of Culture." Pages 3–15 in *The Missionary Movement in Christian History.* Maryknoll, NY: Orbis, 1996.

Watson, N. M. "Risen Christ and Spirit/Paraclete in the Fourth Gospel." *Australian Biblical Review* 31 (1983): 81–85.

Watson, Natalie K. "After Our Likeness (Review)." *Anglican Theological Review* 81, no. 4 (1999): 744–45.

Webster, John. "In the Society of God: Some Principles of Ecclesiology." Pages 200–22 in *Perspectives on Ecclesiology and Ethnography*. Edited by Pete Ward. Grand Rapids: Eerdmans, 2012.

———. *Karl Barth*. London: Continuum, 2000.

Weinandy, Thomas. "Christ and the Spirit (Book Review)." *The Thomist* 59, no. 4 (1995): 656–59.

———. *Does God Change?* Still River, MA: St. Bede's, 1985.

———. "Jesus' Filial Vision of the Father." *Pro Ecclesia* 13, no. 2 (2004): 189–201.

———. *The Father's Spirit of Sonship: Reconceiving the Trinity*. Edinburgh: T. & T. Clark, 1995.

———. "The *Filioque*: Beyond Athanasius and Thomas Aquinas: An Ecumenical Proposal." Pages 185–97 in *Ecumenical Perspectives on the Filioque for the 21st Century*. Edited by Myk Habets. Minneapolis: Fortress Press, 2014.

———. "The Immanent and Economic Trinity." *The Thomist* 57 (1993): 655–66.

———. "Zizioulas: The Trinity and Ecumenism." *New Blackfriars* 83, no. 979 (2002): 407–15.

Welker, Michael. *God the Spirit*. Translated by J. F. Hoffmeyer. Minneapolis: Fortress Press, 1994.

Wiersbe, Warren W. *Be Rich: An Expository Study of the Epistle to the Ephesians*. Wheaton: Victor, 1977.

Williams, David J. *Paul's Metaphors: Their Context and Character*. Peabody, MA: Hendrickson, 1999.

Willis, E. David. *Calvin's Catholic Christology: The Function of the So-Called Extra Calvinisticum in Calvin's Theology*. Leiden: E. J. Brill, 1966.

Wolterstorff, Nicholas. *Reason Within the Bounds of Religion*. Grand Rapids: Eerdmans, 1976.

Wright, Christopher J. H. *The Mission of God: Unlocking the Bible's Grand Narrative*. Downers Grove, IL: IVP Academic, 2006.

———. *The Mission of God's People: A Biblical Theology of the Church's Mission*. Grand Rapids: Zondervan, 2010.

Yamauchi, E. M. "Gnosis, Gnosticism." Pages 350–54 in *Dictionary of Paul and His Letters*. Edited by Ralph P. Martin, Gerald F. Hawthorne, and Daniel G. Reid. Downers Grove, IL: InterVarsity, 1993.

Yocum, John. *Ecclesial Mediation in Karl Barth*. Aldershot, UK: Ashgate, 2004.

Yong, Amos. *Beyond the Impasse: Toward a Pneumatological Theology of Religions*. Grand Rapids: Baker, 2003.

———. "Introduction: Pentecostalism and a Theology of the Third Article." In *Toward a Pneumatological Theology: Pentecostal and Ecumenical Perspectives on Ecclesiology, Soteriology, and Theology of Mission*. Edited by Amos Yong. Lanham, MD: University Press of America, 2002.

———. *The Spirit Poured Out on All Flesh: Pentecostalism and the Possibility of Global Theology*. Grand Rapids: Baker Academic, 2005.

Young, Frances M., and Andrew Teal. *From Nicea to Chalcedon: A Guide to the Literature and Its Background*. 2nd ed. Grand Rapids: Baker Academic, 2010.

Zizioulas, John. *Being as Communion: Studies in Personhood and the Church*. Crestwood, NY: St. Vladimir's Seminary Press, 1985.

———. *Communion and Otherness: Further Studies in Personhood and the Church*. London: T. & T. Clark, 2006.

———. "Human Capacity and Incapacity: A Theological Exploration of Personhood." *Scottish Journal of Theology* 28 (1972): 401–47.

———. "L'eucharistie: quelques aspects bibliques." Pages 11–74 in *L'eucharistie*. Edited by J. Zizioulas, J. M. R. Tillard, and J. J. von Allmen. Paris: Mame, 1970.

———. "The Doctrine of God the Trinity Today: Suggestions for an Ecumenical Study." Pages 19–32 in *The Forgotten Trinity*. Edited by Alasdair I. C. Heron. London: BCC / CCBI, 1991.

Index